# *A* BIBLICAL THEOLOGY *of the* CHURCH

## MAL COUCH
### General Editor

**Contributors**
Mal Couch
Thomas Figart
Arnold Fruchtenbaum
Thomas Ice
Russell L. Penney

Kregel
*Academic & Professional*

*A Biblical Theology of the Church*

© 1999 by Mal Couch

Published by Kregel Publications, a division of Kregel, Inc., P.O. Box 2607, Grand Rapids, MI 49501.

**Library of Congress Cataloging-in-Publication Data**
Couch, Mal.
    A biblical theology of the church / by Mal Couch.
        p.      cm.
Includes bibliographical references and index.
    1. Church—Biblical teaching.    2. Dispensationalism.
    3. Bible. N.T.— Criticism, interpretation, etc.  I. Title.
BS2545.C5C68        1999        262—dc 21        99-33785
                                                      CIP

ISBN 978-0-8254-2411-3

# Table of Contents

## Part 3: How the Church Ministers

# Contributors

**Mal Couch**, M.A., Th.M., Th.D., Ph.D., is founder and president of Tyndale Theological Seminary and Biblical Institute, Fort Worth, Texas.

**Thomas Figart**, Th.M., Th.D., is Distinguished Professor Emeritus at Lancaster Bible College, Lancaster, Pennsylvania.

**Arnold Fruchtenbaum**, Th.M., Ph.D., is a conference speaker and founder of Ariel Ministries. He lives in Tustin, California.

**Thomas Ice**, Th.M., Ph.D., is an author, former pastor, and the executive director of the PreTrib Research Center in Arlington, Texas.

**Russell L. Penney**, M.A., Th.D., is a researcher, writer, and missionary teacher in Santa Cruz, Bolivia.

# Introduction

# The Challenge for the Church

In a certain sense, the world is as it has always been. The vast majority of people know nothing of God's grace that is found only in the Lord Jesus Christ. But in another sense the light of the gospel, and even the basic tenets of biblical Christianity, seem to be diminishing from a brilliance that once was.

## But What About the Church?

As spiritual darkness deepens, this should be the finest hour for the gospel and for the church of Jesus Christ. At every turn there are urgent opportunities to share the truth in both word and deed. The gospel should be going forth as never before, and believers in Christ should be growing in spiritual maturity. The church should be foundationally solid and a strong bastion proclaiming God's sovereignty and will. Local congregations should be centers of light and places of refuge where comfort and hope are dispensed and renewed.

But sadly, few assemblies attain the ideal. Many contemporary churches are posturing to gain acceptance by the very culture they have been called on to oppose. Instead of light, there are compromise and confusion. Thankfully, there are many local congregations that are faithful to their biblical calling.

Yet progressively, it seems as if more and more churches no longer are teaching the Word of God. Many are departing from sound doctrine. Like those in the world, many Christians have adopted New Age enlightenment, accepted spiritual liberalism, and are marching to the drumbeat of secularism and materialism.

## The Challenge for the Church

This book is concerned with the doctrine of the church as revealed in Scripture. If the church is God's vehicle for reaching the world, how should that task be carried out? What is the doctrinal makeup of the church, and what about its organization and function in terms of local assemblies? For the local church to do its job, it must know about its calling. The Word of God must be examined in order to understand what the Lord's purpose is for the body of believers.

This work will reexamine the doctrine of ecclesiology. It will look at every aspect of the church and how it should carry out its commission. Our prayer is that those who study these pages will experience a renewal, a fresh enthusiasm for the task set before us by the Lord. This task is not carried out simply by human strength. Those who are His cannot serve Him unless there is the flow of blessing from Christ who is the Head.

No one can explain better what God is now doing than William Ames (1576–1633). With eloquent words, he well summarizes the urgency, the aims, and the purpose of this book:

> [The church] is instituted by God and Christ alone because men have no power in themselves to institute or frame a church for Christ. . . . Their greatest honor is that they are servants in the house of God. . . . Man, therefore, does not have power either to take away any of those things which Christ has given his church or to add things of like kind. Yet in every way he can and ought to make certain that the things which Christ has ordained are furthered and strengthened. Christ has so instituted the church that it always depends upon him as the head—considered without Christ it is not a complete body. Therefore, the church may not properly make new laws for itself for instituting new things. It ought to take care only to find out the will of Christ clearly and observe his ordinances decently and with order, with greatest edification resulting.[1]

## Part 1

# The Biblical Doctrine of the Church

## Chapter 1

# Dispensational Hermeneutics and the Doctrine of Ecclesiology

Is there seen in Scripture just one people of God who form a thread from the Old Testament to the New Testament? Is there one covenant that determines salvation for one people of God? Or are there two covenants and two peoples? Is the church the Israel of God? When did the church begin?

Is the church simply the New Testament version of the Israel of the Old Testament? Which system best explains ecclesiology and the doctrine of the church, covenant theology or dispensational theology?

These and similar questions hinge on how one interprets the Bible. And interpretation is formulated under the term *hermeneutics*. By the science of hermeneutics, the entire Bible, all specific Scriptures, and each doctrine should be interpreted with a consistent linguistic approach. The laws of interpretation should be applied equally in every part of the Bible.

One's view of the church should be determined by this scientific method of linguistic study. But is there a danger of being biased, unscientific, inconsistent, and subjective when trying to understand God's Word? The answer, of course, is yes! Every interpreter must put aside his preconceived notions about a specific passage or particular truth when attempting to know the will of God from the Bible.

Dispensationalists and covenant theologians agree on many aspects of the scientific approach to interpretation. Covenant theologians would claim they are consistent, but the proof will be in what they write. To begin, it is important to examine the basic definitions concerning hermeneutics. Then, it will be equally important to see how, from the two systems of hermeneutics, the church is set forth and viewed by both covenant and dispensational theologies.

## Definition of Hermeneutics

Ramm writes:

> The word hermeneutics is ultimately derived from Hermes the Greek god who brought the messages of the gods to the mortals, and was the god of science, invention, eloquence, speech, writing, and art. As a theological discipline hermeneutics is the science of the correct interpretation of the Bible. It is a special application of the general science of linguistics and meaning. It seeks to formulate those particular rules which pertain to the special factors connected with the Bible. It stands in the same relationship to exegesis that a rule-book stands to a game. . . . Hermeneutics proper is not exegesis, but exegesis is applied hermeneutics. Hermeneutics is a science in that it can determine certain principles for discovering the meaning of a document.[1]

Zuck points out that Hermes was responsible for transmitting what is beyond human understanding. "Thus the verb *hermeneuō* came to refer to bringing someone to an understanding of something in his language (thus explanation) or in another language (thus translation). The English word *interpret* is used at times to mean 'explain' and at other times 'translate.'"[2]

A. A. Hodge adds:

> Hermeneutics, or the scientific determination of the principles and rules of Biblical Interpretation, includ[es] (1) the logical and grammatical and rhetorical principles determining the interpretation of human language in general, (2) the modification of these principles appropriate to the interpretation of the specific forms of human discourse, e. g., history, poetry, prophecy, parable, symbol, etc.[3]

At the heart of the rules for interpretation is what is termed the *literal method*. This is the starting point for explaining a passage of Scripture, *unless* there are guidelines by word usage or context that would indicate a verse or sentence should be taken figuratively or as an illustration. Tan notes:

> The literal method of interpreting God's Word is a true and honest method. It is based on the assumption that the words of

Scripture can be trusted. It assumes that since God intends His revelation to be understood, divine revelation must be written based on regular rules of human communication. To "interpret" means to explain the original sense of a speaker or writer according to the normal, customary, and proper usages of words and language. Literal interpretation of the Bible simply means to explain the original sense of the Bible according to the normal and customary usages of its language.[4]

Zuck summarizes succinctly, "Hermeneutics is this: It is the science (principles) and art (task) by which the meaning of the biblical text is determined."[5] Hermeneutics is a science in that it has a scientific method for unlocking the meaning of any language, particularly, as this study has already pointed out, the language of the Scriptures. At the heart of that method is literal interpretation or normal meaning. Hermeneutics is also an art in that the interpreter must acquire experience and skill in order to use the scientific method. It is not an art in the sense that it would by governed by the subjectivity of that individual. Biblical truth is not to be found in the personal "taste" of a specific pastor or teacher. As much as is humanly possible, all bias and prejudice must be put aside when interpreting the Word of God. In understanding the nature and function of New Testament ecclesiology, one must begin with orderly and consistent interpretation of key passages.

## Principles of Hermeneutics

Though not meant as an exhaustive list nor detailed explanation, the principles below are accepted by most Bible scholars as the laws for governing sound hermeneutics. Buswell lists some of the most important principles for interpretation:[6]

1. Scripture interprets Scripture. The Bible is a closed volume of literature. It has a historical setting that stands together, and, as a whole, is obviously differentiated from all other writings. In interpreting the Bible we do not ask any favors which we do not believe are proper rules for the reading of any serious literature.
2. The meaning of words is to be established by their usage. The Holy Spirit chose to use known human languages to convey to us the Word of God. Clearly then, these languages convey to us what God wants us to know.
3. Context must be taken into account. Words and thoughts must be understood within the setting, the time frame, the mood of the moment, the culture, etc.
4. A mastery of the historical setting and of the grammar used (a grammatico-historical interpretation) is imperative to comprehending the sense of a given sentence or paragraph. Thus an understanding of the biblical languages is urgent for the interpreter.

Other important rules and principles follow:

5. The interpreter must begin assuming literal or normal interpretation in a passage unless otherwise indicated by common linguistic sense. The simile "the hills skipped like lambs" is obviously poetic. From a literal picture of a frisky lamb playfully jumping about, one can imagine the joy of creation expressing itself in worship to God! In other words, behind the poetry are literal concepts that then in turn give meaning to the poetic language.

6. Thus, as in all languages, the Bible interpreter must use common sense in noting poetry, figures of speech, metaphors, similes, illustrations, etc. But again, even these literary devices are attempting to get across actual concepts.

7. The use of common sense in biblical interpretation is most important. The "human drama" must be allowed to come forth. The interpreter must avoid "wooden-headed literalism" that is so stiff and rigid in meaning that all normal human expression is destroyed.

8. As part of context, factors such as culture, historical background, social setting, and geography all play a part in interpretation.

9. The Bible must be studied dispensationally to see how God dealt with people and nations during various time periods. This means that the student of Scripture must observe carefully the context of a specific period in Bible history to ascertain how God worked in different ways. For example, the Lord dealt with Abraham in a different way than He did Moses and the Jews as they came out of Egypt. He now deals with the nations by grace, but someday He will pour forth His wrath upon the world in the period known as the Tribulation. The Jews under the Law did not know of the full revelation of the death, burial, and resurrection of their Messiah. The object of their faith was simply "Do you believe in God?" Now the object of faith in this grace dispensation is "Do you believe that Jesus is your Savior and that He died for your sins?" To see this difference is to study context carefully and also to observe the different message for each distinct period.

10. Progressive revelation is also important in dispensational hermeneutics. Not everything is given at the beginning of the Bible. Not only does each successive book in the time in which it was written presuppose the biblical books that preceded it, but the earlier books in many passages were clearly intended to point forward to Scriptures that were to come later. God progressively, generation through generation, revealed new truth. Some things, such as the church, were mysteries not previously revealed in the Old Testament. That God would save Gentiles was prophesied in the older testament. But how, when, and by what means was not revealed. Thus the church, its nature, and its structure were revealed from Pentecost (Acts 2) and forward. And that revelation too was progressive. It began with the principal apostle, Peter. He observed through the unfolding of the book of Acts

how the Holy Spirit was operating and building the church. But the full and complete revelation was given exclusively to the apostle Paul.

> *You have heard of the [dispensation] of God's grace which was given to me for you; that by revelation there was made known to me the mystery, . . . to be specific, that the Gentiles are fellow heirs and fellow partakers of the promise in Christ Jesus through the gospel. (Eph. 3:2–3, 6)*

Kaiser adds:

11. "Under the strong impetus of the Reformation there was a renewed emphasis that there is only one sense or meaning to be gleaned from every passage if the interpreter is true to his mission."[7] There are a few cases when the New Testament writers quote an Old Testament passage as an illustration. But the original meaning of the passage is still honored and this rule remains applicable.
12. The process of hermeneutics is threefold: (1) The student of the Word is to *observe* everything he can about a given passage, using all the tools available. (2) The student is then to *interpret* all the data collected as to the meaning and message of the verses under study. (3) Finally there must be *application* of the truths and doctrines discovered in the material. That application is twofold: (a) What did the passage mean to those to whom it was written? (b) What does the passage mean to believers today?

## Requirements for the Interpreter

Ramm lists some of the important spiritual and intellectual qualifications necessary for the student of the Word of God. Though the qualifications he mentions are essential, one can possess them and yet have a blind spot as to how properly to interpret or apply hermeneutics. But these provide an essential basis for interpretation.[8]

1. The interpreter must be born again.
2. The interpreter must have a passion for God's Word.
3. The interpreter must depend on the direction of the Holy Spirit.
4. The interpreter should have a solid educational background. He must know something of history, literature, logic, geography.
5. The interpreter should be competent in the biblical languages.
6. The interpreter must have adequate tools to work with: Lexicons, grammars, language commentaries, an atlas, volumes on biblical background, geography texts.

7. The interpreter must come to the Bible as openly as possible, without any theological bias or presuppositions.

> The Bible student must also approach the Scriptures with sound judgment and reason, seeking to be as objective in his approach to the Bible as possible, without coming to the Scriptures with prejudice or preconceived notions.[9]

8. It is the interpreter's job to represent the text, "not the prejudices, feelings, judgments, or concerns of the exegete. To indulge in the latter is to engage in *eisegesis*, 'a reading into' a text what the reader wants it to say."[10]

In conclusion, Ramm notes:

> Matters of fact cannot be settled solely by spiritual means. One cannot pray to God for information about the authorship of Hebrews and expect a distinct reply. Nor is it proper to pray for information with reference to other matters of biblical introduction expecting a revelation about the revelation.[11]

# Dispensationalism Defined

In a certain technical sense, there is no such thing as dispensational hermeneutics. Dispensationalists hold strongly to the hermeneutical principles given above and argue, if they are consistently followed, one will arrive at dispensationalism. Concerning the doctrine of ecclesiology, the church and Israel will be clearly seen in Scripture as separate bodies. It will be clearly seen as well that the Lord has two distinct plans for the church and Israel.

## *Etymology of the Word*

The word *dispensation* is *oikonomia* in Greek, a compound of *oikos,* meaning "house," and *nomos,* meaning "law." The word implies how one manages and organizes the affairs of a household. The English word *economy* comes from this Greek term. On the biblical usage of the word Ryrie states:

> The various forms of the word *dispensation* appear in the New Testament twenty times. The verb *oikonomeō* is used once in Luke 16:2, where it is translated "to be a steward." The noun *oikonomos* appears ten times (Luke 12:42; 16:1, 3, 8; Rom. 16:23; 1 Cor. 4:1, 2; Gal. 4:2; Titus 1:7; 1 Peter 4:10) and is usually translated "steward" or "manager" (but "treasurer" in Rom. 16:23). The noun *oikonomia* is used nine times (Luke 16:2, 3, 4; 1 Cor. 9:17; Eph. 1:10; 3:2, 9; Col. 1:25; 1 Tim. 1:4). In these

instances it is translated variously "stewardship," "dispensation," "administration," "job," "commission."[12]

"A concise definition of a dispensation is this: A dispensation is a distinguishable economy in the outworking of God's purpose."[13]

Mason defines a dispensation as "a divinely established stewardship of a particular revelation of God's mind and will which is instituted in the first instance with a new age, and which brings added responsibility to the whole race of men or that portion of the race to whom the revelation is particularly given by God."[14]

Couch adds:

> A dispensation is an obvious historical division in Scripture in which God deals in a specific way with mankind on earth, during a specified period. Rather than controlling history, dispensations reflect how God sees human beings by mirroring His view and testing man. . . . All dispensations end in moral failure. . . . To see the overall thrust of the Scriptures, in a literal and consistent sense, leads to a dispensational approach to the Word of God. This is the only way to study the Bible that allows it to make sense in its message to us. A dispensation is not a way of salvation nor is it ironclad with rigid walls. It is simply a way of evaluating God's dealing in a period of history.[15]

The dispensations that most dispensationalists would probably agree upon today are:

- Dispensation of Innocence. Genesis 1:28–3:6.
- Dispensation of Conscience. Genesis 3:7–8:14.
- Dispensation of Government. Genesis 8:15–11:32.
- Dispensation of Promise. Genesis 12:1–Exodus 18:27.
- Dispensation of Law. Exodus 19:1–Acts 1:26.
- Dispensation of the Church (or Grace). Acts 2:1–1 Thessalonians 4:18.
- Dispensation of the Kingdom. Matthew 24–25; Revelation 19:11–22:21.

For the purpose of this chapter, only the dispensations of law and the church will be compared.

**Dispensation of Law:** Will the people of Israel be faithful to their God with a moral and judicial legal code to follow? Will they obey the Ten Commandments and other laws that govern their relationship with God and man?

**The People's Response:** "All that the LORD has spoken we will do. And Moses returned the words of the people unto the LORD " (Exod. 19:8).

**The Failure:** As a nation and as individuals, the Jews could never keep the Law. In time, even in their failure, many of the Jews began to see the Law as a way of salvation—something it was never intended to be! By the time of Christ the people of Israel were hypocritically fooling themselves concerning their ability to be law keepers.

> If you are called Jews, and take comfort in the Law, and make your boast of God . . . do you dishonor your God by breaking the Law? You teach others, do you teach yourself? (Rom. 2:17–23)

> We conclude that a man is justified by trust apart from the works of the Law. . . . Seeing it is one God, who shall justify the circumcision [the Jews] by trust, and uncircumcision [the Gentile] through trust. (Rom. 3:28, 30)

**Dispensation of the Church—the Promise**: By the message of personal salvation through the death and resurrection of Jesus Christ, God graciously offers personal forgiveness of sins, the indwelling of His Spirit, and eternal life. The dispensation of the church is made possible because of the new covenant.

**The Problem:** The heart of men will grow cold and, in time, will even reject the personal offer of salvation.

**The Failure:** This period will end with the Apostasy, the outright personal rejection by men of the offer of salvation. But as well, there will be a great company who appear to be Christian and outwardly religious but they will be apostate. The dispensation of the church closes with the rapture of the church from earth just prior to the coming seven-year period of world tribulation.

## What Are the Essentials?

Benware points out that there are three indispensable elements (*sine qua non*) of dispensational theology. "These three essentials are (1) a consistent literal approach to interpreting the Scriptures, (2) a clear distinction between the church and the nation of Israel in God's dealings, and (3) the glory of God as God's ultimate purpose of history."[16]

Enns shows that dispensationalism will always lead the student of Scripture to premillennialism. He notes that dispensational premillennialism has two important features:

> 1. Literal hermeneutic. Literal interpretation refers to "normal"
> interpretation—understanding words and statements in their
> normal, customary way. Because prophecies concerning Christ's
> first coming were fulfilled literally, it makes good sense to expect

the prophecies concerning His second coming to be interpreted literally. Furthermore, if prophecy can be spiritualized, all objectivity is lost. Dispensational premillennialists emphasize consistency in interpretation by interpreting prophecy literally.

2. Distinction between Israel and the church. The term *Israel* always refers to the physical posterity of Jacob; nowhere does it refer to the church. Although nondispensationalists frequently refer to the church as the "new Israel," there is no biblical warrant for doing so. . . . Israel was given unconditional promises (covenants) in the Old Testament that must be fulfilled with Israel in the millennial kingdom. The church, on the other hand, is a distinct New Testament entity born at Pentecost (1 Cor. 12:13) and not existing in the Old Testament, nor prophesied in the Old Testament (Eph. 3:9).[17]

Theologically speaking, *oikonomia* is used four times in a specific interpretative way (1) to show that a new dispensation of grace (or the church) has come and (2) to make a distinction between the dispensation of Law and the dispensation of grace. The four references are: Ephesians 1:9–10; 3:2–3, 9; Colossians 1:25. By using all the interpretative principles cited above, it can be demonstrated that there are other dispensations in Scripture, though technically they are not called such.

### Ephesians 1:9–10

He made known to us the mystery of His will, . . . with a view to an administration [dispensation] suitable to the fullness of the times, that is, the summing up of all things in Christ.

Mystery means something not previously revealed "which He purposed in Him [Christ]" (v. 9) with the result "that we who were the first to hope in Christ should be to the praise of His glory" (v. 12). In Christ, we who heard the gospel and believed "were sealed in Him [Christ] with the Holy Spirit [who was] promise[d]" that we would be "to the praise of His glory" (vv. 13–14).

Nicoll writes extensively on Ephesians 1:10:

God had His reason for the long delay in the revelation of the "mystery." That reason lay in the fact that the world was not ripe for the dispensation of grace which formed the contents of the mystery. In classical Greek the word *oikonomia* had the two meanings of (a) *administration,* the management of a house or of property, and (b) the *office* of administrator or steward. It was used of such things as the arrangement of the parts of a building . . . , the disposition of the parts of speech . . . , and more particularly of the financial administration of a city . . . . It has the same twofold sense in the NT—an *arrangement* or *administration* of things (in the passages in the present Epistle and in I Tim. 1. 4), and the office of administrator—in particular the stewardship with which Paul was entrusted by God (1 Cor. ix. 17; Col. i.25).

The idea at the basis of the statement here, therefore, as also in the somewhat analogous passage in Gal. iv. 1–11, is that of a great household of which God is the Master and which has a certain system of management wisely ordered by Him. . . . God has His household, . . . with its special disposition of affairs, its *oikonomos* or steward (who is Christ), its own proper method of administration, and its gifts and privileges could not be dispensed in their fullness while those for whom they were meant were under age (Gal. iv. 1–3) and unprepared for them. A period of waiting had to elapse, and when the process of training was finished and the time of maturity was reached the gifts could be bestowed in their completeness. God, the Master of the House, had this fit time in view as the hidden purpose of His grace. When that time came He disclosed His secret in the incarnation of Christ and introduced the new disposition of things which explained His former dealings with men and the long delay in the revelation of the complete purpose of His grace. . . . This "economy of the fullness of the seasons," therefore, is that stewardship of the Divine grace which was to be the trust of Christ, in other words, the dispensation of the Gospel, and that dispensation as fulfilling itself in the whole period from the first advent of Christ to the second.[18]

How different this dispensation is over against the dispensation of Law with all its heavy demands of legal requirements. The writer of Hebrews points out so well how weak and useless the dispensation of the Law had become:

> *Now if perfection [completeness] was through the Levitical priesthood . . . , what further need was there for another priest to arise according to the order of Melchizedek? (7:11)*

> *For, on the one hand, there is a setting aside of a former commandment because of its weakness and uselessness (for the Law made nothing perfect) and on the other hand there is a bringing in of a better hope, through which we draw near to God. (7:18–19)*

> *But now He [Christ] has obtained a more excellent ministry, by as much as He is also the mediator of a better covenant [the new covenant], which has been enacted on better promises. For if that first covenant [the Law] had been faultless, there would have been no occasion sought for a second [covenant]. (8:6–7)*

> *When He [God in Jeremiah 31:31–34] said, "A new covenant," He has made the first [the Law] obsolete. But whatever is becoming obsolete and growing old is ready to disappear. (8:13)*

## Ephesians 3:2–3

> *... if indeed you have heard of the* stewardship [dispensation] *of God's grace which was given to me for you; that by revelation there was made known to me the mystery. . . .*

This "mystery" is concerning Christ (v. 4) and was not revealed previously to the sons of men as now revealed by the Spirit to God's holy apostles (v. 5), specifically, that Gentiles are fellow heirs "of the body" and fellow partakers "of the promise in Christ Jesus through the gospel" (v. 6). To Paul this grace was granted "to preach to the Gentiles the unfathomable riches of Christ . . ." (v. 8).

How much more clear could Paul get? Without question he is referring to the church age or dispensation of grace! The larger context goes back to 2:11–22. There Paul writes of the Gentiles "now in Christ" (v. 13) brought near by His blood. Jesus is the peace who has united Jew and Gentile "into one new man" (v. 15) and reconciled "them both in one body [body of Christ] to God, "and together "we both [Jew and Gentile] have our access in one Spirit to the Father" (v. 18) and are now in Christ "God's household" (v. 19).

## Ephesians 3:9

> *... to bring to light what is the* administration [dispensation] *of the mystery which for ages has been hidden in God, who created all things. . . .*

Paul wraps up his great dispensational teaching by pointing out that the church shows forth the "manifold wisdom of God" (v. 10) and how He had "eternal purpose[s] which He carried out in Christ Jesus our Lord" (v. 11), whereby we have "access through faith in Him" (v. 12). Paul's final verses constitute an anthem to what God is doing in this new church dispensation! ". . . to Him be the glory in the church and in Christ Jesus to all the generations forever and ever. Amen" (v. 21).

## Colossians 1:25

> Of this church I was made a minister according to the steward-
> ship [dispensation] from God bestowed on me for your benefit,
> that I might fully carry out the preaching of the word of God.

This Colossian verse is similar to what Paul writes in Ephesians. He speaks
of the church as a mystery (v. 26) "hidden from the past ages and generations."
But to the saints, "God willed to make known what is the riches of the glory of this
mystery among the Gentiles, which is Christ in you, the hope of glory" (v. 27). Out
of this Paul wishes to present "every man complete in Christ" (v. 28).

Ryrie summarizes:

> Though emphasizing the distinctiveness of the church,
> the dispensationalist also recognizes certain relationships that
> the church sustains. . . . He recognizes believers in this age as
> the [spiritual] seed of Abraham but not the only seed. He seeks
> to be a realist concerning the course of this age and the church's
> program in the midst of increasing apostasy. All his viewpoints
> stem from what he feels to be a consistent application of the
> literal principle of interpretation of Scripture.[19]

## Dispensational Hermeneutics

Though "hermeneutics" should be hermeneutics, this study has focused on
the phrase dispensational hermeneutics to call attention to the need for consistency in interpretation. Dispensationalists believe covenant theologians fail at
this point. They call Israel the church and the church Israel without any objective, biblical evidence. Enns helps sum up the most important principles that
help make up dispensational hermeneutics:

> Dispensationalists use a consistent, literal, normal system of
> interpretation. This approach is applied to all the disciplines of
> theology. By using literal interpretation on Old Testament proph-
> ecies about Christ's first and second coming, dispensationalists
> anticipate His literal return just as His first advent was historic
> and actual, not spiritualized! Dispensationalists hold to the fact
> that God has made unconditional promises to Israel through the
> Abrahamic covenant (Gen. 12:1–3). These promises are both
> physical fulfillments as well as having to do with a spiritual re-
> vival for the Jewish people. Nondispensationalists "spiritualize"
> or allegorize most of these prophecies and relegate them to the
> church.

Dispensationalists never confuse Israel with the church nor call the church "the new Israel." Dispensationalists can show that God has distinct programs for future Israel with the coming Messianic Kingdom but He also has a specific program now for the body of Christ, the church. Dispensationalists emphasize the unifying theme of the Bible is God's glory, where in covenant theology, salvation is the unifying theme. In every dispensation God has shown His glory. This is the unifying theme of all of the Bible.[20]

## The Greek Word *Ekklēsia*

*Ekklēsia* is the common Greek word for church. Often it is translated as *assembly* and *congregation*. Generally, it refers to a religious or even a political gathering. Technically, the word means "the called out ones." *Ekklēsia* is many times used in the Greek Septuagint (LXX) to refer to different assemblies within the Old Testament. In Acts (7:38; 19:32) the word can simply mean a crowd or gathering. However, most often in the New Testament, the word *ekklēsia* is used to describe the entire body of believers, the universal church, or the assembly of Christians in the local church.

## The Church: Universal Spiritual Body of Christ

Many seeing the word *universal* think this is advocating the heresy of "universalism" when instead the word is simply referring to a worldwide fraternity of true believers. Certain words trigger strong reactions, but the one reacting must read on! *There is* a universal spiritual body of Christ! A person in India who has trusted Christ as Savior is a spiritual brother, though one may not speak the same language nor belong to the same "local" church.

"You are the Christ, the Son of the living God" (Matt. 16:16). Upon these confirming, rock-solid words of the apostle Peter, Jesus says He will build His church; and the gates of Hades shall not overpower it (v. 18). Note, it is a single church. But this would not be a single denomination with a governmental hierarchy. It would not be an outward, overwhelming, exclusive system such as the Roman Catholic Church.

This church was to encompass a period of time in which all who place personal faith in Christ will constitute a spiritual unity. Christ is the head of this body. In fact, this is the body of Christ (1 Cor. 12:12–13). But there will also be a local church, a localized cell or community of believers who are just a part of those who have trusted Jesus. As well, it would have a visible leadership, a distinct purpose for local fellowship, and a moral mandate for individual discipline. The New Testament church letters reflect both this spiritual body and the local cell of Christians.

The apostle Paul speaks of the whole body of Christ when he writes, "with all who in every place call upon the name of our Lord Jesus" (1 Cor. 1:2). He likens all believers in Christ, who are many, to the one body, Christ's (12:12). The apostle adds, "whether Jews or Greeks, whether slave or free," all were made to drink from one Spirit. "For the body is not one member, but many" (12:14). Though most of Paul's letters are addressed to local churches, for the most part what he says is applicable to all those in Christ.

For example, he writes, "Do you not know that all of us who have been baptized into Christ Jesus have been baptized into His death?" (Rom. 6:3). He adds, "By one Spirit we were all baptized into one body" (1 Cor. 12:13). And, "He saved us, not on the basis of deeds which we have done in righteousness, but according to His mercy, by the 'again-birthing' of regeneration and the 'remaking' of the Holy Spirit" (Titus 3:5, Greek). This universal body of believers Paul calls the "household" (Eph. 2:19), the building growing into a holy temple (2:21), "in whom you [believers in the local church at Ephesus] also are being built together into a dwelling of God [by] the Spirit" (2:22).

Paul writes further in Ephesians that Christ is the Head and Savior of the church (5:23), that He loved it and gave Himself for it (5:25). In an almost anthem-like verse, Paul summarizes: "And He [God] put all things in subjection under His feet [Christ's], and gave Him as head over all things [relating] to the church, which is His body" (1:22). The New Testament continually emphasizes the singularity of the church. While Peter was in prison, prayer for him was "being made fervently by the [whole] church of God" (Acts 12:5). Overseers (plural) are to "shepherd the [whole] church of God which He purchased with His own blood" (20:28). "I [Paul] persecuted the [whole] church of God" (1 Cor. 15:9).

The principal emphasis in the New Testament is on the church as an organism, a living union of all true believers in Christ. This is the distinctive truth that is presented beginning with the day of Pentecost, with the advent of the Spirit, and concluding with the coming of Christ for His church, in which it will be caught up out of the world and taken to heaven.[21]

## The Church: The Local Congregation

The church, the living organism and the organized cell of believers, is God's way of doing business in local communities in this dispensation. This is a unique period in divine time. In terms of the local church, believers of a given age must see themselves as having a special calling to serve the Lord in their own generation. As much as this may shock some, the local church itself is never instructed in Scripture to evangelize. That is the job of the individual believer. The purpose of the local cell is to arm, equip, and train the Christian to speak out and witness to his circle of influence. But more on this issue later. Chafer further notes:

> It is obviously true that a person may be a Christian and not be a member of a local organized church. In fact, all should be saved before they join a church; and, if saved, it is normal for the individual to choose the fellowship of the people of God in one form

or another. On the earth, the church is seen to be a pilgrim band of witnesses. They are not of this world even as Christ is not of this world (John 17:16), and as the Father has sent the Son into the world, so has the Son sent these witnesses into the world.[22]

In his letters, Paul continually addresses the local congregations, the body of believers who are struggling in a given city or region. Almost all he writes is applicable for today.

In 1 Corinthians (1:2), the apostle makes a separation between the entire church of the Lord and the local body. He writes "to the church of God which is at Corinth." He then adds "with all who in every place call upon the name of our Lord Jesus Christ, their Lord and ours. . . ." At the end of this Corinthian letter, Paul says "the churches of Asia greet you" (16:19), and then also mentions the local church that meets in the house of Aquila and Priscilla (v. 19). In 2 Corinthians he writes about the regional churches "throughout Achaia" and the church there in Corinth (1:1).

## The Dispensational Nature of the Church

God had a distinct dispensational purpose for the nation of Israel in the Old Testament. Through them the Lord's perfect and righteous demands would be displayed through the Law. The temple and all its ceremonies would reflect and foretell the coming of the Redeemer, Jesus the Messiah. And through this nation, Jesus would be born. But as a whole, the Jews would reject their king. God would temporarily set aside His work with the Jewish people as a nation. He would create a new era called the age of grace, or the church age. And in this new period both individual Jews and Gentiles would be saved worldwide and placed into this new body called the church.

Both Jew and Gentile now have a common ground. Both are said to be under sin (Rom. 3:9) and in need of a common Savior. When the Holy Spirit came at Pentecost, the Lord began a new divine program, away from the recognition of a specific people, to an appeal to individuals, Jews and Gentiles alike. The Jews had trouble understanding that their covenants were set aside for a time but would someday still be fulfilled. The writer Luke shows this struggle in the book of Acts.

As a people, and as a nation, the Jews will remain blind in part until the church is called home (Rom. 11:25). Then the Deliverer, the Messiah, will return and restore the Jews to their land. Ungodliness will be turned away from this people when He removes their sins (Rom. 11:26–27). Yet now, individual Jews and Gentiles who respond to the proclamation of the gospel are being added to this new "thing," the church.

God is now forming this one new body (Eph. 2:15). This was a mystery not previously revealed. That God had purposes for the Jewish people distinctly, and that He would someday touch the Gentiles, was no secret. The Old Testament prophesied that Gentiles would someday find Jehovah! But how the Lord would accomplish this was "hid in God."

# Questions for Discussion

1. At what points on interpretation would dispensationalists and covenant theologians agree?
2. What is meant by the literal method of interpretation?
3. As Zuck discusses it, what is implied in the word *hermeneutics?*
4. What is meant by grammatico-historical interpretation?
5. Describe progressive revelation.
6. Why is it important for the interpreter of Scripture to possess certain spiritual qualifications to be a true student of the Word of God?
7. Define and describe dispensationalism.
8. What are the most important essentials of dispensationalism?
9. What is meant by "dispensational hermeneutics"?

# Chapter 2

# The New Dispensation: The Church

## The Church Is Not a New Israel

Some have trouble understanding that Gentiles who become "Abraham's offspring" are not becoming his physical children. To become Abraham's offspring refers to spiritual seed, and it is something God accomplishes because of trust in Christ. Equally so, believers become "adopted sons of God" (Gal. 4:5–6). This is also understood as something spiritual. Nowhere in Scripture is the church seen as the extension of Israel. Neither is the church called Israel! However, some theologians try to say in the Galatians 6:11–18 context that Paul does this. Eadie gives the most convincing arguments against this:

> The apostle is not in the habit of calling the church made up of Jews and Gentiles—Israel. Israel is used eleven times in Romans, but in all the instances it refers to Israel proper; and so do it and *Israelites* in every other portion of the New Testament. In the Apocalypse, the 144,000 sealed of Israel stand in contrast to "the great multitude which no man can number," taken out of the Gentile or non-Israelitish races. . . . the apostle never in any place so uses the name, never gives the grand old theocratic name to any but the chosen people.[1]

## The Church Is Not Added to Israel

Covenant theologian Berkhof defines the Kingdom of God as the church, and even more specifically, the Israel of the Old Testament as that kingdom but also the church simply in an older form! Most covenant teachers would agree. The problem is that all clear and important distinctions are blurred.

Dispensationalists believe in being true to what is observed in the biblical text, otherwise we are telling God what His plans are about instead of listening to what He tells us He is doing in the outline of history.

An additional error covenant advocates make is to read New Testament truths back into the Old Testament. That is, they are interpreting the Old by the New. Instead, the New should be seen as a fulfillment or progression from the Old Testament. Though they would deny it, covenant theologians become slipshod in their observations of covenant and dispensational issues. This particularly impacts the eschatological and ecclesiastical areas of doctrine. For example, Berkhof writes: "The fundamental ideal of the Kingdom in Scripture is not that of a restored theocratic kingdom of God in Christ—which is essentially a kingdom of Israel—as the Premillenarians claim."[2] He had to admit, however, that some of the church Fathers "regarded [the Kingdom] as the coming millennial rule of the Messiah. . . ."[3]

Berkhof looks to Augustine for his confirmation and notes that he "viewed the kingdom as a present reality and identified it with church."[4] As well, Berkhof points out, "The Roman Catholic Church frankly identified the Kingdom of God with their hierarchical institution, but the Reformers returned to the view that it is in this dispensation identical with the invisible church."[5] And finally concerning the church, he writes: "It is impossible to be in the Kingdom of God without being in the church as the mystical body of Jesus Christ."[6]

Does the Bible really see the Kingdom as the church? An important passage on this subject is Ephesians 2:11–22. Many covenant theologians believe these verses are saying that the church was joined to Israel. For example, Nicoll wrongly believes the expression "brought near" (v. 13) means the Gentiles are brought into the camp of Israel by Christ's blood. He writes, "It is probably to be taken, therefore, in the large sense of being brought into the Kingdom of God, made near to God Himself."[7] Though Gentiles are brought near to God, that is not Paul's point here.

What Paul is describing is the fact that the new body, the church, is comprised of both Jew and Gentile. He explains it that way in verse 14. Christ "is our peace, who made both groups into one." This is not an argument for saying the new body, the church, is simply an extension of Israel. Even covenant teacher Charles Hodge understands, at least with this passage, that the church is something new. It is not Israel in a reconstituted form.

Paul writes that the Gentiles were "excluded from the commonwealth of Israel, and [were] strangers to the covenants of promise, having no hope and without God in the world" (v. 12). But Paul adds that "now in Christ Jesus you who formerly were far off have been brought near by the blood of Christ" (v. 13). Jesus is the peace between the two groups, abolishing the enmity, which is the Law of commandments (vv. 14–15).

The apostle then points out that God makes something new with the two groups of people, Jews and Gentiles. He does not simply plug Gentiles into the body of Israel! He Himself "made both groups into one" (v. 14), and He made "the two into one new man" (v. 15). He "reconcile[d] them both in one body [the church] to God through the cross" (v. 16).

Paul then says a new "household" of God is formed whereby we are fellow citizens with believing Jews. This household has

> *been built upon the foundation of the apostles and prophets, Christ Jesus Himself being the corner stone, in whom the whole building, being fitted together is growing into a holy temple in the Lord; in whom you also are being built together into a dwelling of God in the Spirit. (vv. 20–22)*

On this Ephesians passage Hodge writes:

> By abolishing the law of commandments, i.e. the law in both its forms, the apostle says, Christ has, first, of the twain made one new man, v. 15; and secondly, he has reconciled both unto God in one body by the cross, v. 16. . . . The reconciliation itself is expressed by saying, "He made the two one, having removed the wall or enmity between them." The mode in which this was done, is expressed by saying, "He abolished the law." . . . The design of Christ in thus abolishing the law was two-fold. First, the union of the Jews and Gentiles in one holy, catholic [universal] church. And, secondly, the reconciliation of both to God. . . . "In order that he might create the two, in himself, one new man, making peace." . . . They are created anew, so as to become one body of which Christ is the head. . . . The distinction between Jew and Gentile is abolished. . . . There is now one fold and one shepherd. Since the abrogation of the law there is neither Jew nor Greek, there is neither bond nor free, there is neither male nor female; for all believers are one in Christ Jesus. . . . The subjects of this reconciliation are the Jews and Gentiles united in one body, i.e. the church.[8]

Paul goes on and explains in 3:2 that this new thing, the dispensation of the church, was a mystery (something not previously revealed), the mystery concerning Christ (3:4), and that it was a unique revelation given exclusively to him (3:3). In fact, it was hidden from other generations (v. 5). But what is this that is now revealed? "To be specific, that the Gentiles are fellow [together] heirs [with the Jews] . . . of the body, and fellow partakers of the promise in Christ Jesus through the gospel . . ." (v. 6). This was grace "preach[ed] to the Gentiles . . ." (v. 8). To Paul it was given "to bring to light what is the [dispensation] of the mystery which for ages has been hidden in God" (v. 9).

# The Church Rests on the New Covenant

As the Old Testament unfolds by progressive revelation, the new covenant is revealed. It involves an agreement with all the house of Israel (Jer. 31:31), it will contrast with the conditional Mosaic Law (v. 32), it will be written on the hearts of the Jews, and the Lord promises to indeed be their God and they His people in a close and personal way (v. 33). At some future point it can be said "they all know the Lord" (v. 34). But one of the most dramatic promises is "I will forgive their iniquity, and their sin I will remember no more" (v. 34). This certainly implies that the temple sacrifices will no longer be needed and that once and for all God is through with the issue of sin.

Ezekiel and Joel continue, by progressive revelation and the inspiration of the Holy Spirit, to give more details about the new covenant. The Lord will splash (*zaraq*) clean water on the Jews, whereby "I will cleanse you from all your filthiness and from all your idols" (Ezek. 36:25). This must be a spiritual cleansing, since water will not cleanse from idol worship. As well, the Lord promises a new, soft heart that will be responsive to Him (v. 26). And most importantly, He will place His Spirit within (v. 27; 37:14).

Concerning the new covenant and its promise of the coming Spirit, the prophet Joel picks up on this and writes: "I will pour out My Spirit on all mankind" (Joel 2:28). In the same paragraph Joel predicts the display of wonders in the sky, "blood, fire, and columns of smoke . . . before the great and awesome day of the LORD comes" (vv. 31–32). In Acts 2, Peter refers to this entire paragraph when he speaks of the outpouring of the Holy Spirit. He certainly did not understand the issue of the separation of time between the coming of the Spirit and the beginning of the "day of the Lord," the tribulation (Acts 2:14–21). Many dispensationalists and non-dispensationalists have believed that when Peter said "This is what [the coming of the Holy Spirit] was spoken of through the prophet Joel" (v. 16), he was simply saying "this is 'like' what was spoken by Joel."

At Pentecost, when the new covenant is launched, the Spirit would descend upon Jew and Gentile equally. The blessing aspect of the promise to Abraham would come on all! Dispensationalists would say the new covenant was promised first for Israel. Its ultimate fulfillment is in the future kingdom but the Gentiles are presently benefiting from it. As a whole, the Jews are not now benefiting from the new covenant promises unless of course they are part of the body of Christ, the church, by faith. Only those who now trust Christ as Savior are receiving the blessings of the covenant promised them. As a nation, the Jews rejected the work of salvation and the blessings of the new covenant, though it was given first to them.

After the Spirit came at Pentecost, He continued to fall upon Jew and Gentile alike. When Peter visited Cornelius's house and the Gentiles there, "All the circumcised [Jewish] believers who had come with Peter were amazed, because the gift of the Holy Spirit had been poured out upon the Gentiles also" (Acts 10:45). If we look at Joel 2:28 and how Peter quotes it, this makes sense. In 2:28 it is written that God's Spirit would come upon "all mankind." The Hebrew text reads "upon all *basar*." Gesenius says the word is a metaphor for the human race. In Acts 2:17 the Greek quote of the Joel passage reads upon *pasan sarka*, or "every kind of humanity."

Kistemaker, though not a dispensationalist, notes:

> Luke reports that Peter quotes [of the signs and wonders] from Joel's prophecy, but Luke fails to give its application. . . . Luke does not indicate that at Pentecost God fulfilled Joel's prediction of the signs and wonders. He relates that the outpouring of the Holy Spirit occurred in Jerusalem. . . . God opens the way of salvation to all people, both Jew and Gentile. He makes his promise to individual persons and asks them to respond individually. These believers as members of Christ's body constitute the Christian church.[9]

On "this is that which was spoken . . ." Alexander writes:

> The sum of it is: this is not intoxication, it is inspiration, and the fulfillment of a signal prophecy. . . . *all flesh* is an idiomatic Hebrew phrase, . . . more usually [meaning] all mankind (Gen. 6:12).[10]

Hackett also believes Joel's prophecy is being fulfilled here in Acts 2. He writes:

> The Greek identifies this prophecy with its fulfillment. . . . Yet the prophecy has indirectly a wider scope. It portrays in reality the character of the entire dispensation. Those special manifestations of the Spirit at the beginning marked the Economy [the church] as one that was to be eminently distinguished by the Spirit's agency.[11]

On "this is that which was spoken . . ." dispensationalist Toussaint notes:

> This clause does not mean, "This is like that"; it means Pentecost fulfilled what Joel had described. However, the prophecies of Joel quoted in Acts 2:19–20 [blood, and fire, and vapor of smoke] were not fulfilled. The implication is that the remainder would be fulfilled if Israel would repent.[12]

Though sometimes they may not be clear in their arguments, most dispensationalists are saying that the church is presently "benefiting" from the blessings promised in the new covenant. However, they would say that the ultimate fulfillment of those promises for Israel will take place in the Kingdom.

# The Passing of the Law

Hebrews is one of the most Jewish of the books in the New Testament. Some see the book almost evangelistic in that its purpose is to convince the Jews that Christ is better than anything or any person in the Mosaic legal system. Though the debate continues, one thing is certain: the author of Hebrews writes that the new covenant will replace the Mosaic covenant of Law. The author of the book points out, "so much the more also Jesus has become the guarantee of a better covenant" (7:22), that is, the new covenant. This is because as "the Son of God, He abides a priest perpetually" (v. 3).

The dispensation of the Law had so many limitations that it could make no one mature (or perfect) (v. 11). Neither could all the gifts and sacrifices offered up by the sinner make that worshiper mature in conscience (9:9). The Levitical priesthood was hindered in that the human priestly order was made up of sinful men who had moral and physical limitations. But Jesus was of the superior priesthood of Melchizedek that goes back to the period of Abraham (7:1). It was an eternal, unending order that was not confined to any human limitations. In other words, Jesus could be an independent, sinless priest, representing men to God and God to man. And of course the most profound priestly work He performed is that "He offered up Himself (once) for the sins of the people" (v. 27).

Many fail to understand that the Mosaic Law had passed its usefulness. "For, on the one hand, there is a setting aside of a former commandment because of its weakness and uselessness" (v. 18). Neither could the animal blood sacrifices of bulls and goats sanctify the sinner or make his flesh clean from sinning (9:13). Christ became "the mediator of a better covenant [the New], which has been enacted on better promises. For if that first covenant had been faultless, there would have been no occasion sought for a second" (8:6–7).

# Two Ways of Salvation?

Some older dispensationalists have made a few unguarded statements of what Scripture teaches about salvation. Anyone who is intellectually honest will go beyond their few misstatements and look at the overall belief of these dispensational theologians. Ryrie, for instance, states in concise fashion the heart of what dispensational theologians believe about salvation. He writes, "[Dispensationalists teach that] the *basis* of salvation in every age is the death of Christ; the *requirement* for salvation in every age is faith; the *object* of faith in every age is God; the *content* of faith changes in the various dispensations."[13]

This is what C. I. Scofield, Lewis Sperry Chafer, Charles Ryrie, and other dispensational theologians have always held. They never believed that one is saved by the Law. They have always taught that the basis of salvation was the death of Christ.

Are there two ways by which one may be saved? In reply to this question it may be stated that salvation of whatever specific character is always the work of God in behalf of man and never a work of man. This is to assert that God never saved any one person or group of persons on any other ground than that righteous freedom to do so which the Cross of Christ secured. There is, therefore, but one way to be saved and that is by the power of God made possible through the sacrifice of Christ.[14]

Chafer also stated, "The law was never given as a means of salvation or justification."[15] Scofield wrote, "Law neither justifies a sinner nor sanctifies a believer." One of the problems that covenant theologians have with understanding the dispensational teaching is our designation of one dispensation as Law and one as grace. They believe this communicates ways of salvation and cannot understand how the dispensationalist sees Law and grace relating to each other. Thus, as Ryrie relates, it is imperative that dispensationalists show this relationship.[16] Ryrie does just that when he writes, as quoted previously (see p. 34) that the content of faith changes through each of the various dispensations.:

It is this last point, of course, that distinguishes dispensationalism from covenant theology, but it is not a point to which the charge of teaching two ways of salvation can be attached. It simply recognizes that obvious fact of progressive revelation. When Adam looked upon the coats of skin with which God had clothed him and his wife, he did not see what the believer today sees looking back on the cross of Calvary. And neither did other Old Testament saints see what we can see today. There have to be two sides to this matter—that which God sees from His side and that which man sees from his.

Thus, during the dispensation of Law, each person who was justified was justified by faith in God; yet the content of the faith was different. Ryrie adds:

It is entirely harmonious to say that the means of eternal salvation was by grace and that the means of temporal life was by law. It is also compatible to say that the revelation of the means of eternal salvation was through the law and that that revelation (though it brought the same results when believed) was not the same as the revelation given since the incarnation of Christ. Thus, the revelation concerning salvation during the Mosaic economy did involve the law, though the basis of salvation remained grace.[17]

# The Content of Faith

All dispensationalists would agree that the *basis* of salvation, *requirement* for salvation, and *object* of faith for salvation in every age have remained constant. But the *content* of faith has changed in various dispensations. As Enns states:

> God's revelation to man differs in different dispensations, but man's responsibility is to respond to God in faith according to the manner in which God has revealed Himself. Thus when God revealed Himself to Abraham and promised him a great posterity, Abraham believed God, and the Lord imputed righteousness to the patriarch (Gen. 15:6). Abraham would have known little about Christ, but he responded in faith to the revelation of God and was saved. Similarly, under the law God promised life through faith. Whereas the Israelite under the law knew about the importance of the blood sacrifice, his knowledge of a suffering Messiah was still limited—but he was saved by faith (Hab. 2:4). Dispensationalists thus emphasize that in every dispensation salvation is by God's grace through faith *according to His revelation.*[18] (author's emphasis)

The dispensationalist points out the fact that although salvation has always been and always will be by faith, the amount of knowledge one had of the future death of Christ was limited and thus the content of faith was different at different stages of progressive revelation. As Enns observes, the dispensationalist is sensitive to the fact that the *content* of the message in which believers place their faith is affected by the stage of redemptive history or the progress of revelation. Thus, most dispensationalists still believe that the distinctions made by C. I. Scofield in the messages of "good news" or "gospels" are accurate ones and should be maintained. This is especially true in Scofield's distinction of the "gospel of the kingdom of God" and the "gospel of the grace of God." He writes:

> (1) The Gospel of the kingdom. This is the good news that God purposes to set up on the earth, in fulfillment of the Davidic covenant (2 Sam. 7:16), a kingdom, political, spiritual, Israelitish, universal, over which God's Son, David's heir, shall be King, and which shall be, for one thousand years, the manifestation of the righteousness of God, in human affairs. . . .
>
> Two *preachings* of this Gospel are mentioned, one past, beginning with the ministry of John the Baptist, continued by our Lord and His disciples, and ending with the Jewish rejection of the King. The other is yet future (Matt. 24:14), during the great tribulation, and immediately preceding the coming of the King in glory.

(2) The Gospel of the grace of God. This is the good news that Jesus Christ, the rejected King, has died on the cross for the sins of the world, that He was raised from the dead for our justification, and that by Him all that believe are justified from all things. This form of Gospel is described in many ways. It is the Gospel "of God" (Rom. 1:1) because it originates in His love; "of Christ" (2 Cor. 10:14) because He alone is the Object of Gospel faith; of "the grace of God" (Acts 20:24) because it saves those whom the law curses; of "the glory" (1 Tim. 1:11; 2 Cor. 4:4) because it concerns Him who is the glory, and who is bringing the many sons to glory (Heb. 2:10); of "our salvation" (Eph. 1:13) because it is the "power of God unto salvation to every one who believeth" (Rom. 1:16); of "the uncircumcision" (Gal. 2:7) because it saves wholly apart from forms and ordinances; of "peace" (Eph. 6:15) because through Christ it makes peace between sinner and God, and imparts inward peace.[19]

Most dispensationalists hold to these distinctions as a result of their commitment to a normal, natural hermeneutic which forces a recognition of the distinction between God's program for Israel and His program for His church. And as pointed out above, dispensational theologians keep progressive revelation in mind. To be hermeneutically consistent, one must see a different content of faith in various dispensations.

## Salvation Only in Christ

As Ryrie previously stated, Dispensationalists teach that "the *basis* of salvation in every age is the death of Christ."[20] Thus, in this age the content of the gospel message in which those who are to be justified must place their faith is the death, burial, and resurrection of Jesus Christ (1 Cor. 15:1–4).

Ryrie summarizes the dispensational perspective in his chapter on "Salvation in Dispensationalism" in this way:

To show that dispensationalism does not teach several ways of salvation, we emphasized that (1) the law was brought in alongside and did not abrogate the promises of the Abrahamic covenant and (2) there were many displays of grace under the law. Dispensationalism alone among theological systems teaches both the antithetical nature of law and grace and the truth of grace under the law (and, incidentally, law under grace). Grace was shown to be displayed in several ways, but the crux of the matter was the display of grace in salvation.[21]

In examining salvation under the Mosaic Law the principal question is simply, How much of what God was going to do in the future did the Old Testament believer comprehend? According to both Old and New Testament revelation it is impossible to say that he saw the same promise and the same Savior as we do today. Therefore, the dispensationalist distinction between the content of his faith and the content of ours is valid. The basis of salvation is always the death of Christ; the means is always faith; the object is always God (though man's understanding of God before and after the Incarnation is obviously different); but the content of faith depends on the particular revelation God was pleased to give at a certain time. These are the distinctions the dispensationalist recognizes, and they are distinctions necessitated by plain interpretation of revelation as it was given.

If by "ways" of salvation is meant different content of faith, then dispensationalism does teach various "ways" because the Scriptures reveal differing contents for faith in the progressive nature of God's revelation to mankind. But if by "ways" is meant more than one basis or means of salvation, then dispensationalism most emphatically does not teach more than one way, for salvation has been, is, and always will be based on the substitutionary death of Jesus Christ.[22]

## The Doctrine of the Church and Covenant Theology

A closer examination will reveal that the covenant approach to the Word of God is greatly lacking and terribly flawed. James Orr underscores deep hermeneutical flaws in the system of covenant theology:

> It failed to seize the true idea of development, and by an artificial system of typology [and allegorizing interpretation] sought to read back practically the whole of the New Testament into the Old. But its most obvious defect was that, in using the idea of the covenant as an exhaustive category, and attempting to force into it the whole material of theology, it created an artificial scheme which could only repel minds of simple and natural notions. It is impossible, e.g., to justify by Scriptural proof the detailed elaboration of the idea of a covenant of works in Eden, with its parties, conditions, promises, threatenings, sacraments, etc.[23]

What makes covenant theology so disturbing is that the outstanding proponents of the system admit there is no direct scriptural evidence for the two most important covenants in their system, the covenant of works and the covenant of redemption (and/or grace). It is admitted that these covenants must have been revealed in time, but more specifically, they were made in eternity past and outside of Scripture.

## The Covenant of Works

By the candid statements made by Berkhof below, it can be shown that this covenant rests on suppositions.

> The covenant is an agreement between God and Adam that he would obey the Lord in regard to not eating of the tree of good and evil. This obedience incumbent upon Adam shows that it is a covenant, though sovereignly initiated by God alone. In a sense, this was a salvation by works. Covenant theologians argue as to whether this covenant has been revoked and annulled or not. When Adam sinned, "Spiritual death entered instantly, and the seeds of death also began to operate in the body. The full execution of the sentence, however, did not follow at once, but was arrested, because God immediately introduced an economy of grace and restoration."[24]

Dispensationalists answer that nowhere does the Bible call Adam's obedience a kind of covenant. Nor would they agree that this was a form of works salvation. Going by all the biblical evidence from the limited verses about Adam in Genesis, dispensationalists call this the period of innocence in which Adam was sinless and commanded not to eat of a certain tree. God was relating to him in this innocent condition. But in no way, in the normal sense, can this be called a covenant relationship. Dispensationalists have far more evidence to call the period the dispensation of innocence than covenant theologians have for calling it the covenant of works.

About the covenants of works and grace, Benware well notes:

> They are ideas that are not systematized, formalized, and stated by Scripture as covenants. At least the dispensationalist finds the word *dispensation* used of one or two of his specific dispensations (Eph. 1:10; 3:9); the covenant theologian *never* finds in the Bible the terms *covenant of works* and *covenant of grace.*

Benware further writes:

> The existence of the covenants is not found by an inductive examination of passages. . . . Now, if it is permissible for the covenant theologian to base his entire system on a deduction rather than on a clear statement of Scripture, why can he not permit the dispensationalist to deduce the existence of various dispensations, especially when certain of the dispensations are specifically named in Scripture? The dispensationalist has more inductive evidence for the existence of the specific dispensations than does the covenant theologian for his covenants of works and grace.[25]

## Covenant of Grace or Redemption?

In presenting the covenant of grace, there is an immediate conflict between the various covenant theologians. Charles Hodge says there are two distinct covenants, of grace and redemption. But Berkhof insists:

> Though this distinction (between the covenant of redemption and the covenant of grace) is favored by Scripture statements, it does not follow that there are two separate and independent covenants. . . . The covenant of grace and redemption are two modes or phases of the one evangelical covenant of mercy.[26]

Hodge counters:

> Both [covenants] are so clearly presented in the Bible that they should not be confounded. The latter, the covenant of grace, is founded on the former, the covenant of redemption. Of the one Christ is the mediator and surety; of the other He is one of the contracting parties.[27]

He also admits, "The Westminster standards seem to adopt sometimes the one and sometimes the other mode of representation."[28] The Larger Catechism would also say that the covenant of grace was signed and sealed by Christ as the second Adam. He is the second Adam and in Him are all the seed of those who are elected to salvation. Hodge would say that the covenant of redemption was made between the Father and the Son concerning man's salvation.[29] The gospel is the offer of salvation to all men. "In this sense, the covenant of grace is formed with all mankind."[30] Through this covenant,

> Salvation is offered to all men on the condition of faith in Christ. And therefore to that extent, or, in a sense which accounts for that fact, the covenant of grace is made with all men. The great sin of those who hear the gospel is that they refuse to accept of that covenant, and therefore place themselves without its pale.[31]

Ryrie points out:

> There is not one reference from Scripture . . . that deals directly with the establishment of the covenant of grace or its characteristics. There are references concerning the blessings of salvation but none to support the covenant of grace. What is missing is rather significant and revealing.[32]

But dispensationalists would say that salvation comes through the new covenant that was ratified by the shed blood of Jesus. The Lord told His disciples before His arrest and ultimate death, "This cup which is poured out for you is the new covenant in My blood" (Luke 22:20). This new covenant was in seed form when God prophesied through Abraham that all the nations would be blessed through him (Gen. 12:3). This new covenant was meant first for Israel, but the Gentiles would benefit by it during the dispensation of the church. Paul writes:

> *Be sure that it is those who are of faith that are the sons of Abraham. And the Scripture, foreseeing that God would justify the Gentiles by faith, preached the gospel beforehand to Abraham, saying, "All the nations shall be blessed in you." So then those who are of faith are blessed with Abraham, the believer. (Gal. 3:7–9)*

The apostle sees believers now as responsible for sharing the new covenant. He says that God "made us adequate as servants of a new covenant, not of the letter, but of the Spirit; for the letter kills, but the Spirit gives life" (2 Cor. 3:6). The new covenant is the key for the dispensation of the church. And in the 2 Corinthians 3 passage, Paul makes a contrast between this dispensation and that of Law, which he goes on and says was "the ministry of death, in letters engraved on stones, . . . so that the sons of Israel could not look intently at the face of Moses, because of the glory of his face" (v. 7).

Paul nowhere refers to a man-made covenant of grace or redemption. He clearly saw the Law as done away with and yet he points out it had a moment of glory. Now the current dispensation would be hailed as the period of "the ministry of righteousness." "For if the ministry of condemnation [Law] has glory, much more does the ministry of righteousness [new covenant] abound in glory. For indeed what had glory [the Law], in this case has no glory on account of the glory that surpasses it [new covenant]" (vv. 9–10).

## Clear Statement of Scripture

No one concludes the issues better than Ryrie:

> If it is permissible for the covenant theologian to base his entire system on a deduction rather than on a clear statement of Scripture, why can he not permit the dispensationalist to deduce the existence of various dispensations, especially when certain of the dispensations are specifically named in Scripture? The dispensationalist has more inductive evidence for the existence of the specific dispensations than does the covenant theologian

for his covenants of works and grace; and the dispensationalist has as much, if not more, right to deduce his dispensational scheme as does the covenant theologian his covenant scheme.

What the covenant theologian does to make up for the lack of specific scriptural support for the covenants of works and grace is to project the general idea of covenant in the Bible and the specific covenants (like the covenant with Abraham) into these covenants of works and grace. . . . But there remains still the reality that nowhere does Scripture speak of a covenant of works or a covenant of grace as it does speak of a covenant with Abraham or a covenant with David or a new covenant.

Allis calls the revelation of this important covenant in Genesis 3:15 cryptic. This is all very strange and hard to swallow, especially when the biblical covenants with Abraham, Israel, David, and others are so clearly and specifically revealed. Abraham had no doubt that a covenant was being made when God Himself passed between the pieces of the sacrifice (Gen. 15:17–21).

And yet we are asked to believe in the existence of a covenant of grace that was scarcely revealed, although it is the fountainhead out of which even the Abrahamic covenant came![33]

## The First Reference to the Church: Matthew 16:13–20

It would be through the apostle Paul that the full meaning and revelation of the church would come. Jesus first uses the word in Matthew 16:18. Not only is "church" (Greek, *ekklēsia*) first used here in the New Testament, in its context it is used in the technical sense of the coming of the new dispensation of grace that would replace the dispensation of Law.

In the passage, the Lord is preparing His disciples for His coming death. "From that time Jesus Christ began to show His disciples that He must go to Jerusalem and suffer many things from the elders and chief priests and scribes, and be killed and be raised up on the third day" (Matt. 16:21). But just prior to that, He had asked His disciples, "Who do people say that the Son of Man is?" (v. 13). The phrase *the Son of Man* means "the Son related to mankind," and it is a powerful description of the Messiah who would represent humanity before the presence of God the Father.

Peter answered the Lord first by saying, "Thou art the Christ, the Son of the living God" (v. 16). In these words Peter confirmed he understood Jesus was the Anointed King (the Christ) and that He was somehow related to deity ("the Son related to God," Psalm 2). The Lord then called Peter "blessed" because the Father in heaven had revealed these truths to him (v. 17). Jesus then says:

*And I also say to you that you are Peter, and upon this rock I will*
*build My church; and the gates of Hades shall not overpower it.*
*I will give you the keys of the kingdom of heaven; and whatever*
*you shall bind on earth shall be bound in heaven, and whatever*
*you shall loose on earth shall be loosed in heaven. (vv. 18–19)*

There are actually two different subjects in the passage. The first has to do with Christ building His church. The second has to do with another subject, the kingdom of heaven. Grammatically, these two issues can be separated. "'Church' in Matthew 16:18 and 'kingdom' in verse 19 may not be identical in meaning."[34] "The question is raised at once if Jesus does not here mean the same thing by 'kingdom' that he did by 'church' in verse 18."[35] "These words become clear when we note that 'the keys' belong to 'the kingdom of heaven,' and that this kingdom is not identical with 'my church' in verse 18."[36] "Jesus' 'church' is not the same as his 'kingdom' . . . : the two words belong to different concepts, the one to 'people' and the other to 'rule' or 'reign.' "[37]

It is easy to see that two distinct subjects are in view. "I will build My church; . . . I will give you the keys of the kingdom of heaven." One would think that somehow if the two were the same, the passage might read something like: "I will build My church and give to you Peter its keys." Or, "My church is the kingdom I have been teaching about all along." Or still, "Peter, you will be the head over My kingdom the church." But there is no such hint given, in this context nor in the history of the founding of the church, recorded in the book of Acts.

## Who or What Is the "Rock"?

Peter's name *Petros* is a masculine word in Greek. And "upon this the rock *[petra]*" is actually a feminine phrase. Jesus in no way is calling Peter "the girl rock"! Notice that "this the" is feminine. This must be referring back to something already said, but it certainly is not pointing back to the disciple Peter. It must also be pointed out, however, that the feminine form of "rock" can be referring to something said or indicated that in itself is not feminine. The most logical explanation is that it refers to Peter's statement, "Thou art the Christ, the Son of the living God" (v. 16). Jesus acknowledges Peter's words, "Flesh and blood did not reveal this to you, but My Father who is in heaven" (v. 17).

Jesus purposely uses two Greek words which, though not identical, are closely related in meaning. What he said was, "You are
*petros*, and upon this *petra* I will build my church," meaning,
"You are a rock, and upon the rocky ledge (or: cliff) of the Christ,
'the Son of the living God' who was revealed to you and whom
you confessed, I will build my church." If Jesus had intended to

convey the thought that he was going to build his church on Peter he would have said, "and on you I will build my church."[38]

Thus, the church is to be built upon the person of Christ not upon the disciple Peter.

## Kingdom of Heaven/Kingdom of God

In all instances, the expressions *kingdom of God* and *kingdom of heaven* refer to the coming millennial reign of Christ on earth. That this kingdom then goes on into eternity following the one-thousand-year reign of Christ is agreed upon by most dispensationalists. The focus of the kingdom of God issue can be discovered in the Gospels. John, Mark, and Luke use the expression *kingdom of God* exclusively. Yet Matthew uses the phrase *kingdom of heaven* some thirty times and *kingdom of God* only three times.

In the view of most premillennialists and dispensationalists, the two expressions clearly point to the Davidic covenant and the millennial reign of David's Son, Jesus the Messiah. For example, David points out, "[The LORD] has chosen my son Solomon to sit on the throne of the kingdom of the LORD over Israel" (1 Chron. 28:6). And Christ will come through Solomon's line. Though it is the Lord's kingdom (29:11), it is still bequeathed to David's sons and established forever (28:7–8).

Since Peter will help launch the church in Acts 2, what does it mean that he will be given the keys to the kingdom of heaven, especially since that kingdom is not the church? Isaiah 22:20–23, a passage not directly related to the issue, may shed some light on the question.

As Israel faces the terror of the Assyrians during the kingship of Judah's king Hezekiah (approx. 701 B.C.), Isaiah the prophet points out that God places a servant Eliakim in Jerusalem with a certain great prophetic spiritual authority. "He will become [like] a father to the inhabitants of Jerusalem and to the house of Judah. Then I will set the key of the house of David on his shoulder, when he opens no one will shut, when he shuts no one will open" (vv. 21–22).

Almost exactly like Eliakim, Peter would be given a certain open-ended authority over the city of Jerusalem and over the people of Judah, in regard to an issue of judgment in their acceptance and rejection of the gospel message. This authority, if it can be called that, also reflects upon great issues with the house of David and the kingly line. After all, it was Israel's king that was crucified by His own people for their own sins! As Peter preached, the people made judgments against the kingdom and their king.

For example, Peter cried out to the people of Jerusalem, "Repent, . . . that your sins may be wiped away, in order that times of refreshing may come from the presence of the Lord; and that He may send Jesus, the Christ appointed for you, whom heaven must receive until the period of restoration of all things about which God spoke by the mouth of His holy prophets . . ." (Acts 3:13–21).

This is clearly a kingdom offer, though Peter certainly did not know God's timetable for the coming millennial reign. In theory, Peter was unlocking or opening. He was living out the voice of God. And before the Sanhedrin, Peter cried out, "[Jesus] is the one whom God exalted to His right hand as a Prince and a Savior, to grant repentance to Israel, and forgiveness of sins" (5:31). Note how Peter focuses on the Messiah's work as Savior for Israel, the Jewish people!

In time, the message of Christ will slip away from the Jews. Peter's work of judgment against the people will be over. The gospel message will then go to the Gentiles. Israel will be cut off and scattered.

## The Binding and Loosing?

This has already been partly pointed out above. But a closer examination of Matthew 16:19 is important. The text best reads: "I will [future tense] give you the keys of the kingdom of heaven; and whatever you should bind [aorist, active, subjunctive] on earth shall itself have been bound [perfect passive, participle] in heaven, and whatever you should loose [aorist active subjunctive] on earth shall itself have been loosed [perfect passive participle] in heaven."

By the use of two perfect passive participles, the Lord seems to be saying that what Peter does here on earth, with the Jews, with a reference to a kingdom message most applicable to them, the apostle is but carrying out what God has already determined in heaven to be done. In other words, Peter is but an instrument of judgment against the Jews that has been previously determined by the Lord. Peter is the Lord's visible instrument of judgment but the final active authority still rests with God. Thus, he really does not have authority in the way most often thought of. He is but a providential instrument against the Jews and their view of the kingdom of heaven. Once they have been judged through the "instrument" Peter, the work of the Lord through the church increases, as evidenced in the book of Acts.

Is this interpretation correct? Though there are some differences of opinions, many great Bible scholars think so.

"When the perfect participle is given its full force in the Matthean passages, the periphrastic future perfect in 16:19 becomes 'whatever you bind on earth shall have been bound in heaven, and whatever you loose on earth shall have been loosed in heaven' (similarly for 18:18). Thus, as [the grammarian] Mantey insisted, there is no evidence for 'sacerdotalism or priestly absolution' in the New Testament."[39]

## Conclusion

The church on earth carries out heaven's decisions. Heaven is not ratifying the church's decisions.

Seventeen of the early church fathers felt the passage means that the church was built on Peter. This includes Origen and Jerome.

A second view of the church fathers thought that the church was built on all the apostles, not simply upon Peter.

But a majority of forty-five of the church fathers felt that "these words are to be understood of the Faith which St. Peter had confessed, that is, that this Faith, this profession of faith, by which we believe that Christ is Son of the living God, is the eternal and immovable foundation of the church."[40]

This is by far the most customary interpretation and it is attested to by the Eastern church fathers Gregory of Nyssa, Cyril of Alexandria, Chrysostom, Theodoret, and Theophylact. And also it is supported by the Western Fathers such as Hilary, Ambrose, Augustine, and Gregory the Great.

That the rock was Peter would not be fully espoused until Siricius, bishop of Rome, in A.D. 385 wrote a letter to the bishop Himerius of Tarragona, Spain, arguing for the primacy of Peter.

Though it is a faulty hermeneutical argument, Denney believes it can be stated that the interpretation that Christ is the Rock does not take away from the third interpretation, which was held by the majority of the Fathers, that it is upon Peter's confession that the church rests. In fact, some feel that either view is acceptable.

> Hence Dionysius the Carthusian gives the two interpretations as equally expressing the meaning of the words, saying, "And upon this rock, that is, upon the firmness and foundation of his Faith [i.e., upon that of Peter], or upon this Rock which thou hast confessed, that is Myself, the chief corner-stone, the lofty mountain of which the Apostle says other foundation can no man lay, etc."[41]

But one of the major rules of biblical interpretation is that there is almost always just one meaning for a given passage. It would be rare for two very distinct ideas to be embedded in one sentence or short paragraph.

The weight of early church history points to the fact that the church fathers believed Christ's statement in regard to the rock has to do with Peter's confession of who Jesus really is. It is upon that confession that the church will be built.

## The Common View of Roman Catholicism on Matthew 16

Since about 1860, the Catechism of Father Joseph Deharbe has been recognized as the most important doctrinal statement for Catholics throughout North America. Thousands of Catholics cut their teeth on this little volume that carried the imprimatur of John Farley, the Archbishop of New York. In this book, on the basis of Matthew 16, Christ appointed Peter to be the Supreme Head of His church.[42] Deharbe notes:

> We learn from this, 1. That Christ built His church upon Peter, as upon the true foundation-stone; 2. That He gave him in

particular the keys of the Kingdom of Heaven; and 3. That He commissioned him alone to feed His whole flock.[43]

In the catechism the question is then asked, "Who followed Peter upon his death?"

> The Councils, as well as the Fathers of all ages individually have unanimously and most decidedly, by word and deed, acknowledged in the Roman Popes the Primacy and Supremacy of St. Peter. The Ecumenical Council of Florence (1438) referred to "the Decrees of the General Councils, and the Ecclesiastical Statutes," when it declared "that the Bishop of Rome (the Pope) possessed the Primacy over the whole universe; that he was the Successor of the Prince of the Apostles, St. Peter, and the true Vicegerent of Jesus Christ, the Head of the whole church, . . . and whoever refused to recognize the Pope as the Head of the church was at all times considered by all the faithful as an apostate."[44]

The Catholic Church is serious about the Matthew 16 passage of Scripture. From this, it builds an overwhelming system that is meant to control the religious life of all under the church's power. And this power starts with Peter and comes down to every Pope ever placed in office.

The Catechism of Father Deharbe continues, and points out that it is easy to find the visible church because perceptible marks have been left that the world can see. Because of this, all who deny the church are "under pain of eternal damnation" if they do not listen to her.[45] "Non-Catholic Religious Societies (Protestant denominations) are not true because they have no common Head (such as the Pope), and because their founders are not holy."[46] As well, they "have rejected many articles of faith and means of sanctification, as, for example, the Sacrifice of the Mass and most of the Sacraments."[47] The people in these groups are lost "because they cannot produce from among themselves one Saint, confirmed as such by his miraculous power."[48]

The Catechism continues and warns that all must adhere to the decisions of the church. And when the Pope speaks for the church, he speaks infallibly. "The General Council of the Vatican, in 1870, defined that the Pope is infallible when he teaches the church *ex cathedra*."[49] Contrary to what the Catholic Church tries to convey today, the Catechism maintains that non-Catholics stand little chance for salvation unless they come back into the fold of the mother church.

> From the beginning whoever obstinately refused to accept and believe a doctrine of Catholic Faith, when so declared *ex cathedra* by the Pope, was always cut off from the communion of the church, and condemned as a heretic.[50]

## And Who Is a Heretic?

> All those who by their own fault are Heretics, i.e., who profess
> a doctrine that has been condemned by the church; or who are
> Infidels—that is, who no longer have nor profess any Christian
> faith at all; and 2. All those who by their own fault are Schismatics
> —that is, who have renounced, not the doctrine of the church,
> but their obedience to her, or to her Supreme Head, the Pope.[51]

Further, a heretic is one by his own fault, who knows about the Catholic Church, is convinced of her truth but does not join her. But more, he could know her, if he searched, but through indifference and other culpable motives, neglects to do so.[52]

Apart from the church there is no salvation. "Every one is obliged, under pain of eternal damnation, to become a member of the Catholic Church, to believe her doctrine, to use her means of grace, and to submit to her authority."[53]

From the words of Jesus in Matthew 16, the Catholic Church has constructed a system that confines its followers to its own deadly path. In Peter, power was transferred from bishop to bishop, through the centuries, that has created a mountain of belief from which there is no room for challenge nor is there an escape. Those who do not believe all that the church says are lost.

The keys to the kingdom given to Peter have to do with his role of judgment of the Jewish nation and their notion of the reign of the Messiah. Wherever Peter went, he convicted the Jewish leaders about their rejection of Jesus as their Savior and Messiah. Peter was but the instrument in the hands of a sovereign God to carry out this opening and closing of doors (loosening and binding) spiritually for that generation of the Jewish people.

The church is not that kingdom. But the church is built upon the statement of Peter as to the divine person of the Lord. New Testament history seems to best support these views. In great error, the Catholic Church has created a primacy of Peter from the Matthew 16 passage to support their political structure.

# Questions for Discussion

1. What are some of the arguments that the church is not Israel?
2. In what way does the church rest upon the new covenant?
3. How would you explain the "requirement" for salvation, the "object" of faith for salvation, and the changing "content" of faith for salvation?
4. What are some of the main difficulties with the concept of the covenant of works?
5. What are some of the main difficulties with the covenant of grace or redemption?
6. How would you summarize the issues regarding "binding and loosing"?

## Chapter 3

# The Launching of the New Testament Church

## Introduction

The story of the church in Acts is a fascinating study of the work of the Holy Spirit. The Spirit is the Agent of the church and the Comforter (or Helper) whom Christ would send from the Father (John 15:26). But Acts is not only the story of the activity of the Spirit of God, it describes in detail the human drama of the apostles and the salvation of both the Jews and the Gentiles.

Equally important is the fact that the dispensation of the church starts in the book of Acts. As well, the new covenant is launched with the outpouring of the Spirit at Pentecost. The drama concerning the establishment of the "new thing," the church, actually begins in chapter one.

## The Kingdom Postponed

Following His resurrection, Jesus spent forty days teaching His disciples more about the kingdom (Acts 1:3). Which kingdom? The amillennialist would say the church. But searching through the Gospels one can find only one reference to the church (Matt. 16:16–19). What is also interesting is that in Acts 1:3 there is no description as to what the Lord said about the kingdom. And what He is teaching here in Acts is certainly not about the church. Therefore, the only implication left is that He talked about what the Jews were anticipating, and that was the Davidic millennial reign of the Messiah. And clearly the disciples did not take His words as a reference to this "new thing" coming, the church, because they changed the subject and asked, "Lord, is it at this time You are restoring the kingdom to Israel?" (1:6). The Greek word for restore *(apokathistanō)* is a present indicative and can be translated, "'Are You again presently ordaining' the kingdom to Israel?"

The Lord puts off the question the disciples ask and responds:

*It is not for you to know times or epochs which the Father has
fixed by His own authority; but you shall receive power when
the Holy Spirit has come upon you; and you shall be My witnesses both in Jerusalem, and in all Judea and Samaria, and
even to the remotest part of the earth. (Acts 1:7–8)*

Toussaint well explains:

Some conclude from the Lord's response that the apostles had a
false concept of the kingdom. But this is wrong. Christ did not
accuse them of this. If the followers of the Lord Jesus had an
incorrect view, this would have been the time for Him to correct
it. The fact is, Christ taught the coming of an earthly literal kingdom (cf. Matt. 19:28; Luke 19:11–27; 22:28–30). Acts 1:3 states
that the Lord instructed the disciples about the kingdom; He
certainly gave them the right impression as to its character and
future coming. What Jesus discussed . . . was the time of the
coming of the kingdom.[1]

Jesus told the disciples of the soon coming baptism (washing) of the Holy
Spirit "not many days from now" (1:5), and the empowerment of the same Spirit
for witnessing (1:8). These works of the Spirit of God are part of the dynamics of
the new covenant. And this covenant will have its ultimate fulfillment in the
future Davidic kingdom when the Jews are brought back from the *diaspora*, the
scattering. For it is prophesied through the prophet Ezekiel:

*I will take you from the nations, gather you from all the lands,
and bring you into your own land. Then I will sprinkle [slosh]
clean water on you. . . . And I will put My Spirit within you . . .
And you will live in the land that I gave to your forefathers; so
you will be My people, and I will be your God. (36:24–28)*

*. . . I will bring you into the land of Israel. . . . And I will put My
Spirit within you. (37:12b–14a)*

And the prophet Joel further prophesies:

*And it will come about after this that I will pour out My Spirit on
all mankind. . . . I will pour out My Spirit in those days. (2:28–29)*

But previously, the prophet Jeremiah had prophesied of the coming new
covenant. He writes:

*"Behold, days are coming," declares the Lord, "when I will make a new covenant with the house of Israel and with the house of Judah, not like the covenant which I made with the fathers in the day I took them by the hand to bring them out of the land of Egypt, My covenant which they broke, although I was a husband to them," declares the Lord. (31:31–32)*

Jesus told the disciples in so many words that His death would ratify the new covenant. He said at the Passover meal, "This cup which is poured out for you [My death] is the new covenant in My blood" (Luke 22:20). The apostle Paul puts it all together, the coming of the Holy Spirit, and the contrast between the present time of the new covenant and the fact that the Law has been done away with:

*You [Corinthians] are a letter of Christ, cared for by us, written not with ink, but with the Spirit of the living God, not on tablets of stone [the Law], but on tablets of human hearts [the new covenant]. . . . God, who also made us adequate as servants of a new covenant, not of the letter [of the Law], but of the Spirit [the new covenant]; for the letter kills, but the Spirit gives life. (2 Cor. 3:3–6)*

Returning to Acts, it is clear the apostles were to wait for this outpouring of the Holy Spirit and thus the launching of the new covenant. The covenant and the indwelling of the Holy Spirit would be the dynamic of the dispensation of the church age! The saints of the church would benefit from the new covenant but its ultimate fulfillment will come in the yet future millennial kingdom!

## The Launching of the New Covenant and the Beginning of the Church Age

As described in Acts 2, on the Day of Pentecost the Holy Spirit is poured out upon this small band of believers just as Jesus promised. Pentecost was one of four annual Jewish feasts (after Passover, Unleavened Bread, and Firstfruits). It came fifty days after Firstfruits. (According to Paul in 1 Corinthians 15:23, this is a type of Christ's resurrection.) Pentecost was a Greek name for the Jewish Feast of Weeks, so called because it fell seven (a week of) weeks after Firstfruits. It celebrated the wheat harvest (Exod. 23:16). "This day of Pentecost in Acts 2 marked the beginning of the church."[2]

The Day of Pentecost was known as the Feast of Weeks in the Old Testament (v. 1). When it states *the day,* with a definite article, it shows that Pentecost was now to be fulfilled. In other words, the Feast of Pentecost was about to be fulfilled by the events occurring in this particular chapter. The Greek word translated *was now come* means "in the being fulfilled completely." The point Luke is trying to make in using this particular term is to show that by these events, the Feast of Pentecost is about to be fulfilled. If this was observed on a Sunday in keeping with the Mosaic Law, then this day was also a Sunday and the church was born on a Sunday. *They were all together in one place* is taken by some that this was in the Temple Compound and by others as a gathering in the Upper Room as was the case in chapter one.

Christ will now begin to grow this universal fellowship, the spiritual body of Christ that will be dispensationally broad and worldwide in scope. But how will the local churches be formed? How will they be ordered and governed? How will they function in a hostile world? What will be the main purpose of the local assembly? How will it arm the believing Jew and Gentile for a new task and a unique role?

The book of Acts will show the progressive formation of a local polity. The apostles will be the first leaders, followed by the appointing of elders and deacons. It will be the apostle Paul who will see first, and most clearly, the form and function of this new entity, the local church. Inspired by the Spirit of God, Paul will finalize in his Pastoral Epistles and other letters the issue of leadership, the training of that leadership and its teaching responsibilities. But before looking at this in detail, it is important to go back and examine Acts 2, and other passages, in more detail.

All admit that the church begins in Acts 2 with the outpouring and filling of the Holy Spirit (2:1–4). But it will be by "progressive revelation" that Peter and the other apostles will learn of the nature of this new dispensation called the church age or the age of grace. There is evidence that, even with the coming of the Spirit, Peter did not recognize that a new dispensation had begun. It is more than likely he still looked for some immediate period of world tribulation, with the kingdom then coming after.

For example, when Peter on the day of Pentecost quotes the long paragraph of Joel 2:28–32, he includes that fact of the outpouring of the Spirit but also of coming tribulation events such as "wonders in the sky above, and signs on the earth beneath, blood, and fire, and vapor of smoke" (v. 19). Peter did not know when these things would take place. As far as he may have conjectured, they could be happening soon. And then Jesus would return to reign.

When quoting Joel, much has been made of Peter's statement "This is what was spoken of through the prophet Joel" (v. 16). Some dispensationalists believe that Peter is merely using Joel 2 as an illustration or as a second reference. In other words, yes the Spirit will come launching the kingdom, but Acts 2 is really about the beginning of the church age, with no direct connection to Joel. More prominent is the view that Peter quotes Joel 2, understanding that verses 17–19 in Acts are fulfilled there at Pentecost. The tribulation verses 19–20 are yet to be fulfilled. Toussaint again notes:

This is what was spoken by the Prophet Joel. This clause does not mean, "This is like that," it means Pentecost fulfilled what Joel had described. However, the prophecies of Joel quoted in Acts 2:19–20 were not fulfilled. The implication is that the remainder would be fulfilled if Israel would repent.[3]

The new covenant thus begins at Pentecost with the church enjoying the benefits. The ultimate fulfillment will be for the Jews in the kingdom. This in no way makes the church and the kingdom one. They are still two distinct programs of God. But the work of Christ on the cross and the coming of the Spirit would be of benefit and blessing to both, in their proper order—first the church and then for the period of the kingdom and the regathering of restored Israel.

If the church is actually the kingdom, what is interesting is how few times the word *kingdom*, or the implication for the same, is mentioned in Acts. When *kingdom* or an equivalent is referred to, it is seen as something separate from the church. For example, at the Jerusalem Council, elder James notes the way Peter "has related how God first concerned Himself about taking from among the Gentiles a people for His name" (15:14). Peter of course is referring to the church age. But with the next few verses James quotes Amos 9:11–12:

> *After these things I will return, and I will rebuild the tabernacle*
> *of David which has fallen, and I will rebuild its ruins, and I will*
> *restore it, in order that the rest of mankind may seek the Lord,*
> *and all the Gentiles who are called by My name.*

In the Old Testament text of Amos, the verses actually begin with "In that day I will raise up the fallen booth [tabernacle] of David" (Amos 9:11). But James takes doctrinal and contextual liberty and begins quoting the passage with "After these things . . ."—after the period of the church age. *Then* will come the kingdom, the restoration of David's kingly presence in his offspring Jesus. In other words (1) the church age, then (2) the promised millennial kingdom.

In 3:18–21, Peter seems to better understand God's new order of things. He notes that (1) Christ was prophesied to come and to suffer. God "has thus fulfilled" (v. 18). The Jews should then (2) repent and return to the Lord (v. 19a). Next would follow (3) the "times of refreshing" that would come from the presence of the Lord (v. 19b). This would be God sending "Jesus, the Christ appointed for you, whom heaven must receive until the period of restoration of all things about which God spoke by the mouth of His holy prophets from ancient times" (v. 20–21). Few can deny that the "times of refreshing" and the "restoration" are the kingdom.

Paul also refers indirectly to kingdom judgment in his Mars Hill speech. He says in so many words, during this church age, "God is now declaring to men that all everywhere [worldwide] should repent" (17:30) "because He has fixed a day in which He will judge the world in righteousness through a Man whom He has appointed" (v. 31). But as Acts progresses, the apostles increasingly understand that the church is being built and that this church will contain both believing Jew and Gentile. A future kingdom takes a back seat. And toward the end of Acts, the apostles realized they had no idea when that kingdom would come. God was indeed doing a new thing with the church that was quickly spreading out of Palestine to the ends of the earth.

Early on in Acts, Peter seems to have understood that the new covenant and its intangible blessings of forgiveness of sins, a personal relationship to the Lord, and the coming of the Spirit, all go back to the Abrahamic covenant. To a large crowd of Jews, Peter says:

> *It is you who are the sons of the prophets, and of the covenant which God made with your fathers, saying to Abraham, "And in your seed all the families of the earth shall be blessed." (3:25)*

Why did Peter quote only the portion of the Abrahamic covenant that referred to the families of the earth being blessed? (Gen. 12:3). That of course would be the nations and the Gentiles. He then goes on and speaks of the Jews being blessed by God's Servant Jesus (v. 26) and the fact that there is no other name under heaven "that has been given among men, by which we must be saved" (4:12). This verse also would seem to be directed to the Gentiles. In other words, both peoples would at this present time be blessed by the death and resurrection of the Messiah.

Thus the church was launched at Pentecost with the promised coming of the Holy Spirit (Acts 2:33), and the Spirit taking up residence with the believers who accepted Christ as Savior (2:38).

## The Character of the Early Church

The church at Jerusalem exploded in numbers, with three thousand people accepting Christ as Savior in one day (2:41). It is here in this context (2:41–47) that the word *church* is probably first mentioned. We say "probably" because there is a textual problem in verse 47, where in some Greek texts, the word *church (ekklēsia)* is more than likely included. "And the Lord was adding to [the church] day by day those who were being saved." Verse 41 also reads "were added that day about three thousand souls." Everyone agrees that in both verses "to the local church" is certainly meant by context.

In the Jerusalem church "everyone kept feeling a sense of awe; and many wonders and signs were taking place through the apostles" (v. 43). The new converts were also devoting themselves "to the apostles' teaching and to fellowship, to the breaking of bread and to prayer" (v. 42). The Christians sold their possessions and shared together things in common and gave to those who had need (vv. 44–45). Spiritually they were united "with one mind" coming together in the temple. They were "breaking bread from house to house" and were taking their meals together "with gladness and sincerity of heart, praising God, and having favor with all the people" (vv. 46–47).

There has been no period like this since the beginning of the church. These first converts were open to the gospel but they were also open to their newly found comrades in faith. The euphoria must have been electric and the personal commitment total, both to the Lord and to each other. Could this sustain indefinitely? No, because with all things the human spirit cannot maintain gratitude forever. Carnality would in time set in, as it did in almost all the early churches. But since Jerusalem was ground zero for the beginning of the church, it is possible that this spiritual zeal continued longer here than in many places.

The spiritual force of the early Jerusalem church must have frightened the Jewish rulers because, after Peter and John were arrested, they were released "on account of the people, because they were all glorifying God for" the healing of a sick man (4:9, 21). When Peter and John returned to their Christian companions (v. 23), the believing crowd lifted their voices to God in one accord. They recognized what was happening as a fulfillment of part of Psalm 2 that predicts the evil rulers of the nation coming together against the Lord and against His Christ (vv. 24–26).

Since the Jerusalem congregation "were of one heart and soul" (4:32), "all things were common property to them." The believers were selling even their houses and land to provide for those who were needy (v. 34). This was not a form of communism as some have tried to claim because there was no compulsion to do this. The Christians voluntarily carried out the sale of their own goods and property, with the proceeds handed over to the apostles for distribution. But Ananias and his wife, Sapphira, brought only part of their income on the sale of some property to the apostles, yet gave the impression that they were sharing all of it with the needy (5:1–3). Satan had begun to work on this fledgling church by filling the heart of Ananias to lie (v. 3) not only to the apostles but to the Holy Spirit. Both he (v. 5) and his wife (v. 10) suddenly dropped dead because together they had agreed to put the "Spirit of the Lord to the test" (v. 9).

This of course sobered the believers "and great fear came upon the whole church, and upon all who heard of these things" (v. 11). This verse implies that both the Christians and non-believers were stunned at how quickly the Lord moved against their attempt at deception. Again, it should be noted that what was going on was voluntary and did not become a pattern, doctrinally speaking, for other churches.

## Sunday as Lord's Day, Not Sabbath

A few things should also be said about Sunday, since covenant theologians often insist that Sunday is now the Sabbath and Sabbath laws apply to it.

In many circles it has been taught that Sunday worship universally began only in A.D. 321 with the Law of Constantine, or A.D. 364 with the Council of Laodicea. However, the authors of *From Sabbath to the Lord's Day* have shown with excellent documentation that Sunday worship was a universal practice of all churches outside the land of Israel by the beginning of the second century. They also clearly point out that in those early days, while Sunday was viewed as a day of worship, it was not viewed as a Sabbath.

What later church councils did was ratify a practice already common, and only then did they begin to apply the Sabbath rules to Sunday. In the beginning it was not so. Sunday was a day of worship but not a day of rest. As church history developed, more and more Sabbath laws from the Old Testament were applied to Sunday, and this concept is present to this day. So many speak of the "Christian Sabbath," or the "Sunday Sabbath."

However, it is no more correct to speak of a "Christian Sabbath" than a "Jewish Sunday." Charles Hodge, in his *Systematic Theology,* goes to great lengths to insist that all of the Ten Commandments still apply, including the fourth commandment. He also insists, with no scriptural evidence, that the fourth commandment now applies to the first day of the week and not the seventh. His evidences are all derived from the Old Testament, and he insists that the United States government issue laws that will require Sunday observance in a society that may not even believe. His arguments, taken from the Law of Moses, ignore the seventh day emphasis of that same law.

It should be pointed out that Sunday is never called the Sabbath in the New Testament, but always *the first day of the week.* Nor is it ever called "the Lord's Day." Although the early church fathers certainly did use that term for Sunday, it was not so used in the New Testament. The one place where that term appears is in Revelation 1:10, and there is no reason to assume that this day was a Sunday. There is good reason to believe it was not. In this passage, the term "Lord" in the Greek text is not a noun but an adjective. It would be better translated as a *lordly* day. It does not refer to a specific day of the week such as the Sabbath, Saturday, or Sunday. Rather, it was a day in which John was enraptured by prophetic and divine ecstasy, and received divine revelation. It was a day in which he fell under the control of the Holy Spirit and was given prophetic inspiration. For him it was, indeed, "a lordly day."

It is true that by the second century churches observed Sunday as a day of worship. It is also clear that the Pauline churches in the first century observed the first day of the week as a day of worship. This is rather apparent from Acts 20:7–8, 11:

> *And upon the first day of the week, when we were gathered to-*
> *gether to break bread, Paul discoursed with them, intending to*
> *depart on the morrow; and prolonged his speech until midnight.*
> *And there were many lights in the upper chamber where we were*

*gathered together. . . . And when he was gone up, and had bro-*
*ken the bread, and eaten, and had talked with them a long while,*
*even till break of day, so he departed.*

# The Foundation of the Church (Eph 4:7–16)

The apostle Paul describes in Ephesians (4:7–16) how Christ initially gifted the fledgling church with key authorities and leaders. These important men became the pillars for the expansion and maturity of the early church. Continuing (vv. 7–9), Paul quotes Psalm 68:18 as an illustration of how Christ, as a triumphant warrior, sets His conquered people free and then distributes gifts to His followers. He begins by saying "to each one of us grace was given according to the measure of Christ's gift" (v. 7). The "us" is often thought to refer to all believers in Christ. But more than likely it relates just to the leadership Paul will be describing in verse 11. This makes sense when put this way: "To (leaders) was given grace to equip the saints (the other believers in the church)." Paul pictures Jesus as a Prince who *descended* even to the grave in order that He might *ascend* even into the heavens (vv. 9–10). Through this He gives gifts and creates "gifted" men to help mature the church (vv. 12–16). Who are the gifted men? From the Greek text verse 11 should read:

> *Now on the one hand, He Himself [Christ] imparted some [to*
> *be] apostles, and then some [to be] prophets, and then some*
> *[to be] evangelists, and then some [to be] pastors indeed, that is*
> *teachers!* (trans. author's)

## Apostles

> *He imparted some [to be] apostles.*

The word *apostolos* comes from two Greek words combined. *Apo* means "from, away from," and the verb *stellō* means "to send."[4] The word thus means "one sent forth." In classical Greek the word was often used to describe a "ship commander," a "bill of lading," and sometimes a passport, dispatch, or letter. In the New Testament the word describes a delegate, messenger, or an envoy.

Believers in Christ, in a broad and general sense, are seen as apostles. "As for our brothers, they are *messengers (apostoloi)* of the churches" (2 Cor. 8:23). Then there were the original twelve apostles, called by Bauer the super-apostles or "the most eminent apostles" (2 Cor. 12:11).

The apostle Paul was very close in rank to the twelve, for he writes: "For in no respect was I inferior to the most eminent apostles, even though I am a nobody. The signs of a true apostle were performed among you [by me] with all perseverance, by signs and wonders and miracles" (2 Cor. 12:11–12). Finally, there were others in a wider sense recognized as special apostles such as Barnabas

(Acts 19:4, 14), possibly James (1 Cor. 15:7), Silvanus (1 Thess. 2:6), and perhaps also Andronicus and Junias (Rom. 16:7).[5] Concerning the first order of apostles, Hodge writes:

> First, the apostles, the immediate messengers of Christ, the witnesses for him, of his doctrines, his miracles, and of his resurrection; infallible as teachers and absolute as rulers in virtue of the gift of inspiration and of their commission. No man, therefore, could be an apostle unless—1. He was immediately appointed by Christ. 2. Unless he had seen him after his resurrection and had received the knowledge of the Gospel by immediate revelation. 3. Unless he was rendered infallible by the gift of inspiration. These things constituted the office and were essential to its authority. Those who without these gifts and qualifications claimed the office are called "false apostles."[6]

MacArthur adds:

> In its primary and most technical sense *apostle* is used in the New Testament only of the twelve, including Matthias, who replaced Judas (Acts 1:26), and of Paul, who was uniquely set apart as apostle to the Gentiles (Gal. 1:15–17; cf. I Cor. 15:7–9; 2 Cor. 11:5). The qualifications for that apostleship were having been chosen directly by Christ and having witnessed the resurrection (Mark 3:13; Acts 1:22–24). Paul was the last to meet these qualifications (Rom. 1:1; etc.). It is not possible therefore, as some claim, for there to be apostles in the church today. Some have observed that the apostles were like delegates to a constitutional convention. When the convention is over, the position ceases. When the New Testament was completed, the office of apostle ceased.[7]

The apostles may be seen as Stage One in the building of the church and its authoritative structure. But again, as MacArthur so well said, that office is no longer here today. Few would try to claim that there are apostles with us now with the stature and power of a Peter or Paul.

### Prophets
> *. . . then some [to be] prophets.*

The prophets of the Old Testament were inspired by the Holy Spirit to speak and record the full message God intended for the nation of Israel. But, as we shall see, some of the New Testament prophets would be different.

The New Testament "writing" apostles were prophets who delivered the Word of God under the full and complete guidance of the Spirit. These apostolic prophets also, as the prophets in the Old Testament, wrote with absolute divine authority. Thus, they made pronouncement on current problems, gave doctrinal guidance, and verbally judged specific local church issues.

But Paul (Eph. 4:11) is referring to other prophets in the New Testament context besides the apostles. God specially appointed gifted men with the ability to prophesy (1 Cor. 12:10). Their prophecies included some fore-telling of future events but generally was forth-telling, as teaching truths not fully understood nor revealed in complete detail. These prophets spoke *relatively,* not *absolutely,* in that they did not have "full" inspiration by the Holy Spirit. What they said had to be checked and balanced and their teaching could be questioned or corrected. The apostle Paul writes that someday the gift of prophecy would be done away with.

Acts 11:28 gives an example of one of these prophets fore-telling. Again, this is rare in the New Testament: "And one of them named Agabus stood up and began to indicate by the Spirit that there would certainly be a great famine all over the world. And this took place in the reign of Claudius." Agabus also predicted the arrest of Paul in Jerusalem (Acts 21:11).

In 1 Corinthians 14, Paul emphasizes the importance of the gift of prophecy as teaching. In fact, more than likely, the ability of telling future events was no longer with the prophets. The apostle writes, "Desire spiritual gifts but especially prophecy" (14:1); "one who prophesies speaks [in regard to men, Greek] for edification, exhortation and consolation" (14:3); "greater is the one who prophesies than one who speaks in tongues" (14:5); "tongues are for a sign, not to those who believe, but to unbelievers; but prophecy is for a sign, not to unbelievers, but to those who believe" (14:22); "[when] two or three prophets speak, . . . let the others pass judgment" (14:29); through prophecy "all may learn and all may be exhorted" (14:31); and "the spirits of prophets are subject to prophets" (14:32).

The apostle Paul clearly states that the gift of prophecy would disappear: "If there are gifts of prophecy, they will 'in the future be made inoperative' [future passive indicative, *katargeō*]" (13:8). The New Testament prophets were used of the Lord to "teach" the fledgling congregations because all the inspired letters had not been completed or totally circulated. These special men were able to "fill in" truth about the work of God through Christ that had not fully been understood. When the New Testament canon was completed and the inspired books from the apostles began to be circulated, this gift faded.

In conclusion, it may be said that the prophets were speaking and teaching for God but they were not revealing a "new" message from the Lord. The prophets were important, as emphasized by Paul when he placed them in second position after the apostles (Eph. 4:11). But then the office of prophet ceased after the completion of the New Testament, like the office of apostle. The same thing happened with the Old Testament. Those ancient prophets disappeared when that testament was finished about four hundred years before Christ. Jesus is the corner stone and the New Testament apostles and prophets are the foundation upon which the household of God was then constructed (Eph. 2:20).

## Evangelists

> *Then some [to be] evangelists.*

The word *evangelist* comes from two Greek words, *eu,* which means "good," and *angelia,* which means "message." Thus, "the good message" or "good message bearer." The evangelist and pastor are the last two pillars Paul mentions in Ephesians (4:11). It might be argued that the first two roles, the apostles and prophets, have passed away but the last two, evangelists and pastors, are still with us. The verse itself would not indicate that, but other factors may, such as the factual evidence from church history. Yet there must be a caution here.

There can yet be evangelists after the example, say, of Philip. But God is not "authorizing" the message of evangelists today in the same way as He did with Philip. It was said directly of Philip that he performed signs (Acts 8:6), that he was led of the Spirit to the Ethiopian's chariot (8:28), that he was told by the angel to go into Gaza (8:26), and that he was snatched away by the Holy Spirit after he witnessed to the Ethiopian (8:39). By God's continuing providence, He leads all who are serving Him. But this direct guidance, as with Philip, is not how the Lord works today.

Evangelists then are men who go about exclusively sharing the good news of Christ to a disbelieving society. Evangelists will speak with anyone, at any time, in any place. Ironically, the word *evangelist* is only used in two places: Ephesians 4:11 and Acts 21:8. Philip is called an evangelist (Acts 21:8) and Acts (8:4–40) tells of his work of sharing. Philip was one of the few outside the apostles performing miracles as he proclaimed Christ (8:5–7), and the crowds listened hard to his every word (8:6). "There was much rejoicing in the city" from his evangelism (8:8). Philip was led to speak with the Ethiopian eunuch (8:26), and "he kept preaching the gospel to all the cities, until he came to Caesarea" (8:4).

Again, there are parallels between Philip and evangelists today. But Philip's evangelism, as with all the miracle dynamics, is no longer with us. The Scriptures are sufficient for the message of salvation and for living out the Christian life.

Although the office of evangelist is only mentioned in the New Testament twice, young pastor Timothy was encouraged to "do the work of an evangelist" (2 Tim. 4:5). Yet these limited references describe a vital, extensive, and far-reaching ministry, indicated by the use of the verb *euangelizō* (to proclaim the good news) fifty-four times and the noun *euangelion* (good news) seventy-six times. God was the first evangelist, since He "preached the gospel beforehand" (from *proeuangelizomai*; Gal. 3:8). Even the angel evangelized ("I bring . . . good news," [from *euangelizomai*]) in announcing the birth of Christ (Luke 2:10). Jesus Himself evangelized in "preaching the gospel" (Luke 21:1), as did the apostles in "preaching the word" (Acts 8:4).[8]

Church history describes hundreds of evangelists such as D. L. Moody, Charles Spurgeon, Billy Sunday, and Billy Graham. And yet every believer in Christ has the privilege and obligation as a servant to share the new covenant, which is the gospel message of Christ's saving grace (2 Cor. 3:4–8). Because one does not have the gift does not mean one is not responsible for witnessing of his faith.

### *Pastors*

> *Then some [to be] pastors, teachers.*

Because the issue of pastor is crucial, an entire chapter will be given to this important position. (See chapter 15.)

## The First Organization of the Early Church

Despite the first persecution against the ministry and witness of the apostles in Jerusalem, the church kept growing. After Peter and some of the disciples were flogged by the council of elders, they went forth rejoicing (5:41) "and every day, in the temple and from house to house, they kept right on teaching and preaching Jesus as the Christ" (v. 42).

Though their numbers kept increasing, a division arose among the Christians, that is, between native Jews of Jerusalem and Jews who were from Greece. The latter were called Hellenists and had been highly influenced by the cosmopolitan attitudes of Greek society (6:1). The problem was that poor widows in the flock were not receiving daily meals and the Hellenistic Jews were incensed and began to complain.

The twelve disciples called a meeting of the congregation and made mention of how the word of God was going forth through their ministry (v. 2). They were also giving themselves to much time in prayer (v. 4). Since God was blessing these efforts and this dedication, they needed help. They urged the church to select men who could serve tables. They were looking for men "full of the Spirit and of wisdom" to do the task (v. 3). The congregation agreed, choosing seven men from their midst (v. 5). The disciples prayed over them and laid their hands on them (v. 6). Now that some of the behind-the-scenes things were being taken care of, Luke writes:

> *And the word of God kept on spreading; and the number of the disciples continued to increase greatly in Jerusalem, and a great many of the priests were becoming obedient to the faith. (v. 7)*

Though the term *deacon* is not used of these seven individuals, this is the first official "board" or group chosen to perform specific tasks within the body of the local church. The word *diakonia* is used of their activity in verses 1–2. The apostles were acting as elders who were spiritually in charge of the church. Later on in Acts, they would pass the torch of responsibility to men called elders. Though the office of deacon is not mentioned again in Acts, it is noted as a separate working group in Paul's greeting to the church at Philippi (Phil. 1:1). Paul sees the body of deacons, though servants in the church, as a selection of men with high moral and spiritual standards (1 Tim. 3:8–13). (More on the deacon in chapter 16.)

# The Appointment of Elders in Acts

(For a full discussion of church elders, see chapters 15, 16, and 17). Elders seem to appear suddenly in the book of Acts. The apostles were acting as elders in Acts 6 when the issue of feeding the widows arose. The word elder (*presbyteros*) is first used in the early chapters of Acts to refer to the elders of Israel, those ruling the Jewish nation from Jerusalem.

The first reference to church elders comes up in 11:30. It is mentioned in the context that the church of Antioch decides to send a relief contribution with Saul and Barnabas to the elders in Jerusalem. After Paul and Barnabas had proclaimed the gospel to the cities of Derbe, Lystra, and Iconium, they "appointed elders for them in every church, and having prayed with fasting, they commended [the new elders] to the Lord in whom they had believed" (14:23). It is clear from this passage and others that a plurality of elders is assigned for each church.

When the issue of circumcision of the Gentiles and the "custom of Moses" came up, Paul and Barnabas were ordered to go up to Jerusalem to present their opinions before the apostles and the elders of Jerusalem (15:1–2). This phrase "the apostles and the elders" is repeated four more times in this chapter (vv. 4, 6, 22, 23). Obviously, by this time in the book of Acts, the apostles are sharing leadership with the elders at the Jerusalem church. They are brought into the decision-making process concerning this doctrinal problem.

After it was decided that the Gentile believers did not need to be circumcised, "the apostles and the elders, with the whole church," chose Paul, Barnabas, Judas (Barsabbas), and Silas to journey as delegate/missionaries back to Antioch, Syria, and Cilicia to inform these new congregations of their conclusions. In this case, the whole church is in on the decision as to who would speak for them about relieving the Gentiles from law-keeping. When Paul and Timothy start again to other congregations delivering these same "decrees" about circumcision, the Jerusalem apostles and elders for a second time give approval for this mission (16:4).

During Paul's third missionary journey (ca. A.D. 51), the church at Ephesus becomes an important stopover for the apostle. Later, from Miletus, he summons the Ephesian elders to hear a final word of warning. Realizing his days to minister may be cut short, he urges them to be on guard against "savage wolves" who will attempt "to draw away the disciples" to follow after perverse things (20:30). Paul assumes in his discussion that they are now fully mature and responsible for what will happen in that congregation. He says, "The Holy Spirit has made you overseers, to shepherd the church of God" (v. 28). The word *overseer (episkopos)* is one of the title designations for church elder (Titus 1:6–8). The verb "to shepherd" is related to the noun "shepherd" or "pastor." The elders then kneel down and pray with Paul, "grieving especially over the word which he had spoken, that they should see his face no more" (Acts 20:38).

The final reference to the church elders is mentioned in 21:18. Back in Jerusalem, Paul gives a final report about his journeys to the brethren, James, and the elders. It is believed that within the next nineteen years all of the apostles (except John) will have been martyred for their faith and witness to the resurrection of Christ. The elders in all the churches would then have absolute leadership over the spiritual issues in all the churches in Palestine, Asia, and Europe. By the words of the apostle John to the churches in Revelation (chapters 2–3) it is clear that many in leadership failed and did not hold to the truth. The churches were full of unbelievers. Cult activity and apostasy rampant. The legacy of church history will be filled with both the failure and faithfulness of congregational elders. The final story will not be told until the *bema* seat judgment!

## Jesus the Savior

Though complicated questions about the doctrine of salvation arose later in the book of Acts, the simple formula of salvation by grace through faith was preached at the beginning of the church. Faith, in order to receive eternal life through Christ, dominates the Acts both in the verb *(pisteuō)* and noun *(pistis)* form.

All those trusting the Lord were collectively called those "that believed" (2:44). Other believers were added (5:14). Those saved believed "the word" (4:4), believed in their heart (8:37), having believed purified the heart (15:9), believed that Jesus Christ was the Son of God (8:37). As well, they believed that He was the Lord (9:42), in believing they "turned" (11:21), were justified (13:39), and received eternal life (13:48). This faith would be in His name (3:16), and toward the Lord Jesus (20:21).

When Jesus had first revealed Himself to Paul, He told him in a vision that he would be sent as a witness and as a minister (26:16–17), and that those who trusted in Him (26:18) would receive forgiveness of sins, be given an inheritance, and be sanctified. All classes and races accepted Christ, even the Lord's enemies such as the Pharisees (15:5), the Pharisee Saul (later Paul) (9:17), the eunuch from Abyssinia (8:37), Greeks (14:1), Romans (10:43–48), and the Philippian jailer and his family (16:31–34).

Early on in Acts it was established that salvation by simple faith would be extended to those "outside" Israel, the Gentiles. In Peter's vision of the sheet filled with unclean animals the Lord impressed upon the apostle the principle, "What God has cleansed, no longer consider unholy" (10:15). By chapter 15 of Acts, Gentiles in Phoenicia, Samaria, and elsewhere were coming to Christ by the hundreds (15:3). But at the first Jerusalem Council, some Christian Pharisees still thought "it is necessary to circumcise [the Gentiles], and to direct them to observe the Law of Moses" (v. 5). A great debate followed, but Peter stood up and said:

> *By my mouth the Gentiles should hear the word of the gospel and believe. And God, who knows the heart, bore witness to them, giving them the Holy Spirit, just as He also did to us; and He made no distinction between us and them, cleansing their hearts by faith. . . . we believe that we are saved through the grace of the Lord Jesus, in the same way as they also are. (15:7–11)*

Peter's speech will set the pace for defining the gospel from this point forward in the New Testament. He makes it clear that salvation is by faith alone to all who call upon the name of the Lord. It is by trusting Christ apart from works or any other expression of human effort. The norm for personal salvation is set here in Acts and carried forth in the writings of Paul. But quite early in church history, the truth will be twisted. Baptism and infant baptism will quickly begin to dominate and determine who is saved. And deep into the Middle Ages, to receive salvation, or to keep it, one must perform many acts prescribed by the Catholic Church.

## The First Seminary at Antioch

The apostle Paul soon developed a pattern of staying at one location for a season to establish lasting doctrinal roots. For example, when Paul arrived in Philippi, Luke writes that they "were staying in this city for some days" (16:12). After finding Lydia at Philippi, additional days or weeks were added after she "prevailed upon us" (v. 15), and they stayed for many more days teaching (v. 18). At Corinth Paul stayed a year and a half (18:11), and about three years total in Ephesus (19:8, 10; 20:30). Paul and other teachers saw the benefit of plowing the furrows straight and deep with the result, "The word of the Lord was growing mightily and prevailing" (19:20).

But Paul went further in the city of Antioch. There is a tremendous lesson for the church of Jesus Christ today in the way Christianity took hold in that city. The message of Christ and His resurrection would sink deep and root itself in the people of Paul's generation, but more, it would survive for generations after the New Testament times in Antioch and influence for hundreds of years the teaching ministry of Christianity. To comprehend the full picture we must go back to the pagan history of that city.

In early days Damascus had been the natural capital of Syria, which lies to the north of Palestine. But when the Greeks poured into the land after Alexander, it was clear that they wanted the center of their regional government to be closer to the Mediterranean and Asia Minor. Thus the headquarters of the Seleucid Empire was founded not far from the sea, on great roads, and actually on part of an island in the Orontes River. By 175 B.C. and the time of Antiochus Epiphanes, the city had great temples and public buildings.

When the Roman general Pompey overthrew the Greek Seleucid rule, he made it a Roman capital but also a free city. All the Jews who had been enslaved by the Greeks were set free and their possessions returned to them. After a terrible earthquake in A.D. 37, the people quickly restored the town. The city became even more important. Its literature, along with its art and culture, was praised by Cicero. The Jewish historian Josephus called the town the third city in the Empire after Rome and Alexandria. The people were known for their independence, pride, and notorious insolence. A great number of Romans and Jews flocked to Antioch and established large colonies and settlements.[9] But there was a dark side to Antioch.

Poets had spent their youth in Antioch, great generals had died there, and emperors had visited the city and admired it. But, according to Conybeare and Howson, "Its population was a worthless rabble of Greeks and Orientals."[10] The people spent time with frivolous amusements and theater. They were extremely superstitious, following Chaldean astrologers, worshiping in groves of trees with their votaries to the statue of Apollo. The city was a sanctuary for an ongoing festival of vice and lust. It was in this setting that Christianity landed.

The drama concerning Antioch begins in Acts 6:5. One of the first deacons appointed for the young church in Jerusalem is a Gentile proselyte named Nicolas from Antioch. But the story of the metropolis really begins in chapter 11. With the martyrdom of Stephen, persecution against the Jerusalem believers began with a vengeance (v. 19). Many Jewish Christians traveled north along the coast to Phoenicia and boarded ships westward for the island of Cyprus, where there was a large colony of Jews.

As the Jews were being saved on that island, the salvation message was spreading to Cyrene also. Those being saved were speaking the message of Christ to their Greek friends who in turn crossed over to the Mediterranean eastward to speak to other Greeks at Antioch (v. 20). Palestinian Jews took the gospel to Hellenistic Jews who carried it to the Greeks. At Antioch the gospel message exploded with "the hand of the Lord . . . with them, and a large number who believed turned to the Lord" (v. 21).

But when the news reached the mother church in Jerusalem, the leaders there wanted to be sure that what was happening was indeed from God. Barnabas was dispatched to find out (v. 22). Rejoicing, he witnessed the grace of God in that city and urged the new converts "with resolute hearts to remain true to the Lord" (v. 23). Luke summarizes this sudden evangelism by concluding, "And considerable numbers were brought to the Lord" (v. 24).

But the next short verse will change forever the nature of Christianity. It simply reads: "And [Barnabas] left for Tarsus to look for Saul [Paul]" (v. 25). Why? The answer seems quite obvious. Having lived his adult life as a staunch, religious Pharisee, and having been raised in an orthodox, aristocratic family in the Greek city of Tarsus, no one could be better suited to speak to the Hellenistic minds of Antioch. Almost eleven years had passed since the conversion of Paul; surely by now his genuineness as a follower of Christ had been proven.

For a year, Barnabas and Paul "taught considerable numbers, and the disciples were first called Christians in Antioch" (v. 26). About the same time, Luke recalls, Agabus and other prophets came down from Jerusalem and spoke of a coming famine that would be all over the world (v. 28). By now, the congregation of believers in the Lord constituted a large number. A contribution was collected for famine relief for the churches in Judea and Jerusalem (v. 29). This was sent to the elders, probably meaning the leaders in Jerusalem (v. 30). These elders, who had previously been skeptical of Saul when he first came to Jerusalem, would now have to rethink their opinion of him.

Antioch will become Paul's teaching headquarters but also his place of departure for his missionary tours into Asia Minor. He will spend much time here instructing and building up the saints. It is likely that a doctrinal center or seminary was established. Church history will relate how the importance of Antioch as a learning haven will continue for several centuries.

Some fifteen years after Paul's conversion, Luke relates how there was a conclave of "prophets and teachers" residing in Antioch (13:1). Possibly some of these men came from a wealthy background and, like Paul, were from aristocratic families. These were godly men who listened to the prompting of the Holy Spirit to commission Barnabas and Paul "for the work to which I have called them" (v. 2). This commissioning would begin with the first missionary endeavor to Asia and Galatia. Upon their return to Antioch,

> *when they had arrived and gathered the church together, they*
> *began to report all things that God had done with them and how*
> *He had opened a door of faith to the Gentiles. And they spent a*
> *long time with the disciples. (14:27–28)*

It was at Antioch that Jewish legalism and Pharisaism attempted to regain a foothold. Legalists from Jerusalem came to the city preaching that believers in Christ had to be circumcised according to the custom of Moses in order to be saved (15:1). Paul and Barnabas "had great dissension and debate with them" (v. 2), with the result that the church sent them to Jerusalem to bring the issue before the apostles and elders. This first Jerusalem Council ruled through a letter sent back to Antioch that "it seemed good to the Holy Spirit and to us to lay upon you no greater burden then these essentials: that you abstain from things sacrificed to idols and from blood and from things strangled and from fornication" (vv. 28–29). This epistle seems to have had wide circulation even outside of Antioch (v. 23).

When Barnabas and Paul brought this letter back to Antioch, the congregation rejoiced with encouragement (v. 31). Besides reading the edict to the church, two other prophets, Judas and Silas, stayed and "encouraged and strengthened the brethren with a lengthy message" (v. 32). As well, "Paul and Barnabas stayed in Antioch, teaching and preaching, with many others also, the word of the Lord" (v. 35).

The last mention of Antioch of Syria is in 18:22–23. The apostle Paul had returned from his second missionary excursion and spent "some time there." The church would continue to benefit from his teaching and missionary experience, even long after the death of Paul and other early giants of the faith. The believers were blessed more than any other group in the experience of the early church. Though Christianity suffered turmoil and persecution for many decades, scholars would come to Antioch to study, learn, and then teach others what was first expounded by Paul and Barnabas.

It can safely be said that an influential school was established in Antioch. Ramm writes:

It has been said that the first Protestant school of hermeneutics [interpretation] flourished in the city of Antioch of Syria, and had it not been crushed by the hand of orthodoxy for its supposed heretical connections with the Nestorians, the entire course of church history might have been different. The Christian community was influenced by the Jewish community and the result was a hermeneutical theory which avoided the letterism of the Jews and the allegorism of the Alexandrians.[11]

Through the years the school at Antioch produced great Bible expositors such as Lucian, Dorotheus, Diodorus, Theodore of Mopuestia, Chrysostom. Too, it touched Jerome and answered Origen's allegorism.[12] The Antiochian scholars were not dogmatic in their exegesis. They held to the literalness of the Old Testament. They fought allegorists who tried to do away with the historicity of the older testament.[13] And they defended the unity of Scripture.[14]

Ramm concludes:

The result of these principles was some of the finest exegetical literature of ancient times. As [G. H.] Gilbert says, "The commentary of Theodore [of Mopsuestia] on the minor epistles of Paul is the first and almost the last exegetical work produced in the ancient church which will bear any comparison with modern commentaries." Grant observes that this school had a remarkable influence in the Middle Ages and became the pillar of the Reformation and finally became the "principle exegetical method of the Christian church."[15]

# Questions for Discussion

1. What are some of the scriptural arguments for the postponement of the kingdom?
2. What does the apostle James have in mind when he begins his quote of Amos 9:11 with "After these things . . ."?
3. Discuss the maturing character of the church as it flourished and developed.
4. Why is Sunday not the Sabbath?
5. What is so important about Ephesians 4:7–16?
6. What are the characteristics and functions of New Testament prophets?
7. What was the role of evangelists?
8. What seems to be the big misunderstanding about the words "pastors" and "teachers"?
9. What was the lasting importance of the city of Antioch?

## Chapter 4

# How Christ Treats the Church: Ephesians 5:22–32

## Introduction

To understand Ephesians 5 and how Christ deals with the church we must first ask whether the church is a distinct body in this present dispensation. Was the church an issue in Old Testament prophecy? The answer is a loud and firm no! Then the church is not fulfilling Israel's promises, but instead Israel will fulfill them in the future. Therefore, premillennialism with a dispensational viewpoint understands the church as a distinct entity, different from Israel in her beginning, in her relationship to this age, and in her promises.

One of the most important passages that shows how Christ deals with the church is Ephesians 5:22–32. Here the principles are laid out that demonstrate His care and concern for His own, the spiritual body of believers. This section is a masterpiece of literature in that Paul really handles two subjects at once. He shows how husbands should treat their wives as he describes how the Lord relates to His wife, the body of Christ.

Most believe the first application of this passage concerns how husbands are to love their wives. But the other issue is really dominant: In what way does the Lord relate to His wife, the church? Obviously, it is with great care, devotion, and love. Thus, the way Christ treats His own body, His church right now, becomes a prime example for husbands caring for their wives.

Several key phrases and words are used to help fully explain this Ephesian passage. They fall into the category of comparative language. The word *hōs* is used four times (vv. 22, 23, 24, 28), and the phrases *houtōs kai* and *kathōs kai* are used twice (vv. 24, 28). These words can be translated "as," and "so also." Thus, "Wives, be subject to your own husbands, As [if] to the Lord" (v. 22), and "*as* the church is subject to Christ, *so also* the wives ought to be to their husbands" (v. 24). The spiritual relationship Jesus has with His own becomes the pattern as to how husbands should relate to their wives.

## The Issue of Submission

> . . . *the church is subject to Christ . . . (v. 24)*

The wife is to submit to the husband just as the church is to submit to Christ. But this is difficult for this present generation to do. The issue of wife submission today is hotly contested. And yet the Word of God is clear. "Wives, be subject to your own husbands, as to the Lord" (v. 22). Though the verb *submit* is actually not in this verse, it is carried over from verse 21 where it is explicitly used. Lenski points out, "No verb is needed [in verse 22], an imperative, 'let them subject themselves,' being automatically supplied."[1] The Greek word is *hypotassō* and means to "under-attach," or, "to place under," to "subordinate yourself," "to subject oneself," "to serve," "to affix under" as attaching a memo to a document.[2] From this the idea of commitment can also be included. Yet A. T. Robertson notes a stronger meaning: "Old military figure to line up under."[3] "What is insisted on is subordination to a leading authority."[4]

The verb is in the form of a present middle participle which could be translated "be continually submitting yourselves to your own husbands." "This is also voluntary self-subjugation. Moreover, it is Christian: 'as to the Lord,' i.e., as rendering this self-subjugation to the Lord in obedience to his blessed will."[5]

Though Paul gives marriage as an illustration in this passage, his main purpose is to show the relationship between Christ and His church.[6] His strategy is to show how the church is to submit to the Lord. This is a self-subjugation, a voluntary obedience. The members of the body of Christ are to lose their will, their own desires. They are to put aside what they want for the church and seek what Christ wishes.

Verse 24 is one of the most important verses and should read from the Greek text: "Nevertheless as the church is subordinating itself [*hypotassō*, present middle indicative] to Christ, likewise also the wives to the husbands in all things." With *alla* beginning the clause, "Its emphatic force may be brought out by the words *in fact . . . in fact,* as the church is subject to Christ."[7] Christ does not ask His church to submit to Him. It is clearly part and parcel of the relationship. Lenski further notes, "The verb is the middle voice: the church subjects herself voluntarily, joyfully. This is her normal and natural relation to Christ, which could not be otherwise."[8]

## The Issue of Headship

> . . . *Christ also is the head of the church, He Himself being the Savior of the body.* (v. 23)

The Greek text better reads, "For a man [husband] is a head of the woman [wife] just as *(hōs)* also the Christ [is a] head of the church."

In today's revisionist climate, there are those who wish to redefine headship. Headship, some say, simply implies that Christ, the Head, has but a substantive relation with the church, i.e., the body depends on the blood flow and nerves coming from the head. By this they can then say that a husband's headship simply means there is a relationship between the two in the marriage arrangement.

Though this is certainly true, Paul's point is deeper for the following reasons: (1) Since Jesus is the Savior of the church, He has the right to lead it. (2) The very idea of submission in the context implies one is leader over the other. As Christ leads the church, so husbands lead their wives. This is reinforced when Paul writes, "Wives, be subject to your own husbands, as to the Lord" (v. 22). "As to the Lord" means "as if you were subjecting yourself to Him." In marriage, as with Christ, this submission is to be real, not simply through lip service. And yet too, there must be a voluntary attitude with a response that comes from a heart of love rather than from forced compulsion.

> In 1 Corinthians 11:12 Paul has already marked out a hierarchy in which God is seen as the head of Christ, Christ as the head of the man, and the man as the head of the woman. Here he looks at it from another angle. If the head of the woman is the man and the head of the church is Christ (Eph. 1:22; 4:12, 16), then it is permissible to draw an analogy between the wife's relationship to her husband and the church's relation to Christ.[9]

From a study of the word *kephalē,* there is little doubt as to what Paul is intending to say. Balz and Schneider point out:

> The meaning of kephala as *leader, chief, master,* . . . is attested for the Hebrew and Aramaic equivalents . . . . Paul in 1 Cor. 11:3 . . . combine[s] the sociological fact of ancient patriarchalism . . . with the theological idea of origin and rule.[10]

And,

> . . . where the dominance of the husband over the wife (cf. 1 Cor. 11:3) finds its analogy *(hōs)* in the relationship of Christ to the church; *kephalē* is intended to express sovereignty.[11]

Concerning headship, MacArthur points out that the head gives direction and the body responds. "A physical body that does not respond to the direction of the head is crippled, paralyzed, or spastic."[12] He further notes:

> The supreme and ultimate model of submission is Jesus Christ Himself, who performed the supreme act of submission by giving His own sinless life to save a sinful world. Christ is the Savior of the body, His church, for whom He died on the cross. He is the perfect Provider, Protector, and Head of His church, which is His body.[13]

Finally, Hodge suggests, "Because Christ is the head of the church, he is its Saviour; . . . he should not only rule, but protect and bless."[14] And because He is the Son of God, He has an eminency, a superiority in attributes which enable and entitle Him to lead and command. He is greater, stronger, all-sovereign, and bolder in referring to the church. Jesus possesses greater mental and moral capacities which are needed in a leader and head. Thus He is qualified and entitled to command since He exists in the image and glory of God.

The superiority of Christ, as taught in Scripture and observed in the gospel accounts of His life, should cause the church to bow before Him and submit with great joy to His love and care!

## The Issue of Love

> *. . . Christ also loved the church and gave Himself up for her . . . (v. 25)*

Christ proved His love for the church by the fact that He loved (aorist tense) her and gave (aorist tense) Himself up for her (v. 25). His love was demonstrated by His death for His church. He further shows His care by nourishing and "warming" the church (v. 29). This is going on now. Christ is presently nourishing *(ektrephō)* His own. The *ek* on the front of the verb "may point to the careful, continued nourishing from one stage to another, nourishing up to maturity."[15] Alford notes:

> As the woman owed her natural being to the man, her source and head, so we owe our entire spiritual being to Christ, our source and head: and as the woman was one flesh with the man in this natural relation, so we in our entire spiritual relation, body, soul, and Spirit, are one with Christ, God manifested in our humanity—parts and members of His glorified body.[16]

# The Issue of Sanctification

> *. . . that He might sanctify her, having cleansed her by the washing of water with the word . . . (v. 26)*

The words "sanctify" (v. 26) and "holy" (v. 27) come from the Greek verb *hagiazō* and have the force of "to make something unique, special," or "to set something or someone aside" as special. Note that Christ sanctified the church by "having cleansed her by the washing of water with the word" (v. 26). This is positional sanctification that is carried out by the work of the Holy Spirit. It is not accomplished by the ritual of water baptism.

> Probably *water* and *word* are used synonymously. This clearly cannot be a reference to baptism or baptismal regeneration. Just as water washes the body, so the Word of God washes the heart (cf. Ezek. 36:27) . . . the ultimate object for which Christ gave himself. The word "sanctify" shows the immediate object . . . a glorious church.[17]

Hoehner adds:

> This is not baptismal regeneration for that would be contrary to Paul's teaching in this book as well as all his other writings and the entire New Testament. Metaphorically, being regenerated is pictured as being cleansed by water (cf. "the washing of rebirth" in Titus 3:5). The "Word" *(rhemati)* refers to the "preached Word" that unbelievers hear (cf. *rhema* in Eph. 6:17; Rom. 10:8; 17; 1 Peter 1:25). The ultimate purpose of Christ's death is "to present . . . to Himself" the church as radiant or "in splendor."[18]

That the church would be without "spot or wrinkle" and should be "holy and blameless" (v. 27) are all positional issues. Experientially, and in the context of time, the imperfections of the church, even the saved who are daily living out shortcomings in their lives, are clearly seen. No believer in Christ lives a perfect, sinless existence. But holiness and blamelessness in this passage are positional, that is, it is how God sees the saints in their spiritual relationship with Jesus. It is a timeless matter because the application of Christ's sacrifice has eternal consequences. Of course it is the Spirit of God who works all of this together.

The divine purpose of election and predestination is to make those chosen before the foundation of the world to be "set apart," or positionally "holy." Thus Christ is presenting to Himself in all its new perfection His bride! Earthly brides prepare and give themselves to their husbands, whereas the Lord prepares His own bride for Himself.

## The Issue of Mistreatment

> *. . . no one ever hated his own flesh, but nourishes and cherishes it, just as Christ also does the church . . . (v. 29)*

*Hate (miseō)* is an intense Greek word. In this context it sets forth the idea to abuse and mistreat. As a husband would be foolish to do this to his wife, who is part of a oneness with him, how much more the Lord Jesus Christ would not do harm to His own body, the collective believers who have trusted Him for salvation? And yet the Lord may discipline His own in order to bring about correction (Heb. 12:5–11). But He would certainly not allow one of His own children to go without spiritual food to facilitate growth and maturity. And that is what this passage is about.

"Because we are members of His body" (v. 30), He nourishes and cherishes His own, who are a part of that body (v. 29). In the human realm, one may not like the body he has. One could wish to be more handsome, or stronger, or healthier. Yet it is still his own body. It is himself. And therefore he nourishes and warms it for his own good. How much more the Lord Jesus does for His church, His body which He cherishes. Being the One who died for this collection of sinners, He could do no other.

> There is never a moment that Christ does not tenderly watch over his body, the church. We are under his constant surveillance. His eyes are constantly upon us, from the beginning of the year even to the end of the year (cf. Deut. 11:12). Therefore we cast all our anxiety upon him, convinced that we are his personal concern (1 Peter 5:7), the objects of his very special providence.[19]

## The Issue of Oneness

> *For this cause a man shall leave his father and mother, and shall cleave to his wife, and the two shall become one flesh. This mystery is great; but I am speaking with reference to Christ and the church. (vv. 31–32)*

In these two verses, is Paul denying the oneness between husband and wife? Not at all. Though in Genesis (2:24) the full implication is not given, common sense would say it refers to the oneness in conjugal union but surely more. It would also have to do with the oneness of heart, mind, purpose, and thoughts. This is the ideal for the marriage union. And likewise, it is the ideal for the relationship between Christ and His own church. As two people become one, Paul says this is a "great mystery." Hendriksen well explains:

> The union of Christ with the church, so that, from the sweep of eternal delight in the presence of his Father, God's only begotten Son plunged himself into the *dreadful darkness and awful anguish of Calvary* in order ever to dwell in their hearts through his Spirit and at last to present them—even these utterly undeserving ones—to himself as his own bride, with whom he becomes united in such intimate fellowship that no earthly metaphor can ever do justice to it, this even in and by itself is a mystery. Cf. 3:4–6; Col. 1:26, 27. . . . indeed, [this] is the Mystery Supreme![20]

## The Issue of the Church a Mystery

> *. . . the two shall become one flesh. This mystery is great; but I am speaking with reference to Christ and the church. (vv. 31b–32)*

The church is a mystery. Though not actually called such, Ryrie points out that its major elements are specifically designated as mysteries. First, he shows that the concept of Jewish and Gentile believers united into one body forms a new entity, called in Ephesians 3:1–12 a *new man*. Second, there is a new organism, or the idea of "Christ in you," which says that Christ dwells in each believer. This is called a mystery (Col. 1:24–27; 2:10–19; 3:4, 11). Third, Ryrie notes that the church is the bride of Christ which is called a mystery here in Ephesians. Fourth, the Rapture is cited as a mystery (1 Cor. 15:51–52). Ryrie points out that since these four aspects of the church are called mysteries, the church itself is also a mystery. And this was not foreseen in the Old Testament but only revealed in the New Testament.[21]

The church is thus a unique body of believers and saints for this present dispensational age. Ryrie concludes:

1. The church is not fulfilling in any sense the promises God made to Israel.
2. The use of the word *church* in the New Testament never includes unsaved Israelites.
3. The church age is not seen in God's program for Israel. It is an intercalation.
4. The church is a mystery in the sense that it was completely unrevealed in the Old Testament and now revealed in the New Testament.
5. The church did not begin until the day of Pentecost and will be removed from this world at the Rapture which precedes the Second Coming of Christ.[22]

> The greatness of the mystery refers to the two [husband and wife] becoming one flesh. But then Paul returns to mention the

wonderful bond between Christ and the church, which illustrates the love of a husband for his wife.[23]

# Questions for Discussion

1. Why is Ephesians 5:22–32 so important?
2. From Ephesians 5:24, discuss the issue of submission.
3. What are some of the problems being raised over the issue of biblical headship?
4. Discuss Ryrie's conclusions about the uniqueness of the body of believers in this present age.
5. What does it mean to speak of the church as a "mystery"?

## Chapter 5

# Gifts of the Spirit for the Church

## Introduction

Probably no topic has garnered as much attention within the church during the past twenty-five to thirty years as that of spiritual gifts. Baxter writes:

> "Gift Theology," so called, is exploding upon the market place. Whereas prior to 1965 very little was written on "The Gifts of the Spirit," today the situation has reversed. One writer indicates that approximately 80 percent of his books on the subject were written after 1970.[1]

The numerous books, articles, and sermons on spiritual gifts produced in recent times have yielded positive and negative results. The church has been reminded of the fact that there are no second-class Christians. Every believer is endowed with a spiritual gift (or gifts) that is to be used in ministering to the body of Christ. The unfortunate gap between "clergy" and "laity" (neither is a biblical term) in many cases has been narrowed to conform more to the "body life" pattern that characterized the early church. This has been very positive.

On the other hand, the proliferation of material has damaged churches and individuals. An unhealthy preoccupation has resulted in all manner of excess, and a large body of doctrinal truth essential to balance the spiritual life has been neglected.

It is a good rule of thumb that when an area of doctrine is overemphasized it is in danger of causing a distorted picture of the Christian life (and God Himself). This is not the first time this abuse has occurred. As many writers have pointed out, what we have today could be referred to as "Corinth Revisited." In a frighteningly similar way, we have the same misunderstanding of spirituality, and as a result, many of the same excesses.

It is not the intent of this chapter to argue against the theology of certain groups or the validity of certain of the "sign" gifts for the church today. Much has been written that addresses these matters and seeks to resolve the complex issues involved.[2] We will concentrate on the gifts that the majority of evangelicals would agree are still evident in the church today and are important to body life.

## What Are Spiritual Gifts?

A *spiritual gift* is a divinely imparted and empowered ability to carry out a particular task to serve and build up other members of the body of Christ, and thus the church as a whole. Several words are used in the New Testament to express the idea of spiritual gifts. In Paul's first letter to the church at Corinth he deals at length with the proper use of spiritual gifts (1 Cor. 12–14). As he begins this section he uses the term *tōn pneumatikōn* (from *pneumatikos;* 12:1; 14:1, 37), or "the things of the Spirit," or "spiritualities." Walvoord writes, "The word directs attention to the source, the Holy Spirit, and the realm of these gifts."[3] The second noun that Paul uses is *charismatōn* (from *charisma;* 12:4, 9, 28, 30–31; Rom. 12:6; and Peter uses it in 1 Peter 4:10). The noun *charis* is commonly translated "grace"; thus this term emphasizes that it is a gift of grace—a gift given freely.

## Further Definition

Several other things demand our careful attention in the discussion of spiritual gifts. These clarifications will help us not only understand the theology of spiritual gifts more clearly, but also will be helpful later when we discuss the practical outworking of spiritual gifts in the local assembly.

### Spiritual Gifts Are Sovereignly Given

Paul makes abundantly clear in 1 Corinthians 12–14 that the gifts are sovereignly dispensed. He writes, "But one and the same Spirit works all these things, distributing to each one individually just as *He* wills" (1 Cor. 12:11). Edgar writes:

> This entire section assumes the individual did not select his own spiritual gift (1 Cor. 12:12–30). Individuals cannot acquire any gift by their own will. Otherwise why would Paul show so carefully that each gift is important and that the individual must be satisfied with it? Without doubt the "foot" cannot become a "hand" and therefore must be satisfied as a "foot."[4]

Edgar continues:

> With an emphasis on humility and the use of gifts, Romans 12:3–8 assumes that gifts are given by God's choice, not the desires of

people. Verse 3 exhorts believers to think realistically regarding their importance in the body of Christ rather than exalting their importance in their own thinking. The word "for" (Gr. *gar*) connects verses 3 and 4, demonstrating that this tendency to exalt one's own importance is related to the gift that one has in comparison to the gifts that others have. This situation would not arise nor would Paul's reasoning stand if believers could obtain specific gifts by seeking them.[5]

As we see from Scripture, spiritual gifts are sovereignly given throughout the body of Christ by the Spirit Himself. Thus, a prideful attitude toward our gift(s) shows a pitiful ignorance of this doctrinal truth. Humility is the only reasonable response.

### Spiritual Gifts Are Given to Benefit the Body

Spiritual gifts were given so that the body will be edified. Paul writes, "But to each one is given the manifestation of the Spirit *for the common good*" (1 Cor. 12:7). The Greek participle translated as "the common good" (used as a substantive) is *to symferon,* meaning "profit, advantage, for (someone's) advantage."[6] In other words, the spiritual gifts given to each individual are to be used for the advantage of the body. Peter confirms this in his mention of spiritual gifts when he writes, "As each one has received a special gift *(charisma), employ it in serving one another,* as good stewards of the manifold grace of God" (1 Peter 4:10). Peter clarifies that the spiritual gifts were given so that we could use them in serving one another; thus the whole body is built up in the faith. This is important in light of the fact that some claim they use their gift in self-edification. This is impossible to reconcile with Scripture.

### Spiritual Gifts Are Given to Every Believer

Several verses make it clear that every believer in the present dispensation receives a gift or several gifts to be exercised for the benefit of the body. We have already looked at several of these verses. For instance Paul writes, "But to *each one* is given the manifestation of the Spirit for the common good" (1 Cor. 12:7), and again, "But one and the same Spirit works all these things, distributing to *each one* individually just as He wills" (1 Cor. 12:11). And Peter stated, "As *each one* has received a special gift, employ it in serving one another, as good stewards of the manifold grace of God" (1 Peter 4:10). Again, Paul writes in Ephesians 4:16, "From whom the whole body, being fitted and held together by that which *every joint* supplies, according to the proper working of *each individual part,* causes the growth of the body for the building up of itself in love" (Eph. 4:16).

Just as in our physical body each part was placed there by God so that the overall body could function properly, in the same way each individual member of the body of Christ was specially gifted and placed there so that the body as a whole could be built up in love. Thus, if you are a part of the body (a believer) you are a gifted individual.

### Spiritual Gifts Are Given at the Time of Belief

Although there are no references that prove spiritual gifts are given at the point of belief, it is safe to assume that this is the case. It would be odd indeed for all the other ministries of the Holy Spirit to begin in a believer's life at the point of belief and for him not to receive the spiritual gifts that God will use in his life to serve others. For instance, it is clear from Scripture that the Spirit takes up residence in a believer's life at the point of belief (Rom. 5:5; 8:9; 1 Cor. 6:19–20). At the same time the believer is regenerated (Titus 3:5), baptized (Acts 1:5; Acts 11:15–16; 1 Cor. 12:13), sealed (Eph. 1:13; 4:30), and the process of experiential sanctification begins as He starts to conform us to the image of Christ (Rom. 8:28–30).

Some have taken Paul's comments in Romans 1:11, as well as 1 Timothy 4:14 and 2 Timothy 1:6, to mean that he supernaturally gave a spiritual gift, although that is probably not what Paul meant to communicate. In the former passage he is talking about giving a blessing from his ministry, and in the latter two passages he is implying by "the act of laying on of hands . . . simply a solemn recognition of spiritual gifts already imparted by God, and a setting apart to their full exercise."[7]

### Spiritual Gifts Do Not Guarantee Spirituality nor Spiritual Fruit

Spiritual gifts guarantee neither "spirituality" nor "spiritual fruit." This is obvious from even a casual reading of Paul's first letter to the Corinthians. Paul stated that the Corinthians were not "lacking in any gift" (1:7), yet he had to rebuke them for the quarrels and divisions among them (1:11; 3:3), for their arrogance and the immorality among them (3:1–2), for disregarding the sensitivities of weaker brothers in the faith (8:1–13), and for the misuse of spiritual gifts (12–14). In fact, he stated, "I could not speak to you as spiritual men, but as to men of flesh, as babes in Christ" (3:1). This is obviously not a church full of spiritual people, although they were very spiritually gifted.

So what does it mean to be spiritual? First Corinthians 2:15 says, *"But he who is spiritual appraises all things, yet he himself is appraised by no man."* This is a description of the spiritual man. The Greek word translated "appraise" here is *anakrinō*, meaning "to examine, used of judicial hearings, to conduct an examination, to examine and judge, to call to account, [or] to discern."[8] The spiritual man is able to examine and judge all things on the basis of God's Word but he is not understood by others (a natural man) since the actions and attitudes of the spiritual man "are foolishness to him, and he cannot understand them because they are spiritually appraised" (1 Cor. 2:14–15). "If the spiritual believer judges or examines or discerns all things, . . . then *spirituality means a mature, yet maturing, relationship to God*" (italics added).[9] Christ reigns in the life of a spiritual man, and his attitudes and actions are guided and empowered by the Spirit of God. Thus, spirituality has to do with maturity.

It is the spiritual man who produces the "fruit of the Spirit" as well (Gal. 5:22–33). He has learned to "walk by the Spirit" and thus "be led by the Spirit" in yieldedness to God (Gal. 5:16, 18). This is characteristic of mature believers. They have crucified the flesh (Gal. 5:24), and their character exhibits a Spirit-filled life.

The conclusion is that someone can be spiritually gifted without being spiritual and producing the fruit of the Spirit.

## Spiritual Gifts Described in the Bible

As we look at a description of the spiritual gifts, it becomes evident that there is insufficient information to get the thorough understanding of the subject we would like. Edgar writes:

> The New Testament provides us with relatively little detailed information regarding any specific spiritual gift. In fact, in the case of several of the gifts we know only their names. Thus part of the controversy surrounding spiritual gifts is related to the fact that we lack detailed information about them.[10]

All of the information we can glean on the topic of spiritual gifts comes from Paul and Peter. The following passages discuss spiritual gifts: Romans 12:6–8; 1 Corinthians 12–14; Ephesians 4:11; and 1 Peter 4:10–11. Walvoord states:

> A distinction may be observed in the New Testament between spiritual gifts and gifted men. While the two ideas are inseparable, *spiritual gifts* has reference to the supernatural powers possessed by individuals, while *gifted men* has reference to the sovereign placing of gifted men in the church for the purpose of ministering to the body. While the principal thought of 1 Corinthians 12–14 is that of spiritual gifts, we find reference to the bestowal of gifted men on the church in Ephesians 4:11. The two ideas are not strictly separated as indicated by the references in the Corinthian passage to both spiritual gifts and to gifted men. It may be noted, however, that gifted men are normally a gift of Christ or of God, while spiritual gifts are a work of the Third Person.[11]

The New Testament is the source of the lists of spiritual gifts that are found at the top of page 82.

| 1 Cor. 12:8–10 | 1 Cor. 12:28 | Rom. 12:6–8 | Eph. 4:11 |
|---|---|---|---|
| 1. Word of wisdom | Apostle | Prophecy | Apostle |
| 2. Word of knowledge | Prophet | Service | Prophet |
| 3. Faith | Teachers | Teaching | Evangelist |
| 4. Healing | Miracles | Exhortation | Pastor-Teacher |
| 5. Miracles | Healing | Giving | |
| 6. Prophecy | Helps | Leadership | |
| 7. Distinguishing of spirits | Administration | Mercy | |
| 8. Tongues | Tongues | | |
| 9. Interpretation of tongues | | | |

In comparing the lists we see that there are several overlaps. If we count these gifts only once we come up with the following list:

| Temporary Gifts | Permanent Gifts |
|---|---|
| 1. Word of wisdom | Service |
| 2. Word of knowledge | Teaching |
| 3. Healing | Exhortation |
| 4. Miracles | Giving |
| 5. Prophecy | Leadership |
| 6. Distinguishing of spirits | Mercy |
| 7. Tongues | Evangelism |
| 8. Interpretation of tongues | Helps |
| 9. Apostleship | Administration |
| 10. | Faith |

This leaves nineteen spiritual gifts in our list. Because of the brevity of this volume we will deal primarily with those gifts that most agree are exhibited today in the church. Many of the gifts listed above are commonly referred to as sign gifts and seem to have been exhibited only in the first century of the church. This was because the canon of Scripture was incomplete and these miraculous sign gifts were used in confirming the Word of God. Walvoord writes:

> The best explanation of the passing of certain gifts and their manifestation is found in the evident purpose of God in the apostolic age. During the lifetime of the apostles, it pleased God to perform many notable miracles, in some cases quite apart from the question of whether the benefit was deserved. A period of miracles is always a time when special testimony is needed to the authenticity of God's prophets.[12]

Eight of the gifts listed above in the left-hand column are believed by many to have ceased with the passing of the apostolic age; thus we will not deal with them. The gift of apostleship is debated even among conservative scholars, so we will discuss that gift and the differing views. We will then look at the remaining ten gifts and their application to the local church.

# Spiritual Gifts for the Church

### Apostleship

Some have held that the missionary of today is the modern-day apostle of the early church. In light of this, we will look at the way this gift is presented in the New Testament and see if such thinking lines up with Scripture.

Apostles are mentioned in two lists, one in Ephesians 4:11 and the other in 1 Corinthians 12:28. In both instances, they are viewed as gifted men, not as a distinguishable spiritual gift. The word *apostolos*, means simply an "envoy, [or] ambassador."[13] As Edgar writes, "The idea of 'sent' in the sense of a representative is more prominent than any idea of physical travel."[14]

### Apostle in the Official Sense

The term is used in the Gospels of the twelve chosen by Christ. They are referred to as *the* twelve apostles (Matt. 10:2; Luke 6:13; 9:1–10; 17:15). These men had some unique qualifications. Müller writes:

> With the exception of Lk. 11:49, Acts 14:14, Luke applies *apostolos* expressly to the Twelve. They had been called by the historical Jesus to their office (Lk. 6:13; cf. 1:17). They had been with him throughout his ministry from the time of John's baptism. The risen Lord had met them in various appearances (Lk. 24:36ff; Acts 1:3). And so they had the best possible knowledge of what Jesus had said. Before the ascension they had received the promise of the Spirit (Acts 1:4) and the command to evangelize (Acts 1:8). By the event of Pentecost (Acts 2) they were made bearers of the Spirit, the great authorities of early Christianity who, based in Jerusalem, guarded the true tradition which went back to the historical Jesus.[15]

That these conditions were important to maintain is attested to by the fact that when they chose a replacement for Judas, Peter stated, "It is therefore necessary that of the men who have accompanied us all the time that the Lord Jesus went in and out among us—beginning with the baptism of John, until the day that He was taken up from us—one of these should become a witness with us of His resurrection" (Acts 1:21–22). Thus, the term is used in a unique sense of the original twelve chosen by Christ and then of Matthias, who fulfilled the qualifications to replace Judas. Revelation 21:14 shows that these apostles will have a special place in the New Jerusalem.

The term is also used of Paul. In 2 Corinthians 12:11, Paul states, "For in no respect was I inferior to the most eminent apostles, even though I am a nobody. The signs of a true apostle were performed among you with all perseverance, by signs and wonders and miracles." Paul's point is that the signs, wonders, and miracles were specific signs that set him apart as an apostle (cf. Rom. 15:19). Paul also stated in 1 Corinthians 9:1, "Am I not free? Am I not an apostle? Have I not seen Jesus our Lord?" (cf. 1 Cor. 15:8). Paul's point is that just as the original twelve had been witnesses of the resurrected Lord, so had he. This was proof of his apostleship. Not only did Paul perform the signs of an apostle and see the resurrected Lord, he was directly commissioned by the Lord (Acts 22:21; Rom. 1:5; Gal. 1–2; 1 Tim. 2:7).

### Apostle in the General Sense

The term was used of many others, such as Barnabas (Acts 14:4, 14), James (Gal. 1:19), Andronicus and Junias (Rom. 16:7), and Epaphroditus (Phil. 2:25). Here the word is probably used in the general sense of "an envoy or ambassador" for a particular local church and not in the official sense of meeting the qualifications that we have observed in the New Testament.[16]

### The Apostles Laid the Foundation for the Church

It is not surprising that apostleship was a foundational gift. Paul makes this clear in his letter to the Ephesians when he states of God's household (the church) that it has "been built upon the foundation of the apostles and prophets, Christ Jesus Himself being the corner stone" (Eph. 2:20). Edgar comments on this verse:

> Some have interpreted this to mean that foundation that the apostles and prophets laid. The expression "of all the apostles and prophets" is in the genitive case and is plural. The genitive case in Greek may function in many ways, indicating such aspects as content, possession, or relationship. The only way to determine the function of the case is from the context, since the form does not change. Here in Ephesians 2:20 the genitive is definitely the appositional use of the genitive; that is, we may translate this passage as "built upon the foundation *which is* the apostles and prophets."[17] (italics added)

The context of the passage is the universal church, not a local church. Christ became the cornerstone for the church and the apostles were the foundation. Upon this apostolic foundation the church continues to be built. The structure for the church was laid in the apostles. Once that was accomplished there was no need for that gift again or those gifted men again. Thus, these gifted men passed from the scene. The apostolate does not exist in the church today and any so-called restoration of the gift cannot be substantiated from the Holy Text.

The modern missionary could only be referred to as an apostle in the general sense of the word in that he is an "envoy, [or] ambassador" sent out to carry the gospel to areas that have not heard it.

### Service or Ministry

The gift of *service* or *ministry* is listed in Romans 12. *Service* is the translation of the Greek *diakonia* and is apparently distinct from "mercy" (Rom. 12:7) and "helps" (1 Cor. 12:28). This word is used in Acts 6:1 of the "serving" of food to the widows; a similar sense appears in Luke 10:40. It refers generally to loving service in 1 Corinthians 16:15 and Revelation 2:19. That loving service is specifically a collection of money in Acts 11:29; 12:25 (rsv "mission"); Roman 15:31; and 2 Corinthians 8:4; 9:1, 12f. In 2 Corinthians the grace of Christ is clearly the motive).[18] Several uses refer to general ministry of any kind (Rom. 11:13; Eph. 4:12). Baxter writes:

> Since this gift relates to the totality of the practical needs of the local church, it differs from the serving gifts in that it is not necessarily person centered in the service rendered. It is a task oriented gift, with the service directed more to the institution than the individual. Therefore, it is more general in its purpose than the serving gifts, which tend to particularize their ministry to people. . . . Because service is such a general need, this gift usually equips its possessor with a wide range of abilities to meet those needs.[19]

In light of the word's usage in the New Testament, Wagner's definition is a good one. He writes of the gift:

> The special ability that God gives to certain members of the Body of Christ to identify the unmet needs involved in a task related to God's work, and to make use of available resources to meet those needs and help accomplish the desired goals.[20]

### Teaching

This gift is mentioned three times in our lists (1 Cor. 12:28; Rom. 12:7; Eph. 4:11). Two of the passages list gifted men (1 Cor. 12:28; Eph. 4:11), the other lists it as a distinct spiritual gift (Rom. 12:7). In the former passages "teacher" translates the Greek noun *didaskalos*, meaning "teacher or master,"[21] and in the latter passage "teaching" translates the Greek noun *didaskalia* meaning "the act of teaching [or] instruction."[22]

To define this gift it is important to understand how Paul uses the word *teach* in his writings. Moo comments:

> The word *teach* and its cognate nouns *teaching (didaskalia)* and *teacher (didaskalos)* are used in the New Testament mainly to

denote the careful transmission of the tradition concerning Jesus Christ and the authoritative proclamation of God's will to believers in light of the tradition (see especially 1 Tim. 4:11, "Command and teach these things," 2 Tim. 2:2; Acts 2:42; Rom. 12:7). While the word can be used more broadly to describe the general ministry of edification that takes place in various ways (e. g., through teaching, singing, praying, reading of Scripture [Colossians]), the activity usually designated by *teach* is plainly restricted to certain individuals who have the gift of teaching (see 1 Cor. 12:28–30; Eph. 4:11). This makes it clear that not all Christians are engaged in doctrinal instruction. As Paul's own life draws to a close, and in response to the false teaching, Paul is deeply concerned to insure that sound, healthful teaching be maintained in the churches. One of Timothy's main tasks is to teach (1 Tim. 4:11–16; 2 Tim. 4:2) and to prepare others to carry on this vital ministry (2 Tim. 2:2). While perhaps not restricted to the elder-overseer, "teaching" in this sense was an important activity of these people (see 1 Tim. 3:2; 5:17; Titus 1:9).[23]

Walvoord gives us this definition: "[The gift of teaching] is the supernatural ability to explain and apply the truths which had been already received by the church."[24] This gift is not restricted to the elder-overseer but is a qualification to hold the office (1 Tim. 3:2). Although the gift of teaching is mentioned in Romans 12:7, men who possess the gift were mentioned in two other places. In 1 Corinthians 12:28 Paul referred to *teachers,* and in Ephesians 4:11 he referred to *pastors-teachers.* This brings up the question of whether *pastoring* is a separate gift.

The Greek noun *poimēn,* translated "pastor" or "shepherd," is only used seventeen times, and then in reference to the gifted men given to the church in Ephesians 4:11. The word is used in the New Testament to refer to literal shepherds (Luke 2:8, 15, 18, 20), figuratively of spiritual leaders (Matt. 9:36; Mark 6:34; John 10:2, 12; Eph. 4:11), of Christ (Matt. 25: 32; 26:31; Mark 14:27; John 10:11, 14, 16; Heb. 13:1; 1 Peter 2:25). The meaning in our passage is obviously of spiritual leaders. So this is a gift normally given to those in spiritual leadership, and may be referring to what the New Testament calls the *elder* or *overseer.*

Several verses show that the titles *elder (presbyteros), overseer (episkopos),* and our term *pastor-teacher (poimēn kai didaskalos)* are different titles for the same gifted men. In Acts 20:17 Paul called for the elders of the Ephesian church. Then, in verse 28 he tells these same elders *(presbyteros)* to "be on guard for yourselves and for all the flock, among which the Holy Spirit has made you overseers *(episkopos),* to shepherd *(poimainō)* the church of God which he purchased with His blood." Here the three terms are tied together. Again, in 1 Peter 5:1–2 we see the three terms used for the same office. "Therefore, I exhort the elders *(presbyterous)* among you, as your fellow elder and witness of the sufferings of

Christ, and a partaker also of the glory that is to be revealed, shepherd *(poimanate)* the flock of God among you, exercising oversight *(episkopountes)* not under compulsion."

We also see Paul using the words meaning "elder" and "overseer" inter-changeably when giving instructions to Titus. In Titus 1:5 he tells Titus to "appoint elders in every city" and continues in verses 6–9 to give their qualifications. Besides being almost identical to the qualifications he gave Timothy in 1 Timothy 3, he directly refers to the elders as overseers in verse 7, where he says, "For the overseer must be . . ." Since the pastor-teacher is mentioned no-where else in Scripture, the biblical evidence shows that this was not an office distinct from the position of elder but the same office.

So the term *elder* emphasizes who they are, men of age, experience, and wisdom; the term *overseer* emphasizes their general duty, that of overseeing the flock, and the title *pastor-teacher* emphasizes more specifically their major duties as elder, those of shepherding and instructing the flock. With this in mind, it is probable that this gift is given primarily to those God calls to be pastor-teachers or elders in the church. Walvoord writes, "A pastor is one who leads, provides, protects, and cares for his flock."[25]

It is significant that the term *pastor* is linked here with *teacher*. As Walvoord says:

> While it is not necessary for a teacher to have all the qualities of a pastor, it is vital to the work of a true pastor that he teach his flock. It is obvious that a shepherd who did not feed his flock would not be worthy of the name. Likewise in the spiritual realm the first duty of a pastor is to feed his flock on the Word of God. Quite apart from being merely an organizer, promoter or social leader, the true pastor gives himself to preaching the Word.[26]

### Exhortation

The gift of exhortation is just mentioned once in our lists, in Romans 12:8. Here Paul uses the verb form of the Greek word "exhorts" *(parakalōn,* a parti-ciple from *parakaleō)* as well as the noun form of the word translated "exhorta-tion" *(paraklēsis).* In Greek both the noun and verb form of the word could have the meaning of "to exhort" as well as "to comfort and encourage."[27]

Walvoord ties this gift closely to the preaching [teaching] gift. He states:

> As a part of the work of preaching, exhortation fills an impor-tant place. Differing from teaching in that it is an appeal for action, exhortation is the practical aspect of a preaching minis-try. Some are given a special gift in this work, enabling them to lead Christians into the active realization of the will of God.[28]

Walvoord's point is clearly illustrated in passages such as 1 Corinthians 14:30. Here the prophets are required by Paul to speak one after another so that the body will be exhorted from the words of God which they have received. The same example is seen from such writers as Peter, who exhorted the elder to "feed the flock" (1 Peter 5:1–2). The writer of Hebrews wrote to those who were considering returning to Judaism to cling to Christ, "But I urge [exhort] you, brethren, bear with this word of exhortation, for I have written to you briefly" (Heb. 13:22). Thus, this aspect of exhortation deals with a proclamation of God's Word, whether public or private, and an urging to be faithful to its truths. Braumann writes:

> Theologically, . . . Paul gives to exhortation a specific basis. He does not give his readers direct moral instruction, but addresses them through *(dia)* God or Christ, so that the apostle thinks of his admonition as mediated "by the mercy of God" (Rom. 12:1; cf. v. 3), "by our Lord Jesus Christ and by the love of the Spirit" (Rom. 15:30).[29]

The second shade of meaning in the word and in the gift of exhortation is that of "comfort." This aspect of exhortation is brought out in 2 Corinthians, where we read:

> *Blessed be the God and Father of our Lord Jesus Christ, the Father of mercies and God of all* comfort; *who* comforts *us in all our affliction so that we may be able to* comfort *those who are in any affliction with the* comfort *with which we ourselves are* comforted *by God. For just as the sufferings of Christ are ours in abundance, so also our* comfort *is abundant through Christ. (1:3–5)*

Here Paul uses various forms of the word ten times in verses 3–7. Exhortation deals with a proclamation of God's Word, whether public or private, as a balm to heal the hurt of the heart. This could occur in various situations, such as times of repentance from sin and of suffering persecution. As Paul points out in this passage, we are to be channels of God's comfort passing on the comfort we received from God to others who need comfort. Thus, those who are most effective in biblical counseling are those who have the gift of exhortation.

Flynn gives a good summary definition of our findings:

> The gift of exhortation involves the supernatural ability to come alongside to help, to strengthen the weak, reassure the wavering,

buttress the buffeted, steady the faltering, console the troubled, [and] encourage the halting.[30]

## Giving

The word Paul uses in Romans 12:8 is *metadidōmi,* which is used only four other times in the New Testament. Three of those usages are by Paul himself (Rom. 1:11; Eph. 4:28; 1 Thess. 2:8). In Romans 1:11 Paul writes, "For I long to see you in order that *I may impart* some spiritual gift to you, that you may be established." Here, contextually the word carries the meaning "to share." The verse might be more clearly translated, "In order that *I might share* some spiritual gift with you" (i.e. the blessings of Paul's spiritual giftedness). This is confirmed by his clarification in the following verse, where he writes, "But that is, to be jointly comforted with you through each other's faith, both yours and mine."[31] This idea of sharing is also involved in Paul's other usages. The word is used in an almost identical fashion with that of Romans 1:11 in 1 Thessalonians 2:8, that of sharing one's life. And in Ephesians 4:28 the idea of sharing material resources is in view (see also Luke 3:11).

With this analysis in mind, we should be careful to observe that the gift of giving includes but goes beyond the contributing of material resources. The gift of giving manifests itself in the selfless sharing of one's gifts, as well as one's material possessions, to further the Lord's work and meet others' needs. There is also something revealing about the attitude of the person with the spiritual gift of giving—they give with *haplotēti,* that is with "simplicity, sincerity, uprightness, frankness."[32] A contrast in this type of attitude in giving and that of selfish giving is seen very clearly in the story of Barnabas's giving (Acts 4:36) as opposed to that of Ananias and Sapphira (Acts 5:1–11). Flynn writes:

> The person with the gift of giving will give with singleness of mind. No ulterior motive will ruffle the cloth of his mind to make a fold or two in it. He will not give to salve a conscience uneasy because of the way he acquired his money. Nor will he give to gain something in return. Sending a gift, we might sign "love," but never "I am giving this so that you will admire me." Nor do we give for public show, as did the Pharisees who blew trumpets so people would be alerted to watch them bestow their gifts. The person who will not donate unless his name is inscribed on the stained-glass window or engraved on the cornerstone doesn't understand Christ's command not to let the left hand know what the right hand is doing (Matt. 6:3). The gift of giving permits no alloy of self-seeking in the coin of our gift.[33]

### Leadership

The word that is translated "leads" in Romans 12:8 is the Greek word *proistēmi* meaning to "be at the head (of), rule, direct, manage, [or] conduct."[34] Coenen explains:

> *Proistēmi* is found only in the writings of Paul and the Pastorals. First Thessalonians 5:12 has the participle in the plural for those who labour in the church and who are *proistamenous hymōn en Kyriō* (over you in the Lord). They help others to live rightly and therefore deserve special esteem and love. The reference here seems to be to a group exercising leadership in the church.[35]

The word is used of all Christians who are to lead the community in good works (Titus 3:8, 14). In a more official sense, it is used as an activity of those in headship positions in the family (the man; 1 Tim. 3:4 and the church (the elder; 1 Tim. 5:17). In this latter passage it is tied closely to the gift of teaching ("those who work hard in the word *[en logō]* and *teaching*").

The leader must be a model in diligence *(spoudē)*. The word means "eagerness, earnestness, diligence, [or] zeal."[36] Lenski writes of the word, "The word means 'haste' in the good sense: prompt efficiency, no delay, no excuses, no dilatoriness."[37]

Flynn's definition is accurate:

> The gift of government [leadership], then, is the Spirit-given ability to preside, govern, plan, organize, and administer with wisdom, fairness, example, humility, service, confidence, ease, and efficiency.[38]

### Mercy

In Romans 12:8 Paul uses the verb *eleeō*, meaning "to feel compassion, [or] to show mercy or pity"[39] on someone. Vines describes it as follows:

> *Eleos* [the noun form of *eleeō*] is the outward manifestation of pity; it assumes need on the part of him who receives it, and resources adequate to meet the need on the part of him who shows it. . . . *Eleeō* [the verb form] signifies, in general, "to feel sympathy with the misery of another," and especially sympathy manifested in act.[40]

Criswell states of the gift:

> Every Christian is expected to be merciful. This is a role that reflects the fruit of the Spirit. But those with the gift of mercy make

compassion and kindness their life-style. They do not simply react to emergencies, as every Christian is supposed to do. They continually seek opportunities to show pity for the miserable.[41]

This gift is distinct from the gift of service or ministry. It is people-centered and directed more to those who are sick and afflicted. Those with this Spirit-given gift extend mercy with an attitude of cheerfulness *(hilaroteti)*. Such an individual "greets every opportunity for a merciful deed as a great find that makes him jubilant."[42]

### *Evangelism*

The gift of evangelism is only listed once, that being in Paul's list of gifted men in Ephesians 4:11. *Euangelistēs,* here translated "evangelist," is used only three times in the New Testament (Acts 21:8; Eph. 4:11; 2 Tim. 4:5). The word means literally "a messenger of good." That "good" is the good news of the death, burial, and resurrection of Jesus Christ. The cognate noun *euangelion,* "good news" or "gospel," and the verb *euangelizō,* "to bring or announce good news, proclaim, preach,"[43] help describe how this gift manifests itself. Paul stated in 1 Corinthians 15:1–2, "Now I make known to you, brethren, the gospel *(euangelion)* which I preached *(euangelizō)* to you, which also you received, in which also you stand, by which also you are saved, if you hold fast the word which I preached *(euangelizō)* to you, unless you believed in vain."

Thus, the gift of evangelism is a supernatural ability to proclaim the good news of the death, burial, and resurrection of Jesus Christ (1 Cor. 15:3–4), and see people respond. Walvoord writes of the gift:

> By its title it is clear that this gift has reference to effective preach-
> ing of the gospel message to the unsaved, and as such it is to be
> compared to the teaching gift which gives instruction to the saved.
> It is clear, experientially, that knowledge of the gospel does not
> bring with it the ability to preach it with success to others. Men
> may possess the gift of teaching, for instance, without possess-
> ing the gift of evangelism, and vice versa. In some cases, men
> have possessed both the gift of teaching and of evangelism, as
> illustrated in the person of the Apostle Paul. While all are called
> to bring the gospel to the lost by whatever means may be at their
> disposal, and accordingly like Timothy, should do the work of
> an evangelist (2 Tim. 4:5), it is the sovereign purpose of God
> that certain men should have a special gift in evangelism.[44]

The only individual in the New Testament who is called an evangelist is Philip (Acts 21:8). The record of at least Philip's earliest evangelistic activity is recorded for us in Acts 8. Philip is first mentioned in Acts 6 in regard to being chosen as one of the seven men who would coordinate the task of caring for the Hellenistic Jews' widows (Acts 6:1–6). In Acts 8 we find Philip in Samaria as a result of the persecution that had begun in Jerusalem (Acts 8:4–5). Philip proclaimed the gospel in Samaria and many responded (v. 6). A short time later he was beckoned by an angel to go south of Jerusalem to the road between that city and Gaza (v. 26). There he met a eunuch of Ethiopia who was a prominent man in the Ethiopian government (v. 27). Philip shared the gospel with him and he was converted (vv. 28–38). Philip was then supernaturally "snatched" away and taken to Azotus where he continued his proclamation of the gospel message (vv. 39–40).

The apostles Peter and Paul, although not called evangelists, also showed the fruit of the gift of evangelism, as is clear from the thousands converted under their ministry (Acts 2:41; 4:4; 9:42; 10:44–48; 13:48; 16:14, 34; 17:4).

### Helps

The gift of helps is also mentioned only once in Paul's list (1 Cor. 12:28). In fact, the word is found only here in the entire New Testament. The Greek term, antilēmpseis, comes from antilambano, meaning "to take someone's part, to help, to aid." C. Peter Wagner defines the gift of helps:

> The ability that God gives to some members of the Body of Christ to invest the talents they have in the life and ministry of others of the Body, thus enabling that person helped to increase the effectiveness of his or her spiritual gifts.[45]

Baxter writes of those with the gift of helps, "They are the unsung heroes of the church, but not the unrewarded servants of God. As surely as the exercise of every gift brings His 'Well done,' so does the quiet gift of 'helps.'"[46]

The gift is distinguished from the gift of service or ministry in that it does not necessarily involve "identifying the unmet needs involved in a task." In other words, it deals more with simply making talents available whenever a need arises to assist someone. It is broader than the gift of mercy and is not necessarily people-centered but could encompass any task.

### Administration

The last gift we will discuss from Paul's 1 Corinthians 12:28 list is administration. The Greek kybernēseis means "administrations" or "governments." Its cognate, kybernētēs, is used twice in the New Testament where it is translated "pilot" in one instance (Acts 27:11) and "shipmaster" in the other (Rev. 18:17). Lenski writes:

> A kybernētēs is a helmsman who steers a vessel, and thus this gift consists in managing and directing others whether officially as presbyters, pastors, or bishops or in unofficial ways. Some

men and some women of the church, including even young people, have this gift to a marked degree and profit the church not a little by rightly putting it to use.[47]

And Baxter writes of the gift:

Those who have this gift can thereby make the local church alive with activity. They enjoy organizing, overseeing business matters, helping staff relations, dealing with details and generally making sure the work of the local church runs smoothly.[48]

He continues:

The gift may belong to the pastor, but not necessarily so. Many a local church is blessed with laymen who have the gift of administration and who can relieve the pastor of many cumbersome details, allowing him to spend more time in "prayer and the ministry of the Word" (Acts 6:4). A pastor should not, therefore, feel threatened by this involvement by members of his congregation, neither should the laymen become pompous. It is a gift and should neither produce fear nor pride. When properly exercised, the gift [will] glorify God in the smooth running of the local church. [49]

### Faith

Our last gift is faith. This gift of faith is to be distinguished from the act of saving faith. Every believer has some faith which is a gift of God (Eph. 2:8–9), but not a spiritual gift. The Greek word is *pistis,* which means "trust" or "confidence." Walvoord states:

It is manifested not so much in trust in Christ as Savior as in confidence in God in respect to His power and love working in the details of their lives, supplying their needs and guiding their steps.[50]

## How Do I Know My Gift?

To be good stewards of the spiritual gifts God has given us we must first know what they are. Some "spiritual gift tests" are available but most are of little value if you have not been a Christian very long. This is because our gifts usually surface naturally when we are living an obedient, Spirit-filled life. The best way to determine your spiritual gift(s) is to study and meditate on the above explanations of the gifts, pray that God reveal your gift(s) and continue to live out an obedient, Spirit-filled life. It would be helpful to consult other Christian friends and your family, since they may observe your gift before you can discern it.

When you know what your spiritual gift is, be diligent "to employ it in serving one another" (1 Peter 4:10).

Baxter lists the following steps to discovering your gift or gifts:

1. Put the Lord first in your life (Matt. 6:33).
2. Put emphasis on God's will for your life (Rom. 12:1–2; Acts 13:1–4).
3. Know the Scriptures (Luke 6:46–49; 2 Tim. 2:15).
4. Ask God to reveal His particular gifts to you (Matt. 7:7–11; John 16:23–24).
5. Expect confirmation from others.
6. Be prepared to face responsibility (1 Cor. 9:16–17).[51]

## Creating an Opportunity for Expression

Paul stated in 1 Corinthians 12:18, "But now God has placed the members, *each one of them,* in the body, just as He desired." And Ephesians 4:11–16 relates that when these members are doctrinally equipped they cannot be deceived, but will speak the truth in love. This results in the maturity of the body into Christ the head. It is Christ who produces the growth or the "building up" of the body. This is dependent on the "whole body being fitted and held together by that which *every joint* supplies, according to the proper working of *each individual part.*" In other words, Christ's body is designed to function at maximum efficiency when each member, every joint, and each individual part is functioning the way Christ designed it to.

With this in mind, it is imperative that the leadership of the church encourage the discovery and use of each member's gift(s) in the body. They should do this by creating ministry opportunities in which the members can exercise their giftedness. For example, there should be a benevolence ministry for those who have the gift of service, and mercy can be a part. Those with the gift of evangelism should have missions trips and evangelism programs to be involved in on a regular basis. Sunday school teachers and small group leaders should be chosen on the basis of their giftedness in teaching and shepherding.

Everything should be done to encourage that the gifts of the congregation are used for what they were given, for that is service to one another (1 Peter 4:10).

# Questions for Discussion

1. Why do you think there has been an explosion of emphasis on the spiritual gifts?
2. What are the spiritual gifts?
3. How are spiritual gifts given out?
4. Why is there confusion about spiritual gifts?

5. What is the relationship between spiritual gifts and spirituality?
6. How do we demonstrate the fact of "temporary gifts"?
7. Discuss how you would know what your spiritual gifts are.
8. How are spiritual gifts encouraged?

## Chapter 6

# The Church in Prophecy

There are many biblical passages that deal with the church and future events. The majority of these texts deal with the Rapture of the church just prior to the coming terrors of the Tribulation. The *bema* judgment is also highlighted in the writings of the apostle Paul. Both the Rapture and the *bema* judgment are dealt with in chapters 17 and 18. But surprisingly, there are many other contexts that deal with the church and its future.

## "This World Is Not My Home"

Today one could argue that the church is feeling very comfortable in this world. Though believers are not to sit down and do nothing, the purpose of the church is not to carve out a permanent niche in this godless culture. James and the apostle John both warn of getting comfortable with this world system. In exceedingly strong words James writes:

> *You adulteresses, do you not know that friendship with the world is hostility toward God? Therefore whoever wishes to be a friend of the world makes himself an enemy of God. (James 4:4)*

Since James is not writing about the earth or globe, by world (*kosmos*) in this context he means the culture. John writes virtually the same thing when he pens:

> *Do not love the world, nor the things in the world. If anyone loves the world, the love of the Father is not in him. For all that is in the world, the lust of the flesh and the lust of the eyes and the boastful pride of life, is not from the Father, but is from the world. (1 John 2:15–16)*

The world system is the evil kingdom of Lucifer himself. By all the spiritual fraud and mental trickery he can muster, Satan who is "the god of this world has blinded the minds of the unbelieving, that they might not see the light of the gospel of the glory of Christ" (2 Cor. 4:4).

Why would believers in Christ want to settle down and become comfortable in this godless culture? Someday this age is to be judged, condemned, and destroyed. This world indeed is not the home of Christians! Paul punctuates this truth when he writes, "Our citizenship is in heaven, from which also we eagerly wait for a Savior, the Lord Jesus Christ" (Phil. 3:20). This is actually a rapture passage because the apostle writes of the transformation of the body. He says Christ will "change the outer form" *(metaschēmatizō)* of the body of our humiliation to form us together with the body of His glory (v. 21).

The word citizenship *(politeuma)* focuses on the idea of where one conducts one's life. "Christians [should] strive to attain not the earthly *politeuma,* but rather the heavenly community."[1] Lightfoot emphasizes "the state, the constitution, to which as citizens we belong."[2]

But again, though the citizenship is in heaven, believers in the Lord are not to sit down and do nothing. Paul commended the church at Thessalonica for their struggle and the persecution they were undergoing for the sake of Jesus. He writes that they were both serving *and* waiting for God's Son from heaven, "Jesus, who delivers us from the wrath to come" (1 Thess. 1:9–10). The apostle highlights both the working and the anticipation of the coming of Christ to snatch the church away to glory. Paul further puts this into perspective when he writes that this physical, outer man is decaying (2 Cor. 4:16) and yet any present affliction suffered "is producing for us an eternal weight of glory far beyond all comparison" (v. 17). He tries to make the Christian gain a proper focus on this life and its temporal nature. He writes:

> We look not at the things which are seen, but at the things which are not seen; for the things which are seen are temporal, but the things which are not seen are eternal. (v. 18)

Paul sees the whole purpose of the gospel as the Christian's future deliverance out of this life. He writes to the Thessalonians, through the gospel "you may gain the glory of our Lord Jesus Christ" (2 Thess. 2:14). Knowing his time was short, the great apostle wrote to Timothy that he was ready to depart. The Lord "will bring me safely to His heavenly kingdom" (2 Tim. 4:18).

The apostle Peter notes that the believer's pain in this life leads to heaven, for "after you have suffered for a little while, the God of all grace, who called you to His eternal glory in Christ, will restore you" (1 Peter 5:10). Jude adds the fact that those in Christ should be "waiting anxiously for the mercy of our Lord Jesus Christ [that leads] to eternal life" (Jude 21). Luther writes:

Our life should be so ordered that it be nothing more than a constant longing and waiting for the future life, yet so, that such waiting be centered in the mercy of Christ. We must call upon him
with the conviction that he helps us from this into the next life
because of pure mercy and not because of our own work and merit.[3]

Having made it clear that the believer's citizenship is in heaven, Paul lets the
individual Christian know that upon death or the Rapture he is to be transported
instantly into the very presence of the Lord. The apostle writes that now the child
of God is in an earthly tent (2 Cor. 5:1) but awaits "a building from God, a house
not made with hands, eternal in the heavens" (v. 2). Presently Christians are "at
home in the body" but "absent from the Lord" (v. 6), and yet "to be absent from the
body [is] to be at home with the Lord" (v. 8). Whether alive, raptured, or having
died physically, believers will never be away from the presence of the Lord.

Paul writes of the church standing "in the presence of our Lord Jesus at His
coming" (1 Thess. 2:19) and even presented "unblamable in holiness before our
God and Father at the coming of our Lord Jesus Christ with all His saints" (3:13).
In the two passages the word "presence" and "before" are both the same Greek
word *emprosthen* which has the force of "before the face of."[4] Paul often uses the
word "to describe the direct imminence and presence of God."[5]

## Future Judgment Given to the Believers in Christ

Using the future tense, Paul tells the church that it will someday judge (*krinō*)
the world and also be judging angels (1 Cor. 6:2–3). "The saints will be judging
the world . . . and we shall be judging angels." What do these two statements
mean? And at what time will this take place? Does this judgment authority given
to the church have to do with eternity, or is it confined to the Millennium?

With so little evidence on this passage, some premillennialists such as David
K. Lowery confine this judgment of angels to the fallen angels mentioned in
2 Peter 2:4 and Jude 6.[6] Both passages refer to the judgment of those beings, but
the tone is that they are judged by God not the church!

The apostles are promised that when the Son of Man sits on His glorious throne,
they will sit on twelve thrones, "judging the twelve tribes of Israel" (Matt. 19:28).
This is certainly a judgment during the Millennium, but it is not the same as promised to the church saints.

On the 1 Corinthians 6:2–3 passage, Stanley writes:

A time will come when the Christians now so humble and de-
graded in the sight of the heathen world, shall sit in judgment
upon that very world; . . . when once the view of the Christian's
exaltation is opened before the Apostle's mind, it has no bounds,
but extends to the Majesty on High, where Christ sits on the

right hand of God, "angels, and authorities, and powers, being
made subject to Him." Whether good or bad angels are intended
is left undefined.[7]

Edwards believes, "The meaning is that the saints will be associated with
Christ in the act of judging the world at the last day," in other words, at the Great
White Throne Judgment following the one-thousand-year reign of Christ.[8]

Since all things are to be subject to Christ, "His people are to be associated
with Christ in his dominion. They are joint heirs with him, Rom. 8, 17. If we
suffer, we shall reign with him, 2 Tim. 2, 12."[9] On the church judging angels,
Hodge writes:

> [It] may mean, "Know ye not that we are to be exalted above the
> angels, and preside over them . . . ?" This explanation avoids the
> difficulty of supposing that the good angels are to be called into
> judgment; and is consistent with what the Bible teaches of the
> subordination of angels to Christ, and to the church in him.[10]

Concerning this general idea of the saints ruling with Christ, Paul writes,
"We shall also reign with Him" (2 Tim. 2:12). John the apostle repeats this of the
overcomer in Revelation 2:26. He quotes the prophetic words of the risen Christ,
who said to the church at Thyatira, "He who keeps My deeds until the end, to
him I will give authority over the nations." The picture is clearly referring to
present-day church saints during the millennial, kingdom reign of Christ. The
Lord goes on to say, "As I also have received authority from My Father, I give
similar rule to believers that they may reign with a rod of iron" (v. 27). The
language is borrowed from Psalm 2 where almost identical words are used to
describe Jesus judging from the Davidic throne. Church saints will be given co-
authority to reign with Him. This promise is repeated to the church at Laodicea.
Jesus says, "He who overcomes, I will grant to him to sit down with Me on My
throne, as I also overcame and sat down with My Father on His throne" (Rev. 3:21).

Thomas aptly writes:

> This promise is the first definitive reference in Revelation to the
> coming millennial kingdom, which Jesus is to establish when
> He returns to earth. . . . The overcomer will join Christ in de-
> stroying the nations who oppose Him. . . . The genuine Chris-
> tian, the one who overcomes by faith and is victorious over the
> world (cf. I John 5:4–5), will join Christ not only in the great
> eschatological supper, but also will sit with Him on His throne
> to participate in ruling the world. . . . Christ's occupancy of the
> throne of David is a major emphasis of Revelation from its very

beginning to the very end (cf. 1:5, 7; 22:16). It is this throne upon the earth on which the overcomer is promised a place.[11]

# The Church and Revelation 5:8–13

Though some differences of opinion persist, most dispensationalists and premillennialists believe that Revelation 5:8–13 pictures the church in heaven praising God and worshiping the Lamb while the Tribulation rages below on earth. Chronologically, the Rapture of the church probably takes place after chapter 3. In this passage, the saints in heaven, with the twenty-four elders, are almost without doubt the entire church in glory. Church saints are never again seen on earth in Revelation. But there is this heavenly chorus of those "redeemed from all nations," which must be a reference to the body of Christ. Premillennialists such as Walvoord, Scott, Thomas, LaHaye, McGee, and others agree.

McGee notes:

> [Christ] moves to the throne through the Tribulation. He judges the world in righteousness before He reigns in righteousness. He is no longer the Intercessor of the church, for the church is now with Him. He is beginning to act as Judge. . . . Only the church is a priesthood of believers in heaven.[12]

Though in Revelation 6 the Tribulation is about to begin on earth below, Revelation 5:8–13 is a heavenly vision of the church saints who have just arrived via the Rapture. There are many indicators that this is the glorified church in heaven.

First, there is the presence of the twenty-four elders who are always associated with the church in heaven (v. 8). Second, this great company of "saints" (v. 8) is not Tribulation saints because this terrible earthly event does not start until chapter 6. Third, in their song of praise, they mention being purchased for God with the Lamb's blood "from every tribe and tongue and people and nation" (v. 9). Fourth, in the millennial Davidic kingdom, this body of saints will constitute a special entity as a "kingdom" within a kingdom. And in the future, when the kingdom has arrived, they will "reign upon the earth," apparently as Jesus promised in such passages as 3:21, carrying out certain responsibilities of judgment and administration. Fifth, they will also constitute a priesthood (v. 10) that functions separately from the restored Levitical priesthood that will be serving in the revived Temple worship. Sixth, the size of this group gathered around the throne of God would certainly fit the number of redeemed likely to have been saved over the last two thousand years or more. They are described as "myriads of myriads, and thousands of thousands" (v. 11).

This heavenly church chorus is then joined by "every created thing which is in heaven and on the earth and under the earth and on the sea, and all things in them" (v. 13) who bless God and the Lamb with "blessing and honor and glory and dominion forever and ever." This sounds very much like Paul's great anthem to Jesus he penned in his letter to the church at Philippi:

> That at the name of Jesus every knee should bow, of those who are in heaven, and on earth, and under the earth, and that every tongue should confess that Jesus Christ is Lord, to the glory of God the Father. (2:10–11)

## Eating of the Tree of Life

In Revelation 2, the church of Ephesus is promised that they will partake and eat of the tree of life (2:7). The same tree will be for the healing of all the nations in the eternal state (22:2). This promise to the saints of Ephesus cannot be for that individual church alone as it enters eternal glory. The tree and its healing and sustaining properties will somehow be for all. It pertains to life eternal because those not receiving salvation are prevented from partaking of it (22:19).

It is difficult to fully understand the function of the tree of life with its eternal benefit. Is this tree simply symbolic or is there a true, eternal medicinal value in its leaves? Thomas seems to propose the best answer:

> Though eating the fruit of the Tree of Life is unmentioned [in 22:2], the implication is that this is what brings immortality, the same as was true for Adam and Eve originally (Gen. 3:22). Conditions of future bliss will mean a return to the original glories and privileges of God's presence with man, before sin raised a barrier that prevented that direct contact. . . . "Healing" . . . , then, must connote a promoting of the health of the nations such as will be an ongoing service in the new creation.[13]

## The Eating of Manna

The church at Pergamum was promised that overcomers would receive "some of the hidden manna" (2:17). Manna was the miracle food provided by the Lord as Israel wandered in the wilderness (Exod. 16). The word *manna* actually comes from the question of the Israelites, "What is it?" The Jews were commanded to gather in the mornings, except on Sabbath, this bread-like food described as "a fine flake-like thing, fine as the frost on the ground" (16:14). If it was not harvested when and as the Lord commanded, the sun would melt it away (v. 21). Manna became a type, a symbol of God's heavenly provision and care for His people. It was called the "corn of heaven" (Neh. 9:20) and the "bread of the Almighty" (Ps. 78:24).

In the New Testament, Jesus speaks of it as a type of Himself as "the true bread out of heaven" (John 6:32) and "the bread of God is that which comes down out of heaven and gives life to the world" (v. 33). Still using the manna as an illustration, He refers to Himself as "the bread of life" (v. 47), the "living bread" (v. 51), and the bread that gives life forever (v. 58). Further adding to its spiritual implication, the apostle Paul calls it "the spiritual meat" (1 Cor. 10:3), and adds "there is one bread, we who are many are one body; for we all partake of the one bread" (v. 17).

Paul is referring to the spiritual body of Christ. This body, the church, shares the person of Jesus as Savior. The bread represents His body and sacrifice of which we must partake. "Is not the bread which we break [communion] a sharing in the body of Christ?" (v. 16). Some denominations believe the eating of the communion bread is mystical and grants some kind of spiritual presence and effect upon the believer. But since the Lord's Table is but a "remembrance" of Christ's sacrifice of His body (11:24), and since Jesus pictured the taking of the bread as a sign of faith in coming to Him (John 6:35), this ceremony in itself would not be an imparting of some spiritual force or power. In John 6:35, Jesus' words seem to be quite clear: "Jesus said to them, 'I am the bread of life; he who comes to Me shall not hunger, and he who believes in Me shall never thirst.' " The coming to Christ is the satisfying of a hunger, the believing in Him is the quenching of a spiritual thirst.

Thus in Revelation 2:17, the overcomer is one who comes to Jesus as Savior and partakes of Him as bread or manna. Though it seems this is mentioned in a special relation for the church at Pergamum, the promise is really for all believers in Christ. And if the overcomer is but one who is victorious over the tug of the culture and accepts Jesus as Savior, then the verse is simply saying that this person becomes a partaker in the body of Christ. Thomas writes:

> The symbolism of future reward, an allusion to Christ as the true manna, and present satisfaction of believers with this spiritual bread as a foretaste of future fullness are all in the background of "the hidden manna."[14]

Walvoord adds:

> So for the true believer in the Lord Jesus there is the hidden Manna, that bread from heaven which the world does not know or see which is the present spiritual food of the saints as well as a part of their future heritage. This seems to refer to the benefits of fellowship with Christ and the spiritual strength that is afforded by that experience.[15]

Revelation 2:17 also mentions that the overcomer will receive from the Lord "a white stone, and a new name written on the stone which no one knows but he who receives it."

Walvoord hypothesizes that the white stone is

> possibly a brilliant diamond. In courts of law, being given a white
> stone is thought to represent acquittal in contrast to a black stone
> which would indicate condemnation. . . . The real value of the
> stone is the inscription on it rather than the stone's intrinsic worth.
> The stone's value rests in the new name of the recipient which is
> his title to eternal glory. The giving of the white stone to the
> believer here, then, is the indication that he has been accepted or
> favored by Christ, a wonderful assurance especially for those
> who have been rejected by the wicked world and are the objects
> of its persecution. In addition to receiving the stone, a new name
> written on the stone is promised them, the name described as
> one "which no man knoweth saving he that receiveth it."[16]

## Clothed in White Garments

To the church at Sardis the overcomer is prophesied to "be clothed in white
garments" (3:5). Again, this promise must be applicable to all those in this church
age who accept Christ. It is not simply the experience of the believers in Sardis.
White robes in Scripture usually imply the saints being covered by the righteousness of Christ, though sometimes they may refer to the righteous living of
the saints of God (19:8). Righteous angelic beings are also described as clothed
in white (Acts 1:10; Rev. 15:6) as a sign of their unfallen and holy state.

The white robes were also promised to those who would trust Christ, those
who were not saved as yet but who were only part of the visible church at Laodicea.
They were called by Christ "wretched and miserable and poor and blind and
naked" (3:17). But they were urged to buy from Jesus His "gold refined by fire"
so that they could become spiritually rich and be clothed in white garments.
With this the "the shame of your nakedness may not be revealed"; and they
would receive "eyesalve to anoint your eyes, that you may see" (v. 18).

Though the church has already been redeemed and is seen residing in heaven,
saints martyred in the Tribulation are also clothed in white, with their robes having
been washed in the blood of the Lamb (7:14). Since both groups, the Tribulation
saints and church saints, are clothed in white, this does not make them of the same
dispensational group. In the technical sense, the church is residing in glory as
tribulation wrath is poured out on the world below. But by the millions, unbelievers on earth during that horrible seven-year period of terror will turn to the Lord
and be saved, as church saints, by the same substitutionary death of the Messiah.

## A Pillar in the Temple of God

Revelation 3:12 is full of future promises and assurances for the believer in
Christ. Though the verse is addressed to the overcomer in the church of Philadelphia, it stands as a universal promise of being in the presence of the Lord forever.

The verse quotes Christ, who says that the overcomer will be "a pillar in the temple of My God." As well, Jesus "will write upon him the name of My God, and the name of the city of My God, the new Jerusalem, which comes down out of heaven from My God, and My new name."

Thus as the eternal state begins (Revelation 21–22), the body of Christ will be permanent trophies, examples of the grace of God during the dispensation of the church age. Is the verse metaphorical or literal? Thomas provides a meaningful answer:

> The stable relationship to God is guaranteed by . . . ("I will make him a pillar in the temple of My God, and he will not possibly go outside any longer"). The language is clearly metaphorical, as is evident from stylon ("pillar"). Because the person is likened to a pillar, naos ("temple") must be metaphorical also. . . . Hence, this promise is not inconsistent with the later statement that there is no temple in the heavenly Jerusalem (Rev. 21:22). The Jerusalem that comes down from heaven is all temple, and Christ's victorious ones are its living stones and pillars. The Philadelphia Christians will be permanent, like a pillar in the Temple, and will stand when all else has fallen. They are assured of continuance in God's presence throughout all eternity.[17]

Further assurance of eternal life is given by the promise of Jesus that the saved will never again go out from that temple, and that the name of God and the new city of Jerusalem is written upon them.

> The threefold occurrence of onoma ("name") is impressive and amounts to a threefold assurance of his identity with God. To have "the name of My God" was equivalent to belonging to God, being endowed with divine power.[18]

## The New Jerusalem and the Twelve Apostles

In the description of the New Jerusalem (Rev. 21:9–22:5) there are memorials and monuments that are to be remembered eternally, but some descriptions are hard to understand. For example, there is a "great and high wall, with twelve gates, and at the gates twelve angels" (21:12). The twelve gates (gate-towers) may be a continual reminder of the eternal security of those within. The angels likewise may "reinforce the impression of security."[19]

On the gates were written the names of the twelve tribes of Israel (v. 12). Thus the place of the Jewish people is a permanent reminder of their role in the plan of human history. Likewise there are twelve foundation stones supporting the gates with the names of the twelve apostles of the Lamb (v. 14). The human vessels the Lord used to launch the church are memorialized for eternity. For ages to come all the redeemed of all generations will be reminded how God worked in history to bring mankind to Himself.

Walvoord concludes:

> It is noteworthy . . . that not only are the twelve apostles represented but also the twelve tribes of Israel. This should settle beyond any question the matter of the inclusion of Old Testament saints [in the eternal state]. It apparently is the divine intent to represent to the reader that the new Jerusalem will have among its citizens not only the church, or saints of the present age, but also Israel, or saints of other ages, whether in the Old Testament or in the tribulation period. Later on there is mention also of Gentiles. The careful expositor, therefore, on the one hand will not confuse Israel and the church as if one were the other. On the other hand, he will not deny to both their respective places of privilege in God's program.[20]

## Questions for Discussion

1. What should the attitude of the believer be in regard to the world or this culture?
2. Though a citizen of heaven, what is the present task of the child of God who is living in this worldly environment?
3. In the future, whom will believers be judging? Discuss.
4. Will the saints in Christ be ruling? Whom will they rule?
5. What do you think is the purpose of the Tree of Life?
6. What do you think is the significance of the hidden manna?
7. How will a believer, an overcomer, be a pillar in the temple of God?
8. What do you think the apostle John is trying to tell us with the various word pictures he paints in Revelation 2–3?

# The Apostasy
# of the Church

## The Beginning of Spiritual Darkness

In 1921, John Horsch wrote a book that almost became a prophetic classic as to where the visible church is headed. His book *Modern Religious Liberalism* predicted that the twentieth century was rapidly moving toward what the Bible calls the apostasy.[1] By examining religious institutions, churches, and the culture of that day, Horsch felt that the prophesied apostasy of the church was not far away.

This chapter will pick up on some of the thoughts of Horsch. It will be especially controversial because many will say, "Oh, others have predicted we are into the times of the apostasy. No one can guess when the end-times will come."

It is impossible to be absolutely sure of a prophetic timetable. Just as in his day Horsch examined the things happening spiritually at the beginning of the twentieth century, believers in Christ need to look again today at this present generation that is about to go into the twenty-first century. Some very important questions must be asked.

Could the church now be in the era known in Scripture as the apostasy? Could Christianity at the least be at the threshold of that terrible dark period of spiritual blindness? If so, what are the biblical indicators that must be taken into account? We do not want to present an overly dogmatic position and say with absolute certainty that the church is now into the predicted apostasy. However, the contributors to this book believe that the church cannot be far away from what the Scriptures clearly predict about the last days of the dispensation of the age of grace as we know it.

## The Changing Times

Coming into the twentieth century, drastic and momentous changes were shaking the world to the core. These changes were dramatically affecting the church and the moral values that shaped societies. The use of technology was exploding and conflicting philosophies were causing people to put their faith in man more than in God. The human race was becoming the captain of its own destiny, or so a vast number of humanity assumed.

The new was replacing the old. Liberal skepticism was playing havoc with biblical certainty. Supposedly, science was replacing God, and rationalism was supplanting an inerrant Bible that gave the world of the past a certain spiritual hope. The present generation has forgotten how explosive the new thinking was in those days. Liberalism quickly consumed entire church denominations, some Christian universities, and almost all secular universities.

Horsch writes that this change was "so fundamental that it seems to imply the overturn of the whole trend of past philosophies."[2] He adds, "The triumph of liberalism is really a defeat, for it means the destruction of Christianity as Christianity has been known in all ages of its history."[3]

To add drama, Horsch fictionalizes what the worldly critic might say of biblical doctrine that had been held essential up to those days by all believers in Christ. The liberal voices were crying out:

> We destroy much that was formerly accepted by Christian believers. We deny the authority of the Scriptures; we see in Scripture both truth and error. . . . We do not believe [Jesus] was the God-man; we do not believe he was a perfect man. . . . Neither his sayings nor his life are to us authoritative in every respect.[4]

Horsch quotes McCormick Theological Seminary professor Dr. John H. Boyd (*The Christian Register*, December 11, 1919, p. 3), who said:

> I have not pleaded with you to believe in God. . . . I have believed that if you accept the teachings of Jesus Christ and become conscious of your own possibilities, you would grow out and for yourselves find God and spiritual realities. . . . Those who can see the infinite reach of themselves can see God, can strengthen themselves, and the spiritual world is open to them. Men are what they are because of a fatal disbelief in their own divinity.[5]

The monster being fed in these quotes is humanism. Mankind will no longer need God. And when that day fully arrives, the Antichrist, the ultimate, rebellious and evil man, will come and control the world by his new religion.

## "People Simply Think with Their Muscles"

At the turn of the twentieth century, the field of psychology was in the incubating stage in American and European universities. It was sometimes labeled "behaviorism." Horsch points out that it was the "new" psychology and that it was upheld by radical modernists.[6] Behaviorism taught that every thought, feeling, and action was mechanical, nothing more than the result of physical causes. There was no mind, soul, or spirit in human beings. The brain was simply a muscle flexing commands with no rhyme or reason.

> Human volition and responsibility are denied. Behaviorism flatly denies the existence of the soul. The Behaviorists regard man wholly and solely as an animal, and on the basis of evolution, they deny man all qualities and faculties which the animal does now possess. All belief in immortality is destroyed. God is bowed out of existence. He is simply ignored. Here is atheism, pure and simple.[7]

## The Coming Great Compromise

A dispensationalist, Horsch saw all these trends leading western cultures and the church toward the final stages of the age of grace. The world would soon dominate the thinking processes of those who "profess" Christ as Savior. Doctrine would be accepted as it is weighed against the standards of what the society thinks is right. This dispensation of the church would end in biblical and spiritual compromise. Horsch predicted, "The fact cannot be too strongly emphasized that compromise with the new theology means defeat. . . . A position of compromise is a losing position. It means virtually the acceptance of the liberal viewpoint."[8] Though it is possible to disagree with Horsch in his timing of the apostasy, no one can disagree with the essence of this final paragraph from his book.

> The apostasy that is evident on every hand, then, is an unmistakable sign of the times. It should arouse believing Christendom from its lethargy and listlessness to a realization of conditions as they are. In consequence of the apostasy the church finds itself today face to face with a crisis such as it has never passed through in its history.[9]

## The Biblical Doctrine of the Apostasy

Jesus seemed to warn of some far-off day when spiritual service done as unto the Lord would no longer be possible. Apparently addressing His disciples, He said, "We must work the works of Him who sent Me, as long as it is day; night is coming, when no man can work" (John 9:4). He seems to be saying truth has but so long to be proclaimed, and then someday it will be stifled. Because His words appear to be all-inclusive, it is doubtful Christ is simply talking about His own ministry to the Jews. A much larger point of reference seems to be in view.

Though likely referring to events that would take place after he leaves, Paul warned the elders of Ephesus to "be on guard" for the flock because "savage wolves will come in among you, not sparing the flock" (Acts 20:28–29). They will arise, "speaking perverse things" (v. 30). Though clearly pointing to an immediate moment in early church history, the passage sometimes has been used to point out the doctrinal destruction coming upon churches during the age of grace, and to show that the church will be under continue spiritual attack right up to the period of the apostasy.

The most direct verses dealing with the apostasy are in 1 Timothy 4:1–5 and 2 Timothy 3:1–9. In these two sections of Scripture, Paul makes it clear that the apostasy has a specific eschatological orientation. Apostasy is in a certain sense always with the church, but a future distinct period of moral darkness and spiritual deception is also going to take place.

### 1 Timothy 4:1–5

> But the Spirit explicitly says that in later times some will fall away from the faith, paying attention to deceitful spirits and doctrines of demons, by means of the hypocrisy of liars seared in their own conscience as with a branding iron, men who forbid marriage and advocate abstaining from foods, which God has created to be gratefully shared in by those who believe and know the truth. For everything created by God is good, and nothing is to be rejected, if it is received with gratitude; for it is sanctified by means of the word of God and prayer. (1 Tim. 4:1–5)

On this passage, Nicoll well states:

> Although the prophet intends to utter a warning concerning the future, yet we know that what he declares will be hereafter he believes to be already in active operation. It is a convention of prophetical utterance to denounce sins and sinners of one's own time . . . under the form of a predictive warning.[10]

To understand the apostasy is to understand these verses in detail.

*But the Spirit explicitly says* (v. 1). The word *explicitly (rhetos)* in Greek has the force of "expressly, specifically" and was used even within Greek religious writings to punctuate prophetic utterances.[11] The apostle wants to make sure Timothy understands that what he says is truly from the Holy Spirit and not simply from his own thoughts. By this, he is adding importance to the prophecy he is setting forth. Though all Scripture is inspired by the Spirit of God, the use of *rhetos* should make Timothy and other readers in the future give special notice to this prophetic warning.

*In later times* (v. 1). "Later" *(hysteros)* clearly has the idea of the "future times."[12] Paul did not know of the exact moment of the falling away. He simply warns that it will happen some day. Nicoll makes a poignant observation when he notes, "'The later times,' of course, may be said to come before 'the last days.'"[13] What, by the Spirit, does Paul say will happen?

*Some will fall away from the faith* (v. 1). "Fall away" *(aphistēmi)* in both noun and verb form carries a wealth of meaning. It may be translated "to revolt, desert, become apostate, withdraw."[14] Here it is used in a technical sense of the doctrine of the falling away from the faith. Paul is not saying that people will simply depart from their personal belief in the truth. He is arguing that people will still be religious but will no longer commit to The Faith as described in the gospel. In other words, a certain future generation will no longer cling to the truth about Christ and salvation in Him. The verb "fall away" is used in the future middle indicative form and can be translated "some will be removing themselves" from The Faith principle concerning salvation in Jesus.

Paul may be saying that, when this happens, the churches will be full of people who are not really Christians but are simply religious. Barnes speaks of our present day, as if indeed the apostasy is here.

> [The passage] does not mean that, as individuals, they would have been true Christians; but that there would be a departure from the great doctrines which constitute the Christian faith. The ways in which they would do this are immediately specified, showing what the apostle meant here by departing from the faith.[15]

*Paying attention to deceitful spirits and doctrines of demons* (v. 1). It is this clause that gives the impression the apostle is not writing simply about Christians who are fooled or tricked, but he is saying that the churches will be filled with unbelievers who will be religious but who are actually controlled by the under-world realms of demonic powers. Lenski believes the "spirits" are false teachers and spiritual frauds who pretend to be religious but who have long ago given up a belief in the Word of God and its message. The "doctrine of demons" then would be outright satanic lies that promote anti-Christian teaching. "First the impostors, then, coupled with the doctrines they teach, and these Paul calls 'doctrine of demons.'"[16]

*By means of the hypocrisy of liars* (v. 2). In Greek, it literally reads: "in hypocrisy of lie-speakers." This has the force of saying that these who will have fallen away from the faith will act and speak in connection with hypocrisy. They will be as actors on the ancient Greek stage, wearing the mask of a hypocrite. They will claim to be Christians but they will have thrown off all the beliefs that are the very foundation of the faith.

*Seared in their own conscience as with a branding iron* (v. 2). The Greek is literally: "Who are cauterized as to their own conscience." By continually arguing with their conscience, these men have stifled and muted its warnings. In time, their conscience no longer bothers them. They live in rebellion and obstinacy and "their conscience will have been rendered (and thus will be permanently) seared. It will have been made callous."[17] From the pulpits and the denominational publications, these leaders will spew forth lies and contradictions that a majority will not oppose because very few will recognize the difference between false doctrines and the truth.

*Men who forbid marriage and advocate abstaining from foods* (v. 3). Though "to forbid" is acceptable, the first lexical definition is stronger. "To hinder" or "to prevent" may be the better expression in the passage and it might be translated "preventing to be marrying."

On this phrase, Lenski wants to remind his readers:

> These words are prophecy pure and simple. . . . "In later times" does not say how soon this will occur. It is not Paul's object to set a precise date. His object is to warn in advance of coming danger, to have all the churches fully fortified long before the actual danger arrives.[18]

Even though Paul was prophesying beyond his day, he also knew of the ascetic tendencies of the religious Therapeutae of Egypt and the Essenes in the south of Palestine. Even before the days of Christ, for generations these groups confined themselves to the most basic of diets and even condemned marriage. They taught that this brought them a higher degree of blessing in the spiritual life.[19] Paul is warning of an outward religion that will be characteristic of the period of the apostasy. "Religion" will not have died. Though the world has always practiced ceremony, good works, and occultism for an outward religious display, it will be most common and accepted in the period of the "great departure."

Paul concludes by reminding Timothy that God has created all foods to be shared "by those who believe and know the truth" (v. 3b). God has created all good things and they are not to be rejected but received with gratitude (v. 4). He finishes by writing, "For it is sanctified by means of the word of God and prayer" (v. 5).

> In 4:1–5 we have the Spirit's prophecies about these heresies, their devilish source, their contradiction of God's own creation. . . . Dangerous times are ahead; Paul saw them coming when he spoke the words of Acts 20:29, 30.[20]

## 2 Timothy 3:1–9

Paul's second great section on the coming apostasy is 2 Timothy 3:1–9. He tells Timothy again about this period of terror coming upon the outer form of the church. Paul "assured Timothy that persecution and trials were to be expected by all who aimed to lead holy lives, and that it was as certainly to be expected that evil men would become worse and worse."[21] The apostle's reason for mentioning the future perilous times was to preserve, if possible, the purity of the body of Christ. The first five verses read:

> *But realize this, that in the last days difficult times will come. For men will be lovers of self, lovers of money, boastful, arrogant, revilers, disobedient to parents, ungrateful, unholy, unloving, irreconcilable, malicious gossips, without self-control, brutal, haters of good, treacherous, reckless, conceited, lovers of pleasure rather than lovers of God; holding to a form of godliness, although they have denied its power; and avoid such men as these.*

*In the last days difficult times will come* (v. 1). Lenski translates this clause, "In the last days there shall be present seasons grievous."[22] "The one thing revealed is the grievousness of what is in store. . . . Worse times are impending, within the church and without it."[23] The verb "will come" *(enistēmi)* is future middle indicative and can better be translated "shall themselves be threatening, impending."[24] Barnes adds, "Under the gospel dispensation; some time in that period during which the affairs of the world will be closed up."[25]

*Men will be lovers of self, lovers of money* (v. 2). In classical Greek the word *philautos* is often translated "self-respecting," but Paul uses it in a sinful connotation, "self-aggrandizing." "Selfishness, which is evidenced by love of money (silver), the means for gratifying what self wants, this is the mark of people, but it is [going to be] developed to huge proportions."[26]

*Boastful, arrogant, revilers* (v. 2). These three words certainly go together, and though they are not equal in meaning, they often can be seen in one individual who expresses a haughty demeanor and attitude. "Boastful" carries the idea of having a false self-confidence; "arrogance" can be translated "disdainful or proud"; "reviler" is actually the Greek word for blasphemer but here is better interpreted "abusive."

Again, it must be noted that these characteristics of sinful mankind have always been part of the human drama, but they will be amplified and more widespread when the apostasy arrives.

*Disobedient to parents, ungrateful, unholy* (v. 2b). The Greek word meaning *parents (goneus)* is related to the word *knee (gony)*. In other words, parents are the ones to whom one bends the knee or bows before. Children will no longer obey or reverence their parents. They will consider themselves self-sufficient and wholly independent before the appropriate time. On these three words Lenski states:

> Men [will] start young to be "to parents disobedient" (Rom. 1:30), to parents, whom God has placed over their children,

whose very flesh and blood the children are, from whom the children receive countless benefactions. . . . "Ungrateful" for kindness and benefits received pairs well with disobedience. *Anosioi* are "impious [unholy]," who respect and receive and revere nothing that is sacred.[27]

*Unloving, irreconcilable, malicious gossips* (v. 3). "Unloving" *(astorgos)* is an unusual word and is used only here and in Romans 1:31 in a negative sense. Without the Greek *a* (negative) supplied, the word means "to love, have affection," particularly as a mutual response between children and parents. It can be used of the love of a tutelary god for the people, of dogs for their master and sometimes of the love between husband and wife.[28] As Paul uses it, a certain natural and even "anticipated" love will be nonexistent. Hendriksen further notes these religious people will be:

lacking even in natural affection such as parents have for their children, and children for their parents. . . . They show that same callousness all around, also in their relation to their fellowmen. Their feuds never end. In their camp no libation is ever poured out to signify that those who had been at variance with each other have consented to a truce. They are implacable, irreconcilable. . . . These people, then, hurl false and/or hostile epithets and charges at each other. They are slanderers, false accusers, imitators of the great Diabolos (Satan) [as gossips].[29]

*Without self-control, brutal, haters of good* (v. 3b). "Without self-control" literally can mean "without strength; that is, without strength to resist the solicitations of passion, or who readily yield to it."[30] "Brutal" is the Greek word *anēmeros* which is used only here in the New Testament. It can mean "to be severe, harsh, fierce, ungentle." It is the opposite of meekness and gentleness. Without the positive effects of Christianity or its influence on society, men will be coarse and cruel.

*Treacherous, reckless, conceited* (v. 4). The word "treacherous" carries the idea of being a traitor, or one who turns against friends or country. "Reckless" is used only here and in Acts 19:36. Barnes says the word

properly means falling forwards; prone, inclined, ready to do anything; then precipitate, headlong, rash. It is opposed to that which is deliberate and calm, and here means that men would be ready to do anything without deliberation, or concern for the consequences.[31]

"Conceited" literally means "to be puffed up." It has the thought of being inflated, lifted up with pride or self-conceit.

*Lovers of pleasure rather than lovers of God* (v. 4b). The world has always acted this way, probably ever since the fall of Adam. But as the apostle uses the expression, he has in mind that this tendency will only grow worse in the apostasy. Mankind lives only for pleasure. And pleasure can choke out any concept of seeking after or loving God. Sensual pleasures create no restraints, nor do they allow serious pursuits. The self reigns and God is dethroned! "This definitely does not mean that they also love God to some extent. It means that they do not love God at all."[32]

*Holding to a form of godliness, although they have denied its power* (v. 5). The Greek word "godliness" is *eusebeias,* which better translates from the context "religion." Or, "to have the outward form of religion, be religious only in appearance."[33] "They are described as having a form, a mere semblance or appearance (cf. Rom. 2:20) of piety . . . , but denying (literally, 'having once for all denied') its power."[34] Having said this, the apostle comes back into the present for the moment and urges, "Avoid such men as these" (v. 5b).

In verses 6–9 Paul points out that people have been this way in the past and were even the same in his day. However, his point is that such characteristics will grow worse. He prophesies for the future: "Evil men and impostors will proceed from bad to worse, deceiving and being deceived" (v. 13).

Paul continues the thought about the apostasy (noun, *apostasia*) in 2 Thessalonians 2:1–5. Here he gives a proper chronological chain of events. He writes of (1) the rapture of believers: "The coming of our Lord Jesus Christ and our gathering together to Him" (v. 1); (2) the fear within the believers that "the day of the Lord might have already come [but hadn't]" (v. 2); (3) the Day of the Lord (the Tribulation) will not come until the "apostasy comes first" (v. 3a); (4) then, the man of lawlessness, the Antichrist, will come and be revealed (v. 3b); (5) by taking "his seat in the temple of God, displaying himself as being God" (v. 4).

Lenski notes:

> One must certainly be struck by the resemblance between 2 Thess. 2 and Paul's present statements. There the whole great apostasy which is headed by the great Antichrist is revealed, and we are shown how it shall be blasted by the Word and shall finally be utterly destroyed by the Lord's Parousia. [In 1 Timothy 4] Paul warns Timothy only regarding some who will apostasize a little later. We recall 1 John 2:18 where we are told that the great Antichrist is coming and that many little antichrists are already present when John writes his letter. They seem to be advance guards of the great apostasy and the great Antichrist.[35]

### *The Coming of False Teachers*

Peter reminds his readers that as there were false prophets among the Jews in the Old Testament, likewise there will be false teachers who will come among the churches and bring destructive heresies, "even denying the Master who bought them, [and thus bringing] swift destruction upon themselves" (2 Peter 2:1). Again, though this has always happened during this dispensation of the church, more than likely he too is referring to the end times. The mockers mentioned in 3:3 are those same false teachers who will come "in the last days," asking, "Where is the promise of His coming?" (v. 4). They argue that all things continue as "from the beginning of creation." Thus, God is not bringing forth a judgment as expected! Peter reminds his readers that the Lord does not count time as man does (v. 8) and that judgment, the day of the Lord, will come like a thief, suddenly and without warning (v. 10).

Jude reminds his readers of the same thing. There will be mockers "following after their own ungodly lusts" (v. 18) who are "worldly-minded, devoid of the Spirit" (v. 19). As that time of apostasy approaches, Jude makes an earnest plea to believers in Christ to be built up "on your most holy faith; praying in the Holy Spirit" (v. 20). He prepares his readers for this terrible period that will come upon the church in the last days but then gives them hope in the Rapture. "Keep yourselves in the love of God, waiting anxiously for the mercy of our Lord Jesus Christ to eternal life" (v. 21).

## Conclusion

The apostasy will be a period of terrible spiritual confusion. There will be religious activity but the truth will be absent. Few will even grope about to find it. The church could now be moving into this period. If so, it can be expected that our age will grow progressively darker in unbelief and skepticism. Manton summarizes:

> That the scriptures speak much of the evil of the latter times; there [will be] more knowledge, and yet more sin and error. . . . Again, the latter days are as the bottom and sink that receive the dregs of foregoing ages, and as the world groweth old it is much give[n] to dreams and dotage. . . . Well, then, wonder not if you find many scoffing at the authority of the scriptures, Godhead of Christ, day of judgment, the ordinances, fasting and prayer. The latter age will yield such kind of men; and it is one of the arts of Satan, by his instruments, to make things of the saddest and most serious concernment to seem ridiculous.[36]

# Questions for Discussion

1. What does the word *apostasy* mean?
2. What is changing in our world that could lead to the apostasy?
3. Putting all the biblical references together, what is the Word of God telling us about the end-time apostasy of the church?
4. What could Paul be describing when he refers to "The Faith"?
5. Do you feel some of the descriptions of the apostasy fit what is happening in our day?
6. Summarize the doctrine of the apostasy in your own words.

## Chapter 8

# The Rapture
# of the Church

## Introduction[1]

Believers of every generation have longed for Jesus Christ's return. It has generally been understood that Christ would come back to the earth and end all human sorrow. After a general resurrection and judgment, He would initiate a new heaven and a new earth, eternity itself. While the details of how the Lord would come back may not have been defined, a belief in the Second Coming has been held by nearly all Christians.

With the resurgence of the study of Bible prophecy at the beginning of the nineteenth century, students of the prophetic Word noticed that in 1 Thessalonians 4:13–18 the apostle Paul first speaks of a resurrection of those who have died in Christ and then of those caught up together to meet the Lord in the air. Most prominent amillennial scholars ignored the idea that 1 Thessalonians 4 could be any different from other passages that speak of "the coming" *(parousia)* of Christ. In fact, to them the word *parousia* seemed to sum up the doctrine of only one return of Jesus.

Toward the end of the nineteenth century, a greater attention to sound hermeneutics led scholars of prophecy to a better understanding of: (1) how God providentially worked differently in various ages of biblical history; (2) how the end of history had a larger prophetic scheme of things than originally thought; and (3) how important a role interpreting by context played in comprehending the full scope of prophetic truth.

In time, contextual study made it clear that the coming of Christ to "rapture" away the church saints was an entirely different event than was His coming to judge sinners and to rule and reign for a thousand years. Many great Bible teachers of the period saw that both events were to be taken as distinct, literal comings and could not simply be spiritualized away.

By studying various passages, it can be shown that there are two distinct resurrections connected to the Lord's return. There is the resurrection for those in Christ, who will be taken to glory before the Tribulation begins. There is also a raising of the Old Testament saints and the Tribulation-martyred believers to enjoy the blessings of the Lord's one-thousand-year literal kingdom reign. Eleven key elements appear in such passages.

1. Resurrection. Though the resurrection is mentioned in Second Coming passages, these verses and sections of verses reveal certain special elements when they prophesy about those who will be coming forth from the grave (1 Cor. 15:23–24, 51–52; 1 Thess. 4:13–18; 5:1–11).
2. Hope and comfort. These passages give a particular hope and comfort because believers in Christ will be caught away to be at home in heaven with their Lord (John 14:13; 1 Cor. 15:51–52; Phil. 3:20–21; 1 Thess. 1:9–10; 2:17–19; 4:13–18; 5:1–11; 2 Thess. 2:1–2; James 5:7–9; 1 John 3:2–3).
3. Change. A new body is given to those who are resurrected as well as to those who are alive and will suddenly be transformed so they can go home to be with the Lord in heaven (1 Cor. 15:51–52; Phil. 3:20–21; 1 Thess. 4:13–18; 5:1–11; 1 John 3:2–3).
4. Return to heaven (John 14:1–3; Phil. 3:20; 1 Thess. 1:9–10; 3:13; 4:13–18; 5:1–11; 2 Thess. 2:1).
5. Direct involvement of the Lord; people will intimately face Christ at His Coming (John 14:1–3; 1 Thess. 1:9b–10; 2:17–19; 4:13–18; 5:1–11; 2 Thess. 2:1–2; Phil. 3:20–21; James 5:7–9; Titus 2:13; 1 John 2:28; 3:2–3).
6. Expectancy;  people live differently because He is coming (1 Thess. 5:1–11; 5:23; 1 Tim. 6:14; Titus 2:12–14; James 5:7–9; 1 John 2:28; 3:2–3).
7. Imminence; the pronouns *we, you,* and *us* prove the Rapture could have happened in Paul's own generation (John 14:1–3; 1 Cor. 15:51–52; Phil. 3:20–21; 1 Thess. 1:9–10; 2:17–19; 3:13; 4:13–18; 5:1–11; 5:23; 2 Thess. 2:1–2; 1 Tim. 6:14; Titus 2:13; James 5:7–9; 1 John 2:28; 3:2–3).
8. *Parousia* a description of the Rapture (1 Thess. 2:17–19; 3:13; 4:13–18; 2 Thess. 2:1–2; 1 Cor. 15:23–24; James 5:7–8; 1 John 2:8; 3:2–3).
9. Other expressions descriptive of the coming (John 14:1–3; 1 Thess. 4:16; 5:23–24; 2 Thess. 2:1–2; Titus 2:13; James 5:7–9; 1 John 2:8; 3:2–3).
10. Believers go to the Father (John 14:1–3; 1 Thess. 3:13; Titus 2:13).
11. The church involved as those in Christ (1 Thess. 2:17–19; 4:13–18; 5:1–11; 2 Thess. 2:1–2; 1 Cor. 15:23–24; 15:51–52; Titus 2:13).

## Resurrection and the Rapture

The resurrection that takes place at the Rapture has to do with the "dead in Christ," that is, deceased believers who became a part of the spiritual body of Christ in this dispensation.

Four distinct passages link the resurrection of church saints to the Rapture. In the most inclusive rapture passage, 1 Thessalonians 4:13–18, the apostle Paul addresses the issue of those who have fallen asleep in Jesus (4:14). He ties together this "catching away" *(harpazō)*, or the Rapture of living believers, with the resurrection of church saints or those in Christ:

> *But we do not want you to be uninformed . . . about those who are asleep. . . . God will bring with Him those who have fallen asleep in Jesus. . . . The Lord Himself will descend . . . and the dead in Christ shall rise first. Then we who are alive and remain shall be caught up together with them in the clouds to meet the Lord in the air. (vv. 13–14, 16–17)*

The Thessalonian church seems to have been concerned about the death of those who had accepted Christ as Savior. Will they live again? This question had not been answered, and they were grieving as the pagans who had no guarantees about an afterlife (v. 13). The answer is that those believers who have died will in no way miss out on the blessing of the Lord's coming.

Paul states, "In no way, not even, should we precede the ones who have been put to sleep" (v. 15, author's translation). The word "precede" *(phthasōmen)* has a double negative that carries the force of an extra emphatic, "We should *absolutely not* precede those who have been put to sleep!" This is a Greek idiom that effectively takes away any apprehension about the dead in Christ being left out.[2] This idiom has the sense of an emphatic future, "When the time comes this is the sequence of events."[3] The dead in Christ shall rise first.

### Those Awake and Asleep Will Live Together with Christ

In 1 Thessalonians 5:1–10 the apostle Paul writes about the coming Day of the Lord (v. 2), or the wrath (v. 9) that will fall on the lost who are proclaiming peace and safety (v. 3). In verses 2–7 the apostle pictures the birth pangs of trouble and pain that fall suddenly on the lost. They are in spiritual darkness, and they will not escape the terror that will overcome them like a thief (vv. 3–4).

In 5:9–10 Paul comes back to the issue of the Rapture that he began writing about in 4:13–17. He summarizes and restates the fact that both those who are asleep (the dead in Christ) and those awake will live together with Jesus. This was meant to calm their fears during their trials and to correct the error that those who were found alive when He returns would have some priority over those who were dead.

Verse 10 reads:

> *[Christ] died for us, in order that whether we should right now be fully awake or whether we should right now be sleeping, we*

*shall in the future, [and] all at once at the same time, be alive
together with Him.* (trans. author's)

The expression "in the future . . . be alive"[4] prophetically sees the resurrected saints in Christ and those raptured believers living together with Him. The force of the verb could also mean "now and forever" we shall live with Him.[5] The expression "all at once at the same time" sheds even more light on this resurrection and the Rapture. Actually, this represents two expressions joined together: "Together with" *(hama)* and "with Him" *(syn autō)*. Barnes interprets this as "those who are alive and those who are dead—meaning that they would be *together* or would be with the Lord *at the same time*."[6] Hendriksen adds, "Those who are *awake* are those who are *alive,* the survivors, the ones who according to 4:15 are 'left until the coming of the Lord.'"[7]

### Two Resurrections or More?

Even some of the earlier Bible scholars who do not accept a dispensational rapture see two resurrections in 1 Corinthians 15:23–24. In the full context, Paul promises a resurrection in which all in Christ shall be made alive (v. 22). "To explain, each [will be resurrected] in his own order: Christ the firstfruits; next after that, those [believers] who belong to Christ at His coming; after this [will come] the consummation whenever [Christ] [in the future] will be handing over the kingdom to the God and Father [including] whenever He abolishes all rule and all authority and power" (trans. author's).

The whole context is governed by "in Christ . . . made alive."[8] Dispensationally, verse 23 clearly has the church saints in mind and is not describing Jesus' coming to reign over Israel as the Son of Man or His coming to judge the world. He is returning to take the church. Since the kingdom is unquestionably separated in verse 24 from verse 23, the rapture resurrection is the only explanation for this passage.

> There is to be a sequence in the resurrection of the dead, and St. Paul explains this by the three groups: (1) Christ Himself, the first fruits; (2) the faithful in Christ at His coming; (3) all the rest of mankind at the end, when the final judgment takes place. The interval between these two—its duration, or where or how it will be spent—is not spoken of here. The only point the apostle makes concerns the order of the resurrection.[9]

Alford writes:

> The resurrection of the rest of the dead, here veiled over by the general term *to telos* [the end]—that resurrection not being in

this argument specially treated, but only that of Christians. . . . It ought to be needless to remind the student of the distinction between this Parousia [the coming] for those in Christ and the final judgment; it is here peculiarly important to bear in mind.[10]

Robertson and Plummer also believe this passage is open to be interpreted as Christ coming exclusively for His own, the church saints, as separate from another coming in which He raises other dead:

> Of these *tagmata* [each in his own order] there are two, clearly marked, in the present passage; Christ, who has already reached the goal of Resurrection; and Christ's Own [the church], who will reach it when He comes again. Perhaps St. Paul is thinking of a third *tagma* [order], some time before the End. But throughout the passage, the unbelievers and the wicked are quite in the background, if they are thought of at all.[11]

Christ's own, the church saints who have died, are still waiting for the resurrection.[12] This passage shows a sequence in the unfolding of the final events concerning that resurrection. Since Paul was addressing the church, he was not concerned with detailing all future resurrections. He concentrated instead on the church saints who are asleep and on their place in the scheme of things.

## Hope and Comfort

Almost all of the rapture passages speak of the blessing of the Lord's return for His own, or more specifically, the return of Jesus Christ to take His children home to heaven. This is the hope and comfort, and it is a different scenario than that of Jesus coming back to judge the earth, to reign and rule as Messiah. In fact a key to most rapture passages is this going-home joy and anticipation.

### *Going Home!*

In John 14:1–3, Jesus promised His disciples that He was going to prepare a place for them. From the Greek text the passage could read:

> *Let not the heart of each of you be disturbed. All of you together are believing in God; in the same way, all of you continue to trust in Me. In My Father's house are many dwelling places, but if not, I would have told you, because I go to prepare a room for you [to take residence]. And if I am going and preparing a room for you, I will be coming again and taking you along [to My own home], that where I am, I and you [will be together].* (trans. author's)

The hope and comfort in this passage is stated in a kind of a negative, "Let not the heart be disturbed." The reason: Christ is going to prepare a place for them, and He will return to receive them to Himself. This is a rapture passage because it implies that His coming could have taken place at any time. Though death could overtake them, their new bodies would be resurrected and taken home at the Rapture.

The Father's "house" *(oikos)* could not be the location of the earthly kingdom in which Jesus will reign. Jesus would be going soon to His Father's house. He will come for His own and take them back to a location He has prepared. Jesus is not saying that His disciples will simply die and go to the Father's house (although that would be true of their souls if they died before He came for them). Therefore, His coming for them must refer either to the Rapture while they are living or the bodily resurrection that takes place simultaneously. "The dead in Christ shall rise first. Then we who are alive and remain shall be caught up together with them in the clouds to meet the Lord in the air, and thus we shall always be with the Lord" (1 Thess. 4:16–17).

### Waiting Steadfastly

James 5:7–9 may be one of the earliest references to the Rapture, apart from Christ's words in John 14:1–3. Regarding hope and anticipation, verses 7–9 could read from the Greek text:

> *Be waiting steadfastly then, until the time of the visitation [parousia] arrives. Behold, the farmer waits for the precious fruit of the ground, waiting patiently concerning it. . . . You too, be waiting steadfastly, firmly stabilize your emotions, because the visitation of the Lord has progressively been drawing near.*

The phrase "be waiting steadfastly" refers to patience and forbearance.[13] In illustration, it is said that the farmer also "waits." This verb *ekdechetai* has the idea of eager expectation.[14] James urges his readers not only to wait eagerly with expectation for the Lord's coming but also to firmly stabilize their emotions *(kardia)*.

This rapture passage gives confidence and hope despite persecutions falling on the early church. The farmer waits hopefully for the refreshing rains that herald the coming of new crops. So believers can look for the Lord coming for them. Barnes writes, "In due time, as [the farmer] expects the return of the rain, so you may anticipate deliverance from your trials."[15]

### Rescued from the Coming Wrath

First Thessalonians 1:9–10 is a powerful rapture passage that further speaks of an "eagerly waiting" kind of hope. It gives this comfort or hope because it speaks of believers being dragged away from the terror of the wrath that is on its way to this world. In regard to this hope the Greek text literally reads:

*You turned . . . to presently be serving a living and true God, and to presently be eagerly waiting for His Son from the heavens, whom [God] raised from the dead, Jesus, who [will be] dragging [rescuing] us [to Himself] from the wrath which is coming!* (trans. author's)

The verb "be eagerly waiting" *(anamenō)* is given intensity with the preposition *ana.* And it has a continual, or linear, idea, "to keep on waiting."[16] On this hopeful anticipation Hendriksen adds:

The force of the verb to wait must not be lost sight of. It means to look forward to with patience and confidence. . . . It implies (both in Greek and in English) being ready for His return. . . . The thought of His coming does not spell terror for the believer . . . . For it is this Jesus [who] rescues (is rescuing) us from the wrath to come (the coming wrath).[17]

Barnes says:

The hope of his return to our world to raise the dead, and to convey his ransomed to heaven, is the brightest and most cheering prospect that dawns on man, and we should be ready, whenever it occurs, to hail him as our returning Lord and glorious Redeemer.[18]

### Our Hope When He Comes
Paul writes in 1 Thessalonians 2:19: "For what is our hope [anticipation] or joy or crown of rejoicing? Is it not even you in the presence of our Lord Jesus Christ at His coming?" This is an unusual way of speaking about hope and comfort. But Paul is telling the believers at Thessalonica how much he rejoices in their stand for the gospel. In fact their suffering and persecution for the name of Christ was almost overwhelming. When the Rapture occurs, those saints of the Lord will be at that moment Paul's great rejoicing when he stands literally before the face of Jesus. It is with this coming that the Thessalonian believers will be presented as Paul's joy. This is not the coming of Christ to deliver worldwide judgment. This is the Lord taking His own home to be with Him forever—this is clearly the Rapture!

### Comforting One Another
In the most important rapture passage (1 Thess. 4:13–18), the apostle Paul writes to the Thessalonian church about this great miracle event so that they might not grieve as do the rest who have no hope (v. 13). This should be translated "might not be made to grieve." Paul tells believers that if they grieve, it is

because they allow grief about their relatives who are asleep to overtake them, thereby acting as the unsaved who look upon death as final destruction.[19] Trying to correct this erroneous thinking, he pictures the pagan world as having no hope, and he tells of the Christian's blessed assurance of resurrection to glory with the Lord Jesus Christ.

In verse 18, Paul exhorts the believers to find and give comfort in these words from the Lord about the Rapture and the accompanying resurrection. At its root the word "comfort" *(parakaleō)* can mean to call alongside or to counsel. "Likewise, be counseling one another by these words." The present tense and active voice in Greek are used to emphasize that they need to be comforting each other right now and until the Lord comes. This is an exercise in faith in order to recognize the certainty of ultimate triumph.[20]

After writing about the Day of the Lord (5:2) and the wrath to come (5:9), the apostle concludes with the same command to comfort one another because God will not put His own through these days of horror that will come on the world. From the Greek text, Paul writes in 5:11:

> *Therefore, be continually comforting one another and building up one another, even as [I know] you presently are doing.*

Some believers had already fallen asleep in Jesus (4:14–15). Some will be alive when the Rapture takes place (4:17), and they will assuredly miss the terrible Day of the Lord that is coming on the earth (5:9). Thus, the larger hope is that believers will be with their Savior, whether by the Rapture or by resurrection.

### The Day of the Lord Has Not Come

Most believe 2 Thessalonians 2:1 is a reference referring exclusively to the Rapture. From the Greek it could read:

> *Now I am begging you, brothers, concerning the coming of our Lord Jesus Christ even [concerning] our gathering together up to Him.*

A. T. Robertson sees the entire verse as "referring to the Rapture, mentioned in 1 Thessalonians 4:15–17."[21] Paul often writes, "that you may not be quickly shaken from your composure" (2:2). Though the words *hope* and *comfort* are not used here, the apostle is comforting the Thessalonians by saying that the Day of the Lord has not come. The apostasy must come first and the Antichrist (the man of lawlessness) must be revealed (2:3–4).

Paul gives comfort by using two negatives: "Do not totter or waver" *(saleuō)* in your mind, nor "be terrified" *(throeō)* to the effect that the Day of the Lord has come (v. 2). Paul is referring to the Rapture in 1 Thessalonians 4:15–17 and amplifying the assurance that believers will escape the wrath.

### Christ's Resurrection Gives Hope

In 1 Corinthians 15, Paul argues that we have no hope if Jesus was not raised from the dead. "Those also who have fallen asleep in Christ have perished. If we have hoped in Christ in this life only, we are of all men most to be pitied" (vv. 18–19). He gives the great assurance to church saints: "in Christ shall all be made alive" (v. 22). And following Christ's resurrection comes the resurrection of the believers at the Rapture, "after that [the resurrection of Jesus] those who are Christ's at His coming" (v. 23). As He promised (John 14:2–3), Christ will return for those who comprise the church and the dead in Christ will be raised (1 Thess. 4:16).[22]

In 1 Corinthians 15:49, Paul continues his anthem of hope in regard to the resurrection, "as we have borne the image of the earthy, we shall also bear the image of the heavenly." He follows this with the hopeful declaration: "Behold, I am telling you something not before revealed, we shall not all be put to sleep, however, we shall all be changed, in a moment, at a blink of an eye, with the last trumpet; for the trumpet will sound, and the dead ones will be raised imperishable, and we shall all be changed" (15:51–52, author's translation).

These verses truly express a hope and comfort. Saying "behold," the apostle uses a forceful exclamatory to point to a "momentous revelation . . . to which he calls our earnest attention."[23] This is an "emphatic introduction of information of great moment."[24] Paul twice says we shall be changed at some point in the future. The Greek word used has the force of "to alter," or in other contexts, "to change the customs."[25] As well, "to take a new position, one thing for another, to alternate."[26]

Because of the unique dispensation of the church and the fact that living believers in Christ will be changed and translated before the coming wrath, Paul proclaims with great joy this blessed "new" revelation. "That [Paul] did not refer only to those whom he was then addressing, is apparent from the whole discussion. The argument relates to Christians—to the church at large."[27]

### A New Citizenship

One of Paul's most hopeful proclamations is found in the Greek of Philippians 3:20–21: "For our citizenship really exists in heaven, out of which we are waiting expectantly [to welcome] a Savior, the Lord Jesus Christ, who will alter the configuration of our body [that has] a limitation" (author's translation).

We are waiting "expectantly" *(apekdechomai)*. This word can mean "receive, welcome."[28] Paul includes himself in that anticipation. "We wait for, expect, till the event arrives."[29] Paul's heart is in heaven. "'We wait for' . . . vividly pictures Paul's eagerness for the . . . coming of Christ as the normal attitude of the Christian colonist whose home is in heaven."[30]

### Great Expectations

Paul almost shouts his excitement about the possibility of the Rapture in Titus 2:13. From Greek the passage can read: "[We are] excitedly expecting continually the joyous prospect, even [the] glorious appearance of our great God, even [our] Savior, Christ Jesus!" (author's translation).

"Excitedly expecting continually" is often translated simply "looking for" *(prosdechomai)*. And indeed, the present tense makes this "expecting" a continual hope. "This expectation [is] an abiding state and posture."[31] But the word also has the force of "welcome, wait for, expect."[32] The "blessed hope" might be translated "the joyous anticipation." There is no question about this expectation. It is going to come about, and it produces a great joyousness that looks forward to ultimate redemption. "This describes the great expectancy which is the ruling and prevailing thought in the lives of men looking for their Lord's return."[33]

### Having Confidence When He Comes

Christ could reveal Himself by the Rapture at any time. The apostle John expresses similar thoughts to Paul's in his personal love letter, 1 John. In two different contexts he speaks of confidence and hope in regard to Jesus' coming. From the Greek text: "However, now [I want you to specifically] keep on sticking with Him, so that whenever He should be revealed, we might have confidence and not shrink away from Him in shame at His coming" (2:28). "We shall be like-ones with Him, because we shall see Him as He is. And everyone who is having this anticipation of Him, is purifying himself, as that One is [existing as] pure!" (3:2).

Sometimes "confidence" *(parrēsia)* can be translated "joyousness," "courage," or "boldness."[34] By using "we" John implies that even he himself may be alive when Jesus comes and that his generation of believers may not have to die. He encourages them to live the Christian experience by something that could happen while he is alive.

In 3:2, John declares that when a believer anticipates or hopes for the Lord's return it produces a purifying effect within. "One who sets his hope by faith on the Son of God experiences an inward purification that is as complete as Christ's own purity."[35]

## The Change

When the Rapture takes place, believers will instantly receive new, glorified bodies like Christ's, and the resurrection of those asleep in Jesus takes place. This change affects both the living and the dead, in order that they may be brought into the very presence of the living God and His Son. By implication Paul first addresses this in 1 Thessalonians 4:13–18.

### Meeting the Lord in the Air

It is clear the dead in Christ could not be raised (4:16) and that we who are alive could not "be caught up together with them in the clouds to meet the Lord in the air" (4:17) unless we had glorified bodies. The apostle seals this issue with his conclusion, "Thus we shall always be with the Lord" (v. 17).

## *We May Live Together with Him*

Since believers in Christ are not destined for the wrath (1 Thess. 5:9) but are to obtain salvation through His sacrifice, they are raptured to "live together with Him" (5:10). This thought continues the fact that Christians must be changed in order to exist with the Lord.

## *Those Who Belong to Christ*

After thoroughly explaining the need for the resurrection (1 Cor. 15:12–21), Paul summarizes by saying that "in Christ all shall be made alive" (v. 22). He then adds (Greek): "To explain, each [will be resurrected] in his own order: Christ the firstfruits, next after that, those [resurrected] who belong to Christ at His coming" (v. 23). Again, the change is specifically the resurrection. But in 15:51–54, it also includes a transformation physically of the living believers in Christ: "We shall not all sleep [physically die], but we shall all be changed. . . . The dead will be raised imperishable, and we shall be changed. For this perishable must put on the imperishable, and this mortal must put on immortality" (vv. 51–53).

The word *change* in Greek *(allassō)* can mean "to take a new position, one thing for another, to alternate."[36]

## *Conforming Our Bodies*

From the Greek, Philippians 3:21 forcefully explains this needed and dramatic change to our bodies: "[Christ] will alter the configuration of our body [that has] a limitation, into a together-forming with the body of His glory." He does this by the "energizing of His power, even [the ability] to subject all things to Himself."

The word *alter,* often translated "transform" *(metaschēmatizō),* can literally mean to "alter the schematics." Jesus will "turn about" the present body into something new. The word can mean to change the form of a person or thing, to be changed in form, change configuration, change of position or posture.[37]

*Limitation* is often translated "humble state" *(tapeinōseōs).* The word can mean "to lower, reduce, to humble, abase, or a lessening."[38] Paul is speaking about a body that is now less than "the body of His glory." It is earthly, natural, fleshly, perishable (1 Corinthians 15). Sin controls, condemns, and brings about a groaning for release. Thus, we groan "within ourselves, waiting eagerly for our adoption as sons, the redemption of our body" (Rom. 8:23).

The word *together-forming,* often translated "conformity" *(symmorphon),* can literally mean "together-formed." Homer Kent writes:

> The present body is described literally as 'the body of lowli-
> ness' . . . a description calling attention to its weakness and sus-
> ceptibility to persecution, disease, sinful appetites, and death.
> At Christ's coming, however, the earthly, transient appearance
> will be changed, whether by resurrection of those dead or by

rapture of the living, and believers will be transformed and will receive glorified bodies that will more adequately display their essential character . . . as children of God and sharers of divine life in Christ.[39]

### Being Like Jesus

Though it is hard to fully fathom, John says, "We know with certainty that, whenever He should be revealed, we shall be like ones with Him, because we shall see Him as He is" (1 John 3:2, Greek). "'Whenever' sounds uncertain but the grammar construction implies certainty."[40] The Greek grammar literally says "like-ones with Him we shall be." We shall have a body and constitution just like Him! "It is clearly implied here that there will be an influence in beholding the Savior as he is, which will tend to make us like him, or to transform us into his likeness."[41]

## A Return to Heaven

Many of the rapture texts imply or speak directly of a return to heaven. In fact, seven specific contexts let us know our destiny is above. These "catching away" passages are rapture verses.

### To My Father's House

Jesus said to His disciples: "In My Father's house are many dwelling places. I go to prepare a room for you [to live in]. I will be coming again . . . that where I am, I and you [together]!" (John 14:2–3, Greek). Christ actually said, "Again I am coming."

By context, this should be taken as a future present. "I will be coming again."[42] This event "is regarded as so certain that in thought it may be contemplated as already coming to pass."[43]

### Rescued from the Wrath

In 1 Thessalonians 1:9–10, Paul says we wait for God's Son from heaven, "who delivers us from the wrath to come." The implication is that we are taken up so that "we shall always be with the Lord" (4:17). This has to mean we are taken to heaven. Again, this is not the Son of Man coming to reign on earth but to deliver us out of the way when God afflicts earth's inhabitants with an unparalleled series of physical torments.

### Taken Before the Father

In 1 Thessalonians 3:13 the apostle further argues that our hearts will be established unblamable in holiness before our God and Father at the coming of our Lord Jesus with all His saints. As in 2:19 (the presence of our Lord Jesus at His coming), "before" is used of a face-to-face encounter. Note the parallel: "Before (the presence of) our Lord Jesus" (2:19), and "before (the presence of) our God and Father" (3:13). This has to be in heaven.

### *Always with the Lord*

Few would argue that when Paul says,"Thus we shall always be with the Lord," he must be referring to heaven. Bible scholars of all prophetic persuasions have always held this means going home to heaven. This passage in Greek even more strongly suggests this: "We shall be snatched [raptured] into the clouds into the meeting place of the Lord in the air. Thus, altogether we shall ourselves be together with the Lord." Also, Bible teachers concur that Paul is alluding to heaven when he writes, "Whether we are awake or asleep, we may live together with Him" (1 Thess. 5:10).

### *Gathered to Him*

Many believe when the apostle writes of "the coming of our Lord Jesus Christ, even our gathering together to Him," he is still speaking of our going home to heaven (2 Thess. 2:1). Some have called this the muster of the saints to heaven. In fact, the phrase "to Him" can be translated "up to Him."[44]

### *Citizenship in Heaven*

There is no question about what Paul is saying in Philippians 3:20. Christians, while living on earth, have their citizenship elsewhere—in heaven. This contrasts with those who set their minds on earthly things (3:19). "Their mind [the world's] is on earth; our country is in heaven, and to it our affections cling, even during our earthly pilgrimage."[45]

## Taken Directly to the Lord or Intimately Facing Christ at His Coming

This "taking" is not before Jesus as the King of Israel, the Messiah, when He begins His earthly rule. All the contexts of the rapture passages either explicitly state or imply going home to be with the Lord in heaven. But they also indicate that believers will see Jesus instantly by the dynamic Rapture and change upon those living or by the resurrection of the church saints. The purpose for this catching away of the living is so that the wrath may fall on the earth. When He comes to reign in His Second Coming, church saints return with Him.

### *Where Jesus Is, We Are*

In John 14:3 Christ states it clearly: "I will be coming again and take you along [to my home], that where I am, I and you [together]" (author's translation). The Lord's disciples could have been raptured while living, but they died and their souls were taken to heaven. So Christ's coming back with their souls will bring about the bodily resurrection whereby their souls will be joined to their bodies. The disciples will then receive their new bodies. But they could have been snatched away while living and suddenly have met Him in air.

### Waiting for God's Son

Believers are to eagerly await the return of the resurrected Jesus, God's Son, from heaven (1 Thess. 1:10). They will see Him face-to-face! The word *wait (anamenō)* could be translated "to keep on waiting up for His Son." Hendriksen notes:

> The force of the verb to wait must not be lost sight of. It means to look forward to with patience and confidence . . . being ready for his return . . . The thought of his coming does not spell terror for the believer.[46]

### The Judge Is Approaching

When James writes of Christ as an approaching Judge (James 5:9), he is not referring to a judgment of our eternal destiny but of the *bēma* judgment for works. "For we must all appear before the judgment seat *[bēmatos]* of Christ, that each one may be recompensed for his deeds" (2 Cor. 5:10). From the Greek text, James actually says: "The coming of the Lord has progressively been approaching, coming nearer [at hand]" (5:8). Thus, Christ our Judge is brought near, He is at the point of appearing.[47]

### Jesus Who Drags Us Away

Paul writes of "Jesus, who delivers us from the wrath coming" (1 Thess. 1:10). The deponent Greek word *ruomai* has the idea "to deliver, rescue."[48] In some contexts it is translated "saved from the jaws of the lion" (2 Tim. 4:17) and *"delivered* from the power of darkness" (Col. 1:13). Some see this as descriptive of Christ's office, "Our Deliverer."[49] Also, it could be a timeless substantive denoting one of Jesus' characteristics, Jesus who will return as rescuer.[50] In classical Greek the word *erruō* can be translated "drag" or "draw away."[51] Vincent translates *ruomai* with the force of the middle voice, "to draw to one's self," with the specification from evil or danger.[52] The word can also have the force of a prophetic future, "The One who will drag us away [to Himself]" from the wrath that is coming.

### Snatched Away

First Thessalonians 4:17 reads, from the Greek text: "We shall be snatched into the clouds into the meeting place of the Lord in the air." The word *Rapture* comes from the Greek *harpazō,* which indicates being suddenly swooped away by a force that cannot be opposed.[53] Believers are going to meet the Lord in an appointed place in the air. The term "meeting place" *(apantēsin)* has a technical meaning in the Hellenistic world in relation to the visits of dignitaries. Visitors would be formally met by the citizens, or a deputation of them, who had gone out from the town for this purpose. The dignitary would then be ceremonially escorted into the city. In the Rapture, Christ will rescue us (1:10) and snatch us away to the meeting place in the sky, before the wrath of God falls on the earth (5:1–9).

Other passages speak of that face-to-face encounter with the Lord (1 Thess. 2:19). "And we shall always be with the Lord" (4:17). Other like phrases make it clear that when the Rapture comes, we are indeed to be with Him. "Whether we are awake or asleep, we may live together with Him" (5:10). "Our gathering together to Him" (2 Thess. 2:1). "We eagerly wait for a Savior, Christ Jesus" (Titus 2:13). Stay with Him, "so that when He appears, we may have confidence and not shrink away from Him [from His face][54] in shame at His coming" (1 John 2:28). "We shall see Him just as He is" (3:2).

## His People Live Differently

In six distinct passages, godly living is tied to the rapture hope. Critics of the Rapture often claim this doctrine is but an escape for those who teach it. But James and Paul both make it an incentive for living because He could appear to take us to Himself at any moment.

### Do Not Complain Against Another

James pleads, "Do not complain, brethren, against one another, that you yourselves may not be judged; behold the judge is standing, right at the door" (James 5:9). James further warns against swearing and being flippant or profane. The Lord could come at any moment: "Above all . . . do not swear . . . let your yes be yes, and your no, no; so that you may not fall under judgment [when the judge comes]" (5:12).

### Do Not Sleep, Be Sober

After Paul's great teaching on the Rapture and the accompanying resurrection of church saints, he reminds believers in Christ they are not destined for wrath (1 Thess. 5:9). The saints will escape the Day of the Lord (5:2), which will fall with sudden destruction on "them," those who have not trusted in Christ and who are in darkness (5:3–7). But with this reminder, Paul wants the believers to live godly lives. He writes: "We are of the day, let us be sober, having put on the breastplate of faith and love, and as a helmet, the hope of salvation" (5:8). The apostle says the children of light are not to sleep. We must be sober (5:5–6). Paul clearly is talking about how we are to live in the light of His any-moment return for those in Christ.

Paul further prays that God will sanctify the whole person, preserved morally intact and undiminished in light of Christ's return:

> Now may the God of peace Himself sanctify you entirely, and may your spirit and soul and body be preserved complete, without blame at the coming of our Lord Jesus Christ. (5:23)

The word *entirely* could read "quite complete" or "through and through."[55]

"To concentrate, to separate from things profane. . . . Here alone in the New Testament it means the whole of each of you, every part of you 'through and through' (Luther), qualitatively rather than quantitatively."[56]

### Living Without Stain

Paul urges those in Christ to "keep the commandment without stain or reproach until the appearing *(epiphaneias)* of our Lord Jesus Christ" (1 Tim. 6:14). The word stain can refer to a hidden reef or a soiled blemish.[57] *Without reproach* carries the idea of "irreproachable conduct."[58] The apostle seems to refer to issues of money and wealth. He has in view proper moral living in regard to material things, so that his readers might stand spiritually tall when Jesus comes.

### The Blessed Hope and Christian Living

The grace of God should motivate us to look for the blessed hope (Titus 2:12–13). This salvation should assist in denying ungodliness and worldly desires and help us live sensibly, righteously and godly in the present age. And it should produce a welcoming and an expectation of the Lord's soon return. On the two participles "instructing" (v. 12) and "looking" (v. 13): together they would read, "The grace of God has appeared . . . instructing us [that we might live sensibly] . . . [as we are] looking for the blessed hope."

### Do Not Shrink Back

Like Paul, the apostle John urges believers to have confidence and not shrink away from Him in shame at His coming (1 John 2:28). As with us, it may have been easy for the early Christians to forget their Savior. Their lives must have been imperfect. John and Paul tie the believers' lives to the hope of the Rapture so that they might not shrink away from His face with guilt when He arrives.[59]

John adds that just fixing hope on Jesus' return has a purifying effect on the child of God: "Everyone who has this hope fixed on Him purifies himself. . . . One who sets his hope by faith on the Son of God experiences an inward purification that is as complete as Christ's own purity."[60]

## Imminence

Without doubt, the early church and the apostles hoped for Christ's soon return. The use of the terms "we, you, and us" is proof that the Rapture could have happened in Paul's own generation. As with some engagements, a wedding date may not have been set, yet the bride and groom long for and anticipate their coming union. The disciples had this longing but were given no hint as to the time of the Rapture. Since it did not come upon them, we do not question their hope nor the Lord's revelation about the doctrine itself. It simply means that it is yet to come.

## Use of *Parousia* to Describe the Rapture

It is not the purpose of this section to give a complete study on the word *Parousia*. The word can be applied to the Rapture of the church or to the coming of Christ to establish the millennial kingdom. Context is the key issue in determining which coming is in view. The word does not mean simply "a coming." It may, by context, mean a presence, an arrival, a situation, or simply the coming of a dignitary for an official "visit."[61]

Thus, *Parousia* used in rapture passages in no way has to be understood as a "coming to stay." Nor does the word automatically have to relate to the Second Coming of Christ; that is, His coming to earth to reign on the throne of David. By context, then, it may be translated the "event, appearance, or visit." In light of this, the following selected passages are translated from the Greek text.

> *Be waiting steadfastly then, until the time of the visitation arrives. Be waiting steadfastly . . . because the visitation of the Lord has progressively been drawing near. (James 5:7–9)*

> *Are not you in fact [our joy] when we face our Lord Jesus at [the time of] His appearance? (1 Thess. 2:17–19)*

> *That [He may] firm up the hearts of you faultless, . . . in the [very] presence of the God and Father of us with the arrival of our Lord Jesus. (1 Thess. 3:13)*

## Other Expressions for the Coming

In addition to *Parousia,* other words and phrases describe the idea of Christ's rapture return to catch His own away.

### I Will Return

Jesus said, "I will come again, and receive you to Myself" (John 14:3). Actually it reads, "Again I am coming" *(palin erchomai)*. By context and because of the "again," this should be taken as a future present. "I will be coming again." This should be taken as a definite promise.[62] "This use of the present tense denotes an event which has not yet occurred, but which is regarded as so certain that in thought it may be contemplated as already coming to pass."[63] Since He was addressing the apostles, this return could have even taken place while these disciples were alive.

### The Lord's Coming Is Imminent

Besides using the word *Parousia,* James adds that this coming is at hand (James 5:8). From the Greek, the expression "is at hand" *(engizō)* could read, "The coming of the Lord has progressively been approaching, coming nearer, drawing nearer. The word has the idea 'to be imminent' and can be translated 'to be at the point of.'"[64] "The word *engizō* is related to the noun that has the idea of 'in the vicinity of, close by.'"[65]

James further sees Jesus the Judge standing right at the door (5:9). Christ has come right up to the door. By using the perfect tense, the apostle is saying, "He is, as it were, even now approaching the door."[66]

### The Lord Descends from Heaven

In 1 Thessalonians 4:16, the word *descends* means "to come down" *(katabainō)*. "He will [future tense] come down from heaven." The result is that the dead in Christ shall rise first, then we who are alive and remain shall be caught up. But notice, He does not stay here on earth. In fact, we, along with the resurrected, are taken up to Him.

### Gathering Together up to Him

In 2 Thessalonians 2:1, though the apostle Paul uses the word *Parousia* to describe the rapture coming of Christ, he then adds "and our gathering together with Him." Several Greek scholars feel the "coming" and the "gathering" are the same event and thus the passage should read "the coming, *even* the gathering together." Ellicott sees this "gathering" as the "taking up" in 1 Thessalonians 4:14–17.[67] A. T. Robertson adds, "Paul is referring to the rapture, mentioned in 1 Thess. 4:15–17, and the being forever with the Lord thereafter."[68]

### The Blessed Hope and Appearing

Though the noun "appearing" *(epiphaneia)* can refer to the Second Coming of Jesus (2 Thess. 2:8), twice it refers to the rapture coming of our Lord (1 Tim. 6:14; Titus 2:13). As a verb, "appear" is used twice in 1 John to refer to the Rapture (2:28; 3:2), "when He appears."

In Titus 2:13 Paul says we are looking for this appearing of the glory of our great God and Savior, Jesus Christ. "The glory" is a descriptive genitive, translated as an adjective,[69] thus, "the glorious appearance." The "and" between the two phrases "is explanatory, introducing the definition of the character of the thing hoped for. Looking for the object of hope, *even* the appearing of the glory."[70] The Greek connects "the blessed hope and glorious appearing" under one article, suggesting that the reference is to one event viewed from two aspects.[71] The reference to the Lord should read, "the great God *even* Savior, Christ Jesus."[72]

## Being Taken to the Father

Three main passages refer directly to our being raptured to the Father. The first is John 14:1–3. "In My Father's house are many dwelling places . . . I go to prepare a place for you" (v. 2). This house could not be the location of the earthly kingdom in which Christ will reign. Jesus is going *now,* in the historical context of this passage and in reference to the near event of His death, to His Father's house. He will come for His own and take them back to a location He has prepared in heaven.

Thus, this is a specific and personal promise concerning the new dispensation of the church. His coming for them will either be the bodily resurrection or the bodily Rapture. We know now, of course, that they died. They now await the resurrection of their new bodies and the joining of their souls to those bodies.

First Thessalonians 3:13 pictures believers in Christ as kept "in holiness before [in the very presence of] our God and Father at the coming of our Lord Jesus Christ with all His saints." Paul is arguing for the believers' maturity, spiritually and morally, so that they may stand before God *uncensored* by the way they lived.

In a powerful passage on the Trinity and the deity of Christ, Paul writes about the appearing of the glory of our great God and Savior, Jesus Christ (Titus 2:13). Though the Father and the Son are separate persons in the Godhead, they share the same essence and attributes. We are raptured by God the Son and taken to the very presence of God the Father. In the same epistle, Paul says, "God [is] our Savior" (3:4) and "Christ [is] our Savior" (3:6).

## Those in Christ or Allusions to the Church

The Rapture has to do with the dispensation of the church, or those "in Christ." The church age is a unique period with special promises. Those with Him now by faith will not face the coming wrath (1 Thess. 5:9). There was nothing like the Rapture for Old Testament saints, and there will be nothing similar for Tribulation believers.

Most of the rapture passages mention the believer's relationship to Jesus. Paul speaks of our Lord Jesus at His coming (1 Thess. 2:19) and of the dead as those who have fallen asleep in Jesus (4:14), who are now called "the dead in Christ" and who will rise first (4:17). The reason for the Rapture, Paul says, is so we might escape the coming wrath and obtain salvation through our Lord Jesus Christ (5:9). Awake or asleep we will live together with Him (5:10). The apostle continues to punctuate this relationship with our Redeemer when he reminds the confused Thessalonians of this coming of our Lord Jesus Christ and our gathering together to Him (2 Thess. 2:1).

In Paul's great resurrection and rapture section, 1 Corinthians 15:12–28, both events are tightly tied to the believer's spiritual position in Christ. In Christ all shall be made alive, he says (15:21). Jesus is the firstfruits of the resurrection and then those who are Christ's at His coming (25:23). Following the apostle's great description of the believer's change at the Rapture and the resurrection of the dead, he concludes with this triumphant statement, "Thanks be to God, who gives us the victory *because of* our Lord Jesus Christ" (15:57, author's emphasis).

In Titus, Paul calls the Lord "our great God and Savior, Jesus Christ" (2:13).

He gave Himself for us, and thus redeems and purifies a people for His own possession (2:14).

These statements are important because they reveal the unique position the church now has with its Savior that spares it from the coming wrath. Thomas writes, "When God vents his anger against earth dwellers (Rev. 6:16–17), the body of Christ will be in heaven as the result of the series of happenings outlined in [1 Thess.] 4:14–17 (cf. 3:13). This is God's purpose."[73]

Kent concludes:

> At Christ's coming . . . the earthly, transient appearance will be changed, whether by resurrection of those dead or by rapture of the living, and believers will be transformed and will receive glorified bodies that will more adequately display their essential character . . . as children of God and sharers of divine life in Christ.[74]

## Conclusion

These rapture passages form webs of related themes that can be identified and cataloged. Key verses interface with each other and provide undeniable patterns. All the accumulated rapture data strengthen the doctrine and give assurance. These verses spell out that the living believers in Christ will be changed and taken home by the Lord before the terrible period of the wrath begins, and they reveal that the dead in Christ will be resurrected to receive a new, eternal body. Together we go home with the Lord and are presented to God our Father.

## History of the Doctrine of the Rapture[75]

A history of the doctrine of the Rapture is of necessity a history of pretribulationism, since most other views do not distinguish between the two phases of Christ's return, the Rapture and the Second Advent. The partial rapture idea and midtribulationism have been developed only within the past one hundred years.

That the earliest documents (in addition to the New Testament canon) of the ancient church reflect a clear premillennialism is generally conceded, but great controversy surrounds the early understanding of the Rapture in relation to the Tribulation. Pretribulationists point to the early church's clear belief in imminency and a few passages from a couple of documents as evidence that pretribulationism was held by at least a few from the earliest times.

As was typical of every area of the early church's theology, views of prophecy were undeveloped and sometimes contradictory, containing a seedbed out of which could develop various and diverse theological viewpoints. While it is hard to find clear pretribulationism spelled out in the fathers, there are also found clear pretrib elements that if systematized with their other prophetic views, contradict post-tribulationism but support pretribulationism.

Since imminency is considered to be a crucial feature of pretribulationism by scholars such as John Walvoord,[76] it is significant that the Apostolic Fathers, though post-tribulational, at the same time just as clearly taught the pretribulational feature of imminence.[77] Since it was common in the early church to hold contradictory positions without even an awareness of inconsistency, it would not be surprising to learn that their era supports both views. Larry Crutchfield notes, "This belief in the imminent return of Christ within the context of ongoing persecution has prompted us to broadly label the views of the earliest fathers, 'imminent intratribulationism.' "[78]

Expressions of imminency abound in the Apostolic Fathers. Clement of Rome, Ignatius of Antioch, *The Didache, The Epistle of Barnabas,* and *The Shepherd of Hermas* all speak of imminency.[79] Furthermore, *The Shepherd of Hermas* speaks of the pretribulational concept of escaping the tribulation.

> You have escaped from great tribulation on account of your faith, and because you did not doubt in the presence of such a beast. Go, therefore, and tell the elect of the Lord His mighty deeds, and say to them that this beast is a type of the great tribulation that is coming. If then ye prepare yourselves, and repent with all your heart, and turn to the Lord, it will be possible for you to escape it, if your heart be pure and spotless, and ye spend the rest of the days of your life in serving the Lord blamelessly.[80]

Evidence of pretribulationism surfaces during the early medieval period in a sermon some attribute to Ephraem the Syrian entitled *Sermon on The Last Times, the Antichrist, and the End of the World.*[81] The sermon was written some time between the fourth and sixth century. The Rapture statement reads as follows:

> Why therefore do we not reject every care of earthly actions and prepare ourselves for the meeting of the Lord Christ, so that he may draw us from the confusion, which overwhelms all the world? . . . For all the saints and elect of God are gathered, prior to the tribulation that is to come, and are taken to the Lord lest they see the confusion that is to overwhelm the world because of our sins.

This statement evidences a clear belief that all Christians will escape the tribulation through a gathering to the Lord. How else can this be understood other than as pretribulational? The later second coming of Christ to the earth with the saints is mentioned at the end of the sermon.

By the fifth century A.D., the amillennialism of Origen and Augustine had won the day in the established church—East and West. It is probable that there were always some forms of premillennialism throughout the Middle Ages, but it existed primarily underground. Dorothy deF. Abrahamse notes:

> By medieval times the belief in an imminent apocalypse had officially been relegated to the role of symbolic theory by the church; as early as the fourth century, Augustine had declared that the Revelation of John was to be interpreted symbolically rather than literally, and for most of the Middle Ages church councils and theologians considered only abstract eschatology to be acceptable speculation. Since the nineteenth century, however, historians have recognized that *literal apocalypses did continue to circulate in the medieval world* and that they played a fundamental role in the creation of important strains of thought and legend.[82] (italics added)

It is believed that sects like the Albigenses, Lombards, and the Waldenses were attracted to premillennialism, but little is known of the details of their beliefs since the Catholics destroyed their works when they were found.

It must be noted at this point that it is extremely unlikely for the Middle Ages to produce advocates of a pretribulational Rapture when the more foundational belief of premillennialism is all but absent. Thus, the rapture question is likewise absent. This continued until the time of the Reformation, when many things within Christendom began to be revolutionized.

Premillennialism began to be revived as a result of at least three factors. First, the Reformers went back to the sources, which for them were the Bible and the Apostolic Fathers. This exposed them to an orthodox premillennialism. Specifically significant was the reappearance of the full text of Irenaeus's *Against Heresies,* which included the last five chapters that espouse a consistent futurism and cast the 70th week of Daniel into the future.

Second, they repudiated much, not all, of the allegorization that dominated medieval hermeneutics by adopting a more literal approach, especially in the area of the historical exegesis. Third, many of the Protestants came into contact with Jews and learned Hebrew. This raised concerns over whether passages that speak of national Israel were to be taken historically or continued to be allegorized within the tradition of the Middle Ages. The more the Reformers took them as historical, the more they were awakened to premillennial interpretations, in spite of the fact that they were often labeled "Judaizers."

By the late 1500s and the early 1600s, premillennialism began to return as a factor within the mainstream church after a more than one-thousand-year reign of amillennialism. With the flowering of biblical interpretation during the late Reformation Period, premillennial interpreters began to abound throughout Protestantism and so did the development of sub-issues like the Rapture.

It has been claimed that some separated the Rapture from the Second Coming as early as Joseph Mede, in his seminal work *Clavis Apocalyptica* (1627). Mede is considered the father of English premillennialism. Paul Boyer says that Increase Mather proved "that the saints would 'be *caught up into the Air*' beforehand, thereby escaping the final conflagration—an early formulation of the rapture doctrine more fully elaborated in the nineteenth century."[83] Whatever these men were saying, it is clear that the application of a more literal hermeneutic was leading to a distinction between the Rapture and the Second Coming as separate events.

Others began to speak of the Rapture. Paul Benware notes:

> Peter Jurieu in his book *Approaching Deliverance of the Church* (1687) taught that Christ would come in the air to rapture the saints and return to heaven before the battle of Armageddon. He spoke of a secret Rapture prior to His coming in glory and judgment at Armageddon. Philip Doddridge's commentary on the New Testament (1738) and John Gill's commentary on the New Testament (1748) both use the term *rapture* and speak of it as imminent. It is clear that these men believed that this coming will precede Christ's descent to the earth and the time of judgment. The purpose was to preserve believers from the time of judgment. James Macknight (1763) and Thomas Scott (1792) taught that the righteous will be carried to heaven, where they will be secure until the time of judgment is over.[84]

Frank Marotta believes that Thomas Collier in 1674 makes reference to a pretribulational Rapture, but rejects the view,[85] thus showing his awareness that such a view was being taught.

Perhaps the clearest reference to a pretribulational Rapture before Darby comes from Baptist Morgan Edwards (founder of Brown University) in 1742–44. He saw a distinct Rapture three and a half years before the start of the millennium.[86]

As futurism began to replace historicism within premillennial circles in the 1820s, the modern proponent of dispensational pretribulationism arrives on the scene. J. N. Darby claims to have first understood his view of the Rapture as the result of Bible study during a convalescence from December 1826 until January 1827.[87] He is the fountainhead for the modern version of the doctrine.

The doctrine of the Rapture spread through the Brethren movement, with which Darby and like-minded Christians were associated. It appears that, either through their writings or their personal visits to North America, this version of pretribulationism expanded through American Evangelicalism. Two early proponents included Presbyterian James H. Brookes and Baptist J. R. Graves.

The doctrine of the Rapture was taught through Bible conferences, such as the annual Niagara Bible Conference (1878–1909); turn-of-the-century publications like *The Truth* and *Our Hope;* popular books like Brookes's *Maranatha,*

William Blackstone's *Jesus Is Coming*, and *The Scofield Reference Bible* (1909). Many of the greatest Bible teachers of the first-half of the twentieth century help spread the doctrine, such as Arno Gaebelein, C. I. Scofield, A. J. Gordon, James M. Gray, R. A. Torrey, Harry Ironside, and Lewis S. Chafer.

In virtually every major metropolitan area in North America a Bible institute, Bible college, or seminary was founded that expounded dispensational pretribulationism. Schools like Moody Bible Institute, The Philadelphia Bible College, Bible Institute of Los Angeles (BIOLA), and Dallas Theological Seminary taught and defended these views. These teachings were found primarily in independent churches, Bible churches, Baptist churches, and a significant number of Presbyterian churches. Around 1925, pretribulationism was adopted by many Pentecostal denominations such as the Assemblies of God and The Four-Square Gospel denomination. Pretribulationism was dominant among Charismatics in the 1960s and 1970s. Hal Lindsey's *Late Great Planet Earth* (1970) furthered the spread of the pretribulational Rapture as it exerted great influence throughout popular American culture and then around the world. Many radio and TV programs taught pretribulationism as well.

Although still widely popular among Evangelicals and Fundamentalists, dominance of pretribulationism began to wane first in some academic circles in the 1950s and 1960s. A decline among Pentecostals, Charismatics, and Evangelicals began in the 1980s as a shift toward greater social concern emerged. Pretribulationism is still the most widely held view of the day, but it cannot be taken for granted in many Evangelical, Charismatic, and Fundamentalist circles as it was a generation ago.

The doctrine of the Rapture has not been the most visible teaching in the history of the church. However, it has had significant advocates throughout the last two thousand years. It has surfaced wherever premillennialism is taught, especially when literal interpretation, futurism, dispensationalism, and a distinction between Israel and the church are also taught. Regardless of its history, belief in the Rapture has been supported primarily by those who attempt a faithful exposition of the biblical text.

# Questions and Discussion

1. How many resurrections will there be?
2. What does the Greek word *tagmata* mean in relation to the doctrine of the resurrection?
3. What is one of the most important purposes of the Rapture of the church?
4. Is the Rapture a practical doctrine, or is it simply about escaping the terrible times coming upon the earth?
5. How will the body of the believer be transformed at the Rapture?
6. What are some of the forceful and vivid expressions used to describe the Rapture? Discuss.
7. When the apostle Paul warns believers "not to sleep," does he imply they might miss the Rapture?
8. What does the word *Parousia* mean?
9. What does imminency mean when describing the doctrine of the Rapture?
10. How does the doctrine of premillennialism relate to the doctrine of the Rapture of the church?
11. What were some of the earliest references to the Rapture by pioneering prophetic studies?

## Chapter 9

# The Church and the Doctrine of Rewards

## Introduction

One of the most forgotten truths in Scripture for the saints in Christ is the issue of rewards. Since the Reformation, the church has downplayed the fact that Christ will honor His own for being faithful to the gospel. This lack of teaching on the issue may give a certain meaninglessness to the Christian struggle here on earth. No one is suggesting that this is promoting "works salvation" or that the believer ought to be preoccupied with earning rewards and recognition. That could bring about another extreme where Christians are in some sort of race with each other or attempt to out-compete each other for honors. Still, the New Testament has a great deal to say about rewards.

## The Place of Rewards

Several Greek words are used to describe rewards.

### 1. Antapodosis

This word is employed only once in Colossians 3:24. The context has to do with Christian slaves serving well their earthly masters as if "fearing the Lord" (v. 22b). The apostle Paul writes, "Knowing that from the Lord you will receive the reward of the inheritance. It is the Lord Christ whom you serve." One could argue that this "reward of the inheritance" is an exclusive acknowledgment in regard to faithful believing slaves in their earthly service to their masters.

Yet could not the principle broaden out to all the saints in Christ who are faithful to an unpleasant task that they cannot escape? The reason this is possible is that in the context the apostle notes: "Whatever you do, do your work heartily, as for the Lord rather than for men" (v. 23).

## 2. Apodidōmi

This word has the idea of "giving forth," thus "to pay, render," and sometimes "reward." Jesus seems to be speaking of an earthly recompense when He says, in giving your alms in secret remember "your Father who sees in secret will repay you" (Matt. 6:4). The context seems to imply that He will reward and return to one who is faithful a just recognition in this life. This may not be referring to a future, heavenly honor. But Barnes notes the possibility of two views, and writes:

> The encouragement for performing our acts of charity in secret is that it will be pleasing to God; that he will see the act, however secret it may be, and will openly reward it. If the reward is not granted in this life, it will be in the life to come.[1]

In the epistles, Paul uses *apodidōmi* to refer to the Great White Throne Judgment. He sees the lost "storing up wrath . . . in the day of wrath and revelation of the righteous judgment of God, who will render *(apodidōmi)* to every man according to his deeds" (Rom. 2:6). The apostle uses the same word when referring to the *bēma* judgment as he writes about the future giving of "the crown of righteousness which God *shall give [reward]* at His appearing [the Rapture] as the righteous Judge" (2 Tim. 4:8).

The same word again is used of a negative reward when Paul writes about a coppersmith named Alexander who was causing him harm. He says, "The Lord *will reward* him according to his deeds" (v. 14). This will possibly also take place at the *bēma* judgment following the Rapture of the church because it appears as if Alexander is a believer in Christ, though terribly misguided about some of the teachings of the apostle (vv. 15–16).

## 3. Misthos

This Greek word carries the thought of "wages" as well as "reward." Paul uses this word to describe the reward given for those faithful to proclaiming the gospel. "Each will receive his own reward according to his own labor" (1 Cor. 3:8). The apostle reminds his readers that he voluntarily preached the gospel without charge to the hearers and thus will receive a reward for a pure motive (9:18). Though the believer does not serve the Lord for a reward-motive, Paul notes the important principle that "The laborer is worthy of his *wages*" (1 Tim. 5:18).

The apostle John reminds his readers to avoid doctrinal error when he writes: "Watch yourselves, that you might not lose what we have accomplished, but that you may receive a full *reward*" (2 John 8). He apparently is referring to the gnostic cults and the antichrists that denied that Jesus Christ had actually come to earth in human flesh (v. 7). The passage may be teaching that a reward could be removed for those believers in Christ who are careless with truth.

> Because of the appearance of these deceivers, the readers needed to watch out for the disastrous spiritual effects which any compromise with their ideas could lead to. The danger is not loss of salvation, of course, but loss of reward. . . . It should be noted that the phrase *be rewarded fully* shows that failure by the readers would not totally deprive them of reward. God would not forget what they had done for Him (cf. Heb. 6:10). But the fullness of their reward (cf. I Cor. 3:11–15) was threatened by the subversion of the antichrists.[2]

## Does the Judgment of Works Determine Eternal Destiny?

Sometime following the Rapture, the church saints will stand before Christ to be judged for their works. This is not a judgment to determine eternal destiny. That has already been settled once a person accepts Jesus as personal Savior. The believer in Christ is legally acquitted or justified by faith. Paul writes, "There is therefore now no condemnation for those who are in Christ Jesus" (Rom. 8:1). The context of the apostle's statement has to do with the forever forgiveness of *all* of the sins of a believer, based on Jesus' work at the cross. The sins of the child of God are then eternally forgiven, in terms of his "eternal position" in Christ. But the believer's works will stand scrutiny by the Lord who will judge His own and then distribute rewards for service rendered here in this life. Moo well states:

> Condemnation has been removed from the believer, and no more will condemnation of any kind threaten him or her (cf. 8:34). How can this happen for those "in Christ"? Because those in Christ experience the benefits of Christ's death "for us": "He was for us in the place of condemnation; we are in Him where all condemnation has spent its force" (cf. 2 Cor. 5:21).[3]

## All Believers Appear Before the *Bēma*

Paul reminds believers in Christ,

> *For we must all appear before the judgment seat of Christ, that each one may be recompensed for his deeds in the body, according to what he has done, whether good or bad. (2 Cor. 5:10)*

The Greek word for "judgment seat" is *bēma*.

> The word is used as a platform for a public speaker and, in legal contexts, it denotes the place where litigants stood for trial. . . . The word is used frequently in the NT of the platform or dais on which was placed a seat for an official . . . as well as the place where civil officials held session to hear certain legal cases and render judgment in such cases.[4]

Nicholas writes:

> The Greek term *bema*, used to describe this judgment, portrays a seat or raised platform where a judge sits to adjudicate a case, e.g. Matt. 27:19; John 19:13; Acts 18:12. The Greeks employed the same term to describe the platform on which a judge or referee sat during the Isthmian or Olympic games at Corinth. Here the winners of the various athletic events received their rewards. No doubt the apostle Paul had such a scene in mind when he used the phrase, "judgment seat of Christ." Thus, the contexts and the historical background of the term imply that the *bema* is for believers a place and time of rewarding rather than punishing.[5]

The *bēma* judgment of believers should not be confused with the Great White Throne judgment described in Revelation 20:11–15. This judgment is the general judgment of all unbelievers from all generations. Since the blood of Christ has not covered their sins, they must answer for all "their deeds" for the issue of eternal destiny. The description is sobering to see the sea, death, and Hades give up all the lost for this final tribunal of their souls. As given in the description, there is no appeal. All those who stand before the Lord at this judgment are cast into the lake of fire (v. 14), which is the conclusive spiritual "second death." With a horrible pronouncement it is stated, "If anyone's name was not found written in the book of life, he was thrown into the lake of fire" (v. 15).

But as Paul notes, those in Christ "must all appear before the judgment seat of Christ" (2 Cor. 5:10). By the way Paul describes this judgment contextually, he is not speaking of the Great White Throne judgment of the lost. On 2 Corinthians 5:10:

> Salvation is not the issue here. One's eternal destiny will not be determined at the judgment seat of Christ. Salvation is by faith (Eph. 2:8–9), but deeds issuing from that faith (1 Thess. 1:3) will be evaluated.[6]

## The *Bēma* Seems to Follow Quickly After the Rapture

Paul warns saints in Christ not to prejudge each other. He writes, "Do not go on passing judgment before the time, but wait until the Lord comes" (1 Cor. 4:5). James writes something very similar. He urges Christians, "Do not complain against each other" because "behold, the Judge [Christ] is standing right at the door" (James 5:9). Both verses speak of the possibility of the imminency of the Rapture for those to whom the apostles are writing. In other words, Christ's return should be expected. That return could be soon and in the lifetime of those to whom they are writing. And with it, the church saints would suddenly face Him at the *bēma*. On 1 Corinthians 4:5 Hodge notes:

> He will exercise the prerogative of judging the heart and con-
> science; a prerogative which none but an omniscient being can
> rightfully claim or possibly exercise. . . . Paul appealed from the
> fallible judgment of short-sighted men, to the infallible judgment
> of his omniscient Lord.[7]

## The *Bēma* Is for Rewards Done for Christ's Sake

At the *bēma*, "each one may be recompensed for his deeds in the body, according to what he has done, whether good or bad" (2 Cor. 5:10). The Greek word for "recompense" *(komizō)* has the idea of receiving "pay, wages."[8] It is in the middle voice and would better read "he should receive to himself wages." A. T. Robertson notes that it means to "receive as his due."[9] Each believer will stand alone and accountable to the Lord. These deeds are to be judged as to whether they are "good or useless." The word useless *(phaulon)* can mean "worthless, of no account, base, wicked."[10] The wickedness that was in the life of the believer will be exposed as revealed by Christ the Judge.

## The Believer Is to Be Examined as a Servant of Christ

The apostle Paul writes that believers in the Lord should consider themselves as servants and stewards and that being found trustworthy is a most important quality (1 Cor. 4:1–2). He writes that he will not even examine himself, much less should he be judged by the church at Corinth (v. 3). It is the Lord who will bring to light "the things hidden," and He will disclose "the motives of men's hearts" (v. 5). And with perfect fairness, "each man's praise will come to him from God" (v. 5b).

Nicoll points out that the steward "was a confidential housekeeper or overseer, commonly a slave, charged with provisioning the establishment. Responsible not to his fellows, but to 'the Lord,' his high trust demands a strict account."[11]

With the slave-master relationship in mind, Paul further writes, "Whatever you do, do your work heartily, as for the Lord rather than for men. . . . For he who does wrong will receive the consequences of the wrong which he has done, and that without partiality" (Col. 3:23, 25). Christian slaves were enjoined by the apostle to serve out of a "sincerity of heart, fearing the Lord" (v. 22). If they did not, they would receive the "consequences" of wrongdoing. Are these consequences an earthly judgment or one to be administered at the *bēma?* It has been taken both ways by commentators. Eadie writes that it is merely the results reaped by the wrongdoer here on earth. "He does not receive the wrong itself, but the fruit of it, or the wrong in the form of punishment. He shall be paid, as we say, in his own coin. The wrongdoer shall bear the penalty of the wrong."[12]

Paul also wrote that the believing slave would "from the Lord . . . receive the reward of the inheritance. It is the Lord Christ whom you serve" (v. 24). This "inheritance" reward has to refer to the *bēma* heavenly acknowledgment!

## Believers Labor for Christ's Name

When one gives his life to Christ, it is as if he pours a new foundation slab upon which will rise a new building. That foundation is Jesus (1 Cor. 3:11). From the moment of new birth, a child of God is constructing a new life. On that foundation one may build with "gold, silver, precious stones" (v. 12). These valuable elements seem to represent meaningful spiritual service that has lasting quality to glorify Christ.

The believer also may build upon that foundation with "wood, hay, straw" (v. 12). This represents temporal works that are worthless. They do not stand up under the test of eternity. Paul adds:

> *Each man's work will become evident; for the day* [the *bēma* judgment] *will show it, because it is to be revealed with fire; and the fire itself will test the quality of each man's work. If any man's work which he has built upon it remains, he shall receive a reward. If any man's work is burned up, he shall suffer loss; but he himself shall be saved, yet so as through fire. (vv. 13–15)*

The *bēma* judgment for the resurrected saint in Christ will not simply be a positive event. There will be much regret and sadness when the motives of the deeds done are brought to light. It is important to note that the worthless deeds done, represented by the wood, hay, and straw, are consumed. The fire is not for the believer himself but for the worthless deeds he performed not for Christ but for self. Paul seems to indicate that many Christians go through life doing nothing for the sake of their Savior. They will suffer loss and yet escape through the fire (v. 15). But what a terrible day to face the fact that one did nothing out of gratitude to the Lord for the precious salvation given to him through the grace of his Savior! Nicoll may be overstating the case, but he leaves the reader with a sobering picture of the believer who has nothing left but his soul. He has not accomplished anything on earth for the love of his Savior:

Like Lot fleeing from Sodom, his salvation is reduced to a minimum: "He rushes out through the flame, leaving behind the ruin of his work . . . for which, proved to be worthless, he receives no pay" . . . , getting through "scorched and with the marks of the flame" upon him.[13]

## Christ's Love Controls the Believer

The apostle Paul concludes his discussion of the *bēma* judgment by writing that "the love of Christ controls us" (2 Cor. 5:14). The love coming from the Lord keeps us in bounds, constraining us. Believers "should no longer live for themselves, but for Him who died and rose again on their behalf" (v. 15). Paul sets forth the purest incentive to govern the priorities of a Christian in this life.

Nicoll has these observations:

> The[se] words are often quoted as meaning that the love which Christians bear to Christ is the supreme motive of the Christian life; but however true this is in itself, it is not the meaning of the Apostle here. . . . The "love of Christ" here, then, is the love which Christ has for us, not the love which we bear to Him; the constraining power of Christian ministration and service is more effective and stable than it would be if it sprang from the fickle and variable affections of men (cf. John xv. 16).[14]

Hodge adds these thoughts:

> The connection is plain. The love of Christ here means Christ's love for us, not the love of which he is the object. This is obvious, because the apostle goes on to illustrate the greatness of Christ's love to us, and not of our love to him. . . . The word *synechō* means also to restrain, a sense which many adopt here. "The love of Christ restrains me from acting for myself." . . . It coerces, or presses, and therefore impels. It is the governing influence which controls the life. This is a trait of Paul's experience as a Christian. . . . A Christian . . . is so affected by a sense of the love of this incarnate God as to be constrained to make the will of Christ the rule of his obedience, and the glory of Christ the great end for which he lives.[15]

## The *Bēma* Judgment Will Include Rewards

Since the concept of the *bēma* is taken from or related to the Greek games, there are rewards to be distributed to the saints in Christ for their service in relation to His name. Paul uses the figure of the victorious athlete who is rewarded for his accomplishments. The purpose of the judgment is to recompense those who serve Christ. "The believer's works will be examined (1 Cor. 3:13) whether done by self-effort or by God through the individual. If the believer's works do not endure, he is saved but receives no reward (1 Cor. 3:15)."[16]

The apostle pictures his life as an athlete who exercises and disciplines himself not to receive a perishable wreath "but . . . an imperishable" (1 Cor. 9:25). He writes of "that day" when the Lord will appear at the Rapture (2 Tim. 4:8) and give to him a crown of righteousness presented by "the righteous Judge." For elders, there is the crown to be given for being examples to the flock (1 Peter 5:3). Peter writes, "And when the Chief Shepherd appears, you [elders] will receive the unfading crown of glory" (v. 4) for shepherding "the flock of God among you, exercising oversight . . . voluntarily, according to the will of God" (v. 2).

Finally, there is the crown that will be given for how one lived the Christian life, in self-glory or humility, being double-minded or without reproach (James 1:5–10). James continues to write about endurance that produces maturity, "lacking in nothing" (v. 4). He then concludes his exhortation by writing:

> *Blessed is a man who perseveres under trial; for once he has been approved, he will receive the crown of life, which the Lord has promised to those who love Him. (v. 12)*

## Questions for Discussion

1. In your opinion, why is there little discussion in Scripture about Christian rewards?
2. Define *bēma* and describe the *bēma* judgment.
3. Is the *bēma* judgment a place of rewards or punishment?
4. Will Christians have regrets as they stand before the *bēma*?
5. What should be the motive in striving for rewards?

# Part 2

# The Governing of the Church

## Chapter 10

# The Development of Church Polity

## Introduction

The church was founded by the Holy Spirit at Pentecost. Its purpose was to unite all believers into one spiritual body. This new organization was to rely upon God for its guidance and its growth, following the pattern established in the book of Acts. The Holy Spirit, who indwelled each believer, would illuminate the truth of the Word of God to bring the believer to a position of maturity and usefulness in the church. It was within this arrangement that the church was to meet its own needs by taking care of proper family structure and function, physical needs, and spiritual needs. In this manner the members would support and walk with each other through the joys and sorrows of human existence. The church would identify with God and demonstrate complete reliance on Him to meet its needs.

In the beginning, the church was under the direct supervision of the apostles. In due time others were selected to assist in the work of the church. These men became known as deacons. In Acts 6, the apostles instructed the people:

> *And the twelve summoned the congregation of the disciples and said, "It is not desirable for us to neglect the word of God in order to serve tables. But select from among you, brethren, seven men of good reputation, full of the Spirit and of wisdom, whom we may put in charge of this task. But we will devote ourselves to prayer, and to the ministry of the word." (Acts 6:2–4)*

This was a natural result of the rapid growth of the church, and of the apostles having too much to take care of. Thus they told the disciples to select seven qualified men to be in charge of the physical needs of the church (Acts 6:1–6; 1 Tim. 3:8–13).

## Elders Appointed

Bishops and elders were appointed later in the church at Jerusalem (Acts 14:23; 20:28; Titus 1:5; 1 Peter 5:2). They were assigned specific responsibilities of ruling the church (1 Tim. 3:4–5; 5:17). They defended the church from moral and theological error (Titus 1:9). Although the first elders were appointed by the apostles, new churches, as they matured, made their own appointments as spiritual qualities developed to  make an individual suitable for such an important place of leadership.

Philip Schaff quotes J. B. Lightfoot, who noted in his discussion of ministry:

> It is certain that throughout the first century, and for the first years of the second, that is, through the later chapters of the Acts, the Apostolic Epistles, and the writings of Clement and Hermas, Bishop and Presbyter were convertible terms, and the body of men so-called were rulers—so far as permanent rulers existed—of the early church. . . .
>
> We proceed to the officers of local congregations who were charged with the carrying forward in particular places the work begun by the apostles and their delegates. These were two kinds, Presbyters or Bishops, and Deacons or Helpers. The terms Presbyter (or Elder) and Bishop (or overseer, superintendent) denote in the New Testament one and the same office, with this difference only, that the first is borrowed from the synagogue, the second from the Greek communities; and that the one signifies the dignity, the other the duty.[1]

In the middle of the second century, the word *bishop* became restricted to a chief presbyter. This seemed, as Lightfoot pointed out, to follow the almost universal law. He gives the example of the monarchical rule that was prevalent in that section of the world. This led to the natural elevation of a single presbyter in a given locality.

This second-century church organization gave rise to the early third-century move to a complete hierarchical system. During this period it was customary to apply the term *priest* directly to Christian ministers, especially those who were bishops. The word *clergy* also came into use, referring to the ministry as one of special relationship to God. As well, the word *laity* distinguished those selected for that special function of clergy from those who were not.

Schaff points to the rise of the clergy and the tendency to separate them from the laity. This was accomplished by insulating them from involvement in secular business, and from social relations (marriage). Therefore, they were represented to the people as totally independent of Christian society, and devoted exclusively to the service of the sanctuary.

The church organization established in the third century became solidified in the fourth century. At the fourth council of Carthage (A.D. 398) laymen were prohibited from teaching in the presence of clergy without their consent. Charlemagne enacted a law that laymen were not to recite a lesson in the church, nor even to say "hallelujah." The century ended with what is now known as Catholicism well entrenched.

The next change in the organization of the church occurred during the Reformation. Two leaders were Martin Luther and John Calvin. Centralized church government was abhorrent to Luther. Schaff summarizes Luther's position:

> How far we must ask here, did Luther recognize the dominion of the papacy as a part of the true catholic church? He did not look upon the Pope in the historical and legal light as the legitimate head of the Roman church; but he fought him to the end of his life as the antagonist of the gospel, as the veritable Antichrist, and the papacy as an apostasy.[2]

Schaff continues with Calvin's views:

> He (Calvin) agreed with Luther that the papacy was an invention of the Devil; that the pope was the very Antichrist seated in the temple of God as predicted by Daniel (11:36) and Paul (2 Thess. 2:3), and the beast of the Apocalypse; and he would be soon destroyed by a divine judgment.[3]

The organization of the church was sure to change. Three different systems of church function came out of this period. These different organizations are known as the Episcopal, the Presbyterian, and the Congregational.

The differences in these three types of church governments are as follows:

> **Episcopal**. "The Episcopalian system is the government of the church by bishops *(episkopoi)*. Episcopalians recognize the threefold ministry of bishops, priests, and deacons as basic to the life of the church. The only minister entitled to ordain is the bishop, to whom belong certain functions originally associated with the apostles themselves. The elaborate Episcopalian system, as known today, is not to be found in the NT except in embryo."

> **Presbyterian**. "The term derives from the word 'presbyter.' Its reference is primarily to a church which is governed by presbyters, usually elected by the people of the congregation or of a group of congregations."[4]

> **Congregational**. This may be traced back to the reign of Queen Elizabeth I, whose objective for the church of England was an

enforced uniformity. There were those, however, who thought otherwise. Puritans wanted to see the national church reorganized on presbyterian rather than episcopalian lines. A few others repudiated the whole concept of a state church and favored the "gathered church" principle. These became known as "Separatists" and were the forerunners of those who later were termed "Congregationalists." They contended that the church should consist only of those who had responded to the call of Christ and who had covenanted with Him and with each other to live together as His disciples.

The officers of a Congregational church are usually a minister, a diaconate, and a church secretary and treasurer. The call to a minister to assume the pastorate of a local church is issued by the church meeting. Deacons are elected by the membership to assist the minister in the administration of the church and also to share with him the pastoral responsibilities.[5]

In the early church, the bishop was one of the presbyters (elders) who was a member of the local church. In the second century one presbyter was elevated to bishop or overseer of the church. It was only later that this person was acknowledged as overseer of other local churches. The modern Episcopal bishop has taken on a more apostolic position.

The Presbyterian type of church government is more closely representative of New Testament teachings. However, it too falls short of Scripture. Calvin made it a three-tiered system. While it uses the elder system for spiritual leadership and deacons to handle the material needs of the church, Calvin adds to the scriptural pattern by having two other officers of the church: pastor and doctor or teacher. These offices have a debatable scriptural base.

The Congregational form of church government takes the position of an autonomous organization. The local church is ruled by democratic vote of all the members of the congregation. This is equivalent to the sheep telling the shepherd what to do. This type of organization must assume that all its members are actually filled with the Holy Spirit, whom they faithfully depend on for guidance. This has led to a liberal approach in the outworking of the Congregational system.

The modern church bears little resemblance to the organization that was brought into existence by the Holy Spirit at Pentecost. The problem can be identified as the departure of the church from its God-ordained structure. A plurality of elders were to govern the church while being assisted by a plurality of deacons who handled the physical affairs of the church body. A careful examination of the Scriptures will clearly show that this was the pattern to be followed.

# Questions for Discussion

1. How were elders selected in the New Testament?
2. Discuss how this is different from the way most elders come into the position today.
3. What are the three most common types of ecclesiastical government found among churches today? Discuss.

# The Doctrine
# of Biblical Eldership

## The Principle of Biblical Leadership: Elder

### Jewish Elders During the Time of Paul

There are many parallels between the concept of the Old Testament elders and the body of elders in the dispensation of the New Testament. But there are differences as well. What this chapter will focus on is the similarities that, under the guidance of the Holy Spirit, the apostle Paul picked up and instituted in the local churches.

The scattering of the Jews (the Diaspora) brought about the system of the synagogue with communal leaders consisting of elders *(presbyteroi)* and *archōns*. The *archontes* (the arch ones, the higher leaders) were probably also considered part of the elder body. Some see the archons as the executive committee of this leadership. "It therefore seems probable that the traditional Jewish communal representation in Judaea formed the chief model for the Diaspora centers, although undoubtedly various modifications took place in them in the course of time."[1]

There appears also to have been a chief officer of the synagogue called the *archisynagōgos* (head of the synagogue). In the Syriac and Aramaic versions of the Gospels, this title is rendered by the word *rabbi*. Thus, it is presumed that the head of the synagogue was the community's spiritual leader and authoritative scholar. Talmudic sources call holders of this title "Head of the *Keneseth*" ("gathering"). It is understood that this head of the synagogue was appointed for life. In some locales he is called "the for-life head-of-the-synagogue." More than likely this was a title with a permanent office possibility, but not necessarily so.

In the capital of Rome, Jewish synagogue archons are mentioned, but elders are not. Most scholars believe the term *archōn* was usually synonymous with *elder.* Women were not given this appointment. Outside of Rome, the designation *elder* appears in the rest of Italy, Spain, Cyprus, Alexandria, and Asia Minor. In the city of Elche, at a later date, archons and elders are mentioned in records together. By Justin Martyr's writings in the mid-second century, *archōn* may have become generic for all synagogue offices: "the *archōns* of the people." These men figured in the public affairs of the community and may have been the contacts for dealings with the Gentile world. In the *Pseudo-Chrysostom,* though lifetime commitments seem to have been possible, appointments were made annually. Practical considerations may have limited the terms of office. Yet too, if an elder or archon wished to remain in his leadership position, it appears that he was able to do so. Appointment by other elders seems to be the rule. There are no indications of a system of popular election as known today in most churches in America.

The synagogue leaders, such as at Antioch-in-Pisidia, carried out introductory functions in the worship and life of the assembly. By these men visitors were invited to speak. In the synagogue, "after the reading of the Law and the Prophets the officials sent to [Paul and John], saying, 'Brothers, if you have any word of exhortation for the people, say it'" (Acts 13:15). As well, the head of the synagogue took the intellectual leadership of the group. Sometimes they were open for controversy. Paul knew this when he went into the synagogue at Ephesus. Paul "entered the synagogue and reasoned with the Jews. And when they asked him to stay for a longer time, he did not consent" (Acts 18:19b–20).

In Rome and Alexandria, at least one more term was used to describe Jewish leadership and that is the *hazzan.* The word is related to the concept of shepherd or sheep-keeper. Some think the office was similar to that of the church deacon. The *hazzan* acted as an official in the house of prayer, made announcements, took care of the sick, and assisted the poor. He also kept order during the services and could even administer corporal punishment on community or synagogue law-breakers. The *hazzan* was educated and was often a reader, a *shamash.* In Judea they served on the town councils.

It would be a mistake to see every detail of the synagogue system transferred to the church, first of all because those synagogue offices were not "inspired" by the Lord in the Old Testament. They came about by need. Secondly, the Jews were a racial community whereas the churches would be a racially mixed group with some similar needs but many that would be different. And finally, the positions of elders and deacons were ordained by inspiration of the Holy Spirit and then authenticated and explained in Paul's letters.

### The Elder System of the Old Testament

The most common word for elder in Hebrew is *zāgān,*which means chin or beard. From this word comes *zāgēn,* which is translated as "old or to become old." This word is also used to describe a decrepit old man or a "camel that lets her lip hang down."[2] These "bearded-ones," or elders, gathered in each village and formed councils to serve as local rulers. They functioned as a city council. Usually they were heads of families and were to be wise and experienced community leaders.

All pagan cultures of ancient times had an elder system. Pharaoh had elders (Gen. 50:7), as did the Midianites, Moabites (Num. 22:7), and Gibeonites (Josh. 9:11). The Arab, Greek, and Roman worlds also functioned through an elder system.

Observing an Arab goat-market today in Israel, one can get a glimpse of elder rule in place. The older men, the elders, stand against the shaded wall with their hands behind their backs. There are no women or even young girls mixing with the men, boys, and goats in the enclosure. Around the elders are the middle-aged men, forty to fifty years of age. Beyond them are the men in their thirties holding the hands of their young sons. The conversation of the younger men can be loud and even confrontational. They often curse and hit each other in the head with their hands. The older men just smile and talk. But the younger ones are absorbing every word their elders say. And no one would defy or go against their utterances. There is a fixed order as to where everyone stands or walks. The boys often will drag a fat, heavy sheep over to the older men for them to utter an opinion over the health of the animal. Everyone knows his place and position. In what looks like chaos to visitors, there are order and rank. And even more, the respect for the village elders is clear. None of the younger men would break ranks and violate the boundaries and established ground rules. So it is in almost all cultures. And so it was in ancient Israel.

The elders of Israel are first mentioned in the Egyptian captivity (Exod. 3:16). They are mentioned in the Old Testament 162 times. There are two groups cited: those tribal elders who sat in judgment on national issues and those elders who ruled in the towns and villages. The village elders sat at the gate of the city where they could exercise judgment on the caravans and traders who entered the city. Also, they could scrutinize the strangers who entered into their midst. The task of the elders was to look after the welfare of those in their charge. They could give approval and pass judgment.

For example, parents could bring delinquent sons before the elders, who could order them to be stoned (Deut. 21:18–21). In today's view this would seem a harsh punishment for juvenile problems, it certainly deterred criminal behavior. Elders felt responsible for the sins of the people. When Israel was defeated at Ai, the elders fell before the ark and lamented (Josh. 7:6). The elders judged the correctness of Boaz making Ruth his wife (Ruth 4:11). When Saul had disobeyed the Lord in sacrificing the sheep, he begged the prophet Samuel to restore his honor before the elders (1 Sam. 15:30). Rehoboam defied the elders of Israel by laying a heavy burden on the people when he began to rule. "He forsook the counsel of the elders which they had given him, and consulted with the young men who grew up with him and served him" (1 Kings 12:8). By bypassing wisdom and authority, he accepted the ill advice of "yes" men around him.

When King David took a wrongful census out of his own self-reliance, God pronounced judgment through the angel of the Lord. "Then David and the elders, covered with sackcloth, fell on their faces" (1 Chron. 21:16). When Jerusalem was invaded by Nebuchadnezzar (586 B.C.), the elders became cowards and departed. "Elders were not respected . . . [the] elders are gone from the gate" (Lam. 5:12b, 13b). For Israel's sins, "judgment [fell] against the elders and leaders" (Isa. 3:14). After Judah arrived in Babylon to begin their seventy-year captivity, Jeremiah addressed a letter to the priests and people. But out of respect, the elders were mentioned first in his prophecy. "The letter which Jeremiah the prophet sent from Jerusalem to the rest of the elders of the exile" (Jer. 29:1).

Elders held great responsibility for the people in their community, but they could turn from the Lord and act with evil intent. Amos and Zechariah both speak of justice lost at the gate because of sinful elders (Amos 5:10–12; Zech. 8:16).

The elders seemed to occupy a continuing place of importance throughout the history of Israel, from their sojourn in Egypt to the postexilic period when they gave orders to assemble the people to deal with the question of foreign marriages (Ezra 10:8).

> Nothing is said about the organization of the councils of the elders of the tribes. Their number probably depended on the size of the local community; there were seventy-seven at Succoth (Judges 8:14). It is quite unlikely that there was a council of elders of the entire nation selected from the elders of the various tribes.[3]

It is quite clear that the elders of Israel, whether they were national or local leaders, had more than social or civic responsibilities. They had to judge on the basis of practical wisdom and on the guidelines of the Laws of Moses. Their opinions often had tremendous spiritual and judgmental repercussions. The basic idea is that wise men had to possess the insights of experience and of age. Elders could go bad. They could compromise with the king or foreign enemies. Though evil can persist in elder rule, no nation or community can survive long without the guidance of experienced moral leadership.

## "Civic" Eldership in the Time of Christ

Civic eldership in New Testament times was much the same as what we see in the Old Testament, and what they did had the same moral and spiritual overtones as well. In the Gospels there apparently were religious elders who were part of the leadership in Jerusalem. They must have been honorary members of the ruling body of the Seventy, the Sanhedrin. Jesus had little good to say of these men.

The Pharisees and scribes often said to Christ, "Why do Your disciples transgress the tradition of the elders?" (Matt. 15:2). From the time of the last attack by the Pharisees, "Christ began to show His disciples that He must go to Jerusalem, and suffer many things from the elders and chief priests" (16:21). The elders of the Temple even came to Jesus and said, "By what authority are You doing these things?" (21:23). The elders of the people were in on the plot to capture and kill the Lord (26:3–4). In Jerusalem these elders were often linked with the chief priests against Christ (26:47; 27:3, 12; 28:12).

However, it must be remembered that in the New Testament there are examples of godly and sincere Jewish elders. Most believe Nicodemus was an elder, a member of the ruling Sanhedrin when he came to Jesus inquiring about spiritual matters (John 3). Later, he was numbered with the disciples who came to Christ's tomb bringing myrrh and aloes (19:38–39). In the story of the centurion's sick slave, there are indications that the elders of Capernaum believed Jesus was the Messiah. They begged the Lord to heal this man. They appeared to have a firm faith that He could save the man from death. The "Jewish elders ask[ed Christ] to come and save the life of [the centurion's] servant" (Luke 7:1–10). Finally there is the elder Gamaliel, a member of the Sanhedrin and the renowned teacher of the Law, who urged this body of rulers to be careful concerning the teachings about the resurrected Christ. In frank sincerity he told the ruling Council: if this message about Jesus "is of God, you will not be able to overthrow [the disciples and their speaking]; or else you may even be found fighting against God" (Acts 5:39).

## The Principle of Biblical Pastoring

### *Introduction*

What is a pastor? The Greek word *poimēn* can be translated "pastor or shepherd" (The English word *pasture* is related.). The root meaning is "to protect."[4] However, the noun is used but *once*, in Ephesians 4:11, to refer to an officer of the local congregation. That's right. The man in today's church pulpit is called *pastor* only once in the New Testament. Yet, dozens of times he is called teacher, overseer, or elder (more on this later).

Though the noun for pastor is used but once, the word *shepherd* is often used in other contexts. For example, Jesus called Himself "the good shepherd" (John 10:11), He said that he, the shepherd, would be struck down, and the sheep would scatter (Mark 14:27), and, when He returns as King and Messiah to sit on the throne of David, He will remove evil men "as a shepherd divides His sheep" (Matt. 25:32). Our Lord is called the great Shepherd (Heb. 13:20) and the Shepherd and Bishop (Overseer) of our souls (1 Peter 2:25).

The verb *poimaino* means to "feed the flock" and is related to the noun *poimēn*. Sometimes the word is translated "to rule" as over the flock. Christ told Peter to "feed My flock" (John 21:16). The overseers (or elders, pastors) are told by the verb "to shepherd" the church of God (Acts 20:28). Peter repeats this to the pastor-elders he is writing to and urges them to "feed the flock of God among you, exercising oversight" (1 Peter 5:2). When Christ returns as King, "He will rule [shepherd] the world with a rod of iron" (Rev. 2:27). The righteous before God's throne now are "shepherded" by Jesus the Lamb (Rev. 7:17).

### Characteristics of Sheep

After watching countless sheep and shepherds in Israel, Mal Couch makes this observation:

> Having taken 23 trips to Israel and the Middle East, I spent a lot of time watching Arab shepherd boys tend their sheep in the deserts of Palestine and other Arab countries. I probably clocked around 300 hours watching sheep and shepherds just for curiosity. But too, I directed many documentary films made in those lands and ended up with a lot of first-hand observations about the little woolly ones and their keepers! . . . First of all, it is true! Sheep are really dumb animals! They have been known to die of thirst standing just a few yards from water. They have very poor eyesight. They seem to have little or no personality and have to be led everywhere. When traveling along a hillside, their heads are down and they simply follow the tail right in front of them! In fact the hills of Palestine are scarred with "sheep ruts." They always plod the same old rutty paths! Finally, sheep are beasts of self-imposed habits but appear to be in no way "trainable," as are many of the four-legged creatures of the animal kingdom. Since the Lord calls us sheep, the above description gives us a rude awakening as how we must really be spiritually. Helpless, hopeless, and untrainable by nature! Thus, we need shepherds.

### Lessons from Shepherds

With this as a brief fix on what sheep are like, how should shepherds herd their sheep? Though we realize that human shepherds do not match up to the perfect shepherd found in Christ, there are still important lessons to learn from them.

*Shepherds should not "baby" the sheep.* The pictures of Jesus cuddling sheep is not based on reality. Sheep need strong shepherds, not pampering ones. American Christians do not want affirmative pastors. They want leaders who will baby them. Somehow this is supposed to show patience and love. But the shepherds of Israel do not coddle their sheep. They are in charge of leading their flock in the right direction. Sometimes that requires toughness.

*Shepherds should pick the right pastures.* The sheep eat the grass the shepherd leads them to. If the sheep stop to munch something they should not, with a long stick the shepherd will "spook" them to move on. He is responsible for their feeding. Some pastors today are giving the sheep what they want, not what they need.

*Shepherds should look ahead to where the sheep are going.* The Arab shepherd, standing or squatting on the ridge of a hillside, sometimes may appear passive as to the direction his flock of sheep are heading. But then the boy picks up a stone and throws it in front and to the left of where the sheep are moving. Slowly, the flock begins to move to the right. He "oversees" what is ahead and what the flock will encounter. He knows where to find the best grass and the most ideal pools of still water. Church pastors are responsible for giving their people the best spiritual food. There can be no cultural compromise. They need to look intently as to where the sheep are moving. A pastor of people needs to ask: What are the people being tempted with and what should I do to counter error?

*Shepherds may have to be tough with the sheep.* In the Arab sheep market sometimes the sheep become immobile. They bunch up and won't move. Often they do not respond to commands, though they can recognize the voice of their shepherd. The shepherd sometimes must pull them by the hind legs or straddle their backs and tug them along by the neck or ears. Or he will push and shove the sheep when they need to be moved. The apostle Paul urges young pastor Titus to do the same when the sheep in the church become doctrinally confused. With tough language Paul writes that "empty talkers" must "be silenced" because they are upsetting whole families. He adds ,"for this cause reprove them severely that they may be sound in the faith" (Titus 1:10–13). Many pastors are afraid of losing the sheep to supposed greener pastures. Many fear the sheep will not like them. But a good shepherd must do what is right no matter what the cost. The safety or health of the entire flock can be at stake.

Then there is the other side of this issue. Christians, like sheep, are stupid and helpless, and need constant guidance and attention. When the sheep have sinned and need mercy, the shepherd must respond in kind, that is, with love and compassion. For this, Christ *and* the Father are both seen as the good and faithful Shepherds!

Jesus says He is the "good shepherd" and the sheep know Him and respond to His voice (John 10:14). He calls us, the sheep, by name and leads us out to green pastures (10:3–4). The Lord speaks of the viciousness of the sheep robbers (10:8, 10), the scattering of the sheep by the wolves (10:12), and the carelessness of the hireling (10:12). But Christ goes even further and pictures Himself as the sheep-gate that protects the flock (10:7–9), and the one who so cares for it, He would lay down His own life for its security (10:11). In this passage (John 10) are some classic verses on the Good Shepherd:

> *I am the door; if anyone enters through Me, he shall be saved, and shall go in and out, and find pasture. . . . I came that [the sheep] might have life, and might have it abundantly. (10:9–10)*

In contrast to the unfaithful shepherds, the Lord God describes Himself as an over-shepherd, the one who has other shepherds serving Him. But He ultimately is "the shepherd who cares for his herd" (Ezek. 34:11). Through Ezekiel, Jehovah pronounces strong prophetic words against these careless leaders. And He promises another shepherd, "My servant David . . . And I will make a covenant of peace with them and eliminate harmful beasts from the land, so that [My flock] may live securely in the wilderness and sleep in the woods" (34:23–25). "Behold, I Myself will search for My sheep and seek them out" (v. 11).

All of these verses give "job descriptions" of what the pastors-teachers over local churches should be, how they are to serve, and what kind of heart they must have for the sheep. God Himself and His Son Jesus are examples as the ideal Shepherd.

### The Most Important Way the Pastor Pastors

Many mistakenly think there are five distinct founding pillars of the church mentioned in Ephesians (4:11). Actually, there are only four. The Greek grammar best reads: "Some [to be] pastors, *indeed* teachers *(didaskalous)*." MacArthur notes, "Often the word *and (kai)* means 'that is' or 'in particular,' making teachers in this context explanatory of *pastors*."[5] Nicoll adds:

> The absence of the *tous de* before *didaskalous* indicates also that the [pastors] and the [teachers] were not two distinct men . . . in different functions, the former defining them according to the office of oversight, the latter according to their office of instruction and guidance.[6]

Other scholars, such as Alford and Robertson, add:

> It would seem the two offices were held by the same persons.[7] Here Paul groups "shepherds and teachers" together. All these gifts can be found in one man.[8]

H. A. Meyer notes:

> Every presbyter (elder) was at the same time [teacher], and had to be endowed with this gift; hence Paul here (in Ephesians 4:11) puts together [pastor and teacher], and, in 1 Tim. 3:2, it is laid down as the requirement of an [overseer or bishop] that he should be [teacher].[9]

John Gill says:

I rather think [the two words] intend one and the same office, and that the word *teachers* is only explanative of the figurative word *pastor* or shepherds; . . . because if the apostle had designed distinct officers, he would have used the same form of speaking as before; and have expressed himself thus, *and some pastors, and some teachers* whereas he does not make such a distribution here.[10]

John Calvin adds:

*Pastors* and *Teachers* are supposed by some to denote one office, because the apostle does not, as in the other parts of the verse, say, *and some, pastors; and some, teachers.* . . . Chrysostom and Augustine are of this opinion.[11]

And Vincent:

The omission of the article from *teachers* seems to indicate that pastors and teachers are included under one class. *The two belong together.*[12] (italics added)

*No man is fit to be a pastor who cannot also teach.* And, "Pastors and teachers were stationary ministers appointed for the continuous edification of the flock. They represent, not two classes of office-bearers, but two aspects of one and the same office."[13] "[The two words] refer to two characteristics of the same person who is pastoring believers (by comforting and guiding) while at the same time instructing them in God's ways" by being an overseer and elder who is able to teach them.[14]

*And finally*: In Ephesians (4:11), pastor *(poimēn)* is used with the word *teacher.* The Greek construction indicates that the two terms go together, and we might hyphenate them in English as pastor-teacher. The emphasis is on the pastor's ministry of teaching.[15]

"Pastors and teachers" are grouped together in such a way as to suggest that the two roles are regarded as complementary and often coordinated in the same person. Pastors (literally, "shepherds") probably included presbyters and bishops; they were entrusted with the nurture, protection, and supervision of the flock.[16]

## Conclusion

Without doubt, this passage is telling us that the pastor pastors by being a teacher. This will be demonstrated over and over again. It is a terrible tragedy for the propagation and teaching of the gospel to realize that we have lost sight of the major role the local pastor is to assume. Some shepherds will not like this message. They have taken a position of leadership without the intellectual discipline and preparation required and prescribed in Paul's writings. But more on this in later chapters.

### Pastors, Teachers, Elders, Overseers

The New Testament makes it clear that pastors are described with all of the above nouns. Clear evidence points to the fact that all four terms refer to the same office. For example, 1 Timothy (3:1–7) gives the qualifications for the "overseer" (bishop). But in another qualification list given in Titus (1:5–9), the elder and overseer are described as the same person.

In 1 Peter 5:1–2 the apostle puts all three times together, telling the elders to be mature overseers as they pastor.

> *Therefore, I exhort the elders* [presbyteros] *among you, as your fellow elder and witness of the sufferings of Christ, and a partaker also of the glory that is to be revealed, shepherd* [poimainō] *the flock of God among you, exercising oversight* [episkopeō] *not under compulsion, but voluntarily, according to the will of God.*

The word *elders* is the most common way to describe pastor-teachers. But the nouns and verbs of the other three words are interchanged continually in the New Testament: "Shepherd the flock," "exercise oversight," "teach the Word." MacArthur well summarizes, "Acts 20 also uses all three terms interchangeably. In verse 17, Paul assembles all the elders *(presbyteros)* of the church to give them his farewell message. In verse 28, he says, 'Be on guard for yourselves and for all the flock, among which the Holy Spirit has made you overseers *[episkopos]*, to shepherd *[poimainō]* the church of God.'"[17]

*Elder* emphasizes who the man is, *bishop* speaks of what he does. *Pastor* deals with attitude and character. All three terms are used of the same church leaders, and all three identify those who feed and lead the church; yet each term has a unique emphasis.

*Episkopos* was the secular Greek culture's equivalent to the historic Hebrew idea of elder. Overseers or bishops were those appointed by the emperors to govern captured or newly-founded city-states. The bishop was responsible to the emperor, but oversight was delegated to him. He functioned as a commissioner, regulating the affairs of the new colony or acquisition. *Episkopos* therefore suggested two ideas to the first-century Greek mind: responsibility to a superior power, and introduction to a new order of things. Gentile converts would immediately understand those concepts in the term.[18]

The New Testament bishop, or overseer, was in a unique leadership role in the church and was specifically responsible for teaching (1 Tim. 3:2), feeding, protecting, and generally nurturing the flock (Acts 20:28). Biblically, there is no difference in the role of an elder and that of a bishop. The two terms refer to the same group of leaders, *episkopos* emphasizing function and *presbyteros* emphasizing character.

## The Plurality of Elders

### *Elders of the Church Are Referred to in the Plural*

In historical narrative in the New Testament, the churches always had more than one elder or pastor-teacher. Though it is possible that one or more may be paid for his services and the other elders in that church body are not. The main point, however, is that they are all equal. When the door is closed and they must make decisions, their opinions are all the same in weight. No one is "head" pastor or elder in a hierarchical or superior sense. One may have more training than the others, say a seminary education, for example. Yet all must act together and rule over the spiritual affairs of the church equally.

How do some denominations and churches justify having no elders or simply calling the pastor "the" elder? Churches that violate the biblical guidelines do so on the basis of *tradition*. "This is the way we've always done it," is their only reply.

### *Are Elders to Receive Financial Support?*

The Scripture is clear that elders are entitled to financial compensation. First Timothy 5:17–22 sets forth the various functions of the elders. But it also addresses the question of whether elders (pastors-teachers) are to be financially compensated. Paul states, "Let the elders who rule well be considered worthy of double honor, especially those who work hard at preaching and teaching" (1 Tim. 5:17). The word here translated "honor" is the Greek word *timēs,* which has the primary meaning of "price" or "value" in a financial sense.[19] Additionally, verse 18 confirms that Paul is talking about taking care of the elders' physical needs: "For the Scripture says, 'You shall not muzzle the ox while he is threshing,' and 'The laborer is worthy of his wages.'"

Earle writes that Paul is making a point that workmen should receive compensation, "a financial remuneration."[20] Gill adds, "This is to be understood both of that outward respect that is to be shown [teaching, preaching elders] by words and actions; and of a sufficient maintenance that is to be provided for them."[21] "For their oversight all elders received a stipend; but those who excelled in this ministry of leadership were to be considered 'worthy of double honor,' or twice the remuneration as the rest."[22] Barnes notes: "Nothing would be more reasonable than that, if their duties in the church interfered with their regular employment in their secular calling, their brethren should contribute to their support."[23]

Patrick Fairbairn says, "There can be no doubt, from what follows in the next verse, that [double honor] includes pecuniary remuneration."[24] Hendriksen notes that C. Bouma and Chrysostom held this passage was referring to honor and honorarium. Moffatt believed this meant ample pay, a salary, and comments, "The work should also be rewarded in a material way." Hendriksen summarizes, "A man who spends all his time and effort in kingdom-work certainly deserves 'a good salary.'"[25]

In Paul's letter to the Galatians he states, "And let the one who is taught the word share all good things with him who teaches" (Gal. 6:6). In fact, Paul seems to indicate that those who do not take care of the financial needs of their elders may be directly affected in what they reap (Gal. 6:7–8). Paul also says to the church at Corinth that he has every right to be compensated for his labor with them. In 1 Corinthians 9 he deals with the issue extensively, concluding in verse 14, "So also the Lord directed those who proclaim the gospel to get their living from the gospel." He uses the examples of the soldier, vine grower, shepherd (v. 7), ox (v. 9), a farmer (v. 10), and the Old Testament priests (v. 13). Clearly, the elders have a right to be financially compensated.

But can they choose to forgo this right? Paul makes it clear that in some cases the elders can do so. Paul himself gave up his right in certain cases, such as here at Corinth (1 Cor. 9:15, 18; Acts 18:3) and at Thessalonica (1 Thess.2:9; 2 Thess. 3:8).

Some believe Paul is continuing the idea of financial compensation in two other letters he writes. In 1 Thessalonians 5:12 he says, "We request of you that you *appreciate* those who diligently labor among you, and have charge over you in the Lord and give you instruction" (italics added). He adds in 1 Corinthians that three men, Stephanas, Fortunatus and Achaicus supplied some of his needs, refreshing his spirit, "therefore *acknowledge* such men" (16:18, italics added). Monetary reward should not be the first goal of elders. Yet by the apostle's words there is nothing wrong with it; if possible, money should be supplied.

Applying this to church situations today, it is obvious that many small churches cannot afford to support more than one elder. The natural choice for this compensation would be the teaching elder (1 Tim. 5:17), who would then have the time to study and prepare appropriately to feed the people. He would then carry out more of the teaching responsibilities, but not all of them. It is a tremendous benefit to have at least one man who can spend the time in studying the Scripture to feed the flock and carry many of the shepherding responsibilities.

## What Is the Main Source for the Doctrine of the Local Church?

Though the issue of the local church is mentioned in all of Paul's letters (and the books of Acts, Hebrews, 1 Peter, and others), the most prevalent and pointed instructions come from 1 and 2 Timothy and Titus. These books are called the Pastoral Epistles.

Timothy had traveled with Paul as a missionary. This younger man had been well spoken of by fellow Christians in Lystra and Iconium (Acts 16:1–3). After some training, Paul sent him about as an ambassador and even traveling elder who would be working with, appointing, and directing local church elders. In the context of the 1 Timothy letter, Timothy had been left in charge of the work in Ephesus and Asia Minor. Paul wrote this epistle probably from Macedonia (1:3) and was on his way to Nicopolis (Titus 3:12). First Timothy was written around A.D. 63.

Second Timothy was penned in A.D. 66 with Paul alone in a cold dungeon facing death in Rome. Nero's persecution of Christians had begun. Paul continues his encouragement of Timothy to be "a good soldier of Christ Jesus" (2:3), and urges him to continue his elder responsibilities.

All three letters are applicable to us today in understanding the doctrine of the local church. The instructions are timely, inspired directives for all churches everywhere. These epistles carry full apostolic authority. Though traveling about, Timothy and Titus were both acting as Paul's representatives. They went forth with elder power and ability. They apparently remained in certain areas for a time and became the local church's authority until other elders could be appointed. They were to pass on doctrinal, spiritual, and practical knowledge to others. And, with those they felt were qualified and called: "The things which you have heard from me [Paul], entrust to faithful men, who will be able to teach others also" (2 Tim. 2:2). "Remind [the believers] of these things, and solemnly charge them in the presence of God" (2:14).

Contrary to the opinion of some, there is very little in these books that would be termed "cultural" and not applied to situations today. Some, with very poor biblical training, try to say that Paul's instruction concerning women not teaching men (1 Tim. 2:9–15) was a local, historic issue and does not impact our times. But it is amply clear that the apostle's instructions that women are not to teach or exercise authority over a man is a doctrinal issue not simply a cultural one. Paul says the reason for this injunction is doctrinal, because "Adam was created first, and then Eve" (v. 13). He adds that Adam was not deceived but Eve was "quite deceived" and fell into the transgression (v. 14). Paul, under the inspiration of the Holy Spirit, argues on a doctrinal issue that has to do with order in creation. Thus, his point still carries doctrinal authority in the churches to this very hour.

# Questions for Discussion

1. In the Jewish assembly or synagogue, what kind of leadership government was practiced?
2. As far as we can tell from the Old Testament, what kind of leadership government was in place?
3. What is the basic thought behind the word *shepherd*?
4. What is the basic thought behind believers in Christ being called sheep?
5. What is so startling, and important, about Ephesians 4:11? Discuss.
6. What is behind the description of overseer?
7. Why is it important to see church leadership as plural?
8. Can the elders/pastors be paid for their ministry?
9. What differences do you see in the way most churches are structured today from what the Bible says?
10. Is it important that churches be organized along biblical lines? Or do you feel it does not matter?

## Chapter 12

# The Qualifications for Elders and Deacons

## The Biblical Ideal

God desired from the beginning that the church would have strong pastoral leadership. Yet in church history there has been an oscillation between extremes of anti-pastor to pastor, or clergy dominating the laymen and the laymen rebelling against the leadership. This is unfortunate in light of the clear structure and spiritual qualifications given in Scripture. Though certain characteristics are listed throughout Paul's letters, 1 Timothy 3:1–7 and Titus 1:6–9 give us specific qualifications. The two lists are similar and describe the pastor-teacher by the descriptive titles *overseer* and *elder*. In some ways the lists are not simply moral requirements. They lay down issues of maturity, experience, character, and temperament in reference to dealing with others and exercising leadership.

What is interesting is that, in both lists, the apostle uses a long series of present tenses in describing what the elder is to be. In essence, Paul is saying, "He is to be right now this way." In other words, his past may have been one thing, but what is he like presently?

Along with the importance of noting Paul's use of the present tense, several vital mistakes are made when examining the apostle's lists of qualifications. The first, is to presume a man has had a perfect, sinless past. Also, to believe that a prospect for elder-pastor perfectly fits all the requirements is not realistic and does not comply with the facts. No one can come up to the standards laid down by Paul. Nevertheless, they are high biblical ideals no one can question. Without doubt, his lists remain as important goals. But too often they have been used against godly men who will indeed walk with imperfections. The lists can be turned into weapons of legalism to judge, condemn, and remove men who need to be corrected but not necessarily replaced.

# The Position of Pastor-Teacher

With 1 Timothy (3:1–7), Paul begins by writing, "The word is faithful! If one is himself reaching forth, longing after [for a position of] overseer (bishop), he is desiring of a noble accomplishment" (Greek).

The apostle sees nothing wrong in pursing this position. To be a pastor-teacher is the highest calling possible. These offices in the local church require the most skilled and dedicated leadership. It is not simply a position of honor or influence. Instead, it is a labor of dedicated service that brings forth the best in men.

The one seeking this role in the local church must have the right intention. It should not prompt carnal and personal ambitions but the aspiration of a heart that has itself experienced the very grace of God. The elder-overseer longs to see others coming to the Lord and share in the saving love of Christ.[1]

# The Qualifications of a Pastor-Teacher

From verse two Paul describes the kind of man a pastor-teacher should be.

*"It is necessary for him to be right now* [present infinitive] *irreproachable [anepilēmpton]"* (v. 2), that is, irreproachable in conduct. No charge can be laid against him presently. He walks uprightly, and he is transparent in character.

The force of the present infinitive verb "to be" continues: *"It is necessary for him to be right now a one-wife man"* (v. 2)—a husband of one wife. Taking into account only the words themselves, there might seem to be no reason to look beyond the current marital relationship to any that existed in the past.[2] Fairbairn points out that many scholars believe the issue in this passage is polygamy, not divorce, as devastating as that might be. This interpretation would certainly open the door for restoration, no matter what issue led to a past divorce. According to Fairbairn:

> Thus Chrysostom: "He (St. Paul) speaks thus . . . to restrain undue license; since among the Jews it was lawful to enter into double marriages, and have two wives at the same time." So, too, Theodoret: "Concerning that saying, *the husband of one wife,* I think certain men have said well. For of old, both Greeks and Jews were wont to be married to two, three, and more wives at once. And even now, though the Imperial laws forbid men to marry two wives at one time, they have commerce with concubines and harlots. They have said, therefore, that the holy apostle declared that he who dwells in a becoming manner with a single wife is worthy of being ordained to the episcopate." . . . Theophylact . . . : "[Paul] said because of the Jews, for to them polygamy was permitted." Even Jerome, with all his ascetic rigor, speaks favorably of this interpretation (in his notes on the passage in Titus); he states that, according to the view of many and worthy divines, it was intended merely to condemn polygamy, and not to exclude from the ministry men who have been twice married.[3]

*"It is necessary for him to be right now non-addicted to wine (nēphalion)"* (v. 2). Paul addresses moderation in the use of intoxicating liquor. Some believe the word is best translated "sober." Because the apostle will mention wine again in verse 3, some say he is actually speaking here of "lust" addiction.

But if it is a reference to drinking: In all cultures (except in America since the Industrial Revolution), wine was permissible for Christians. However, because of a moral stigma now among believers concerning drink, the principle of "doubtful things" would come into play.

Paul writes elsewhere in respect to the weaker brother who may stumble if he sees his pastor-teacher drinking wine. Paul puts it this way: "The stronger should bear the weaknesses of those without strength and not just please ourselves" (Rom. 15:1). "It is good not to eat meat or to drink wine, or to do anything by which your brother stumbles" (14:21).

*"It is necessary for him to be right now self-controlled [sōphrona]"* (v. 2). This and related words can mean "thoughtful, mental soundness, reasonableness." "Properly a man of a sound mind; one who follows sound reason."[4] He is not "ready to accept the nonsense which was being disseminated by the errorists at Ephesus."[5]

*"It is necessary for him to be right now 'down to earth' [kosmios]"* (v. 2). Yes, this word is related to the Greek word "world" *(kosmos)*. What does Paul then mean by it? The Greek lexicons translate the word "respectable, honorable."[6] In a positive sense, one of the related words *(kosmeō)* can mean "to adorn, put in order, make attractive." I think the ultimate idea is to be sensible, in the proper sense "related to this world," thus, "down to earth." The pastor-teacher knows what he is doing. He is respected in a "goodly" worldly way. People respond to him because he knows how to "put things in order."

*"It is necessary for him to be right now hospitable [philoxenon]"* (v. 2). The word *friend* or *friendly* can be seen in this word, *philos*. Because the believers were traveling extensively in Paul's day, this was a very important quality. Ungodly manners prevailed in places of public stay. Christians needed to find a kindly reception and a proper fellowship as they traveled about and spread the gospel. The pastor-teacher was to open his home to those on the road.

*"It is necessary for him to be right now 'skilled in teaching' [didaktikon]"* (v. 2). He must be "didactic." He must be able to logically present clear, rational, linear truth that builds a doctrinal framework in the mental processes of the believer in Christ. The pastor *must* be a teacher.

In verse 3, Paul addresses two important social ills of that day.

*"It is necessary for him right now not to be a drunkard [paroinon]"* (v. 3). This sounds much like the injunction in verse two. But this term may be more intense. He could be thinking what the non-Christian might be thinking when he sees the pastor-teacher sitting before a heavy drink. Barnes comments:

> [The word] means, properly, *by wine;* i.e., spoken of what takes place *by* or *over* wine, as revelry, drinking songs, etc. Then it

denotes, as it does here, one who sits *by* wine; that is, who is in the habit of drinking it. It cannot be inferred, from the use of the word here, that wine was absolutely and entirely prohibited. It means that one who is in the *habit* of drinking wine, or who is accustomed to sit with those who indulge in it, should not be admitted to the ministry.[7]

Fairbairn concludes:

[The word means] rather *not a brawler,* or *of vinous temperament,* not given to such impetuous and violent behavior as is wont to be exhibited by persons under their cups.[8]

*"It is necessary for him right now not to be a fighter [plēktēn]"* (v. 3), or, one who strikes out. Or, one who is inclined to natural outbursts with an almost violent temper. One with this problem would only hinder the service of Christ. It is one thing to have righteous indignation against sin and show proper anger toward human injury, but it is another thing to constantly be showing an uncontrolled spewing forth of verbal venom.

*"It is necessary for him right now to be gracious [epieikas]"* (v. 3). The Greek word can also imply "gentleness, yielding, forbearing."[9] Hendriksen puts it this way: "Though he never compromises with respect to the truth of the gospel, he is willing to yield when it comes to his own rights, in the spirit of 1 Corinthians 6:7, 'Why not rather suffer wrong?'"[10]

*"It is necessary for him right now not to be quarrelsome [machomai]"* (v. 3). The word *maxa* means to "go to battle, fight with weapons, be in dispute." We might say the pastor-teacher is not to be "in running disputes." When he takes up the cross, he is to "lay his [human] weapons down."

*"It is necessary for him right now NOT to be a lover of silver [aphilargyros]"* (v. 3). The pastor-teacher is not to be tempted with money. He is to resist showing favors to the wealthy in church. He is to resist showing favoritism to the rich in the congregation. Fairbairn states:

Few things, indeed, are more certainly fatal to the position the [pastor-teacher] ought to occupy in men's regard, and the spiritual ends he should aim at accomplishing, than a perceptible fondness for worldly treasure. He must be known to love his work for its own sake, not for the incidental earthly benefits that may or may not come in its train.[11]

Next (vv. 4–5), the apostle turns to issues at home. The force of the "to be" present infinitive continues with a series of participles.

*"He is to be managing correctly his own house."* The Greek word for "manage" is *proistēmi*. It has a broad range of meaning: "To be the head of, directing, being concerned about."[12] At its root the word means to "before place [in proper order]." The word "correctly" *(kalōs)* is a forceful adverb meaning: "beautifully, appropriately, in the right way, splendidly, commendably, beneficially."[13] The pastor-teachers are to have their house shipshape. These men hold a position resembling a father who properly sustains his household.

The participle "managing" means "to superintend," to be first or at the head of his own household. "Any Christian man should be able to function well as the head of his own home; one who fails in so simple a requirement is not fit to be elevated to the ministry."[14] With stern words, Gill adds:

> . . . keeping a good decorum in his family, obliging his children to observe his orders and especially the rules of God's word; and not as Eli, who did not use his authority, or lay his commands upon his sons nor restrain them from evil, or severely reprove them for their sins, but neglected them, and was too mild and gentle with them.[15]

*"[His] children, having [them] in under-attachment [hypotagē]"* (v.4). *Hypo* means "under" and *tagē* comes from *tassō*, which means "to attach," thus, to under-attach, "to subject, put in subordination, have under control, have in obedience."[16]

Note the phrase that follows, "with all dignity" (v. 4). *Semnotētos* means "with all gravity" or decency of deportment, "having, in short, a well-ordered and properly trained household."[17] Barnes well notes that the force of this phrase really falls on the pastor-teachers. Their children may not in a one-hundred percent way conform to what is right. But with their families, these fathers are *doing* what is right. The passage does not mean that he should be severe, stern, morose—which are traits that are often mistaken for gravity, and which are as inconsistent with the proper spirit of a father as frivolity of manner—but that he should be a serious and sober-minded man. He should maintain proper dignity, he should maintain self-respect, and his deportment should be such as to inspire others with respect for him.[18]

Paul then asks the all-important question: "But if a man does not know how to manage his own household, how will he take care of the church of God?"

By using the words "take care of" in reference to the church, we may have an important clue as to *how* the pastor-teachers are to carry out their leadership. The words "take care" (v. 5) are two Greek words put together. *Epi* means "upon, over." And *melō* has the idea of "to care for, be concerned about, to be attentive." In the good sense this can be translated "to overly care for." Paul wants these men to pay careful attention to all that is happening to the flock, just as they would their own family. And if they cannot exercise this same concern at home, they cannot do it with the church of the Lord.

Then (vv. 6–7) Paul deals with the issue of maturity, and especially since the elders must deal with the outside world.

*"It is necessary that he must not be right now a neophyte [neophytos]."* There is no way a new convert to Christ can handle local church issues. Though this man may be older and possess some natural wisdom, his position and power may go to his head and destroy his witness and ministry. Over and over again this has happened to those having natural talent. But this natural ability is not the "new" working of the Holy Spirit within the new Christian. He will easily think his work comes from his own resources. It does not. It must be "gifted" from above. Note what can happen to him:

> He can become conceited, actually "clouded, smoked or all steamed up" *(typhoomai)* and a judgment may come about at the instigation of the devil! The fall he experiences may happen in such a way as to bring dishonor on the ministerial character. His life will be such as to give men occasion to reproach the cause of [Christianity]. The snare which the devil lays [may] entrap and ruin the ministers of the gospel and all good men. If the minister has any *propensity* which is not in entire accordance with honesty, Satan will take advantage of it and lead him into the snare.[19]

*"It is also necessary that he right now have a good witness before the outsiders"* (v. 7). Even with the outside the prospective overseer, and also the overseer who is already in office, must have a good reputation. It frequently happens that non-Christians with whom the overseer does business know a lot about his character. Their judgment is important because the body of Christ seeks to exert a godly influence for Christ upon the world, leading sinners to Jesus. An overseer's bad reputation with the world will not be of any help in achieving this purpose.

## The Elder As Overseer

In Titus 1:5–9, the apostle Paul has a similar list of qualifications he shares with missionary elder Titus. This is an important support section that tells us clearly elders and overseers were actually the same men. Paul says "appoint elders *(presbyteros)*. . . , for the overseer *(episkopos)* must be . . ." (1:5, 7). The designations were two because they were derived from two different quarters. *Presbyteros* was Jewish in origin and had a point of reference in the synagogue generations before the Christian period. The word passed into the Christian church with but little variation.

Originally the term implied an issue of age. For the religious community, the leaders were supposed to be the seniors, experienced and venerated in the body of believers. But in time, the etymology shifted to simply mean the presiding head of the group. More than likely, though, older men still normally took the office of pastor and elder. Most churches were planted where there was great Greek influence and the word *episkopos,* "overseer," already was a popular term for the corresponding city office. It was easy to transfer the idea of the *episkopoi* from the civil realm to the spiritual.

This paragraph actually begins, "For this reason I left you in Crete that you might set in order what remains, and appoint elders in every city as I directed you."

There are some important things to note in verse 5. As Paul's emissary, and acting as a roving elder, Titus was to finish the work started on the island of Crete. The foundational work probably included evangelism and a long period of extended teaching about the Christian faith. Titus was instructed to "set in order" or "set in the right path" the remaining important issues, especially of appointing elders (plural) in each city (singular). The word "appoint" in Greek is *kathistēmi* which can be translated "to accordingly place." The Lord intended elders or pastors to be appointed, but this was not simply a human arrangement. Christ Himself gifted His church with "pastors indeed teachers" and overseers assigned by the Spirit of God for instructing the flock (Eph. 4:11–12). Titus and Timothy both were told by Paul what traits were needed in qualified leaders for the oversight of the churches that were being planted.

Paul lists their qualifications (vv. 6–9). Again, he will consistently use a present tense. The elder "is to be right now." This list is much like 1 Timothy 3 with some characteristics repeated and a few that are different.

*"He is to be right now above reproach [anenklētos]"* (v. 6). Literally, this word means "above-called." An elder-pastor has a higher calling, thus he is to be "irreproachable, blameless."[20] Lenski translates it "unaccused." This word is also used to describe the qualifications of a deacon (1 Tim. 3:10).

*"He is to be right now the husband of one wife"* (v. 6; see 1 Timothy 3:2).

*"He is to right now have children who believe [faithful children]."* Some excellent commentators have noted that this could not mean the children are necessarily converted. Salvation is a sovereign matter in the hands of the Lord. Gill states it well:

> By faithful children cannot be meant converted ones, or true believers in Christ; for it is not in the power of men to make their children such; and their not being so can never be an objection to their being elders, if otherwise qualified; at most the phrase can only intend that they should be brought up in the faith, in the principles, doctrines, and ways of Christianity.[21]

As well: *"He is not to have children who are accused of dissipation or rebellion [asōtias or anypotakta]"* (v. 6). Barnes notes the first word can be translated "excess" and the second "unruly, insubordinate, ungoverned."[22]

In today's culture the difficulties with children have become more and more of a problem. Again, the rule of thumb is not to be too legalistic. This is an important standard laid down by inspiration of the Holy Spirit. And yet, few Christian fathers will be found today who are not in a crucial moral struggle with their teenagers. They may have done everything properly in raising their children, but the hedonistic cultural tug on this generation of young people is awesome.

*"The overseer [elder] is to be right now above reproach [in regard] to being God's steward"* (v. 7). Though writing about elders, Paul switches words to "overseers," since the words are interchangeable. "Steward" is *oikonomon* from which we get the word "economy" and "dispensation." Gill says:

> One appointed by God over His household and family, the church, to give to every one their portion of meat in due season; one that dispenses the manifold grace, or various doctrines of the grace of God, and mysteries of Christ; and of such an one it is required, that he be faithful, both to his Lord and Master.[23]

Fairbairn writes:

> [Steward] showing at once the original identity of elder and *episkopos*, by the substitution here of the one name for the other, and the weighty reason why he should be of irreproachable character, since by the very nature of his office he has to manage the things of God. . . . Presbyters settled over each church, and these presbyters each and all, bearing the name of *bishop*-pastor, or overseer of the flock.[24]

*"He right now is not to be self-willed [authada]"* (v. 7). The word can mean "stubborn, arrogant." The word is used only here in the New Testament and can mean "self-complacent, assuming, imperious."[25]

*"He right now is not to be quick-tempered [orgilon]"* (v. 7). *Orgilon* conveys an inclination to anger.[26] The pastor-teacher cannot be hot-headed. He cannot explode with unjust rage. Caution: Neither should the pastor-teacher be effeminate. He must occasionally stand up in righteous indignation when believers harm each other with gossip and other sins. He must speak out forcefully against heresy and evil. The Reformers displayed proper moments of anger against evil.

*"He right now is not to be addicted to wine, not pugnacious, not fond of sordid gain"* (v. 7, see 1 Timothy 3:3).

Some more important positive characteristics are listed (1:8): *"He right now is to be hospitable"* (v. 8). See 1 Timothy 3:2. *"He right now is to love what is good [philagathos]"* (v. 8). Barnes rightly observes, "[This] may apply to any thing that is good. It may refer to good men, as included under the general term *good;* and there is no more essential qualification of a bishop than this. A man who sustains the office of a minister of the gospel, should love every good object, and be ever ready to promote it."[27]

*"He right now is to be sensible"* (v. 8). See 1 Timothy 3:2.

*"He right now is to be just [dikaion]"* (v. 8). This may refer to his character, that "he lives a righteous life." Or it may refer to the way he treats others, that "He provides justice to everyone." This man will be fair to all. He will give you an honest hearing and he can be counted on to do what is right.

*"He right now is to be devout [hosion]"* (v. 8). *Hosion* implies more than "sanctification" or "holiness." The elder-overseer is conscious of his walk with the Lord. *Hosios* presents the idea of "pleasing to God, or pious," one who is greatly "devoted to his God."[28]

*"He right now is to be self-controlled [enkratē]"* (v. 8). "Having power over all his passions."[29] "Temperate abstaining from those things which might be lawfully used, though inexpedient, for the sake of the weak, the peace of the church, and the glory of God."[30]

# The Role of Deacon

To be true to the Bible the local church must have elder/pastors and deacons. In fact the word *deacon* should better be translated "servant." By calling the deacons "servants," the men who serve can gain a proper perspective on what their role is with the church.

## *The Greek* Diakonos

Bauer notes that *diakonos* can refer to those who wait on tables. As a participle, it can mean "waiter" (Luke 22:26). The idea is to serve as a helper; one who renders service. The word can refer to one who distributes alms, charity support, or one who helps with a collection for the needy. General service and charity dominate both broad usage and definition. Some have conceptualized the deacon as a "go-between" in word (such as a courier or messenger) and in work (an authorized agent).

> The emphasis, . . . is not on the humble, menial character of the service rendered, but on its in-between, representative nature. If this is correct, then it is right to see the deacons as the assistants of the overseers. Yet one wonders if the antithesis has not been drawn too sharply. After all, the diakonos who operates as an agent is still called to a lowly and subordinate role, however exalted the person he represents.[31]

In a wide sense, all believers in Christ Jesus are called "servants" or "ministers." In Romans 12:7 Paul says, "On *ministry (diakonia),* (let us wait) on (our) *ministering.*" He adds, "Since we have this *ministry,* as we received mercy, we do not lose heart" (2 Cor. 4:1). Peter continues, "It was revealed to them that they were not *serving* themselves, but you, in these things" (1 Peter 1:12). God has "also made us able *ministers* of [the] new covenant" (2 Cor. 3:6). Finally, Paul says God gave to the church apostles, prophets, evangelists *and* "pastors *indeed* teachers," *for* the equipping of the saints for the work of *ministering (diakonia)*, to the building up of the body of Christ (Eph. 4:11–12).

In a more specific sense, there is the "board" of *servants* who are officially part of the leadership that functions in a "serving" capacity in the local assembly. The first reference to the calling and function of these men is given in Acts 6:1–7.

As the early church grew in Jerusalem, the problem of charity began to surface and apparently became a major issue. In Acts, the author Luke notes: "At this time while the disciples were increasing in number, a complaint arose on the part of the Hellenistic Jews against the native Hebrews, because their widows were being overlooked in the daily serving of food. And the twelve [disciples] summoned the congregation of the disciples and said, 'It is not desirable for us to neglect the word of God in order to serve tables'" (6:1–2).

## The Great Urgent Purpose

Teaching of the Word was the most important task of the disciples in this early setting of explosive church planting, evangelism, and soul winning. To firm up and make solid these new cells of believers was a paramount issue with the apostles. But gathering around these study groups were people who did not have enough to eat, especially widows. They had to be taken care of in order to be faithful to the concept of true Christian love.

The disciples then urged the church fellowship, "Select from among you, brothers, seven men of good reputation, full of [controlled by] the Spirit and of wisdom, whom we may put in charge of this task. But we will devote ourselves to prayer, and to the ministry of the word" (6:3–4). Note that these men were "put in charge" of this work of *serving (diakonos)* (6:1). From this will come the idea of the *deacons*.

Were these men "voted" on in the good old American tradition of democracy? Some Bible teachers think so, but most reject the idea. The apostles were acting as the elders of this assembly. Later, other godly men will come alongside the disciples, learn from them, and in time become the pastor-teachers of the various mushrooming congregations. Thus, in this passage we see:

1. The division of roles: "We will teach the Word, and they will daily serve."
2. The apostles will "put these men in charge of this [charity] task." In other words the apostles/elders will give the *servants* their charge and responsibility.
3. The servants were brought before the disciples for approval (v. 6). The disciples then prayed over them and laid their hands on them (v. 6).

What then was the role of the congregation? And, how did they respond? (1) They "selected" the brothers (v. 3). (2) They found "approval" with the apostles' words (v. 5). And (3) they "chose" out the seven men (v. 5). The key to all of this is the word "select" *(episkeptomai)*. The preposition *epi* means "over" and *skeptomai* comes from the word *skopos,* "scope." Put together, the words could be translated "to look over," or "to skeptically analyze."

In classical Greek the word *episkopeiō* means "inspect, look at, observe, examine, review, consider."[32] The related word *skopeō* may be translated "contemplate, examine, inspect, watch suitably to a purpose." The koine Greek lexicon defines *episkeptomai* as "look at, examine, inspect."[33] Nowhere is the word *skeptomai* in any form used in the sense of voting. The people in the newly created Jerusalem church set forth those they felt were capable of doing the job of church servants. The apostles approved those selected, prayed over them, and directed them in their task.

"That we may 'put [them] in charge' of this task [of charity]" (6:3). Note that the servants are working under the direction of the apostles. As elders/pastors, the disciples were responsible for the overall spiritual focus of the church. They must have then supervised the work of the servants in the congregational setting.

In Greek, 6:5 reads: "And the 'word' [statement spoken] before the entire congregation pleased [them], and they 'called out' Stephen." The word "called out" is *eklegō.* The people summoned certain ones they felt were "controlled" ("full," *plēreis*) of the Spirit and of wisdom (6:3). On this "out-calling," Kistemaker writes of Acts 6:

> How the people instituted and regulated the search for these men is not known. Luke says nothing about casting the lot (compare 1:26), but the verb *to choose* indicates that a selection was made based on the rules stipulated by the apostles. Incidentally, Christ chose the twelve apostles (including Matthias; see 1:24), but the church chooses the seven men whom the apostles installed.[34]

## The Doctrine of Servants and the New Testament

Interestingly enough, the office of servant (deacon) is mentioned in Acts only here in chapter 6. But the fact that it became a viable office in the local assemblies is proved in Philippians where Paul writes: "To all the saints who are in Philippi, including the overseers [pastors-elders] and deacons" (1:1). The office of servant is distinct from the office of elder.

Some churches, especially Baptist, try to get around this obvious fact. They incorrectly see the pastor as the only elder (singular) in the church with a group of deacons who only act as an advisory board (though many deacon boards do have practical functions to carry out). This arrangement is not biblical. And if it is not biblical, the local assembly cannot carry out its purposes as God intended. Either the patterns laid down in Scripture by the Holy Spirit are followed or they are not. Because so many churches violate the patterns for church polity, this could be one of the key reasons there is dysfunction in the local assembly.

A. T. Robertson puts all of this together in commenting on Philippians 1:1:

> In the second century *episkopos* (Ignatius [points out]) came to
> mean one superior to elders, but not so in the N.T. The two New
> Testament church officers are here [in Phil. 1:1] mentioned (bish-
> ops, or elders and deacons). The plural is here employed because
> there was usually one church in a city with several pastors (bish-
> ops, elders). *And deacons (kai diakonois).* Technical sense here
> of the other church officers as in 1 Tim. 3:8–13. The etymology
> [of deacon] *(dia, konis)* suggests raising a dust by hastening.[35]

## The Qualifications of the "Servant"

The apostle Paul lays down the standards for the servants in 1 Timothy 3:8–13.
He has just described the qualifications for the overseer/elder/pastor in verses 1–7.
By using the word "likewise" *(hōsautōs)*, Paul implies the calling of the servant
in the local church ministry is as important as of the elder. *Hōsautōs* can be
translated "in the same way, similarly."[36] The list of characteristics the apostle
gives for the deacon is very much like what he gives for the elder. Deacons
likewise must be, "Men of dignity" (3:8). Or, men "worthy of honor" *(semnos).*
This is almost the same word used to describe the overseer in verse 4. Both
words carry the idea of "reverence, seriousness, respectfulness." Our English
expression is: You can take this person seriously.

*"Not double-tongued"* (v. 8). Literally, not "two-worded." The servant speaks
only one thing. You can trust what he says. He will not claim one thing on one
occasion and change his words in another situation. Lightfoot suggests this means
"a tale-bearer." Perhaps the word "insincere" may be meant here.[37]

*"Not to be addicted to much wine"* (v. 8). This is similar to but more broad
than the phrase addressed to overseers. The overseers are not to be "addicted to
wine." The servants are not to be "addicted to much *(pollō)* wine."

Not to be *"fond of sordid gain"* (v. 8). A better translation is "shameful gain
or advantage." The issue is not the source "whence the gain comes, but in the
setting of gain before one as an object in entering the ministry."[38] The servants
were open to be tempted, since some of them were probably the treasurers for
the local assembly.

*"Holding to the mystery of the faith with a clear conscience"* (3:9). "That
great objective truth which man of himself knows not, but which the Spirit of
God reveals to the faithful: and even [this is] Him who in fact *is* that mystery, the
great object of all faith."[39]

*"First be tested"* (v. 10). The Greek word is *dokimazō*, which carries the
idea "to examine, prove." Bauer shows the word is used with the meaning of "to
approve what is essential," or, "to test oxen for their usefulness."[40] The servants
need to be confirmed as to their abilities to handle their office. The verb is in the
present tense: "They need to be examined over a period of time."

This testing of fitness for the office of deacon may have been effected either by (a) a period of probationary training or (b) by the candidates producing what we should call testimonials of character.[41]

*"Let them serve if they are beyond reproach"* (v. 10), or have a calling that is beyond doubt or question. "It means one who is unaccused, free from any charge at all. Christlike conduct is required of deacons."[42]

*"Women must likewise be dignified"* (v. 11). Ryrie notes, "Most likely a reference to the wives of the deacons, rather than to a separate office of deacon-ess, since the qualifications for deacons are continued in verse 12. If he had a different group in mind, it would seem more natural for Paul to have finished the qualifications for deacons before introducing the office of deaconess."[43]

Feminists today try to squeeze out of this passage an official office for women in the local church. But no precedent for this can be established. (Romans 16 will be handled later in the section dealing with women in the church.) At no time in church history were women considered servant leaders in the local as-sembly, as a "board." Though a few of the church fathers such as Pliny thought this was an official women's deacon group, they are the exception. Just physi-cally speaking, men carry more of a leadership presence. Though it is not "politi-cally correct" to speak this way today, the fact is men are far better equipped to lead and guide than women.

Gill concludes, "It is better to interpret the words of the wives of the dea-cons, who must be as their husbands, which will reflect honor and credit to their husbands."[44]

The wives, *"not malicious gossips"* (v. 11), actually, diabolic *(diabolous)*. This is the same Greek word describing Satan. *Dia* refers to "constantly, con-tinually." *Bolos* is translated "throw." The English expression might be "do not be constantly slamming" someone. The wives of the deacons must be careful as to how they speak.

The wives are to be *"temperate"* (v. 11). The same Greek word (*nēphalios*, "they are not to be") is used in verse 2. They are not to be intemperate.

The wives are to be *"faithful in all things"* (v. 11). "As in the marriage-bed, so with whatsoever else they are entrusted with in the family, and civil concerns of their husbands."[45]

*"Let deacons be husbands of only one wife"* (v. 12; see above discussion related to elders, v. 4). Earle states:

> Some have interpreted this as meaning "married only once." By the end of the second century this interpretation was being pro-mulgated, under the influence of an asceticism that led to cleri-cal celibacy in the Roman Catholic Church. Bernard defends this view emphatically. He writes of the phrase here [in 3:4]: "It excludes from ecclesiastical position those who have been

married more than once." But most commentators agree that it means monogamy—only one wife at one time.[46]

Deacons should be *"good managers of their children and their own house-holds"* (v. 12). This is similar to what is said about the elders in 3:4–5.

Paul concludes with a summary about the servants: "For those who have served well as deacons obtain for themselves a high standard and great confidence in the faith that is in Christ Jesus" (v. 13).

## Conclusion

Putting it all together, it is obvious that the standards for both elders and deacons are close in terms of requirements. There must be a body of Christian qualities that all Christian leaders strive for. The lists, seen together, point toward five major areas of concern.

In regard to the candidate himself, he needs to be self-controlled and mature, including dealing with such issues as drink, tongue, temper, and money. In regard to family, he needs to be true to his present wife, to control his children. In relation to Christian brothers, he needs to be hospitable and gentle. And in regard to the outside world, he should be highly esteemed. Finally, in regard to his trust in the Lord, he ought to hold high the truth of the gospel and be gifted in teaching doctrine.

Stott remarks:

> Although some commentators disparage these . . . qualifications for the pastorate as pedestrian, and as suitable for secular leader-ship, they have far-reaching Christian implications, as we have seen. And if Paul's standards are regarded by some as compara-tively low, we need to reflect that contemporary standards are lower still! For the selection procedure of many churches today does not include an examination of candidates in these . . . areas. They continue a necessary, comprehensive and challenging test.[47]

The standards are high for both elders and deacons of a local assembly. Be-cause of the use of the Greek present tense and present infinitive in the verses describing the elders and deacons, it is clear that Paul is saying, "The elders and deacons are to be right now. . . ." Since most of the men selected were either from a Jewish or pagan background, they needed time and seasoning for growth. More than likely, as younger men they had moral and spiritual problems. They had to learn over a period of time how to walk with Christ. They were sinners and made mistakes but *now* spiritual maturity must be seen in their walk.

It may also be assumed that their present Christian walk was not perfect. Even as leaders they would have blind spots and make mistakes. More than likely by a raising of hands, the elders or deacons could dismiss one of their own mem-bers who was stubborn and unrepentant for sin.

In fact Paul makes it clear that an elder could be accused with the testimony of two or three witnesses (1 Tim. 5:19). For those who were continuing in sin, they could be "rebuke[d] in the presence of all, so that the rest also may be fearful of sinning" (v. 20).

Common sense would dictate that the lists giving the qualifications of elder and deacon must not be used in an absolute legalistic way. The lists stand as the inspired ideal. But no one can walk in spiritual perfection.

When elders or deacons are to be appointed, here are some important questions to ask: (1) Are these men growing in grace and maturity? (2) Are there sins that are overwhelming to their character and life and would hinder their effectiveness as leaders? (3) Are they sensitive to their failures and weaknesses and do they strive to contain that which would cripple their walk before others?

Yes, the lists of qualifications must be honored with fear and trembling. But it is also important to choose men who are humble in regard to their imperfections and are growing stronger in their daily walk with the Lord.

Finally:

> The corresponding encouragement is that the pastorate is a noble task, a beautiful undertaking, a laudable ambition. It involves giving oneself to the service of others. Besides, the words *episkopos* and *diakonos* are both applied to the Lord Jesus in the New Testament. Peter called him "the Shepherd and Overseer *(episkopos)* of your souls, and he applied to himself the verb *diakonein*. Could there be any greater honour than to follow in his footsteps and share in some of his *episkopē* and *diakonia* which he is willing to delegate to us?[48]

# Questions for Discussion

1. Do you feel that most church leaders fit the qualifications Paul lays down?
2. In what areas do you feel most leaders come short?
3. Do most churches practice a biblical balance in the offices and functions carried out by elders and deacons?
4. Is it possible to appoint an elder or deacon who is qualified and mature in all areas? If not, what should be done? Discuss.
5. What does it mean when Paul so consistently uses the present tense in describing the present qualifications of elders and deacons?
6. Would it help us to better understand the role of the deacon by using the term "servant"?
7. Should elders and deacons be lifetime positions? Should they be rotated out of office? Discuss.

**Chapter 13**

# The Choosing of Pastors-Teachers-Elders and Their Primary Task

## Introduction

First of all it must be made clear that pastors-teachers-elders are not chosen or voted upon in the good old American tradition. They are to be appointed, as Paul urges Titus: "I left you in Crete, that you might 'set in the right path' *(epidiorthoō)* what remains and 'put in place' *(kathistēmi)* elders in every city as I directed you" (Titus 1:5).

Paul reminds Timothy of the holy process by which Timothy had been commissioned an elder: "Do not neglect the spiritual gift [of pastor-teacher] within you, which was bestowed upon you through prophetic utterance with the laying on of hands by the presbytery [elders]" (1 Tim. 4:14). Some think this commissioning by the elders was for Timothy's evangelism ministry.[1] But this was probably not his gift since he was but urged "to do the work of an evangelist" (2 Tim. 4:5).

Since Timothy was carrying out pastor-teacher functions, this is likely what Paul is writing about. The laying on of hands was not something magical. Barnes writes, "We are not to suppose, therefore, that there was any mysterious influence —any *virus*—conveyed by the act of ordination, or that that act imparted any additional degree of holiness."[2] It simply is a sign of comradeship, companionship in a mutual ministry. It shows a brotherhood of men committed to the service of Jesus Christ. But they are not to consider themselves aloof or more spiritual; they do not live on some higher plane above the average believer in Christ. An elder should generate respect, but he lives and walks with the flock.

# First Reference to Church Elders

The first mention of local congregation elders is in Acts (11:30). The believers at Antioch put together a collection for the relief of the Christian brothers in Judea and Jerusalem. The collection was to be taken by Barnabas and Paul to the Jerusalem elders. Later, Paul and Barnabas appointed elders (plural) in every church (Acts 14:23). They did this after much prayer and fasting. Then they "commended them to the Lord in whom they had believed." (Some say the word "appointed," which means "to raise the hands," proves they voted in the New Testament church. More on this later.)

When some of the Jewish believers began to say Gentiles needed to be circumcised in order to be saved, Paul and Barnabas had a great debate against this. It was determined that Paul and Barnabas should go up to Jerusalem "to the apostles and elders concerning this issue" (Acts 15:1–2). By this time certain appointed elders were working alongside the apostles in making decisions. The apostles in Jerusalem probably meant to pass the torch. The elders would continue on when the apostles had departed or had been killed.

When arriving in Jerusalem, Paul, Barnabas, and the elders and apostles came together to discuss the matter of circumcision (15:6). This first Jerusalem council ruled Gentiles did not have to be circumcised in order to be saved. Thus, "it seemed good to the apostles and the elders, with the whole [Jerusalem] church, to choose men from among them to send to Antioch with Paul and Barnabas" (Acts 15:22). Note the order of leadership: apostles, elders, and the congregation. Only the apostles and the elders are mentioned with authority: "The apostles and the brothers who are elders, to the brothers in Antioch" (Acts 15:23).

In a sense, Paul and Barnabas are like returning missionaries going back to Antioch. The whole church could "choose" to approve of their going. The Greek word "to choose" is *eklegomai*. *Ek* means "out," and *legomai* means "to call, speak." Technically, the word should be translated "to call out." Again, this is not like our popular political voting, where politics come to play and favorites are selected. In this passage, the apostles, elders, and congregation unanimously "called forward" these men to represent them in Antioch.

This is most important, because churches today try to justify their voting processes for selecting their leadership. Again, the rule: the sheep do not pick their shepherds.

Later Paul would travel to Derbe and Lystra. While passing through the cities with Timothy accompanying him, "They were delivering the decrees, which had been decided upon by the apostles and elders who were in Jerusalem, for [Gentiles] to observe" (Acts 16:4). From Miletus, Paul sent to Ephesus and called to him the elders of the church (20:17). When these men arrived, Paul enjoined them: "Be on guard for yourselves and for all the flock, among which the Holy Spirit has made you *overseers* [bishops], to *shepherd* [pastor] the church of God" (20:28). When Paul returned to make his report in Jerusalem, Acts tells us "James, and all the elders were present" as he began to relate the things which God had done among the Gentiles (21:18–19). And finally, Peter writes of the elders ruling among the dispersed Jewish believers (1 Peter 5:1) he urges younger men to be subject to the elders (v. 5).

Elders appear in a normal fashion among the people. We know Titus was told to "appoint" elders in Crete. We know too, they are in the churches within a plurality. This safeguards leadership and the decision-making process. No one man can dominate and neither can he be bullied by a congregation. If there is opposition to a specific elder's words, the local church must face the leadership of *all* the men rather than just the one.

The Lord designed the local church in this way in order to create proper leadership authority. Most churches "vote" on elders and deacons. Some see the pastor as the one and only elder in the church. Both extremes are biblically wrong and fly in the face of what God through the apostles has set forth.

But what about Acts 14:23? Does not the passage prove the elders were voted on by the congregation?

One must look carefully at the passage to see exactly what it says. First of all it is talking about Paul and Barnabas who had just returned to Lystra, Iconium, and Antioch. They then "appointed elders for them in every city." Did Paul and Barnabas actually take a hand-raised vote and then mutually decide on key men to fill the elder positions?

The Greek word for "appoint" is *cheirotoneō,* and it is used twice in the New Testament (also 2 Cor. 8:19). It is a word used for voting among the Greek city-states by the elite of the population. The word hand *(cheir)* is actually in the word.

Some would say Paul and Barnabas actually took a vote among themselves as to the selection of these elders. They could argue that "voting" seems to be the idea when the word is used of the selection of Titus as a missionary to travel with Paul. "[Titus] has also 'been appointed' to travel with us in this gracious work." There is no problem if the churches selected their own missionaries or even voted on them. But the question remains, did two men, Paul and Barnabas conduct a popular vote as an appointment procedure for elders?

The answer is no. The reason: in all languages a word may have a certain origin, a particular beginning, but that word can evolve and change with usage or *context.* In fact, often context is more important than any consideration. Paul and Barnabas talked about the men who were potential elders, examined them, prayed about them, and then made a mutual decision or appointment. Barnes writes:

> That imposition of hands *might* have occurred in setting apart afterwards to this office [of elders] is certainly possible, but it is not implied in the word employed here, and did not take place in the transaction to which this word refers.[3]

Hackett adds:

> The verb used here, *to extend the hand,* signifies properly to
> elect or vote by extending the hand, but also, in a more general
> sense, to choose, appoint, without reference to that formality
> [of raising the hand].[4]

McGarvey continues:

> It should be observed that a plurality of elders were appointed
> in "every church;" and this, so far as we are able to trace the
> facts, was the universal practice of the apostles. In appointing
> these, Paul and Barnabas were but following the example of
> the older apostles, by whom this office was instituted in the
> churches of Judea.[5]

## Conclusion

Though discussions were carried on as to who would be elders, no one can
honestly and fairly prove these men were voted on in a popular congregational,
electoral fashion. The best indication we have from Scripture is that they were
appointed for their positions by other elders/leaders. Shepherds should be able to
spot shepherds. They are given the responsibility to make important spiritual
decisions. This is the role of leadership. More than likely they had been Jewish
elders before they received Jesus as their Messiah and Savior. They perpetuated
elder leadership roles by appointment of other elders.

## What Is the Most Important Task of the Pastor-Teacher?

### Introduction

To teach. To set forth doctrine and truth. This is the force of Ephesians 4:11:
"[Christ] gave some as pastors *indeed* teachers." The apostle Paul sets the standards for those men desiring to serve the Lord. Though he was a master teacher,
he also lived the life of an evangelist.

Paul refers to this and makes a profound statement in Romans 15:16 that is
not clear in our English texts. The Greek actually says, "I am to be a 'ministering
priest' of Christ Jesus unto [the service] of the Gentiles, [this is] 'priestly serving' [forth] the Gospel of God." In this, Paul could not be stopped in his mission
as an evangelist. He carried his proclamation of Christ from Jerusalem to Illyricum
on the eastern shore of the Adriatic Sea (now Croatia) (Rom. 15:19).[6] He adds, "I
have fully 'gospelized' about Christ. I aspired to 'gospelize,' not where Christ
was already named, that I might not build upon another man's foundation" (15:20).

For those who would remain in one area and function as pastors-teachers, they were to be living examples of good works, "with purity in doctrine, sound in speech which is beyond reproach" (Titus 2:7–8). Though the word *doctrine* *(didaskalia)* has a basic and simple meaning in Greek, the theological implication as used by Paul is awesome. The lexicon defines the word as "teaching, instruction, to impart." But a deeper meaning would be "to present logical, clear, linear truth that impacts a life and gives reason and order to that truth."

The apostle's aim for pastors-teachers was that they would carry out a "noble process, with a glorious goal." All was to be aimed at nothing short of an accepting community of believers with a mature reliance on the Head, Jesus. In Acts, we can feel the pulse, the heartthrob of this great teacher Paul. His aim was to inform the mind, awaken the understanding, stir the reason, quicken the judgment. Paul *expounded* (28:23), *exhorted* (20:1), *disputed* (9:29), *reasoned* (19:8–9), *persuaded* (28:23), *discoursed* (20:25), *admonished* (20:31), *commended* (20:32), *rehearsed* (21:19), and *made defense* (24:10).

Kuist gives us Paul's mind and heart. And no doubt, this author points out, Paul would desire that pastors-teachers follow him in like patterns for ministering to others. There is no room for weak pastors who may be unsure in their teaching convictions. Kuist writes:

> St. Paul directed the mind to the most ennobling and exalted thoughts. "Finally, brothers, keep in mind whatever is true, whatever is worthy, whatever is just, whatever is pure, whatever is attractive, whatever is high-toned, all excellence, all merit" (Phil. 4:8, 9 Moffatt's translation). Yet he warned against speculation: "Avoid the profane jargon and contradictions of what is falsely called knowledge" (1 Tim. 6:20, Moffatt's translation). "Shut your mind against these profane, driveling myths; train for the religious life" (1 Tim. 4:7). "Shut your mind against foolish, popular controversy; be sure that only breeds strife." His Pharisaic conservatism crops out: "But hold to what you have been taught, hold to your convictions, remember who your teachers were, remember you have known from childhood the sacred writings that can impart saving wisdom by faith in Christ Jesus" (2 Tim. 3:14, 15). He aimed to train in exactness and readiness of thought: "Learn how to answer any questions put to you" (Col. 4:6). He sought also to make individuals independent in their thinking: "Let no one deceive you with specious arguments; these are the vices that bring down God's anger upon the sons of disobedience" (Eph. 5:6). He encouraged application in study: "Give diligence to show thyself approved unto God, a workman that needeth not to be ashamed, handling aright the word of truth" (2 Tim. 2:15 RV).

Paul's aim as a teacher was also spiritual. He sought to spiritualize life by bringing men into fellowship with God by faith in Jesus Christ. "My aim," said he, "is to make the Gentiles an acceptable offering, consecrated by the Holy Spirit. Now in Christ Jesus I can be proud of my work for God" (Rom. 15:16). He aimed to touch and cultivate man's spiritual nature: "We interpret what is spiritual in spiritual language. The unspiritual man rejects these truths of the Spirit of God; to him they are 'sheer folly,' he cannot understand them. And the reason is, that they must be read with spiritual eye" (1 Cor. 2:14).

St. Paul's aim was also volitional. He sought to move men to action. One need but note the almost continual use of the imperative mood in his speeches and letters to be convinced of this. He also aimed at firmness of will: "Well, then, brothers, stand firm and hold to the rules which you have learned from us orally or by letter." He endeavored to establish stability of purpose: "Watch yourself and watch your teaching; stick to your work; if you do that you will save your hearers as well as yourself" (I Tim. 4:16). He endeavored also to educate weak wills to follow after truth: "Only we must let our steps be guided by such truth as we have attained" (Phil. 3:16). To this end he invited imitation of himself: "Practice also what you have learned and received from me, what you heard me say and what you saw me do" (Phil. 4:9).[7]

### Pastor-Teachers Afraid to Speak Out?

By writing to young pastor-teacher Timothy, Paul reminds him that to be a good servant of Christ is to be continually "nourished on the words of the faith and of the sound [healthy] doctrine [teaching] which you have been following" (1 Tim. 4:6). He goes on and tells Timothy he must fight against error by "giving orders [commanding] and teaching these things" (4:11). Pastor-teachers too often are silent or afraid to speak out. They become fearful of the flock. The apostle strikes hard against this and strongly urges Timothy, "Let no one look down on your youthfulness, but rather in speech, conduct, love, faith and purity, show yourself an example of those who believe" (4:12). No one could argue against what Timothy said if he lived out the things he taught.

Paul goes on and urges that sound doctrine be taught. "Until I come, give attention to the public reading of Scripture, to exhortation and teaching" (4:13). "Take pains with these things [I have spoken about]; be in [the Scriptures], so that your [going forward] may be evident to all" (4:15).

The apostle requires of Timothy self-examination as well as an examination of what he is teaching. "Pay close attention to yourself and to your teaching"

(5:16a). He says literally, "'Stay on top of' these things [looking at yourself and what you are teaching]; for as you do this you will insure salvation both for yourself and for those who hear you" (5:16b).

Paul does not use the idea of salvation (Greek, *sōzō*) here in reference to eternal, spiritual salvation but in reference to "delivery, rescue, sparing" in the sense of sparing the life, or not ruining the life by making tragic mistakes. He uses *sōzō* to speak of women "rescuing" their lives, "preserving" or "sparing" themselves through child-bearing. So here (4:16b), "By solid teaching of the Word of God, you will insure a 'deliverance in life' for yourself and others!"

The apostle further explains the results of solid doctrinal teaching. He says the teaching of the Word will not be "blasphemed" when Christian slaves honor their masters (6:1). He continues and calls for believing masters as well to be respectful to their slaves. Mutually, the two should be seen together as "believers and beloved." By using two present imperatives in the Greek text, he then urges "these things, be continually teaching *(didaskō)* and be continually counseling *(parakaleō)*" (6:2).

After telling Timothy how to handle slaves and masters, Paul calls for more instruction, this time to the rich: "Instruct the rich not to be conceited or to fix their hope on the uncertainty of riches, but on God, who richly supplies us with all things to enjoy. Instruct them to do good, to be rich in good works" (6:17–18).

The apostle reminds Timothy to "retain the standard of healthy words. Guard through the Holy Spirit who dwells in us, the treasure [of truth] which has been entrusted to you" (2 Tim. 1:13–14). Further, Timothy is to follow Paul's teaching, conduct, purpose, and faith (3:10). He is to continue in the things he has learned (3:14). Paul brings to Timothy's mind that from "childhood you have known the sacred writings which are able to give you the wisdom that leads to salvation through faith which is in Christ Jesus" (3:15).

It is only through the Scriptures that the pastor-teacher (the man of God) will be "able to meet all demands" and be equipped for every good work (3:17). The reason the man of God can be so affected is that "All Scripture is inspired by God and profitable for *teaching,* for reproof, for correction, for training in righteousness" (3:16).

### The Unpleasant Task

Paul was unusual in that he "was appointed [by God] a 'proclaimer' and an apostle as a teacher of the Gentiles [for them to receive] faith and truth" (1 Tim. 2:7). But to the churches, teaching was paramount in his thinking. He wrote to the church at Thessalonica, "We request and exhort you in the Lord Jesus, that, as you received from us instruction as to how you ought to walk and please God [just as you actually do walk], that you may excel still more" (1 Thess. 4:1). Teaching was so important to Paul that he later wrote them, "If anyone does not obey our instruction in this letter, take special note of that man and do not associate with him, so that he may be put to shame. And yet do not regard him as an enemy, but admonish him as a brother" (2 Thess. 3:14–15).

## Shepherds May Not Be Popular

Paul instructed that pastors-elders must carry out this unpleasant work. It is not popular. And the sheep may no longer "like" their leaders. But Paul argues that it must be done. To teacher Timothy he writes, "I solemnly charge you in the presence of God and of Christ Jesus, proclaim the word; be ready in season and out of season; reprove, rebuke, exhort, with great patience and doctrine" (2 Tim. 4:1–2). In giving the reason why, Paul describes a future generation that will reject "healthy" teaching:

> *For the time will come when they will not endure sound doctrine; but wanting to have their ears tickled, they will accumulate for themselves teachers in accordance to their own desires; and will turn away their ears from the truth, and will turn aside to myths. (4:3–4)*

Could Paul be drawing a picture of this *now* generation? Could this generation we are into be the Apostasy? No one can say for sure, but there are parallel patterns we can see in our culture that may tell us we have arrived at that day. Lenski notes:

> Paul is not speaking of a change in the temper of the world in general but of a condition that will appear in the churches. Some churches will do what he here foretells; we have them today. "Heap up for themselves" like haycocks refers to the number of elders which each congregation had: these congregations will be set on filling their presbytery (elder boards) with only such men and at every election will turn down sound men." [Note "election." As stated above, elders are not to be voted on but appointed by other elders.][8]

Fairbairn adds:

> Accordingly, the more the church grew [over the centuries] as an outward institution—growing in that respect, indeed, far too rapidly—the fewer always became the number who would endure sound doctrine, till they were found only in holes and corners. There is enough of this itching after false doctrine in the scattered communities of Protestantism to humble and sadden any Christian heart; the signs of the times give no doubtful indication of even more yet to come; but it is in the bosom of the great apostasy that the more marked and mournful exemplification of the apostle's prediction is to be met with.[9]

Finally, Barnes says Paul is describing apostates who at the time would seek a kind of instruction more comfortable to their wishes and feelings. They will seek such kind of preaching as will accord with their carnal desires; or such as will palliate their evil propensities, and deal gently with their vices.[10]

## *Growing Up a Church*

Paul wants pastor-teacher Timothy to pass on his teachings "entrusted to faithful men who will be able to teach others also" (2 Tim. 2:2). This would imply an appointing process, not an election or voting on new elders. Those who are teachable and who can lead will be the next generation of elders. In this passage the apostle is actually saying "pass along my instructions to faithful men who will 'begin to teach' [aorist infinitive] others also."

The apostle warns the road will not be easy for those leading immature new flocks. He writes (2 Tim. 2:3–10), "Suffer hardship with me, as a good soldier of Christ Jesus." "Consider what I say, for the Lord will give you understanding in everything." Though often imprisoned, he says, "The word of God is not imprisoned"! (v. 10).

How are the pastor-teachers to grow up a church? By teaching the things that are healthy (sound) in doctrine (Titus 2:1–10). Paul dramatically illustrates the results if the Word of God is properly taught by the elders to answer life issues. Paul says there will be a change in the older men (v. 2). Older women (v. 3) will turn around and encourage the younger women (vv. 3–4), and likewise the younger men will become more sensible (v. 6). If elders-pastors want change in their people, this is the apostle's formula. Here Paul gives Timothy instructions as to his own method of teaching, showing what kind of doctrines he should inculcate, and what kind of instructions he should give to the various classes of his hearers. He was, in general, to speak only such things as became sound doctrine.[11]

The notion of healthy teaching is common in the Pastorals (cf. 1 Tim. 1:10; 6:3; 2 Tim. 1:13; 4:3; Titus 1:9, 13; 2:2). So also is the idea that certain behavior befits sound doctrine, and other behavior does not (cf. 1 Tim. 1:10; 6:3). The victims of false teachers (cf. Titus 1:16) were out of harmony with sound doctrine; but now Paul would describe the right sorts of behavior.[12]

Fairbairn well notes that the pastors-teachers must teach what is wholesome, because it does not run out upon fables and frivolous prescriptions of human invention, but bears throughout with practical energy upon the duties of everyday life. Christianity is primarily, indeed, a doctrine, but only that it may be in the true sense a life; and the two can never be kept apart from each other in the public teaching of the church without imminent peril to both.[13]

Paul concludes this section in Titus 2 by writing: "These things [practical and doctrinal issues] speak and exhort and reprove with all authority" (v. 15a). This is the greatest single responsibility of the pastors-teachers.

# Questions for Discussion

1. What is the most important task of the pastor/teacher?
2. What is one of the main reasons pastors/teachers are afraid to speak out?
3. Why is the role of pastor/teacher so difficult? Discuss.
4. Though not mentioned in the chapter, list some of the "pains" inflicted on the pastor/teacher by our church culture today.

## Chapter 14

# Response to Doctrinal Error in the Church

## Introduction

The apostle addressed doctrinal deviation head-on. Paul didn't mince words, and he refused to back down from controversy. He also was not afraid to call names and be specific in handling the destructive nature of error. Throughout his letters he made it clear that the way to silence heterodoxy was to teach doctrine and to instruct with truth. By the power of the Holy Spirit and sound words, Paul felt the mind had to be changed by the input of new spiritual guidelines.

The early church was full of heresy and error. For example, (1) pure, raw paganism was infiltrating the assemblies of the early church. This began slowly with individuals dabbling in personal idolatry. But by the time of the writing of the book of Revelation, it apparently was taking over many congregations, with a mixture of Christian doctrine and pagan belief. (2) The false religion of Gnosticism was apparently rampant in the early church setting. Again, this was the manifestation of pagan religions which could, in a sense, disguise themselves to a degree as Christian, and then add large doses of mysticism, secret rituals, and worship of nature. (3) As well, the apostle Paul considered Jewish legalism as heresy that had to be addressed with all speed lest it destroy the truth of justification by faith through grace alone. Over the centuries, a steady but certain "assimilation" or syncretism of paganism and Christianity would assert itself in Catholicism. The Reformers would have a painful and limited success in ridding the church of its deeply rooted paganism.

## Assimilation of Paganism and Christianity

The most conspicuous mixing of paganism and Christianity mentioned in the New Testament is found in the book of Revelation. By some accounts of the church fathers, the Nicolaitans (Rev. 2:6) were a licentious sect advocating free love. They also promoted a hierarchical religious system that could have led to the concept of the Roman Catholic priesthood. John the apostle hints that some in the church of Pergamum had fallen back into idolatry (2:14), and a large number tolerated Jezebel, who led many others astray to acts of immorality and sacrifice to idols (2:20). Later, many churches fell even deeper into idolatry and pagan practices. Walvoord writes:

> . . . the Ephesian church is commended for hating the deeds of the Nicolaitans. Much scholarly speculation has arisen concerning the precise nature of this group's error. The Nicolaitans apparently were a sect, and some have interpreted their name as meaning "conquering of the people" from *nikaō,* meaning "to conquer" and *laos,* meaning "the people." This view considers the Nicolaitans as the forerunners of the clerical hierarchy superimposed upon the laity and robbing them of spiritual freedom. Others have considered them as a licentious sect advocating complete freedom in Christian conduct including participation in heathen feasts and free love.[1]

It is common knowledge that, after the New Testament period and early in the development of the church during the early Middle Ages, Christendom was assimilating with paganism. Mariolatry was the most obvious doctrinal deviation from biblical orthodoxy. Dave Hunt writes:

> The only "queen of heaven" mentioned in Scripture is an idol which was worshipped by the pagans and to which the Jewish women gave offerings, bringing the wrath of God upon them.
>
> *The children gather wood, and the fathers kindle the fire, and the women knead their dough to make cakes to the queen of heaven, and pour out drink offerings unto other gods, that they may provoke me to anger. (Jer. 7:18)*
>
> *Because you have burned incense [to the queen of heaven] and because you have sinned against the Lord . . . therefore this evil is happened unto you. (44:15)*
>
> Far from being embarrassed by such pagan connections, Rome flaunts them. Many Catholics boast that Mary has taken the place of "Maia, the nymph of Greek mythology, who was the mother of Hermes by Zeus, the sky god." The month of May was named after Maia, who was known as the queen of May

... [and] the Jesuit effort to turn the Queen of May into the Virgin Mary was successful.[2]

## Gnosticism

The Gnostics were the New Agers of their day. Though we don't know of all that the gnostic groups taught, they did for certain believe they were gifted to receive revelation others could not know. Thus the word "Gnostic," to know what others cannot fathom or to have special knowledge. Many Gnostics held to strict asceticism, prophetic utterances, the deity of human beings, and that there were many paths to God. They also denied the true humanity of Christ.

## Jewish Legalism

In Galatians, Paul counters Jewish legalism head-on. Even some Christian Jews were apparently arguing that faith in Christ *plus* keeping the law was necessary to obtain salvation. They were arguing law-keeping for gaining and then living out their salvation. Paul becomes quite angry about this issue because it polluted the gospel. There could be no mixing of law and grace.

## Jude and the Apostle Peter

It was not only the apostle Paul who responded to error in the churches, but Peter and Jude had much to say as well. In their eschatological books of 2 Peter and Jude, the two apostles give strong warning about those who will lose heart and possibly compromise truth. In reality they are writing about unbelievers who have infiltrated the churches and are wreaking havoc in the midst of the saints.

Both of these men spoke out about being on guard and not being carried away by the error of "lawless" men (2 Peter 3:17). Peter says these "false prophets" came in "among" the believers (2:1). By coming into the churches they "cleansed" themselves outwardly and escaped "the defilements of the culture" (2:20). They had an outer acceptance of Christ but then "turned away" from the truth (2:21). One of the characteristics of those in cults is that they can look like believers in Christ. They can appear religious and pious. But Peter in no uncertain words says they never knew the Lord in personal terms.

Jude writes that these false prophets "crept into the churches unnoticed who were marked out long ago for condemnation." He adds they were ungodly men who turned God's grace into "debauchery" (Greek *aselgeia*) (v. 4). He goes on to write that they went after the error of Balaam (v. 11) and were "hidden reefs" [of destruction] in their love feasts (v. 12). Jude further describes them as "trees without fruit," "doubly dead, uprooted" (v. 12). He forcefully concludes:

> *These are grumblers, finding fault, following after their own lusts; they speak arrogantly, flattering people for the sake of gaining an advantage. (v. 16)*

> *These are the ones who cause divisions, [they are] worldly-minded, devoid of the Spirit. (v. 19)*

Peter says they are "self-willed," and indulge the flesh while despising authority (2:10). He says they are hedonistic (living in the now), living in luxury; they are stains and blemishes and speak "arrogant words of vanity [and] entice by fleshly desires, by sensuality," promising freedom while they are slaves of corruption (2:18–19).

In terms of eschatology, Peter adds that "in the last days mockers will come . . . following their own lusts, and saying 'Where is the promise of His coming? . . . [since] all continues just as it was from the beginning of creation'" (3:3–4). The apostle tells us they say this because they have their own selfish agenda (their own lusts) whereby they want the world to continue as it is (3:3).

## Paul's Response to Doctrinal Error

### Galatians

In Paul's first letter (A.D. 49–55), the apostle blasts Jewish legalism. He calls the gospel "the grace of Christ" (1:6) and warns of those teaching a "different" gospel (1:6), disturbing the believers and distorting the gospel message (1:6–7). He calls "accursed" any who preach a contrary gospel, no matter if the message-bearer is from heaven or earth (1:8).

In his profound commentary on Galatians, Luther points out that, in all of Paul's arguments against false teaching in the church, his motive is protecting the gospel message from pollution and error. In fact Luther points out that this is the central doctrine of the church and must be kept pure at all costs. Coming out of a Europe that had been kept in the dark about the gracious way of salvation in this dispensation, Luther and other Reformation leaders argued that this truth must flourish. The gospel is ultimately to the glory of God and must be protected at all cost. Luther writes in his *Galatians* introduction:

> We have to fear as the greatest and nearest danger, lest Satan take from us the pure doctrine of faith, and bring into the church again the doctrine of works and men's traditions. Wherefore it is very necessary, that this doctrine be kept in continual practice and public exercise both of reading and hearing. And although it be never so well known, never so exactly learned, yet the devil our adversary, who continually rangeth about seeking to devour us, is not dead; likewise our flesh and old man is yet alive; besides this, all kinds of temptations vex and oppress us on every side. Wherefore this doctrine can never be taught, urged and

repeated enough. If this doctrine be lost, then is also the whole knowledge of truth, life and salvation lost and gone. If this doctrine flourish, then all good things flourish, religion, the true service of God, the glory of God, the right knowledge of all things and states of life.[3]

Paul makes it clear that the pure gospel is not from men and that it came by revelation (1:11–12). The apostle makes no bones about the fact that he is the Lord's exclusive, first-line message-bearer, and that he received this truth from the Lord, outside of himself. Its origin is not from men (1:11). Paul explains that opposition comes from "false brothers" who have sneaked in and spied out the church's liberty, "which we have in Christ Jesus," with the intent of bringing believers into "bondage" (2:4).

Paul further reminds his readers that he submitted his gospel message to the church at Jerusalem. The Lord Himself guided Paul to share the "revelation" he received from Christ to the apostles in private (2:2). James, Peter, and John recognized the grace that had been given to Paul (2:9). Later, though not preaching heresy, Peter was not consistent in his practicing the gospel of grace. In time, Peter was convinced of his error.

In the heart of his Galatian letter, Paul argues that law and grace may not be mixed, either in the issue of salvation or in the Christian life (3:1–5). He speaks strongly that "God would justify the Gentiles by faith . . ." (3:8), and he adds that by being under the Law, one is cursed! (3:10). Salvation *and* the promise of the Spirit only come through faith (3:14). The apostle adds that God has "hemmed in, enclosed, confined, imprisoned" (Greek) all men under sin, that the promise by faith in Jesus Christ might be given to those who believe (3:22). No argument could be more clear than what Paul puts forth here in Galatians.

But into the believers' camp comes opposition. Paul writes of those who are attempting to "persuade" the churches differently (5:8). He speaks of those who are "hindering," "disturbing," and "troubling" the body of Christ. He argues that their ultimate goal is to "make a good showing in the flesh" by trying to Judaize the Gentile Christians back into circumcision (6:12). On verse 12:

> The apostle now shows up the hollowness of the Judaists, and utters his last warning against them. . . . They were not conscientious in insisting on circumcision as indispensable to salvation. Their motive was to screen themselves from persecution, and to gain a good report among the Jews. The enmity of these Jews toward those of their brethren who made a Christian profession was greatly modified by the thought, that they had not only ceased to observe the Mosaic ordinance themselves, but were actually forcing it on Gentile converts.[4]

## Romans

As Paul closes this book he urges his readers to watch carefully certain brothers in the Lord and "turn away from them" (16:17) because they "cause dissensions and hindrances." Importantly, he argues that they are acting "contrary to the teaching which you learned" (16:17), and he adds, "for such men are slaves . . . of their own appetites" and deceive the hearts of the unsuspecting by "smooth and flattering speech" (16:18).

## 1 Corinthians; 2 Corinthians

The assembly at Corinth had more problems than any other church. Paul addresses their divisions (1:10) and quarrels (1:11) and then focuses on the power of the gospel for salvation (1:18) and the great need in the Christian life to grow up (chapter 3). He closes 1 Corinthians with few specific warnings but does remind the readers, "Be on the alert, stand firm in the faith" (16:13). As well, he comes down hard on anyone who does not love the Lord by saying "let him be accursed" (16:22).

## Ephesians

Paul has only one paragraph warning of apparent error. He writes, "Let no one deceive you with empty words, for because of these things the wrath of God comes upon the sons of disobedience. Therefore do not be partakers with them" (5:6–7).

## Philippians

Paul is furious at the inroads made by the Judaizers. He detests the mixing of law with grace. He writes a stinging rebuke and says, "Beware of the dogs, beware of the evil workers, beware of the false circumcision; . . . put no confidence in the flesh" (3:2–3).

Most commentators believe the term "dog" is referring to the Judaizers who claimed circumcision as necessary for salvation, though dog was generally a word reserved for pagan Gentiles. In a paraphrase, Lightfoot puts in the mouth of Paul what he believes the apostle is trying to get across:

> I [Paul] reverse the image. We [believers in Christ] are the children, for we banquet on the spiritual feast which God has spread before us: they are the dogs, for they greedily devour the garbage of carnal ordinances, the very refuse of God's table [the laws].[5]

## Colossians

Paul takes to task those who were "defrauding" the Colossian saints (2:18). They were mystics who worshiped angels, had visitations from them, and had an egotistical, self-inflated mind. Paul writes that these people were not "holding onto the head," Christ, who brought about spiritual growth (2:19).

The apostle also writes against ascetics who looked at the physical as sin: "Handle not, taste not, touch not!" (2:21). Ascetics followed their own commandments, which appeared wise but were really practices of "self-made religion." Their maltreatment of the body did not help conquer temptation (2:23). Paul urges his readers to rise above the false doctrines swarming about and to focus on the eternal (3:2).

## 1 Thessalonians; 2 Thessalonians

The apostle closes 1 Thessalonians by commanding all in the church to "admonish the impulsive, cheer up the small-souled, help the sick [of heart]" (5:14). Besides this, he urges the church to appreciate those working among them and who "give you instruction" (5:12).

The church at Thessalonica was suffering terribly from persecution. But Paul was still concerned about error, apostasy, and doctrinal departure and about those who lived undisciplined and lazy lives. At the end of 2 Thessalonians he writes, "Keep away from every brother who leads an undisciplined life" (3:6). With even harsher words, he says, "If anyone does not obey our instruction in this letter, take special note of that man and do not associate with him, so that he may be put to shame. . . . Yet do not regard him as an enemy, but instruct him as a brother" (3:14). The apostle was determined to create a strong, mature church that could withstand any onslaught of error.

## 1 Timothy

In the Pastoral Epistles, the apostle comes down still harder on doctrinal drift. In 1:3, Timothy was told to stay at Ephesus in order to "'command with authority' (parangeilēs) certain men not to teach 'heterodoxy' (heterodidaskalein) nor to pay attention to mere speculations that do not further the work of God by faith!" These men, he says, have strayed from "commands given by authority" (parangeilēs) and have "limped" (exetrapēsan) toward fruitless discussions (1:5–6). He says these men are "legalists" and do not "mentally reason" (noountes) what they are saying and know nothing of the things they seem confident about.

The apostle does not mind mentioning the names of those who have drifted from the truth. He writes of two men named Alexander and Hymenaeus who became shipwrecked in faith (1:19). Alexander was delivered over to Satan because of his blaspheming (1:20). Further, this man "vigorously opposed our teaching," Paul adds (2 Tim. 4:15).

Paul also went beyond his day to this present time. In 4:1, he addresses our apostate church with his strong words:

> For the Spirit emphatically is saying that in later times some will themselves "apostasize" (apostēsontai) away from The Faith,[6] turning one's mind (prosechontes) to "impostor spirits" and to

*demonic didactics. . . . [They are doing this by the influence of
those] liars with "inferior discernment" (hypokrisei) who have
been seared by their own conscience. (4:1–2)*

The apostle adds that Timothy will be a good servant to point out "these things
to the brothers" (4:6) who need to be continually nourished on the words of the
faith and of the sound doctrine "which you [Timothy] have been following."

Paul urges young pastor Timothy to avoid "worldly babblings" (4:7) and
"empty chatter" (6:20), as well as heretical arguments that were falsely labeled
"knowledge"—by which some went astray (6:21).

The apostle concludes this letter to Timothy with strong words:

*Be teaching and counseling with these principles! If anyone
[teaches] heterodoxy (heterodidaskalei), and does not set forth
sound words, those of our Lord Jesus Christ, and with the doctrine conforming to godliness, he is conceited and understands
nothing; but he has a morbid interest in controversial questions
and disputes about words, out of which arise envy, strife, abusive language, evil suspicions. (6:2c–4)*

## 2 Timothy

Because of the rejection of doctrine and of the gospel, Paul warns Timothy
of the struggle he must endure for truth. Paul points out that all in Asia turned
away from him (1:15). He uses phrases like "suffer hardship as a good soldier,"
"compete as an athlete," "the hard-working farmer," "enduring all things," "persecutions and sufferings," "imprisonment as a criminal though the word of God
is not imprisoned."

Timothy was to remind those drifting to stop "wrangling" about words, which
is useless, and "leads to the ruin of the hearers" (2:14).

In this epistle also Paul is not afraid to call names. He mentions again Hymenaeus
along with a Philetus, who had "gone astray from the truth" and had "upset the faith
of some" (2:18). These men were teaching that the resurrection had already come
and gone with the result that many were spiritually shaken within. Paul also urges
Timothy to "reprove, rebuke, exhort, with great patience and instruction" (4:2),
because the time will arrive when men will not endure sound doctrine (4:3). They
will want their ears tickled and desire teachers who will tell them what they want to
hear. These men will turn away from the truth to myths (4:4).

In this book the apostle also warns of the last days when hard times will
come. "Men will be self-lovers, lovers of money, boastful, arrogant, revilers,
disobedient to parents, ungrateful, unholy, . . . holding a form of godliness but

denying its power" (3:1–5). They will be those who are ever "learning and never able to come to the knowledge of the truth" (3:7).

### Titus

In many ways Paul is tougher on error in this letter to Titus than in any of his other writings. In giving the qualifications for the elder, the apostle says that Titus should be "exhorting with 'healthy' doctrine and exposing those who argue" (Greek, 1:9). In a lengthy diatribe the apostle lashes out against "rebellious men," "empty talkers," and "deceivers" (1:10) who "must be silenced because they are upsetting whole families, teaching things they should not teach, for the sake of sordid gain" (1:11). He adds, "Reprove them severely that they may be sound in faith" (1:13). He goes on: they teach the commandments of men "who turn away from the truth" (1:14).

In contrast, Titus is to "speak the things which are fitting for sound doctrine" (2:1). Paul then addresses the spiritual and practical needs of older and younger men and women. He ties "good deeds" together with "purity in doctrine" (2:7). He again urges Titus to speak "these things and exhort, reprove with all authority" (2:15). In doing so, "Shun foolish controversies and genealogies and strife and disputes about the Law" (3:9), for such discussions are worthless, he says. And finally, "Reject a factious man after a first and second warning, knowing that such a man is perverted and is sinning, being self-condemned" (3:10–11).

## Answering and Confronting Error

How would the apostles of the New Testament answer pastors today who are clearly compromising with the culture and who are flirting with doctrinal slippage?

1. Paul and James would say, "No matter the cost, you teach doctrinal truth."
2. John would say, "Truth is never sacrificed in place of love. Both are proclaimed and bonded together."
3. James and John would say, "We are at war with the culture. We can never compromise and assimilate biblical truth with the philosophies of the world!"

For example:

1. James argues, "If any among you strays from the truth, and one turns him back, let him know that he who turns a sinner from the error of his way will save his soul from death, and will 'remove from sight' a multitude of sins" (James 5:19–20). The writer of Hebrews adds, "Do not be carried away by varied and strange teachings" (Heb. 13:9). Paul goes on, "If anyone does not obey our instruction in this letter, . . . do not associate with him, . . . put him to shame. [And yet] admonish him as a brother" (2 Thess. 3:14–15).

But Paul goes even further in his argument for teaching strong doctrine. He writes in 2 Timothy 3:16–17: "All Scripture is God-breathed [Greek, *theopneustos*]" and is useful for:

- **teaching**—a body of doctrinal propositions.
- **reproof**—a statement of negative reprimand.
- **correction**—getting back on course.
- **training in righteousness**—a new path in living.

Paul concludes with a solemn charge: "Start proclaiming the word; be ready in season and out of season; reprove, rebuke, exhort, with great patience and instruction" (2 Tim. 4:2).

2. The apostle John emphasizes the issue of Christian love and doctrine. He does not simply say "love everybody," nor does he argue only doctrine. He calls for both. "Let us not love with word or with tongue, but in deed and truth" (1 John 3:18).

He continues, "[To those] whom I love with truth; and not only I, but also all who know the truth, for the sake of the truth which abides in us and will be with us forever" (2 John 2). "Grace and mercy from God the Father and from Jesus Christ, the Son of the Father, in truth and love" (v. 3). He adds that he is glad to find the believers "walking in truth" (v. 4), and notes that this was commanded by God the Father.

John says he is so glad to hear from other believers that those he wrote to were "walking in the truth." He states further, "I have no greater joy than this, to hear of my children walking in the truth" (3 John 4).

3. Finally, the church is at war with the culture. The world is coming into the church and taking over the lives of believers. This is possibly one of the most alarming and frightening events happening. Discernment is gone. Pastors and people no longer seem to know the difference between the influence of the world and biblical truth.

James and John speak to this issue head-on. John first reminds his readers they are strong because "the word of God abides in you" (1 John 2:14). But he reminds the Christians, "Do not love the world [culture], nor the things in the world," because the one who loves the culture cannot have the love for God the Father within (2:15). He adds that the philosophy of the world and all it offers is not from the Father (2:16). From the culture we are tempted by the "cravings" (lust) of the flesh, the "cravings" of what our eyes long for. As well, we are tugged by the culture toward the pretentious pride of living (Greek, *bios*).

In certain terms James blasts believers who sleep with the world. "You adulteresses, do you not know that a friendship with the culture is 'war with God'?" (James 4:4). "Therefore whoever wishes to be a friend of the culture makes himself an enemy of God." James then pictures God as a jealous husband. He has placed His Spirit within us because He desires to have an exclusive and intimate relationship as a husband with his wife (4:5).

Finally, James writes that God has given us a "greater grace" to overcome the temptation of the culture. Worldly temptation is fueled by a selfish pride which God is not committed to *(antitassō),* but instead, He will grant grace to those who humble themselves and repudiate the world and all its glitter (4:6).

## Conclusion

A line is being drawn in the sand. Many pastors and conservative evangelicals are realizing that compromise can no longer be tolerated. It is time for the church to stand. The apostles apparently acted decisively against error and foolish doctrinal deviation. They urged others to take the lead and act with determination. Today, with American democracy so influencing the church, many feel that no word can be said to challenge the varied opinions of others. But if Paul were here, he would speak with a loud, clear voice against the biblical drift that is so obvious in a great many Christian circles. The challenge is stated so perfectly by these three great Bible scholars:

Lenski writes:

> Titus should do but one thing with these people, namely gag them, stop their mouths and silence them by force. Paul does not say how this was to be accomplished; [but] in 1 Tim. 1:4 he wants Timothy to order them to stop their contrary teaching.[7]

Calvin notes:

> If we do not turn away from the simple doctrine of the gospel, if we wish to be governed by the will of God; if we are not carried away by our . . . passions, if we do not walk by our groveling appetites; in short, if we are good scholars of our God, and reckon it enough to have received the doctrine which He teaches us; if that be the case, we shall be fortified against all evil![8]

Closing with John Gill:

> "Sound in the faith" (Titus 1:13) means "healthy" in faith. Thus we speak wholesome words of Christ to create strong and robust and healthy believers. What about those who are weak and sickly in their profession of faith? We should rebuke those who are infected with bad principles and practices, like the physician removing the causes of disorder; and with rebukes, admonitions and censuring. This is ultimately for the good of those corrected.[9]

# Questions for Discussion

1. How should false teaching be handled in the church?
2. Does the apostle Paul write much about heresy and false teachers in his letters?
3. Discuss the guidelines for answering and confronting error.
4. In general, how do people in our churches today react to confrontation?
5. Should leadership teach more about false beliefs and error in the church?

## Chapter 15

# Women in the Church

## Introduction

During the past several decades volumes have been published dealing with the position of women in Christianity and specifically, their role in the operation of the local church. In one volume, for example, over forty pages are devoted to the study of the Greek word *kephalē*, "head." In one chapter, therefore, it is unrealistic to attempt more than a summary of this doctrine from a biblical standpoint. There are several possible approaches to the discussion that have been employed. One writer certifies that Paul taught the headship of man over woman, but that Paul was wrong. Another chooses to use rather obscure definitions of crucial words to prove a point rather than take the usual definitions. From this comes a third emphasis: applying the obscure definitions without proper reference to the context in which the word is used.

The first of these three methods is in reality a repudiation of the inspiration of Scripture. If Paul is in error here, he could just as easily be wrong on other doctrines. Thus we, as uninspired humans, become judges of one who had apostolic authority. The second and third approaches are unfair and unacceptable applications to the interpretation of scriptural passages. The old adage remains true: "The beginning of understanding rests upon precise definitions, used in proper context."

## The Establishment of Headship

### 1 Corinthians 11:3

The male/female relationship began in Genesis 2:18–24, but it might be wise begin with a step beyond this to the statement of 1 Corinthians 11:3. There three "headships" are dogmatically asserted, yet without any animosity whatever. Here we read, "But I would have you know that the head of every man is Christ; and the head of the woman is the man; and the head of Christ is God." In the highest order of headship, God is the head of Christ. It is true that absolute equality

214 A BIBLICAL THEOLOGY OF THE CHURCH

exists among the three Persons of the Trinity; this, however, does not rule out differences of function, along with the voluntary agreement on the part of the Son to assume submission in order to execute such functions.

Pastors often pray, "Father, we thank you for dying on the cross for our salvation," a blatant assertion of patripassionism; yet, if some of those pastors were asked, they would immediately deny that the Father came down from heaven, took upon Himself human flesh, and submitted to crucifixion. It was Christ who hung upon the cross; it was a voluntary submission to the Father, recognizing the headship of the Father over the Son. In John 8:29 Jesus said, "I do nothing of myself; but as my Father hath taught me, I speak these things. And he that sent me is with me. The Father hath not left me alone; for I always do those things that please him." In the scope of these few words, Christ affirms three times that He does and speaks only as the Father directs Him. In Philippians 2:5–8 the classic statement of the humility and submission of Christ who "humbled himself and became obedient unto death" is mentioned, in spite of the fact that He was "equal with God."

Now the whole point of this is to recognize that there can be submission to headship without any thought of inferiority, and so also is the second headship; Christ is the head of man, and the third, which is of equal importance, the man is the head of the woman. This will be considered in detail later. Yet, some have said that the word *kephalē* ("head") does not carry the idea of authority over someone, but merely "source." The forty-page article previously mentioned concludes:

> All the lexicons that specialize in the New Testament period, including two very recent ones, list the meaning "ruler, authority over" for *kephalē*—it appears to be a well-established and valid meaning during the New Testament period. . . . On the other hand, the evidence for the meaning "source" is far weaker, and it is fair to say that the meaning has not yet been established. . . . Therefore there is no linguistic basis for proposing that the New Testament texts which speak of Christ as the head of the church or the husband as the head of the wife can rightly be read apart from the attribution of authority to the one designated as "head."[1]

### Genesis 2:18–25

Does the role of Christ in submission to the Father connect in any way with the role of man and woman in creation? First, it establishes the paradox of headship within absolute equality of the image of God in both man and woman (Gen. 1:26–27), but does not nullify the position of man as the *head* and woman as the *helper* in Genesis 2:18: "And the LORD God said, 'It is not good that the man should be alone; I will make him an help fit for him.'" Thus there emerges a second aspect of this paradox, namely, that while the woman is recognized as "one flesh" (2:24) with the man because she was created from his rib, at the same time this very method of her creation indicates that Adam had not only *chronological* priority, but also *positional* priority as the head of the woman. Paul states clearly in 1 Corinthians 11:8–9, "For the man is not of [*ek-*, "out of"] the woman, but the woman of [*ek-*, "out of"] the man. Neither was the man created for [*dia-*, "for the sake of"] the woman, but the woman for [*dia-*, "for the sake of"] the man." The NASB puts it even more succinctly: "For man does not originate from woman, but woman from man; for indeed man was not created for the woman's sake, but the woman for the man's sake."

All of this comes from Genesis 1–2, not from Genesis 3. Whatever happened at the Fall did not change the creation order of male and female. At worst, it made things harder, such as childbirth and physical labor, but it did not alter the headship of man. Genesis 3:16 only informs the woman that there may well be *difficulties* in her relationship with her husband. In fact, she may desire to master her husband, but at the same time this will only cause him to enforce his rule over her. It is evident that this verse does not include the wonderful power of the Holy Spirit in the life of the believer to overcome the effects of sin, so that the husband can love his wife even as Christ loved the church and that the wife can be submissive as the church submits to the headship of Christ (Eph. 5:25–33).

### Galatians 3:28

If the headship of 1 Corinthians 11 and Genesis 1–2 teach a role of man over the woman, then what does Paul mean when he says that in Christ "there is neither male nor female, for you are all one in Christ"?

It is always necessary to consider passages of Scripture in their contexts. In this case Paul is seeking to show that all Christians are equally "sons of God" in Christ. Among those things which the passage does *not* discuss are male and female distinctions in the leadership and ministry of the church, headship as it should exist between the husband and wife, and the exercise of spiritual gifts by either men or women. In short, this passage has nothing to do with the continuing controversy concerning the responsibilities of the male and female genders. What it *does* teach is the absolute equality of each *individual* in the body of Christ regardless of national, social, or sexual differences. When the parallel passages are consulted, it is clear that none of them includes the gender distinctions (Rom. 10:12; 1 Cor. 12:13; Col. 3:11); but as a matter of interest, Col. 3:11 presents two heretofore unmentioned contrasts, namely the religious (circumcision or uncircumcision) and the cultural (barbarians and Scythians) distinctions.

Ironically enough, Paul begins Galatians 3:26 by saying, "For ye are all the *sons* of God. . . ." Are we to suppose that the "daughters" are omitted? Certainly not! The term *huioi* ("sons") is a contrast to *tekna* ("children") in Galatians 4:1 and refers to the *huiothesian* ("son-placing") in Galatians 4:5, which is the *positioning* of those already "born" children as *adults* in the body of Christ. This is the egalitarianism of Galatians 3:28. The attempts of the feminists to redefine or reinterpret the words to mean anything other than this are not valid.

One quotation will suffice to show that some would even go so far as to say that Paul taught the headship of the male, but that Paul was wrong:

> Furthermore, in reasoning in this way, Paul is not only basing his arguments exclusively on the second creation narrative, but is assuming the traditional rabbinic understanding of that narrative whereby the order of their creation is made to yield the primacy of the man over the woman. Is this rabbinic understanding of Gen. 2:18f. correct? We do not think that it is, for it is palpably inconsistent with the first creation narrative, with the lifestyle of Jesus, and with the apostle's own clear affirmation that in Christ there is no male and female (Gal. 3:28).[2]

Responding to this interpretation of Galatians 3:28, one noted Christian theologian who supports the evangelical feminism movement has said, "Surely Professor Jewett does not wish to leave it for each group of professing Christians to decide for itself how sexual egalitarianism is to work. And if there is no male or female, how will he oppose homosexuality?"[3]

### Ephesians 5:21

Ephesians 5:21 reads, "Submitting yourselves one to another in the fear of God," and at first reading, the verse seems to teach that all Christians should be submissive to one another. The appeal would be to compare it with Philippians 2:3, "Let each esteem others" (*allēlous,* the same word used in Eph. 5:21 for "one to another"). There are, however, considerations that qualify the mutual submission of the total congregation.

It may be that Ephesians 5:21 is the general statement concerning submission and that 5:22–6:5 show how this submission is "exemplified in these three relations in which one must yield to another."[4] Thus, "5:21 is limited by 5:22–6:5 to submission of wives to husbands, children to parents, and slaves to masters. As a corollary to this, the meaning of the verb *hypotassō* ("be in subjection") is always one-directional in its reference to submission to an authority."[5] This footnote goes on to show that the order is never reversed; husbands are never told to submit to wives, nor parents to children, nor masters to slaves. In a number of verses reciprocal submission would not make sense, even though *hypotassō* is used, including Revelation 6:4, "that they should kill one another," since this would mean that all those killed should kill their enemies. Then, in Galatians 6:2, "Bear one another's burdens" means that "*some* who are more able should help bear the burdens of *others* who are less able."[6]

When these things are taken into consideration, Ephesians 5:21 is consistent with the establishing of the headship of the husband over the wife.

## The Extent of Leadership

### *Elders/Bishops and Deacons (1 Tim 3:1–13; Titus 1:5–8)*

While it is true that 1 Timothy 2:11–15 includes a statement concerning women not usurping authority over men, it also mentions the gift of teaching, so that this passage will be considered under the subject of the exercise of spiritual gifts. Here in 1 Timothy 3 it deals directly with the two church offices of *bishop* and *deacon* and gives specific requirements in each case. Among these requirements in both 1 Timothy 3:2 and Titus 1:6 is that the bishop (*episkopos*, or "overseer"), who is also called the "elder" *(presbyteros)* in Titus 1:6, as well as the deacon *(diakonos)* in 1 Timothy 3:12 must be "the husband of one wife" *(mias gynaikos andra)*. It has been argued that this referred to the prohibition of polygamy, or that a church official should be a "one-woman man." Either way, the absolute condition is that the officer must be a male, never a female. Further, in 1 Timothy 2:4–7 the pronoun "he" or "his" is used seven times in English to describe the gender of the bishop; similarly plural masculine endings indicate the gender of the deacon in 1 Timothy 3:8–13.

It is significant that Paul K. Jewett *never* mentions 1 Timothy 3 or Titus 1 in his book entitled *Man as Male and Female,* and only mentions Philippians 1:1 with this notation:

> While it is true that the apostle addresses this church as constituted with bishops and deacons, all of whom were males (Phil. 1:1), one can hardly reason that he simply used Lydia's conversion and hospitality as a means of establishing a bridgehead with men in the community.[7]

This constant reference to something more than is in the text is rather typical of the feminist agenda.

### *Acts 6:1–6*

Some have interpreted this passage as the appointment of the first deacons; but even if it is so, there were no women included in the seven chosen for the task. Further, the actual word *deacon (diakonos)* does not occur in the paragraph, though the word *diakonia* ("ministration") and the infinitive *diakonein* ("to attend") are used in 6:1–2. Then, in 6:5, the word *diakonia* is actually used of the ministry of the *Word* by the apostles themselves. These seven men were appointed to meet a specific need, but this does not necessitate the conclusion that they were church officers. The actual title of elder is not used until considerably later in Galatia in Acts 14:23 and in Ephesus in Acts 20:17, 28. The title of deacon is mentioned only in Paul's later epistles, Philippians 1:1 and 1 Timothy 3:8.

### 1 Timothy 3:11 and Romans 16:1–2

Was there a third official position in the church known as "deaconess"? The statement in 1 Timothy 3:11 literally translated from *gynaikas hōsautōs* is "even as women," and then certain qualifications of these women are given. Who are these women? One would expect differing opinions concerning this subject, depending upon the historical development of a particular denomination. But any historical argument must inevitably be superseded by the direct exposition of the passage involved, and some of these arguments become convoluted. After an extended discussion of the problem, Charles C. Ryrie reached the following conclusion:

> What, then, can we say of these women? If deacons were concerned with the physical and material needs of the community, what would be unnatural about their wives sharing in these ministries as they concerned other women? This accounts for what otherwise would be an intrusion of verse 11 into the discussion about deacons.[8]

Ryrie quotes J. A. Robinson on Romans 16:1–2: "Of Phoebe, then, we may say with sincerity that she is a witness of the important service rendered by women in the primitive church; but in tracing the history of the diaconate it will not be wise to assume that the word *diakonos* is used of her in the strictly official sense."[9] Ryrie adds, "Thus we conclude, . . . the case of Phoebe does not present evidence of an order of deaconesses at that time in the church."[10]

*Thayer's Greek Lexicon* indicates that *diakonos* can be used with either a masculine or feminine article (just as other words, such as *kamēlos* (camel) or *kaminos* (furnace),[11] so that Paul would have used the feminine article with *diakonos* when he spoke of Phoebe as a deaconess, rather than the general connotation of *diakonos* as "servant."

## The Exercise of Stewardship

When the word *stewardship* is used, it means more than financial stewardship. In 1 Corinthians 4:1–2 Paul speaks of himself as a *steward* of the mysteries of God. We are using the word here in the sense of one who has been bestowed with spiritual gifts by God. With regard to women, are there any spiritual gifts withheld from them? Some writers have pointed to Romans 16:7: "Greet Andronicus and Junias, my kinsmen and my fellow-prisoners, who are of note among the apostles," assuming that Junias was a woman and an apostle. The NASB translates that they were "outstanding among the apostles."

## Women Apostles

Various authorities have been quoted including Chrystostom (A.D. 342–407) who stated that Junias was a woman, and Epiphanius (A.D. 315–403) declared that the use of "of whom" (masculine relative pronoun) indicates that Junias was a man. Origen, who died around 252, used Junias, a Latin masculine singular nominative, to translate the Greek name to Latin.[12] Piper and Grudem, who made these investigations, conclude that there is no way to be dogmatic, yet, there does seem to be more evidence from the Greek form of the name. In Greek, the name is *Iounian,* with the circumflex accent over the Greek *alpha (â),* signifying masculine, whereas the feminine would have the acute accent over the Greek *iota* immediately preceding the *alpha (ía).* The critical apparatus gives overwhelming support for the masculine reading.[13]

Another factor, admittedly less weighty, is that Paul mentions Andronicus and Junias as "fellow prisoners," which would seem less likely if Junias were a woman.

The second matter concerns whether or not these two were apostles. Actually, the Greek text itself does not necessitate such a conclusion. It reads *hoitenes eisen episēmoi en tois apostolois,* which can be translated, "Such ones as they are stand out as men of note among the apostles." Lenski writes:

> In fact, they stand out as men of note not only in Paul's estimation, but in the estimation of the apostles. . . . It is rather extravagant to regard "illustrious *en tois apostolois*" as meaning, "as apostles among the apostles" and to think of a host of apostles and regard as such all who carried the gospel anywhere.[14]

## Women and the Gift of Prophecy

Like the gift of apostleship, the gift of prophecy was a "sign gift," given for the purpose of imparting new revelation from God while the New Testament was in formation. Some have equated this with preaching, but it is not so. True prophecy was also for edification, exhortation, and comfort just as the gift of teaching, but though a prophet could teach, a teacher was not necessarily a prophet. Both foretelling and forthtelling were within the realm of prophecy, but forthtelling was the limit of the teacher. Therefore, while there are instances of women with the gift of prophecy (1 Cor. 11:5; Acts 21:8), this is irrelevant to the present-day controversy since this gift is no longer given to men or women.

## Women and the Gift of Pastor/Teacher

Another common mistake is to declare that while we no longer have the prophetic *gift,* we can still have the prophetic *office* as part of the responsibility of the pastor/teacher, who is also an elder. Nowhere in the New Testament is a prophetic *office* mentioned. There are only two offices, the bishop/elder and the deacon, and as stated before, the *gift* of prophecy is no longer in existence. Further, it is incorrect to equate the *office* of the elder with the *gift* of pastor/teacher, even though the elder must also be gifted as a pastor/teacher.

Some hold that Paul's list of elder qualifications indicates that the office of elder/pastor is limited to men. At the same time, however, it is held that there are no gender distinctions in the distribution of spiritual gifts.[15] It might be clearer to say that the office of elder carries with it the qualification that he must be "apt to teach" (1 Tim. 3:2). To this could then be added that the *one* gift which is limited to the masculine gender is "pastor." The Greek noun *poimenas* translated "pastor" occurs only in Ephesians 4:11 when referring to gifts given to the church. The verb form *poimainō,* translated "feed," is used only three times: in John 21:16 by Jesus saying to Peter, "Feed my sheep"; in 1 Peter 5:2 by Peter as an elder to other elders, "Feed the flock of God which is among you"; and by Paul to the Ephesian elders in Acts 20:28, "Take heed . . . to feed the flock over which the Holy Spirit hath made you overseers (*episkopous,* "elders"), to feed (*poimainein*) the church of God." Thus, the pastor or "shepherd" is the "elder." This word is masculine and is never used of a spiritual gift to a woman.

One seeming contradiction is that though the gift of prophecy was given to women, a woman could pray or prophesy as long as her head was covered (1 Cor. 11:4). Yet in that same epistle (1 Cor. 14:34–35) women were to keep silent in the churches. After wading through seven unacceptable resolutions to this apparent discrepancy, D. A. Carson presents an interpretation that verifies both commands by Paul and avoids all of the theological pitfalls:

> Paul has just been requiring that the church in Corinth carefully weigh the prophecies presented to it. Women, of course, may participate in such prophesying; that was established in chapter 11. Paul's point here, however, is that they may *not* participate in the oral weighing of such prophecies. That is not permitted in any of the churches.[16]

### Women and the Gift of Teaching

This leads naturally to Paul's admonition in 1 Timothy 2:11–13. He places two restrictions on women: "But I do not permit a woman to teach, nor to usurp authority over the man, but to be in silence." A practical application of these admonitions is the teaching of 1 Corinthians 14 that women cannot evaluate prophecies given by either men or women, since that would violate both restrictions: They would be (1) teaching the local church and (2) usurping the authority to determine the truth of these prophecies 14:29.

Again, much investigation has gone into discerning the proper meaning of "usurp authority" *(authentein).* An entire three-hundred-page book is devoted to this one text, 1 Timothy 2:9–15. This worthy volume established two historic positions, namely, that women are to be in subjection and not to usurp authority over men, and that they should remember the original headship of Adam over Eve at creation. The crux of the matter is presented as part of the conclusion to chapter five:

> Moreover, women should not arrogate a teaching role for them-
> selves when men and women are gathered in public meetings. . . .
> The creation of Adam before Eve signaled that men are to teach
> and exercise authority in the church. . . . Women, Paul reminds
> his readers, will experience eschatological salvation by adher-
> ing to their proper role, which is exemplified in giving birth to
> children.[17]

In an article written by a woman, the author concludes similarly:

> The principle of male headship was violated through the rever-
> sal of authority roles in the Fall with devastating consequences,
> and Paul wanted the believers to avoid such a role reversal and
> its consequences in the church. Despite the results of this rever-
> sal of roles in the Garden of Eden, women who fulfill their God-
> ordained roles as women and who have the inner adornment of
> a godly character may expect to receive future perfection of
> salvation with its accompanying reward.[18]

### Summary

In summary, apostleship and prophecy were temporary "sign" gifts, and are no longer in existence today. Therefore, all the arguments with regard to whether women had these gifts are irrelevant today. However, the *offices* of elder and deacon are permanent, and both of these have the qualification, "husband of one wife," which automatically excludes women from these positions of authority in the church. We have also seen that the gift of pastor (*poimenas,* "shepherd") is used of men only. What, therefore, *can* a woman do in the church? Without watering down biblical inspiration, without violating biblical hermeneutics, with-out employing erroneous exegesis, women can discover many areas of ministry clearly exhorted by Scripture and personally exemplified in Scripture by godly women who were used mightily in service for their Lord in both the Old and New Testaments.

## The Biblical Latitude

Although it is obvious that the Scriptures put prohibitions on women in the church in certain positions, there is tremendous latitude for women's ministry in the local church, including areas of teaching. But as H. Wayne House writes, "Women who teach, whether in conformation to the Scriptures or otherwise, are under the same divine scrutiny and ultimate accountability as are men" (James 3:1).[19] The spiritual qualifications of a woman in a leadership position such as children's church director, or a Sunday school teacher should be as high as those for the men, since in these positions they need to exhibit responsibility as well as teach through word and deed. They need to be an example of mature Christian womanhood for those whom they teach. It is for this reason that House suggests that candidates for these positions should be measured by the qualifications given in 1 Timothy 3:1–13 and 2 Timothy 2:21–26.

In light of the prohibition of 1 Timothy 2 and the other passages looked at, it is probably best to lay down some guidelines for when boys become "men." This is very pertinent to the Sunday school in the local church. Ideally, at twelve or fourteen years old, boys reach puberty and become men. Since the best way to become a godly man is to pattern your life after a godly man, it is preferable at this age for young men to receive spiritual instruction from godly, mature men. Some argue for an earlier age, and this is preferable. If several ages of classes have to be combined because of a lack of committed, qualified men, then so be it. We need to remember that many boys have no example of what a godly man should be; it is important that they see godly manhood modeled in the spiritual training they receive at church.

The question arises, "What are other areas in which women can serve in the local church?" The possibilities are numerous. Here is a modest list of some areas where women can exercise their spiritual gifts.

1. Teaching women (small groups, large groups, conferences)
2. Teaching children (boys until puberty)
3. Writing
4. Authoring Bible-study materials (especially for women and children)
5. Personal evangelism and discipleship (especially among young women)
6. Visitation to the sick
7. Counseling women and children
8. Children's church director
9. Children's ministry director
10. Church secretary
11. Assisting deacons in benevolence ministry
12. In cross-cultural missions, all of the above would apply

This is only a partial listing. In each church or missions situation the elders should examine the job profile in light of the biblical injunction and be convicted that the principle of women not "teaching or exercising authority over a man" is not being violated.[20]

## Conclusion

Even allowing for the efforts of extremists of both genders, when the sincere men and women in the body of Christ adhere to the admonitions directed to both sexes, there will be little difficulty in fulfilling the proper principles of headship, leadership, and stewardship of gifts.

# Questions for Discussion

1. Describe in your own words the issue of headship.
2. What does the book of Genesis imply in regard to the issue of headship?
3. Does Paul get rid of headship when he says, "There is neither male nor female, for you are all one in Christ"?
4. What does Paul mean when he dismisses gender distinctions?
5. Why is there such confusion today over the issue of women as pastors/ teachers? Isn't the Bible clear on this issue?
6. Why do some people still resist what the Word of God is saying on the subject?

# Part 3

# How the Church Ministers

## Chapter 16

# Discipline in the Church

## Introduction

As Ryrie states, "Christ's purpose for the church is to sanctify it and present it to Himself without spot or wrinkle (Eph. 5:26–27). All the activities of a church should also aim at this goal, including discipline, for it too is designed to produce a holy character in the one who has to be disciplined."[1]

## God's Discipline of His Children (Heb. 12:3–13)

### God Disciplines His Children

For a proper perspective on the discipline that should be administered in the church, we need to understand how God disciplines us individually. The author of Hebrews explains how God disciplines and instructs His children in Hebrews 12. He quotes the Septuagint version of Proverbs 3:11–12 (Heb. 12:5–6). The Christians were encouraged not to "regard lightly" (*oligōreō;* "make light of," "neglect") the benefit of the Lord's discipline.[2] The Greek noun translated "discipline" is *paideia,* which in the Greek world denoted the upbringing and handling of a minor child. It included direction, teaching, and chastisement.[3]

Thus, "the Lord's discipline refers to that instructive and correctional training that the Lord administers."[4] As Rienecker points out, "In Judaism a father was required to provide for the instruction of his sons and daughters and to teach them good behavior. Whipping was accepted, along with other disciplinary measures."[5]

The Lord's discipline is more than what we would call "chastisement" or "spanking," although this is included in the idea of *paideia.* Especially in our passage that is obvious from the use of the Greek *mastigoi,* translated "scourging" in Hebrews 12:6. It means "to beat with a whip."[6] As Kent writes, "Proper training must include correction of faulty behavior."[7] This idea is very much in line with the Old Testament idea of discipline with the emphasis on chastisement (Deut. 21:18; Prov. 13:24; 19:18; 23:13; 29:17). So the overall idea is that the suffering of the Hebrews was sovereignly allowed by God and was used in their training process. Kent states, "In times of affliction caused by opponents to their faith, God's people are to realize that persecution is actually overruled by God and used for the training of believers."[8] The bottom line idea here is that suffering brings growth. Whether it be correction for a wrong, suffering unjustly, or every-day struggles, suffering fits into God's training program for his sons (Rom. 8:28).

### The Motivation of God's Discipline

Hebrews 12:5–6 states, "My son, do not regard lightly the discipline of the Lord, nor faint when you are reproved by Him; for those whom the Lord loves He disciplines, and He scourges every son whom He receives." The motivation for the Lord's action in discipline is *love*. At the point of salvation we became "sons of God" (Rom. 8:14–15; Gal. 3:26; 4:5–7) and were placed in God's family (1 Cor. 12:13). Because we are sons, God is committed to train us to be obedient.

The very fact that Christians experience chastisement is proof that they are God's own. It is those who don't experience God's chastisement who are "illegitimate." We should endure in the face of persecution and suffering, realizing God is in total control and is using it for our instruction. As F. F. Bruce states, "A father would spend much care and patience on the upbringing of a true-born son whom he hoped to make a worthy heir; and at the time such a son might have to undergo much more irksome discipline than an illegitimate child for whom no future of honor and responsibility was envisaged"[9] (Heb. 12:7–9).

The key to growing through chastisement, suffering, and everyday trials is being in "subjection" (v. 9). The Greek verb here is *hypotassomai,* meaning "to be in submission or subjection," or "to submit oneself to another." In this case that "other" is our heavenly Father. This can mean not running from difficult situations and also reacting to times of chastisement and suffering with a submissive attitude toward God, knowing He is in control.

Before the foundation of the world God set His love on us and chose us to be His children (Eph. 1:4–5). He is committed to conforming us to the image of His Son (Rom. 8:29). His training process will bring us to that point some day, and it is all motivated by His incredible love for us (Heb. 12:6).

### The Result of God's Discipline

Continuing the comparison between our earthly fathers and our heavenly Father ("the Father of spirits," v. 9), the writer points out that our earthly fathers' discipline was "for a short time." This "short time" would have been from birth until we reach the age of adulthood. In contrast, God's discipline of us is for a lifetime. In the case of our earthly fathers, they were limited in their knowledge of what discipline we needed to grow up to be morally and ethically responsible adults. Since they were imperfect themselves, they could not give us perfect discipline. "Our heavenly Father, in the perfection of His wisdom and love, can be relied upon never to impose any discipline on us that is not for our good. The supreme good that He has in view for His children is this, that they may share His holiness."[10] This is not referring to the positional holiness that we receive at salvation on the basis of which we can be referred to as saints (Rom. 1:7; 1 Cor. 1:2; 2 Cor. 1:1; Eph. 1:1), but rather the writer here is referring to the holiness "which is the goal for which God is preparing His people—that entire sanctification which is consummated in their manifestation with Christ in glory."[11]

Chastisement is never pleasant. In fact, in most instances the pain of chastisement seems extremely unpleasant and sorrowful (Heb. 12:11). Those who have endured chastisement with a submissive attitude, looking for God's instruction in the circumstances, are fully trained by it (*gymnazō,* meaning "to exercise or train," and the perfect tense indicates completed action). The result is spiritual maturity. The training culminates in the "peaceful fruit of righteousness." This is probably the inner peace of knowing that all is right between us and God.

# Discipline in the Church

### *The Process of General Church Discipline*
In Matthew 18 Christ addresses the subject of discipline within the church (*ekklēsia*) or "church." Christ's hearers, at this point, had poor technical understanding of the *ekklēsia* as a Spirit-baptized body of believers in Christ (1 Cor. 12:13), including Jew and Gentile. The word was used in the general sense of an "assembly," "meeting," or "gathering." D. A. Carson writes:

> Whenever *ekklēsia* in the Septuagint is translating Hebrew, the Hebrew word is *qhl* ("assembly," "meeting," "gathering"), with reference to various kinds of "assemblies" (cf. E. Jenni and C. Westermann, eds. *Theologisches Handworterbuch zum Alten Testament,* 2 vols. 3 ed. [Munchen: Chr. Kaiser Verlag, 1978–79], 2:610–619), but [it was] increasingly used to refer to God's people, the assembly of Yahweh.[12]

Since the church is a mystery in the Old Testament (Eph. 3:1–12), Christ's listeners would have probably taken this as instruction to those who made up the assembly of believers in Christ as Messiah. At the same time, although the church would not be born until the coming of the Spirit at Pentecost, it is true that the apostles along with the prophets made up the foundation of the church (Eph. 2:20), and any instruction given them about the *ekklēsia* would carry over to their instruction for the church.

*The First Step*

Christ states that the first course of action is to go to the brother who is in sin and "reprove him in private" (v. 15). The intention of the heart is important. We have already seen that the Father's motivation in disciplining His children is love (Heb. 12:6). In Galatians 6:1 Paul writes, "Brethren, even if a man is caught in any trespass, you who are spiritual ["walking by the Spirit" (Gal. 5:25)], restore such a one in a spirit of gentleness; each one looking to yourself, lest you too be tempted." As well as being motivated by love our attitude must be one of humility, realizing that we could fall into sin just as he has. In this way we fulfill the law of Christ (Gal 6:2), which is to love others as Christ loved us (John 13:34). Paul warns against pride in discipline in Galatians 6:3. Entering into discipline with a haughty spirit means that the person is deceiving himself into believing he could not fall as well.

*The Second Step*

In Matthew 18:16, Christ says that if the brother does not listen we are to take a second step. This involves taking one or two more witnesses to confront him. Christ quotes from Deuteronomy 19:15, showing this is the same principle used in the Old Testament. It states, "A single witness shall not rise up against a man on account of any iniquity or any sin which he has committed; on the evidence of two or three witnesses a matter shall be confirmed."

*The Third Step*

If the brother still refuses to listen and repent, his case is to be brought before the whole church (v. 17).

*The Fourth Step*

If the brother refuses to accept the godly counsel of the elders and the church as a whole and chooses to persist in his sin, there is only one other course of action left. He is to be excluded from fellowship with the church (v. 17). Hopefully this action will only be necessary for a short time as the Holy Spirit convicts the heart of the saint and pushes him to repentance. Then he can be restored to full fellowship. This action of the corporate body carries out the decision that has already been made in heaven. Christ calls such a decision to exclude someone from the fellowship of the body "binding" and "loosing" (v. 18). The idea of binding and loosing has the force of forbidding and permitting. "The phrase was used in Christ's day by Israel's religious leaders regarding what was forbidden (bound) and what was permitted (loosed)."[13]

The Greek verbs "bind" *(deō)* and "loose" *(lyō)* are in the perfect tense here. Thus, a more literal translation would be, "Truly I say to you, whatever you forbid on earth *will have already been forbidden* in heaven; and whatever you shall permit on earth *will already have been permitted* in heaven." How would church leaders know what to forbid and what to permit among the brethren?

Their guideline was simply God's eternal Word. When a brother or sister was excluded from fellowship, it was on the basis of something they were involved in that violated God's Word and from which they would not turn. The church's authority did not overstep the bounds of God's Word.

## The Objectives of Discipline

The primary objectives of church discipline are at least four. They include:

1. To restore him/her to proper fellowship with God and the church (2 Cor. 2:5–11).
2. To remove the leavening, the corruptive influence, from the presence of the other members of the congregation (i.e., false teaching, immorality, etc.) (1 Cor. 5:6–8; Titus 1:10–16).
3. To correct doctrinal error (Titus 1:13).
4. To prevent the sin from spreading to other members of the congregation and to challenge them unto godliness (Gal. 6:1; 1 Tim. 5:20).

One might add to this list the fact that such action may protect the reputation of the church as well as that of the individual in the community, and thus maintain his or her ability to be effective in witnessing.

## Examples of Discipline in the Early Church

Ryrie lists seven kinds of people (some of which overlap) who received discipline in the early church:

1. An accused elder (1 Tim. 5:19–20)
2. A sinning brother (Matt. 18:15–20)
3. An overtaken brother (Gal. 6:1)
4. An unruly brother (2 Thess. 3:6)
5. False teachers (Titus 1:10–16)
6. Factious people (Titus 3:8–11)
7. The immoral brother (1 Corinthians 5)[14]

### 1. An accused elder (1 Tim. 5:19–20)

The discipline of an erring elder will be discussed below.

### 2. A sinning brother (Matt. 18:15–20)

The general steps to be taken in the process of church discipline are carried out deliberately, with the goal of restoration.

### 3. An overtaken brother (Gal. 6:1)

Paul writes in Galatians 6:1, "Brethren, even if a man is caught in any trespass, you who are spiritual, restore such a one in a spirit of gentleness; each one looking to yourself, lest you too be tempted." The Greek verb translated "caught" *(prolambanō)* means "to overtake by surprise," or "to overpower before one can escape."[15] Ryrie states:

> This refers to someone tripped up by sin in an unguarded moment, rather than persistent sin. He needs the help of someone mature to readjust his life and make it usable again (the word "restore" is used also in Matt. 4:21, "mending"; Eph. 4:12, "building up"; and 1 Thess. 3:10, "complete").[16]

### 4. An unruly brother (2 Thess. 3:6)

Paul writes, "Now we command you, brethren, in the name of the Lord Jesus Christ, that you keep aloof from every brother who leads an unruly *(ataktōs)* life and not according to the tradition which you received from us" (2 Thess. 3:6). The Greek adverb translated "unruly" is a military term meaning to be out of step or "out of rank."[17] These were those who were not following the "traditions" or authoritative teaching of the apostle Paul (2:15). The context of this passage indicates that these individuals were "leading undisciplined lives, doing no work at all, but acting like busybodies" (3:11). Paul's advice was to cut them off from any support that the church may be bearing. The rule was "if anyone will not work, neither let him eat" (3:10). Rejection of Paul's instruction to these undisciplined individuals should lead to a dissociation with them but with continued admonishment along the way as to a brother (3:14). Constable writes:

> The faithful were not to have social contact with an idle person till he repented. The purpose of this social ostracism was to make the offender feel ashamed ["be put to shame"; NASB] of himself so that he would repent. The design of divine discipline is always to produce repentance, not division. Social pressure can be effective in helping an erring person come to his or her senses. This is exactly what Paul advocated in this case. Ostracism from the body of believers should help such a person be ashamed and feel his separation from fellowship with the Head of the body, Jesus Christ.[18]

### 5. False teachers (Titus 1:10–16)

In 1 Timothy, Paul says he "delivered over to Satan" Alexander and Hymenaeus "so that they may be taught not to blaspheme" (1 Tim. 1:20). He says that they had rejected their "faith and good conscience and suffered shipwreck" (1 Tim. 1:19). Later we see Hymenaeus and Philetus involved in teaching the error "that the resurrection had already taken place" (2 Tim. 2:17–18). Paul says this error had "upset the faith of some." So clearly there are times when discipline needs to be carried out to protect the rest of the flock. Ryrie writes:

While Paul dealt severely with false teachers, he showed considerable patience with people who were misled doctrinally. He did not counsel excommunication for those in Corinth who denied the resurrection; rather he patiently taught them the truth. Presumably if they had then rejected what he taught and in turn promoted heresy he would have disciplined them in some way.[19]

## 6. Factious people (Titus 3:8–11)

It is unfortunate that occasionally there are people who are simply "factious" (*hairetikon*) (Titus 3:10). This Greek word "designates one whom Simpson describes as 'an opinionative propagandist who promotes dissension by his pertinacity.'"[20] This is the person who always has a hidden agenda. Instead of going to the leadership with his dissenting views on side-issues, he spreads them among the brethren and causes division. Paul says "to reject" (*paraiteomai*) such a man. Guthrie says of this term, "It is a vague term (cf. Tim. iv. 7) which does not convey the idea of excommunication, but means merely 'to leave out of account.'"[21] This man should be "rejected" or avoided after a first and second warning (Titus 3:10).

## 7. The immoral brother (1 Cor. 5)

In writing to the Corinthian believers, Paul is outraged by the fact that there is a man in the church who is involved in incest (1 Cor. 5:1). Apparently the man and his father's wife (his stepmother) were living together. Notice, Paul says their reaction should have been one of mourning over such a sin instead of becoming arrogant (5:2). He should immediately be "removed from their midst" (5:2). Paul's prescribed punishment was to "deliver such a one to Satan for the destruction of the flesh" (5:5). This meant they were to exclude him from the fellowship of the church and turn him over to the world, Satan's domain (1 John 5:19). If he continued in his sin, it could result in the destruction of the flesh through sickness or even death (1 Cor. 11:30; 1 John 5:16–17). Paul points out in his discussion that anyone who behaved like that and called himself a Christian is "an immoral person, or covetous, or an idolater, or a reviler, or a drunkard, or a swindler" (1 Cor. 5:11). He is to be cut off from fellowship ("[do not] even . . . eat with such a one").

# Discipline of Elders (1 Tim. 5:19–22)

In Paul's first letter to Timothy, he addresses the process of disciplining an elder. If elders are chosen on the basis of the qualifications given in chapter 3 of this same letter, this disciplining process will not have to be exercised often, but sadly enough, it will be needed occasionally. Paul gives us some brief but important guidelines for this process. First of all, an accusation is not even to be taken into consideration unless it is brought against the elder by "two or three witnesses" (1 Tim. 5:19). This obviously protects against those who may have personal biases against an elder. But when a legitimate complaint is brought against an elder, the natural course of action would be for the other elders to try to re-solve the issue in a discreet fashion and thus restore the brother (Gal. 6:1). If the fellow elder continues to sin, he is to be brought before the entire congregation and rebuked (1 Tim. 5:20).

Paul says that one of the positive results of this discipline is "that all will be fearful of sinning." Obviously, showing that even an elder is not above spiritual correction when needed will have a positive effect on the church. It is always a danger that the elders might be more tolerant of sin in the case of a fellow elder and may overlook things in the elder's life that need to be addressed. But notice that Paul issues a strong warning against this, "I solemnly charge you in the presence of God and of Christ Jesus and of His chosen angels, *to maintain these principles without bias, doing nothing in a spirit of partiality*" (1 Tim. 5:21). Paul's warning in 5:22 may be taken two different ways. Some interpret this to mean that as Timothy's best way to prevent having to discipline an elder is to be careful in his choosing of the elders. In light of the context, a better interpreta-tion might be that Paul was pointing out the need for a period of time when the one who is being disciplined is examined to see if his repentance is genuine. In other words, Paul is warning against immediate restoration, especially since the elders are living examples whom the flock is following. Restoring one who has not repented of his sin may lead to that elder being an example that leads others of the flock into the same sin (1 Tim. 5:22). Guthrie writes:

> It was of utmost importance to safeguard innocent men from false accusation, and as Jewish law required the agreement of two witnesses before a man might be called upon to answer a charge (cf. Dt. xix. 15) so it must be in the church (cf. Mt. xviii. 16; 2 Cor. xiii. 1), especially when *an elder* is implicated. He must be protected against malicious intent; but if there are real grounds for accusation, then disciplinary action should be taken before the whole church (unless *all* here means all the elders). Such action could not fail to have a salutary effect upon the commu-nity (that others also may fear) by drawing attention to the need for Christian purity. The abuse of discipline has often led to a harsh and intolerant spirit, but neglect of it has proved a danger almost as great. When faced with sinning elders a spineless attitude is deplorable.[22]

# Questions for Discussion

1. Why does the Lord discipline His own?
2. Is discipline sometimes painful?
3. What should be the results of discipline?
4. What are some of the first steps in church discipline?
5. What are some of the first examples of discipline in the early church?
6. Can leaders and elders be disciplined? How and when?
7. Discuss whether you feel churches today are over- or under-zealous in discipline.

## Chapter 17

# Building Leadership in the Church

## Introduction

How should churches today prepare mature leadership for tomorrow? Is there really a place for leadership training in the local church setting? What are the biblical patterns for training leaders? And what is there to learn from the New Testament epistles about preparing mature men for such positions of spiritually leading a congregation?

As the church began in the book of Acts, the prominent leadership and teaching ministry in the Jerusalem church was in the hands of the apostles. But because of the growing numbers of widows joining the church, the disciples had to "put in charge" men who would do the work of charity so that the teaching of the Word could continue unhindered (Acts 6:3–4). These servants would later be called deacons.

About nineteen years after Pentecost, elders are suddenly found ministering with the apostles in the church at Jerusalem (15:22). Thirteen years later (A.D. 62), Paul is giving the moral and character qualifications for those men who are becoming the elders/overseers (Titus 1:5–9; 1 Tim. 3:1–7) and deacons (1 Tim. 3:8–13) in the new congregations. By the time all of the apostles are gone, local church leadership will be found mainly in these two offices. But the New Testament seems to give small hints of others serving the churches in both formal and informal ways. Only fragments and small glimpses give any meaningful information.

Most Bible scholars feel it is appropriate today to develop leaders outside of the parameters of Scripture, as long as those functions do not violate what the Bible indicates about leadership. In other words, the churches today are free in a certain pragmatic way to do what has to be done to help the local body do its job. But the scriptural guidelines must be honored first.

# The Many Ministers of Christ

Quite a few passages of Scripture describe an army of servants, beyond the official circle of elders and deacons, carrying out tasks within the local assembly. However, these leaders are overseeing what the servants are doing.

The writer to the Hebrews closes his letter by urging, "Obey your leaders, and submit to them; for they keep watch over your souls" (13:17). Are these "leaders" the elders? The word *leader* is in a participial form from the Greek verb *hēgeomai* and can be translated "the ones who are guiding" your souls. Some argue that the passage is simply referring to the elders. There is strong evidence for this, yet it could also be referring to others such as talented teachers of the Scriptures who are part of the congregation and are assisting the elders/pastors. These seem to be the same as those who are leading the church (v. 7), "who spoke the word of God to you." Saphir writes, "Verses 7 and 17 show that there was a stated ministry, that there were recognized and regular teachers and pastors in the congregation, whose gifts not only, but whose office was acknowledged."[1]

### The Teacher/Readers

Through John the apostle, the Lord Jesus in Revelation addresses the angel *(angelos)* of each church that held a visible position in Asia (Rev. 2–3). Though *angelos* generally refers to an angel, most believe the word in this context should be translated *messenger*. In the early churches "readers" (members who could read and write) were called upon to read aloud the letters to their congregation. These men became the scribes who wrote to other churches, copied incoming letters, and passed the original messages on. After reading the letters aloud, they explained the meaning of spiritual letters and theological treatises before the assembly.

### The Traveling Ministers

There were those in the congregations who were willing to travel for the sake of the ministry. For example, almost eight years before he became a pastor, Titus was used of the apostle Paul as a courier of messages for transferring of charity funds for the church in Jerusalem. Paul writes that God "comforted us by the coming of Titus" (2 Cor. 7:6), and Titus was used to carry the collected charity monies from the churches in Macedonia to Jerusalem (8:1–6).

Traveling with Titus is an unnamed brother in Christ "whose fame in the things of the gospel has spread through all the churches" (8:18). Some believe this fellow Christian is Trophimus, who was appointed by "the churches to travel with us in this gracious work" (v. 19). He must have been a faithful evangelist or teacher of the Word of God. All the churches vouched for his effectiveness.

### The Counseling Ministers

Not in the formal sense, but in a very personal way, the early church was truly a caring society. Second Corinthians 1:3–11 indicates there was extensive counseling taking place both to solve problems and comfort those who were hurting. In this passage Paul points out that God "comforts us in all our affliction with the comfort with which we ourselves are comforted by God" (v. 4). The Greek word for comfort is *paraklēsis* and from its verb form means "to call alongside." The same word is used of the Holy Spirit in which various versions have translated the personal noun form *paraklētos* as "Helper, Advocate, and Comforter" (John 14:26; 15:26). The word *counsel* or *counselor* could also be used to translate *paraklētos*.

Some argue today that only elders or pastors should counsel in the local church environment. But the 2 Corinthians passage seems to indicate that many others in the congregation were used to help those afflicted. The passage speaks of "us in all our affliction," "so that we [all] may be able to comfort," "our suffering," "we are comforted," "we were burdened excessively," "we despaired even of life." By the pronouns "we" and "us" it is clear many were used to counsel those suffering (v. 6). Without a doubt, much of the discouragement came from persecution. Nevertheless, there was a tremendous sharing of encouragement given out by average laymen, even to the apostle Paul.

### The Teaching Ministry

The teaching of the Word seems to have been the number one ministry in the New Testament churches. There were teachers at the church school in Antioch (Acts 13:1–2). Pastor Titus was to teach the older men about doctrine but also about living the Christian life in a moral and sound manner (Titus 2:1–2). And whether formally or informally, older women were to teach the young women about practical issues in the Christian marriage (2:3–5).

In Paul's hall of fame of Christian service (Rom. 16), he has much to say about both men and women serving the churches, even endangering their lives to do so. He speaks of Phoebe as a servant and helper (vv. 1–2), of Priscilla and Aquila as fellow workers (v. 3) who risked their lives for his sake. He references "all the churches of the Gentiles" who likewise "risked their own necks" (v. 4). Paul mentions a Mary who "worked hard" (Greek *kopiaō*, "to struggle, strive") in the gospel, along with many others whom he cited as fellow workers.

Many of these of course were laboring in an informal capacity, i.e., they were simply serving from their heart's desire and held no formal position as elder or deacon. But there had to be leaders-in-training, even if this was carried out in an informal way. More than likely it was done by discipling. The word *disciple* implies "a learner," one who is more than likely learning spiritual leadership by the example of another. In the early church this was done by the apostles, for certain Peter, John, Paul, Barnabas, and others. There was also a clear sense of the need to "pass it on." One will train another by example, who will train another.

## Expectations of Leaders

Besides the qualifications listed in 1 Timothy and Titus, Paul spells out what is expected in practical leadership behavior, as he does in most of his letters. He concentrates his thoughts in the Pastoral letters and appears to focus on elders and pastors. But his words can apply to other leadership roles.

## The Charge to Leadership

What commands does Paul issue to those leading? The ultimate responsibilities for leaders are laid out in the charges made to pastor/elders Timothy and Titus. These important requirements are given first to these younger men but are certainly applicable to those guiding local assemblies today. Beneath the elders are the ranks of evangelists, Sunday school teachers, and youth directors who must be trained and discipled to handle the tough business of dealing with the problems in congregations.

This section will assume that there is a ladder upon which younger dedicated workers must climb in both position and maturity, in order to serve the local body of believers. We will also deal with other directives of the apostle besides the requirements he has already spelled out for the elder (1 Tim. 3:1–7; Titus 1:5–9) and deacon (1 Tim. 3:8–13). Those requirements stand as the standards and the goals for all growing and developing leadership. Below are some, but not all, of Paul's injunctions to leadership:

1. *Instruct certain men not to teach strange doctrines* (1 Tim. 1:3). The apostle "first deals with the disturbers of the faith; they must be stopped. This properly comes first" as an urgent issue for those in leadership positions. Heresy in the local assembly must be addressed.[2] At the same time, leaders and teachers of the Word must not become trapped in futile dialog. Many times in writing to Timothy, Paul urges him not to "wrangle about words, which is useless" (2 Tim. 2:14), and "avoid worldly and empty chatter" (v. 16), because such words lead to "foolish and ignorant speculations, knowing that they produce quarrels" (v. 23).

2. *You may fight the good fight, keeping faith and a good conscience* (1 Tim. 1:18–19). "Faith fitly goes first; for it is this which provides the Christian combatant with his only valid standing-ground for the conflict. But a good conscience is here faith's necessary handmaid."[3] The leader "who would do battle for the truth of God must be responsive in his inmost soul to the claims of divine truth, and render it clear as day that he identifies himself with its interests—is ready, in a manner, to live and die in its behalf."[4]

3. *Let no one look down on your youthfulness, but rather in speech, conduct, love, faith and purity, show yourself an example of those who believe* (1 Tim. 4:12). Timothy had been called to leadership beyond his years. Paul is not concerned now with error and its detection, but with truth and

how it could be commended, for older members often accept a young person as leader only with reluctance.[5]

4. *Give attention to the public reading of Scripture, to exhortation and teaching* (1 Tim. 4:13). Leaders have a great obligation to make certain, no matter what other tasks they are performing, that the Word of God is going forth and that it is applicable to the needs of the flock. There is an unmistakable issue of teaching and understanding the Scriptures. "Thus Paul urges a public ministry that reads the scriptures to the gathered Christians, exhorts them to respond appropriately, and teaches them its principles."[6]

5. *Do not neglect the spiritual gift within you* (1 Tim. 4:14). If one is called to church leadership, he more than likely has an appropriate gift to serve the assembly. The call of God for a leader is "thus recognized by the church, and the approbation of the [elders] expressed by setting him apart to the office, should be regarded by Timothy as a part of the 'gift' or benefit."[7] Barnes notes that the gift is not some mysterious influence, or a "virus," but is a benefit that must be cultivated to the highest degree.[8]

6. *Pay close attention to yourself and to your teaching; persevere in these things* (1 Tim. 4:16). A leader must concentrate on his calling, his gift, his training, and his duties. He must count it a privilege to give forth the depths of God's promise. The Lord has special rewards for His faithful ministers of the Word.

7. *Do not sharply rebuke an older man, but rather appeal to him as a father, to the younger men as brothers, the older women as mothers, and the younger women as sisters, in all purity* (1 Tim. 5:1–2). A church leader has a trying task in dealing continually with different ages and personalities in the congregation. This can be emotionally testing and frustrating. "The wise church ruler must understand how to deal with his people individually. Each age and condition needs separate treatment: old men, young men; old women, young women."[9]

8. *Do not lay hands upon anyone too hastily and thus share responsibility for the sins of others; keep yourself free from sin* (1 Tim. 5:22). Though directly aimed at Timothy in his appointing of other elders, this stands as an important principle for all those rising to the occasion of leadership. The apostle is urging caution until everything is fully in place with these potential leaders. Make sure that these candidates are capable and will become sound, well-informed teachers of God's Word.

9. *Guard what has been entrusted to you, avoiding worldly and empty chatter and the opposing arguments of what is falsely called "knowledge"* (1 Tim. 6:20). Leaders have an obligation to point out error, but they must not become sidetracked and go about answering all false doctrine. They must also teach that which is positive and true. The word *knowledge* (Greek, *gnōseōs*) may refer to the false "sciences" of Paul's day, false doctrine, or pseudonymous knowledge. Today churches are being invaded by New Age

concepts and cultic doctrine. After due warning and exposure, church leaders must teach sound doctrine!

10. *Retain the standard of sound words which you have heard from me* (2 Tim. 1:13). The Greek word *standard* can be translated "model, example, prototype." Paul is urging up-and-coming elder leadership such as Timothy to follow his example in speaking and teaching. "Pay careful attention to the patterns you hear from me and the content of truth I share with others." "This sketch, model, or pattern consisted of the words which he had heard from Paul. Let him hold on to these, ever using them as his example, never departing from them."[10]

11. *Guard, through the Holy Spirit who dwells in us, the treasure which has been entrusted to you* (2 Tim. 1:14). Paul says: "guard, keep, preserve" that "deposit" entrusted to you, Timothy. Most believe that this deposit is the "sound words" mentioned above. Paul exhorts Timothy to guard the good deposit, knowing that the Holy Spiritwill be the one through whom Timothy carries out the exhortation.[11] Elders and leaders are committed to this charge. They are responsible for the preservation of doctrine.

12. *Be strong in the grace that is in Christ Jesus* (2 Tim. 2:1). The Greek word "be strong" is *endynomai*, and carries the idea of "to be capable within." With Timothy being a maturing leader and pastor, Paul is intense and anxious as to how this younger man will behave in his future conduct in the church. But Timothy simply cannot draw on his own personal talents. "Grace here has its simplest theological meaning, as the divine help, the unmerited gift of assistance that comes from God."[12]

13. *And the things which you have heard from me . . . entrust to faithful men, who will be able to teach others also* (2 Tim. 2:2). As was carried out in Antioch, Paul puts in place the concept of a "seminary," a pattern of teaching and training others, who in turn can teach the church. For "growing" leadership, "this has come to be called 'the ministry of multiplication,' and it is God's method for propagating the good news of Jesus Christ."[13]

14. *Suffer hardship with me, as a good soldier of Christ Jesus* (2 Tim. 2:3). Paul emphasizes the strenuous task of perseverance required of leaders, referring to it more than once in 2 Timothy. As a soldier in combat, the apostle pictures a deadly struggle in which the minister "in active service" (v. 4) cannot entangle himself with the affairs of living. He must please the one who enlisted him. He must compete as an athlete seeking a prize (v. 5) or struggle as the hard-working farmer (v. 6). Leaders must prepare to "suffer hardship even to imprisonment as a criminal" (v. 9), following Paul, who "endure all things for the sake of those who are chosen" (v. 10).

15. *Be diligent to present yourself approved to God as a workman who does not need to be ashamed, handling accurately the word of truth* (2 Tim. 2:15). The minister of the Word must know the Word. He must make every effort to

be thoroughly trained and prepared for sharing the truth. If one is called to the position, he is also called to the process of preparation.

16. *Flee from youthful lusts, and pursue righteousness, faith, love and peace, with those who call on the Lord from a pure heart* (2 Tim. 2:22). Leaders, young and old, sometimes must work hard at avoiding temptations, which may be from sexual or monetary enticement. A leader young or old must always be on guard. "Since these inordinate desires often assert themselves more turbulently in youth than in old age—as he grows older a Christian rises above them through the sanctifying grace of the Holy Spirit, bring him gradually to spiritual maturity."[14]

17. *Preach the word; be ready in season and out of season; reprove, rebuke, exhort, with great patience and instruction* (2 Tim. 4:2). Though not knowing when the apostasy would come, Paul had this in mind, for he continues on and writes, "For the time will come when they will not endure sound doctrine" (v. 3). Leaders are to be tenacious with their teaching and preaching, whatever their situation. As a leader, Timothy was "to be right there, namely with the Word, to herald it 'in good season,' when things seem favorable, 'in no season,' when it does not seem seasonable at all."[15]

18. *Speak the things which are fitting for sound doctrine* (Titus 2:1). With the verses that follow, Paul shows leadership the results of "healthy" teaching. It will strengthen older men (v. 2), stabilize older, mature women (v. 3) that they may in turn encourage young women to care for their homes, husbands, and children (vv. 4–5). Teaching will filter down to create sensible younger men (v. 6).

But Paul comes back and reminds Timothy that he must . . .

19. *Show [yourself] to be an example of good deeds, with purity in doctrine* (v. 7). The Greek word *hygia* ("purity") can mean "undamaged, unbroken." Solid doctrine and teaching *must* be coupled with an example of living and of loyal service to Christ. Leaders must be living out truth, with the practice of that truth.

20. *Urge bondslaves to be subject to their own masters, in everything, to be well-pleasing, not argumentative, not pilfering, but showing all good faith that they may adorn the doctrine of God our Savior in every respect* (Titus 2:9–10). Though slavery as seen in the times of the New Testament is not prominent today, some application can be made here to the relationship of employee to employer. Some disagree but it seems plausible to make that connection. Pastors and those leaders working with men's groups need to remind Christian brothers laboring in spiritually disturbing environments that they have a witness to maintain. Sometimes the workplace can be harsh and even unfair in the way Christians are treated. But while in that position, believers in Christ must remember that they represent Him, and what they believe (the doctrine of God) must match up with how they do their job (being well-pleasing).

21. *Remind* [the people] *to be subject to rulers, to authorities, to be obedient, to be ready for every good deed* (Titus 3:1). As an elder and leader, Titus must remind the local church of its image before the culture as a whole, but also before government. "Though Christians are a 'special' people elected by God, redeemed from the world and no longer dependent upon it, they are not above the necessity of getting along with the civil authorities who govern them."[16]
Paul expands this injunction and adds, remind them "to malign no one, to be uncontentious, gentle, showing every consideration for all men" (v. 2).

22. *I want you to speak confidently, so that those who have believed God may be careful to engage in good deeds* (Titus 3:8). The verb "speak confidently" *(diabebaioomai)* in Greek carries the idea of "to confirm, insist."[17] It is related to the verb *bebaioō*. This and other related words speak of "confirmation, being firm, establishing, strengthening."[18] With the prepositional prefix *dia* added, the word here in Titus can be translated "be thoroughly confirming" these things, with the results that the believer in God will be engaging in good works.

Leaders are to speak with strength and determination. They are to "insist" on the truth! Confidence must be their hallmark. Lenski adds, "Titus is to affirm what is sure, what he knows to be so. His own confident assertions are not to rest on his own convictions but on this Word and its real and objective contents."[19]

23. *Reject a factious man after a first and second warning, knowing that such a man is perverted and is sinning, being self-condemned* (Titus 3:10–11). By "factious" the apostle refers to a man who causes divisions or is heretical.[20] Leadership has a great responsibility toward the congregation of believers even to the point of driving them out of the assembly if necessary. Doctrinal purity regarding critical issues must be maintained. Knight writes:

> One can take the radical action of dismissing such a person from the Christian community because the refusal of a "heretical person" to respond to two admonitions gives the grounds for such action and indicates the necessity for it. As in Mt. 18:17, the basis for taking the last difficult step is such a person's self-indictment ("being self-condemned," *autokatakritos*).[21]

## Conclusion

In these pastoral letters, Paul pours out his heart to Timothy and Titus. He continually (1) warns against false doctrine and heretical teachers, (2) urges these men as leaders to instruct and exhort the saints, and (3) instructs and encourages these men as leader/teachers to be tenacious in their calling, realizing that it will be a continual struggle against error and sinful personalities. Finally, (4) he reminds Timothy of a future apostasy that will be a horrible period in which "religion" will prevail but spiritual truth will all but vanish. In a positive note to Titus, (5) the apostle reminds him of the grace of God that brought salvation to all (2:11) but that also leads us to be "looking for the blessed hope and the appearing of the glory of our great God and Savior, Christ Jesus" (v. 13).

Despite all the efforts through the centuries of those who love the Lord and in the human sense lead the church, a departure will take place! And only the Rapture will spare those remaining from the terror of the wrath of God. Church leadership must warn and teach, but also proclaim the hope of the return of Christ.

# A Model for Building Church Leadership

### *Leadership Training*

How should church leaders be trained today? Since the body of Christ does not know the day or the hour of His Coming, believers must continue to serve until that glorious event takes place. And future leadership must continue to be in training. Below are some prudent and practical guidelines to build leadership. These principles are based on Scripture. But where the Bible does not speak as to the details of how to prepare men for serving as deacons and elders/pastors, there can be room for innovation and for training programs that work. Some may wish to adjust what is given below to fit their own local church circumstances.

For those engaged in Sunday school or evangelistic work, an ongoing study program should be put into place. This would also include young men who may be called in the future to be deacons in the assembly. How should they be selected as Sunday school leaders and teachers?

1. Of course, they first should be those who can profess a personal faith in Christ as Savior.
2. They should not be new converts. At least several years should pass after their conversion before they are allowed to be teachers of the Word and leaders.
3. They should agree with the doctrinal statement of the church.
4. Their lives should progressively be maturing and moving in the direction of Paul's guidelines for elders (1 Tim. 3:1–7; Titus 1:5–9) and deacons (1 Tim. 3:8–13).
5. They should understand Paul's additional directives for leadership as listed above.
6. They should be in agreement with certain demands of discipline as laid down by the teaching elders. Though these directives may not be biblical, they are seen as important by the present leadership. And those coming up in the ranks must respect this. These guidelines are to be prudent and wise

so that any future leader can agree to them. For example, leadership will support the teaching ministry of the church, be on time as a teacher, attend training sessions, etc. They should show some direct and personal concern for those they teach. They should contact their students if they are absent or sick.

7. They should show discipline in study habits and teaching preparation. There should be some teaching talent shown but more importantly, the teacher should have a heart for the Lord, a thirst for His Word, and exhibit an enthusiasm for sharing His truths. These issues should come before talent.

Leadership training should include (by monthly church classes or attendance at a conservative Bible school) courses in:

1. **Hermeneutics and inductive Bible study** (issues in interpretation and personal Bible study). Suggested texts are:

   Zuck, Roy B. *Basic Bible Interpretation: A Practical Guide to Discovering Biblical Truth*. Wheaton, Ill.: Victor, 1991.
   Ramm, Bernard. *Protestant Biblical Interpretation*. Grand Rapids: Baker, 1970.

2. **Personal discipleship.** Texts to consult:

   Penney, Russell L. *Equipping the Saints: The Basics—Division I*. Ft. Worth, Tex.: Tyndale Biblical Institute, 1996.
   Penney, Russell L. *Equipping the Saints: Basic Bible Knowledge—Division II*. Ft. Worth, Tex.: Tyndale Biblical Institute, 1997.

3. **Basic evangelical and conservative doctrinal study.** Recommended text:

   Chafer, L. S. *Major Bible Themes*, rev. John F. Walvoord. Grand Rapids: Zondervan, 1974.

4. **Principles for the Christian home.** Leadership should be aware of the problems that can arise in the family. The issues of raising children, the roles of husband/father and wife/mother must be continually stressed. Many fine books are available in these subject areas.

5. **Evangelism.** Leaders should practice evangelism when possible. They should know the issues and major verses of Scripture for personal witness. As well, they should be sharing these in their training classes or Sunday

school sessions. There is a variety of evangelism-training literature available for this purpose. See for example:

Story, Dan. *Engaging the Closed Minded: Presenting Your Faith to the Confirmed Unbeliever.* Grand Rapids: Kregel, 1999.
Moyer, Larry. *Larry Moyer's How-To Book on Personal Evangelism.* Grand Rapids: Kregel, 1998.

## Appointing Deacons and Elders

In selecting deacons and elders, what one striking quality stands out? When the time comes, those men who have been faithful in the ministries given them will become obvious and they will form a pool of mature men for potential leadership. Meanwhile, they "stand and wait" until called of the Lord, through circumstances, to move up in responsibility. It only makes sense that one would take a position of deacon before becoming an elder/pastor. If one is faithful and demonstrates maturity in that office, it seems right that he would someday become an elder.

Though they may have bypassed the role of deacon, it seems clear from Scripture that Titus and Timothy served an apprenticeship under Paul before taking on the office of pastor. The apostle writes of Titus having "previously made a beginning" of gracious work for the saints (2 Cor. 8:6) and having earlier given himself to ministering for the Lord and serving under Paul by the will of God (v. 5). Titus traveled for Paul as a comfort to others and as a faithful servant (7:13–14) and was called by Paul "my brother" (2:13), "my partner and fellow worker" for ministering to the church at Corinth (8:23).

Along with Paul, Timothy had preached the Son of God to the local assembly at Corinth (2 Cor. 1:19), had joined the apostle in writing to that congregation (1:1), and had traveled often to that body of believers at Paul's request, in doing the "Lord's work" (1 Cor. 16:10). Thus, one of the final most important principles of leadership: discipling and mentoring a younger brother as to how to serve Christ.

A great part of that leadership training is imitating the godly and spiritual qualities of those presently leading. Paul urges the carnal church at Corinth to imitate him (1 Cor. 4:16, 11:1), and he called on the Ephesian congregation to imitate God (Eph. 5:1). He also mentions that the church at Thessalonica imitated him and other disciples and the Lord also, "having received the word in much tribulation with the joy of the Holy Spirit" (1 Thess. 1:6).

Finally, the greatest compliment that can be given to leaders is that those coming up behind them learned great spiritual truths by simply watching how they lived their Christian walk before the world.

# Questions for Discussion

1. List the kinds of ministries we see in the New Testament.
2. Is it all right to have other ministries besides those listed in Scripture?
3. Looking at the instructions and guidelines for leaders in this chapter, do we take leadership as seriously as we should?
4. Is it possible that today churches are too "democratic" to properly respect and follow biblically mandated leadership? Discuss.
5. Discuss the seven guidelines for leaders today. Should there be additional issues addressed along with these?
6. In your opinion, what one or two characteristics really stand out that indicate one is truly a spiritual leader?

# Chapter 18

# Missions

## Introduction: The Mission of the Church

> Christian missions make sense only in the light of an existing
> abnormality or emergency and in the conviction that an answer
> to and remedy for such a malady is available. . . . The emer-
> gency is the fact of *sin* in the world which has overpowered and
> infected the human race and which threatens the very existence
> of mankind. There would be no need for Christian missions if
> sin were not a serious reality. Neither would the doctrine of
> soteriology make sense without the presence and awfulness
> of sin. Sin made salvation necessary and sin makes Christian
> missions necessary.[1]

To understand the Christian mission one must start with the character of the
Almighty. God's holiness and justice seen against the sinful state of humankind
set the stage for understanding God's redemptive work through the sacrifice of
His Son. Because God is holy He cannot have a relationship with sinful human
beings unless their sin is dealt with first. In light of this, God provided from the
foundation of the world His Son as a substitute for the sins of the world (Acts 2:23;
John 3:16). Although the plan of God was conceived outside of time, the fruition
of the substitution occurred in time. Thus, although men have always been saved
on the basis of the shed blood of Christ and have had a limited understanding of
the Redeemer, it was not until the crucifixion that this became the unique content
of their faith. Until then men were saved by grace on the basis of their faith in
God and were credited with righteousness on the basis of the death of Christ (for
example, Abraham, Gen. 15:6). But only after the death, burial, and resurrection
of Christ did this become the central content of the gospel message that the
church proclaims (1 Cor. 15:3–4).

Thus, the mission of the church is to proclaim the gospel of the death, burial, and resurrection of Jesus Christ, God's Son, until He returns.

## Is the Great Commission Directed to the Church?

Some dispensationalists have argued that the Great Commission given in the Gospels (Matt. 28:18–20; Mark 16:15; Luke 24:44–49) is not given to the church, especially since the church was not established until the coming of the Holy Spirit in Acts 2. It is agreed that the birth of the church did not come until the advent of the Holy Spirit. This is confirmed by the fact that the body is created by the Holy Spirit's ministry of "baptizing" or placing each member "in Christ's body—the church" (1 Cor. 12:12–13). This ministry of Spirit Baptism did not commence until the coming of the Holy Spirit at Pentecost (Acts 1:5; 2:1–4; 11:15–16). Thus, the church was not formed until Acts 2.

At the same time it must be admitted that although technically the dispensation of grace (or the church) had not yet commenced, the program of God had already changed focus from the nation of Israel to the nations as a whole. This is evident in contrasting the Great Commission as given in Matthew 28:18–20; Mark 16:15; Luke 24:44–49; John 21:15–17; and Acts 1:8 with Christ's previous commission to the disciples in Matthew 10:5–7. In the former passages they are to take the message of the gospel of the death, burial, and resurrection of Christ (1 Cor. 15:3–4). The outreach is to all the world. In the latter passage the content of the gospel is to prepare for the kingdom by recognizing Christ as the King. The limit of the proclamation is the nation of Israel.

The period after Christ's resurrection and before His ascension was a transitory time between the two dispensations of law and grace. Christ gave His disciples needed encouragement and instruction for their tremendous task of proclaiming His death, burial, and resurrection to the world. Although the twelve disciples were first given the commission to take the gospel of the kingdom to the nation of Israel (Matt. 10:5–7), when the nation rejected the kingdom and their King (Matt. 21; The Triumphal Entry, esp. 21:43; also Matt. 23:37–39), they became the foundation of the church (Eph. 2:20).

Thus Enns, a dispensationalist, writes:

> The foundational command for evangelism in the world is Matthew 28:18–20. The work of the church in the world is to make disciples (learners), baptize them, and bring them into the fellowship of believers. The ministry of evangelism was not carried on by a select few but by ordinary believers as well (Acts 8:4). The central message the early church proclaimed was Christ (Acts 8:5, 12, 35; 9:20; 11:20); moreover, they took the message beyond the Jewish boundary, crossing previously rigid cultural barriers (Acts 2:41; 4:4; 5:14; 6:1; 8:12; 10:48; 11:24; 13:48; 14:1, 21).[2]

Lightner, another dispensationalist, states:

> In broad outline Christ's great commission sets forth the answer
> to the question, Why does the church exist? The evangelization
> of the lost is a major responsibility of the church (Matt. 28:19).
> "Go ye therefore and teach all nations" [KJV] is better translated,
> "Go therefore and make disciples of all nations" [NASB].[3]

# The Great Commission (Matt. 28:18–20)

## *The Authority of the Commission (Matt. 28:18)*
Jesus stated, "All authority has been given to Me in heaven and on earth."
This statement that preceded Christ's commission was of incredible value. At
this point, some of the disciples were "still doubtful" (28:17). In light of this,
Christ's words in verse 18 are extremely important.

## *The Content of the Commission (28:19–20a)*
Christ's command is, "*Go* therefore and *make disciples* of all the nations, baptizing them in the name of the Father and the Son and the Holy Spirit, teaching
them all that I commanded you." His first command is to "go." Although Matthew
uses an aorist participle here instead of an imperative, many Greek grammarians
believe that this is a rare case of a participle being used to issue a command.[4] Christ
meant for His church to be an aggressive, outgoing organism that saw their goal as
proclaiming the gospel "to the remotest parts of the earth" (Acts 1:8).

We should note, though, that the main verb in the commission is "to make
disciples." This Greek verb is *mathēteuō* and the noun form is *mathētēs,* which
can be translated "disciple," "learner," or "adherent"[5] in the New Testament. Bauer
indicates that the verb means, "to make a disciple of, or [to] teach [someone]."[6]
Thus, the disciples were commanded to go and make disciples. But how were
they to carry out this command? Christ was clear about how to accomplish this
task. He followed this imperative with two modal participles (sometimes referred to as "participles of manner"). A modal participle "signif[ies] the manner
in which the action of the main verb is accomplished."[7] Thus, the making of
disciples involves "baptizing" and "teaching." Barbieri writes:

> Their field was to include all nations, not just Israel. They were
> to make disciples by proclaiming the truth concerning Jesus.
> Their hearers were to be evangelized and enlisted in Jesus' fol-
> lowers. Those who believed were to be baptized in water in the
> name of the Father and of the Son and of the Holy Spirit. Such
> an act would associate a believer with the person of Jesus Christ
> and with the Triune God. . . . Those who respond are also to be

taught the truths Jesus had specifically communicated to the Eleven. Not all that Jesus taught the disciples was communicated by them but they did teach specific truths for the new church age as they went abroad.[8]

The disciples were not only to teach the facts of what Christ had taught them to new converts, but they were also to teach them "to observe" all these things. The Greek term *(tērein)* used here can be translated "to guard" or "to keep."[9] Thus, the intent of the command was to make disciples by teaching them by word as well as deed. This is the pattern that Christ left us in the Gospels through His own disciples.

### The Support of the Commission

As we have seen, we are to make disciples by leading them to faith in Christ (baptizing)[10] and by teaching them to observe doctrinal truth (teaching). But the question that the disciples may have been asking at this critical point is, "How can a tiny band of followers have any hope of fulfilling such a overwhelming task?" Christ states, "And lo *(idou),* I am with you always, even to the end of the age." In light of the doubts the disciples had, Christ assures them that He will be with them. The Greek particle *idou,* translated "lo" in the NASB, is a demonstrative particle which has no exact English equivalent. It is often used to "emphasize the size or importance of something."[11] A good English translation of this last phrase might be, "and *look,* I am with you every day, until the completion of the age!" This would assure them that they were not alone in this endeavor, but the One with all authority in heaven and on earth (28:18) would be walking with them every day until the completion of the age—thus the completion of their task (28:20).

# The Pattern of Missions in the Early Church

One might ask, "Why study the pattern of missions in the early church in a book setting forth a practical strategy of missions for today?" Tucker, in her book *From Jerusalem to Irian Jaya,* writes:

> Paul's extraordinary accomplishments in the field of missions have prompted a number of missiologists to argue that his methods should be closely, if not precisely, emulated today. . . . It is difficult to overemphasize the significance of the apostle Paul in laying a pattern for effectively reaching the lost, and *to a degree the successes or failures of missionary work since can be attributed in part to the adherence to or deviation from his own personal example and the general guidelines that he set forth.*[12] (italics added)

Thus, let us look at the "missions strategy" of the early church.

## Dissemination of the Gospel from Jerusalem

Fifty days after the Jewish Passover and the crucifixion of our Lord, as the Jews celebrated the feast of Pentecost, the church was born. The coming of the Holy Spirit on the day of Pentecost inaugurated His ministry of baptism. He began to take believers and place them into the body of Christ (1 Cor. 12:12–13), creating the church. The dissemination of the gospel on this birthday of the church was *centripetal* (the people came to the proclaimer), as it was primarily in the Old Testament. On the day of Pentecost the crowd included Parthians, Medes, and Elamites, residents of Mesopotamia, Judea, and Cappadocia, Pontus and Asia, Phrygia and Pamphylia, Egypt and the districts of Libya around Cyrene, as well as visitors from Rome, Cretans, and Arabs. Although from their viewpoint they had come to celebrate the Jewish feast of Pentecost, from God's viewpoint they were there to see and hear the manifestations of the Holy Spirit and to hear the proclamation of the gospel message by Peter. Many of these took back with them the gospel to their own section of the Roman Empire.

But it took persecution and the stoning of Stephen for the thrust of the gospel to go beyond Jerusalem and to become more *centrifugal* (blasting the proclaimer toward the unreached). When believers scattered to the surrounding regions, Philip took the gospel to the Samaritans (Acts 8:5–25) and the Ethiopian eunuch (vv. 26–40). Although the events at Pentecost and Philip's evangelism resulted in growth and a dissemination of the gospel, neither were technically "missions" (a result of zeal to carry out Christ's commission). One wonders how much dissemination beyond Judaism would have occurred had God not scattered the believers through persecution. Thus, although it was Philip who showed the first real zeal for evangelism, Paul and Barnabas were the first called into full-fledged missionary activity (13:2). They give the divine pattern for that activity.

## Missions from Antioch

It was not long after the stoning of Stephen that the scattered believers made their way to Antioch (Acts 11:19). There a large church was established and time was spent to ground them in the faith (vv. 20–26). The center of missionary activity soon shifted to this growing church in Syria. We will look at a few important principles of this evangelistic work.

Paul's missionary activity began when he and Barnabas were chosen by God and set apart by the leadership of the Antiochian church (13:2). The *first* principle we see is that the *leadership* recognized those that God had chosen to be sent out. *Second,* it should be noted that those who were sent were not among the "least" qualified from the church but two of the "most" qualified. Paul and Barnabas undoubtedly exhibited spiritual maturity, a must for the missionary going to represent Christ on the field. Does this not make sense in light of the main task of the missionary to baptize, teach, and establish leaders in new churches?

A *third* key principle is that Paul and company, in approaching the evangelization of an area, primarily considered the province rather than the city. Roland Allen writes:

> Both St. Luke and St. Paul speak constantly of the provinces rather than the cities. Thus St. Paul was forbidden to preach the word in Asia [Acts 16:6], he was called from Troas not to Philippi, or to Thessalonica, but to Macedonia [Acts 16:9–10, cf. Acts 18:5, 19:22; 2 Cor. 1:16, 2:13, 7:5, Phil. 4:15, etc.]. Speaking of the collection for the saints at Jerusalem St. Paul says that he boasted that Achaia was ready a year ago [2 Cor. 9:2]. The suggestion is that in St. Paul's view the *unit* was the province rather than the city.[13] (italics added)

The *fourth* principle is that evangelism moved from urban centers outward. Allen writes:

> St. Paul's theory of evangelizing a province was not to preach in every place in it himself, but to establish centres of Christian life in two or three important places from which the knowledge might spread into the country round. . . . [Thus Paul] intended his congregation to become at once a centre of light.[14]

Allen points out that Paul's strategy was to evangelize a province by evangelizing the important cities of the province, the centers of commerce and trade. "[As well], through some of them the commerce of the world passed. They were the great marts where the *material* and *intellectual* wealth of the world was exchanged" (italics added).[15] Although this is an important principle, it is not an end in itself. This strategy has failed frequently because another important principle was neglected: The *fifth* principle is that the gospel must be proclaimed in a way that the one who receives it can both understand and personally proclaim. The message must be entrusted to him for that purpose. "Concentrated missions, at strategic centres, if they are to win the province, must be centres of evangelistic life."[16]

Finally, the *sixth* broad principle is the converts must be taught. We are reminded of the command in the Great Commission we studied earlier, ". . . and teaching them all that I commanded you." The disciples were not only to teach the facts of what Christ had taught them to new converts, but they were also to teach them "to observe" all these things. As stated before, the Greek term *(tērein)* used here can be translated "to guard" or "to keep."[17] Thus, the intent of the command was to make disciples by teaching them by word as well as deed. This is the pattern that Christ left us in the Gospels with His own disciples. A stern warning must be given here, for it is here where many missionary efforts fail. The missionary must impart truth by teaching the converts through word and deed and pushing them to take responsibility for their own ministry. Allen comments:

> St. Paul did not go about as a missionary preacher merely to convert individuals: he went to establish churches from which the light might radiate throughout the whole country round. The secret of success in this work lies in beginning at the very beginning. *It is the training of the first convert which sets the type for the future.* If the first converts are taught to depend upon the missionary, if all work, evangelistic, educational, social is concentrated in his hands, the infant community learns to rest passively upon the man from whom they receive their first insight into the Gospel. Their faith having no sphere for its growth and development lies dormant. A tradition very rapidly grows up that nothing can be done without the authority and guidance of the missionary, the people wait for him to move, and the longer they do so, the more incapable they become of any independent action. Thus the leader is confirmed in the habit of gathering all authority in to his hands, and of despising the powers of his people, until he makes their inactivity an excuse for denying their capacity. The fatal mistake has been made of teaching the converts to rely upon the wrong source of strength. Instead of seeking it in the working of the Holy Spirit in themselves, they seek it in the missionary. They put him in the place of Christ, they depend upon him.[18] (emphasis added)

Missionaries who understand this fact spend much time training and equipping the new converts to be able to evangelize and teach (make disciples of) their own people. Paul, on his first missionary journey, was able to establish elders who could care for a congregation. He taught them how to evangelize and teach the others in that province (Acts 14:23). This was accomplished, according to Ramsey, in as brief a time as five to six months.[19] In many of these congregations Paul's involvement from that point on amounted to personal letters, which passed along further instruction and addressed specific local issues. Paul's methods were so effective in his own estimation that,

> Ten years after his first start from Antioch, he told the Romans that he had "fully preached the Gospel of Christ from Jerusalem and round about Illyricum," and that he had "no more place in these parts."[20]

## Summary of Principles

These broad principles can be summarized:

1. Leaders recognized those God had chosen to be sent out.
2. Those who were sent were not among the "least" qualified from the church; rather they were two of the "most" qualified.
3. In approaching the evangelization of an area, Paul and company considered the province rather than the city.
4. The goal was to evangelize a province state, region by establishing centers of Christian life in two or three important places, from which knowledge might spread. The gospel, then, would most effectively be proclaimed by the native peoples of the province.
5. The gospel was proclaimed in a way understandable to the region, so that the one receiving it could understand it and understand how to proclaim it. "Concentrated missions, at strategic centres, if they are to win the province, must be centres of evangelistic life."[21]
6. Missionaries made disciples of the nationals in order to equip them to take over responsibility for evangelizing and teaching. Indigenous Christians become a light that radiates throughout the whole country. Their dependence is on Christ, not on individual missionaries or sending bodies.

## Guidelines for the Local Church

From the above principles, we might establish some guidelines for the local church to use in choosing and commissioning missionaries from their flock. In light of the first two principles, leaders of the church are central to this process, assuming they have been appointed on the basis of biblical standards and are among the most spiritually mature (1 Timothy 3). They should be the ones who recognize those qualified for the mission field.

Being among the most spiritually mature, these men should be able to discern if a person's life reflects the Christian maturity and scriptural knowledge and wisdom needed for effective missionary service. If the prospective missionary has shown this maturity, knowledge, and wisdom in his life and service in that local body, then he is a worthy candidate. Generally, it will be the missionary who will feel the desire to go to the mission field. At this point, it is a good idea to send that prospective missionary on several short-term mission trips. This will help him confirm whether this is really God's leading.

In light of the fact that the *most* qualified are the ones God used in the early church, the missionary being sent out should have the discipleship skills needed to proclaim the gospel and establish someone in the faith. This implies considerable theological training. This training may be formal or informal, but it is essential to success on the field. A final note on this point of theological education. This author realizes in the complexity of modern-day missions there are places in mission agencies for non-theologically trained support workers. Today, anyone who has a heart for missions, from a mechanic to a computer programmer, may benefit the frontline missionary as a support worker. Here we are dealing with the frontline missionary who is in a key position to reach unreached peoples and plant churches as Paul did.

The final four principles deal with work on the field. In approaching the mission of creating disciples, one must remember Paul's strategy of looking at a province. In practical terms this would mean approaching a state, region, district, or in some cases a particular people group. Once this is decided, the strategic points of trade and commerce, as well as the place of intellectual wealth, should be the target. The goal must be to make disciples here by baptizing as well as teaching, and it must be done in a way that the new converts understand that the gospel is a deposit that must be shared. The gospel is entrusted to them for that purpose.

Although space has allowed for only a brief discussion of missionary principles and strategy, these are the foundational principles that if overlooked will bring frustration and disaster to many missionaries and missionary endeavors. Too many times the church has overlooked these divinely ordained principles, saying that they are simply *descriptive* of Paul's journeys and not necessarily *prescriptive* for today. This author believes that history shows those who took them *prescriptively* made the wiser choice.

# Financial Support of Missionaries

In light of the fact that the church is commissioned to "go and make disciples," it is important that we understand what the Bible teaches about the church's responsibility to support the missionaries they send out. This is especially true in light of the different ways various groups approach this element of missions.

### *Avenues of Support for God's Servants*

Let us first look at a typical "faith mission" financial policy for wisdom in the handling of finances. Since every mission is a bit different, we will check the accuracy according to Scripture of this example, the financial policy statement of International Teams, a faith mission with headquarters in Prospect Heights, Illinois.

1. Never go into debt.
2. Stop ministries rather than go into financial deficit.
3. Give generously to others.
4. Strive for excellence without extravagance.
5. Take deliberate steps of faith.
6. Make specific needs known and ask for response.
   - Don't pressure.
   - Don't plead.
   - Don't beg.
7. Believe spiritual coldness hampers support raising.
8. Don't lock into any one method just because it works.[22]

To approach an understanding of the biblical soundness of this typical "faith mission" approach, let us take a look at the Scripture, which broadly presents two approaches to financial support. They are:

1. God's full-time servants are supported by those who directly benefit from their ministry.
2. God's full-time servants are supported by those who believe in them and who desire to be colaborers with them through financial giving.

## Support by Those Who Receive the Benefit

### The Old Testament Principle
This is a principle that we see throughout Scripture. The Old Testament pattern is seen as early as Numbers 18:21–24:

> And to the sons of Levi, behold, I have given all the tithe in Israel for an inheritance, in return for their service which they perform, the service of the tent of meeting. And the sons of Israel shall not come near the tent of meeting again, lest they bear sin and die. Only the Levites shall perform the service of the tent of meeting, and they shall bear their iniquity; it shall be a perpetual statute throughout your generations, and among the sons of Israel they shall have no inheritance. For the tithe of the sons of Israel, which they offer as an offering to the Lord, I have given to the Levites for an inheritance; therefore I have said concerning them, "They shall have no inheritance among the sons of Israel."

As we see, early on God established the principle that those who rendered full-time service for Him on behalf of others were to be supported by those who received the benefit. Among the nation of Israel the Levites were given no inheritance in the land, they were to receive the tithe. It was to sustain them "in return for their service which they perform" (Num. 18:21).

### The New Testament Principle
This same principle continues into the New Testament as we see in Jesus' ministry, as characterized in Luke 8:1–3:

> And it came about soon afterwards, that He [Christ] began going about from one city and village to another, proclaiming and preaching the kingdom of God; and the twelve were with Him, and also some women who had been healed of evil spirits and

*sicknesses: Mary who was called Magdalene, from whom seven
demons had gone out, and Joanna the wife of Chuza, Herod's
steward, and Susanna, and many others who were contributing
to their support out of their private means.*

During Christ's ministry He allowed others to provide *physically* and *materially* for His needs. He was not embarrassed to receive support from others, whether goods, possessions, or property. We also read, "and the twelve were with Him." So as Jesus and the twelve apostles were involved in full-time ministry, they were provided for by those to whom they were ministering. When the Twelve were sent out by Jesus we read in Matthew 10:5–10:

*These twelve Jesus sent out after instructing them, saying, "Do
not go in the way of the Gentiles, and do not enter any city of the
Samaritans; but rather go to the lost sheep of the house of
Israel. And as you go, preach, saying, 'The kingdom of heaven
is at hand.' Heal the sick, raise the dead, cleanse the lepers, cast
out demons; freely you received, freely give. Do not acquire gold,
or silver, or copper for your money belts, or a bag for your journey, or even two tunics, or sandals, or a staff; for the worker is
worthy of his support."*

Jesus specifically told these missionaries not to take anything with them, but to depend on the support of those to whom they ministered. He states the principle: "For the worker is worthy of his support." We see the same principle in passages such as Galatians 6:6–10 where we read, "Let the one who is taught the word share all good things with him who teaches." Paul tells Timothy in 1 Timothy 5:17–18:

*Let the elders who rule well be considered worthy of double
honor, especially those who work hard at preaching and teaching. For the Scripture says, "You shall not muzzle the ox while
he is threshing," and "The laborer is worthy of his wages."*

Here Paul quotes Deuteronomy 25:4 and Luke 10:7 showing that the principle spans dispensational distinctions. This support clearly shows the biblical pattern stated above, that being: God's full-time servants are supported by those who directly benefit from their ministry.

### *Support by Co-Laborers*
Normally the principle of the ministered-to providing for the ministerers does not work very well on the cross-cultural mission field. So, where does a

missionary to a foreign properly go for support? Is there precedent for raising support among Christians back home who believe in and desire to colabor with those on the mission field? In Philippians 4:15–20 we read:

> And you yourselves also know, Philippians, that at the first preaching of the gospel, after I departed from Macedonia, no church shared with me in the matter of giving and receiving but you alone; for even in Thessalonica you sent a gift more than once for my needs. Not that I seek the gift itself, but I seek for the profit which increases to your account. But I have received everything in full, and have an abundance; I am amply supplied, having received from Epaphroditus what you have sent, a fragrant aroma, an acceptable sacrifice, well-pleasing to God. And my God shall supply all your needs according to His riches in glory in Christ Jesus. Now to our God and Father be the glory forever and ever. Amen.

It is clear from this passage in Paul's letter to the Philippians that they "colabored" with him by sharing materially with him as he ministered to others (i.e., the church in Thessalonica). Here we have a much closer pattern to what we see today in faith missions, where God's full-time servants (Paul and his companions) are supported by those who believe in them and desire to be colaborers with them through financial giving.

### Missionaries Should Ask for a Response

Many missionaries struggle with allowing their needs to be known and then asking for a response. In fact, there are mission agencies that teach this is unscriptural and that we need simply to pray and trust God. Their desire in doing this is to honor God, but what does Scripture teach us about the pattern of Paul? In 2 Corinthians 1:15–16, Paul relates:

> And in this confidence I intended at first to come to you, that you might twice receive a blessing; that is, to pass your way into Macedonia, and again from Macedonia to come to you, and by you to be helped on my journey to Judea.

Here Paul mentions to the Corinthians that one reason for his passing through Corinth on the way to Judea was to "by you be helped on my journey to Judea." The Greek infinitive *propemphthēnai,* here translated "helped on my journey," means "to outfit for a trip."[23] So Paul is voicing his desire for them to help him out materially in his ministry. He is clearly letting them know that he has a financial need in his ministry and that he desires them to help him with it. In a similar way, Paul lets the Roman church know he has a need and wished them to help meet that need in his letter to that church. In Romans 15:24 we read:

> *. . . whenever I go to Spain—for I hope to see you in passing, and to be helped on my way there by you, when I have first enjoyed your company for a while.*

Here again Paul uses the same Greek infinitive which expresses purpose. The word is *propemphthēnai* from the verb *propempō,* which means according to Bauer, "[to] *help on one's journey* with food, money, by arranging for companions, [and] means of travel, etc."[24] In this case it is a church Paul had never even visited although he did know many of its members (Rom. 16:3–16). Thus, Paul makes specific needs known, but nowhere does he make specific *amounts* known in his appeals.

## Support for Missionaries Summary

So we have established the following from Scripture:

1. God's full-time servants are supported by those who directly benefit from their ministry.
2. God's full-time servants are supported by those who believe in them and desire to be colaborers with them through financial giving.
3. God's full-time servants let believers know about their needs and directly ask them to help meet those needs.

We believe that faith missions, such as the one we listed above, are biblically sound as they "make specific needs known and ask for a response."

## Conclusion

The church of Jesus Christ has been called to make disciples by going to all nations, baptizing and teaching all those who come to Him. The leadership of churches should be commissioning, training, and sending out those who feel a desire to go to the mission field and show the Christian maturity, knowledge, and wisdom to be effective on the mission field. The apostle Paul's divinely ordained strategy was to evangelize provinces by establishing churches in the major cities of material and intellectual wealth. These then became centers of light to the surrounding countryside. He did this not just by teaching the converts but by imparting the ministry to them in a way they understood the "how to" of making disciples themselves. As well, they understood that it was their responsibility to impart the same message and skills to others. Paul and his companions were supported by those who directly benefited from their ministry, as well as those who desired to be colaborers with him in his missionary work. Paul, like Christ, was not embarrassed to let his needs be known and communicate his desire that certain saints share in meeting his needs. As history has shown, those who have followed these principles have by their success testified of their validity as time-tested principles, which are effective even today.

## Some Practical Suggestions

### General Suggestions

1. Churches should keep the need for foreign missionaries ever before the people. This helps remind them that our command to make disciples is to "all nations." The church that does this is constantly reminded of God's bigger program and is less apt to become ingrown and have the goal of just "building a bigger local church." Some ways to accomplish this objective would include:
   a. Missionary newsletter display board
   b. Missions sermons
   c. Publications (missions books, "Operation World," etc.)
   d. Missions Sundays
2. Local churches need to make it a practice to have missionaries speak on a regular basis. This should include home and foreign missionaries.
3. Local churches should strive to have a significant percentage of their budget committed to missions work beyond their local work.
4. Local churches should only be commissioning missionaries who exhibit spiritual maturity and possess the biblical wisdom and knowledge to be effective on the field. The leadership should make sure that those who express a desire to serve on the mission field:
   a. Are active and effective in their local church
   b. Exhibit Spirit-filled lives (show spiritual maturity; a passion for holiness, Eph. 5:18; Gal. 5:22–23)
   c. Have a good grasp of the Scriptures (This demands some theological training either within the church or at a Bible school or seminary. Since most local churches cannot provide the quality of training that a Bible school or seminary can give, the latter would normally be the best option.)

### Requirements for Long-Term Missionaries

1. Spiritual maturity (Eph. 5:18; Gal. 5:22–23; 2 Peter 1:4–9)
2. Doctrinal proficiency (2 Tim. 2:15; Titus 1:9)
3. An understanding of biblical missions strategy
4. Training in language acquisition
5. Financial commitment from the church

### *Requirements for Short-Term Missionaries*

1. Doctrinal proficiency (2 Tim. 2:15; Titus 1:9)
2. An understanding of the clearly defined goals and training to meet those goals
3. An understanding of the differences in their culture and the host culture (This involves information that can be obtained from missionaries already on the field or from the State Department. Be culturally sensitive for the sake of the gospel [1 Cor. 9:19–23].)
4. Use of simple sentences, avoiding idioms or figures of speech that an interpreter will find difficult to translate (this makes for a smoother presentation when teaching and sharing the gospel and goes a long way toward preventing possible misunderstandings.)
5. Humility (The missionary goes as a servant, not a master.)

# Questions for Discussion

1. Is missions really a responsibility for the church?
2. Summarize the main issues set forth in the Great Commission.
3. How did the early church carry out the commandment to evangelize?
4. Is missions simply evangelization or is it also discipleship? Discuss.
5. Discuss the six important principles for missionaries listed in this chapter. What other principles may be added?
6. In your opinion, why is mission support often neglected or downplayed?
7. In your own opinion, how could missions strategy be improved and made more important in the thinking of the church?

# Chapter 19

# Pastoral Care

## Pastoral Care in the Local Church

In the decades to come, the modern Church Growth Movement and the megachurch concept could easily destroy the most essential work of the elders/pastors. Everywhere there are signs that evangelical Christians have adopted the view that "bigger is better." Also, many have come to believe that the local church must have a Madison Avenue appeal to attract the "boomers." Thus, to accommodate a younger mindset and integrate biblical truth with cultural marketing methods, true biblical pastoral ministries are in danger of disappearing.

No one is suggesting that a local church cannot be contemporary in much of its teaching methods and in its use of new technology. But this is not the ground upon which the struggle is taking place. At risk is doctrinal purity, honest teaching about living the Christian life from the Bible, and genuine personal spiritual growth and change that should be taking place in the experience of the individual child of God.

Some would argue that in modern times the approach to pastoral care should be different from the past. It is true that certain practices and methods can be replaced, but the substance of pastoral care is the same. And the source must be the same—the Word of God. But many are drifting from this and substituting psychology for biblical and spiritual comfort.

Os Guinness warns that the new trends, especially the movement toward the megachurch, is bringing on a "flirting with modernity." He notes that megachurches have adopted "one-stop shopping" that provides features such as movie theaters, weight rooms, saunas, and roller rinks.[1] With this environment some feel evangelism is easier but "discipleship infinitely harder."[2] Guinness adds:

> The problem is not that Christians have disappeared, but that Christian faith has become so deformed. Under the influence of modernity, we modern Christians are literally capable of winning the world while losing our own souls.[3]

He further notes that modernity has changed evangelicals into those who do not think.[4] Churches are in danger of being professionally orchestrated into single purpose environments and so preoccupied with technique, rational solutions, and secular approaches, they can lose their hearts.[5] Churches are pandering to a consumerist mentality. All needs must now be met on demand. True spiritual needs are reinterpreted to meet surface or simply physical needs.[6]

Guinness writes about what he calls the six character types of modernity.[7] First is the "pundit" through whom everything can be known by simply providing information. Second is the "engineer," who argues everything can be fixed or produced. Then there is the "marketer," the one who says everything can be sold or marketed through enough effort. Fourth is the "consultant" who would say everything can be better organized or managed. Fifth is the "therapist," the one who believes everything may be healed or adjusted. Finally, there is the "impresario," the one who knows how to change everything into an advantage.

From this, he argues that there is a new professionalism with the power to prescribe.

> All that has changed is the type of authority. Traditional authorities, such as the clergy, have been replaced by modern authorities—in this case, denominational leaders by church-growth experts. . . . In most cases all that has changed is the type of clergy. The old priesthood is dead! Long live the new power-pastors and pundit-priests![8]

Despite how some are now beginning to ignore the directives of Scripture, what does the Word of God say about how the elder/pastor must relate to and treat the flock? What does the Bible say about practical pastoral care? Who is to carry this out? And who is most responsible for the spiritual health of the local congregation? Though there is a new, modern era of thinking, does this mean that the doctrine of the local assembly and how it is to be constructed and function is to change?

Practical new methods and forms for ministering to a modern local assembly may be practiced. But that new approach must conform to scriptural guidelines and directives. It cannot violate basic biblical doctrines. To see what the Bible says on these matters, this chapter will divide pastoral care into areas of responsibility: public, benevolence, counseling, and family equipping.

When speaking of the leadership of the local church, the epistles always mention the elders in the plural. Thus, each assembly has a body of elders or pastors who are to be the teachers "for the equipping of the saints for the work of service" (Eph. 4:11b–12). The word *overseer* is also another job description for this same group of leaders. Though their qualifications are spelled out, it is understood that not all these men will have the same abilities or insights. And some, who obviously are giving full-time to their pastoral work and who "work hard at preaching and teaching," may receive double honor or some sort of financial remuneration (1 Tim. 5:17).

This body of men is seen as responsible for the congregation, the flock of believers entrusted to them. Spiritually speaking, Jesus portrayed Himself as the great Shepherd of His own, the sheep (John 10). Before His ascension, the Lord told Peter to "feed My sheep" (21:16). From the Greek word *shepherd (poimēn)* comes the word "to feed, care," or "rule" over a flock. The elders then are in charge of "feeding" "the church of God" (Acts 20:28) and they are to "shepherd the flock of God among you" (1 Peter 5:2).

To carry out their shepherding, the elders have:

# Public Responsibilities

### Teaching the Word

The elder/pastors are charged with clearly setting forth and explaining the Word of God. Paul reminded Titus that elders should be "holding fast the faithful word which is in accordance with the teaching" (Titus 1:9), and he urged Timothy to "preach the word . . . with great patience and instruction" (2 Tim. 4:2). The word "instruction" is *didachē* or doctrine.

Many today are arguing for shorter public teaching gatherings in favor of small care groups. But the New Testament seems to indicate there is value in the coming together of the entire congregation to hear the Word of God taught. This coming together also provides a sense of unity. Paul was well aware of the importance of this spiritual and physical cohesion.

When he and Barnabas arrived back in Antioch from their first missionary tour, the whole church gathered to hear their report of "all things that God had done with them" (Acts 14:27). At Troas, Paul gave a long message to the entire gathered church that did not *begin* until midnight (20:7). His long talk ended at daybreak (v. 11)! At Corinth, the great apostle taught the believers for six months in the house of one named Titus Justus, whose residence was next to the local synagogue (18:7–11). As well, he reminded the Ephesian elders how he went about "teaching you publicly and from house to house" testifying about "faith in our Lord Jesus Christ" (20:20–21). Four other house churches are mentioned besides the one in the house of Justus (Rom. 16:5; 1 Cor. 16:19; Col. 4:15; Philem. 2). One can imagine strong, healthy teaching of the Word going forth from those dwellings.

Regardless of the size of the congregation or the setting in which it must meet, the Word of God must be taught. This is the central mandate given to the elder/pastors. But few in contemporary times are giving exegetical teachings from God's Word. Too often, the "pulpit ministry" is given over to shorter devotionals or simply topical messages. Yet for the church to be healthy, doctrinal content cannot be ignored.

## Reading the Word

Many churches do just this each Sunday morning before the assembled congregation. Pastors feel that the mere sound of scriptural words is sufficient to fulfill this command, so they wander into a devotional sermon that has little direct connection to the text that was read. The Bible becomes a launching pad for human thoughts and wisdom.

But as Paul commands the reading of Scripture, he says, "Until I come, give attention to the public reading of Scripture, to exhortation and teaching" (1 Tim. 4:13). The translators of the *New American Standard* have actually supplied the words "to Scripture" and "public" to help make better sense of the verse. This addition is justified, but the passage literally reads: "Give attention to reading, to exhortation, to teaching." By using three dative phrases, Paul shows scriptural reading, exhortation, and teaching to be equally important for the spiritual growth of the body.

The elder/pastors are responsible for explaining the Word of God and seeing to it that, as it is read, the words and thoughts are applicable to the needs of believers. This pattern of teaching the Scriptures is also found in the Old Testament.

When the exiles had returned to Jerusalem from Babylon, Nehemiah 8:1–8 records that Ezra the scribe gathered both men and women "as one man" in a square in the city and read them the law of Moses. "All who could listen and understand" from morning until noon "were attentive to the book of the law" (v. 3). Ezra stood on a high wooden podium and opened the Torah in the sight of all the people (v. 5). But the scrolls were not simply read, they were explained to the crowd (v. 7). Since this new generation had come from Babylon, they did not know the Hebrew that the law of Moses was written in. Therefore, the Scriptures were interpreted. "And they read from the book, from the law of God, translating to give the sense so that they understood the reading" (v. 8).

Earlier in Deuteronomy, Moses had called the gathering of men, women, children, and the stranger to hear the reading of the law (31:11). But this was not simply an auditory exercise of only hearing the sounds of words being read. God explained to Moses that the people should "hear and learn and fear the Lord your God, and be careful to observe all the words of this law" (v. 12).

Despite criticism from some who feel it is old-fashioned, the reading and explaining of the Scriptures is essential for spiritual maturity. This is why the elders need as much biblical training as is feasible, to be able to explain properly what the Word of God says.

## Preaching the Word

The Greek verb *kēryssō* and the noun *kērygma* have been translated "preaching," "to publish, proclaim," or "to preach." Generally speaking, the word is applied to the proclamation of the gospel message itself, and it relates almost exclusively to the issue of salvation. From Acts on, the word *kēryssō* is used to declare that (1) Christ preached (Acts 8:5; 9:20; 15:21; 19:13; Rom. 16:15;

1 Cor. 1:23; 15:12; 2 Cor. 1:19; 11:4; Phil. 1:15); (2) the gospel preached (Gal. 2:2; 1 Thess. 2:9); (3) the word of faith preached (Rom. 10:8); and (4) "the gospel that you have heard" was proclaimed in all creation" (Col. 1:23).

A pastor should make certain that the gospel is presented in a clear fashion in whatever setting he finds himself. But for those who are saved, the pastor should concentrate on the teaching and explaining of doctrine that is absolutely essential for spiritual growth and maturity. Some pastors focus only on a repetitive presentation of the salvation message.

### *Overseeing by the Word*

The pastor/teacher is also to be an overseer, one who is concerned with what is happening spiritually, morally, and maybe even in terms of error creeping into the congregation. The basic word is *episkopos* and means literally "to oversee." Other forms of the word are also used in the New Testament epistles.

Paul told the Ephesian elders that they were made overseers by the Holy Spirit. The Greek text reads, "Be continually alert for yourselves and for all the flock, among which the Holy Spirit has Himself placed you as overseers, to be pastoring the church of God which He purchased with His own blood" (Acts 20:28). The apostle addresses both the overseers (or elders) and deacons in the church at Philippi (Phil. 1:1) and says they must be morally blameless (1 Tim. 3:2; Titus 1:7). The word is used by Peter when he exhorts the elders to "pastor" the flock of God, " 'exercising oversight' *[episkopeō]* [but] not with compulsion" (1 Peter 5:2).

The word *episkopos* and its variations can have the idea of "looking at or paying attention to a person or thing."[9] The word can mean "to inspect or investigate closely." In classical Greek it is often translated "review, superintend, or examine."[10]

Brown notes, "Early on oversight became the task of a special office."[11] The word reflected

> The need for pastoral oversight to keep the church in the way of faith . . . for bishops were linked with a particular place and church. But at first it was probably synonymous at least with that of shepherd *(poimēn)* and elder *(presbyteros)* and the ideas associated with them.[12]

The elders/pastors/overseers then must be men of wisdom who are looking out for the best interest of the assembly. They look for error and insidious cults that can mislead the flock. They must pass judgment on doctrines and make certain the Word of God is taught properly. They need to warn the local church of cultural philosophies that are leading families and youngsters away from the truth. They must be looking forward to what is coming that is satanic in nature. From this insight and wisdom, they must teach with relevancy. They must make the Word of God applicable to current issues and temptations.

## Conclusion

In order to carry out the pastoral ministry of teaching and preaching publicly, the church leaders should accomplish the public teaching through (1) Bible book studies with verse-by-verse exposition. Though unpopular today, this approach has been at the heart of the evangelical pronouncement for generations. Of course this can take place from the pulpit and in the Sunday school classroom. Next, (2) doctrinal teaching series are appropriate in order to focus on issues and truths that need to be reinforced. For special occasions, there is nothing wrong with (3) topical messages, word studies, or Bible character sermons. (4) Devotionals should be used sparingly. But the teacher should always take the audience into the Bible itself.

The passing out of study notes, the use of the overhead projector, or the implementation of computer-generated illustrations and graphics are certainly appropriate to reinforce the hearing/visual learning process. The use of such helps to the pulpit ministry should not get in the way of the power of the Word of God. They are legitimate instruments that help explain what God is communicating to His own flock. But if any approach waters down or tampers with the message of Scripture being taught, it should not be used.

# Benevolence Responsibilities

Throughout Scripture God places high priority on care for the weak and helpless. In the societal laws given to the nation of Israel, God states of those who afflict a widow or orphan, "I will surely hear his cry; and My anger will be kindled, and I will kill you with the sword; and your wives shall become widows and your children orphans" (Exod. 22:23–24). How a society treats the widows and orphans, or the helpless in general, shows the spiritual health of that society. God takes our care for the orphans and widows very seriously since, "A father of the fatherless and a judge for the widows, is God in His holy habitation" (Ps. 68:5). Lenski writes, "Like orphans, widows are in a special way under the protection of God. To hurt them is listed among the greatest crimes (Ex. 22:22; Deut. 14:29; 24:17, 19; 26:12; 27:19; Job 24:3; Ps. 68:5; Prov. 15:25)."[13]

James, in his painfully practical book, states, "This is pure religion in the sight of our God and Father, to visit orphans and widows in their distress" (James 1:27). The word translated "visit" *(episkeptesthai)* carries with it more than the idea of dropping by. Throughout the New Testament the word means "to provide for" or "to care for"[14] (cf. Matt. 25:36, 43; Acts 7:23, 15:36). Clearly the New Testament church recognized a responsibility to their own widows and orphans.

## The Care of Widows

Early in his account of the early church, Luke shows the responsibility of believers for the widows among them. In fact, the first complaint recorded in the church was over the care given to the widows in the Jerusalem church. In Acts 6:1–6 Luke records:

> *Now at this time while the disciples were increasing in number, a complaint arose on the part of the Hellenistic Jews against the native Hebrews, because their widows were being overlooked in the daily serving of food. And the twelve summoned the congregation of the disciples and said, "It is not desirable for us to neglect the word of God in order to serve tables. But select from among you, brethren, seven men of good reputation, full of the Spirit and of wisdom, whom we may put in charge of this task. But we will devote ourselves to prayer, and to the ministry of the word." And the statement found approval with the whole congregation; and they chose Stephen, a man full of faith and of the Holy Spirit, and Philip, Prochorus, Nicanor, Timon, Parmenas, and Nicolas, a proselyte from Antioch. And these they brought before the apostles; and after praying, they laid their hands on them.*

The church in Jerusalem was growing very rapidly. On the day of Pentecost three thousand souls were saved (Acts 2:41), and the church continued to grow quickly in the weeks and months to follow (Acts 2:47; 4:4; 5:14). It was not long until the first problems came as a result of this rapid growth. The church was made up of Hellenistic Jews and native Hebrews. The Hellenistic Jews were those who had adopted the Greek culture. They were likely raised abroad or had parents who came from outside of Israel (Acts 2:5–11). As a result they would speak their native dialect and Greek. The native Jews were those who grew up in Israel and spoke Greek and Aramaic, the native tongue of the Jews living in Israel.

The twelve apostles responded to the complaints by calling a meeting of the congregation and saying, "It is not desirable for us *to neglect the word of God in order to serve tables*" (Acts 6:2). The apostles were staying very busy praying, as well as teaching and preaching the Word of God to such a large congregation. The complaint of the Hellenistic Jews was certainly valid, but to neglect the teaching of God's Word would also be harmful to the congregation. As a result, they appealed to the congregation to choose seven men for the task at hand.

The phrase "to serve tables" (6:2) is a translation of the Greek phrase *diakonein trapezais*. This infinitive comes from the verb *diakoneō*, meaning "to care for" or "take care of."[15] The phrase here is used figuratively for ministering to the widows by the daily serving of food, and probably meeting other basic needs of the widows (6:1).

The church by this time had fifteen thousand to twenty thousand members, so others must have already be helping the apostles with this task by dispensing the aid. But apparently the logistics had become so much work that some of the widows were being neglected. As a result, men had to be chosen to keep a list of all the widows and to calculate how much food and other supplies were needed to be bought and distributed daily. In addition, they would have to make sure that there were men and women to dispense this aid to the widows. In a church so large, that would be a major task. The job would require men of wisdom and commitment. As a result, they chose "seven men of good reputation, full of the Spirit and of wisdom." These men were put in charge of the task. Many, if not most, conservative scholars believe this was the precursor to the office of deacon.

Thus, the church has a responsibility to care for the widows among them who are not in a position to care for themselves or do not have family to care for them. (This will be discussed further in the next section.) According to this passage in Acts, it is the deacons of the church who are to identify the widows in their church who have needs and to organize a strategy to meet those needs.

In Paul's first letter to Timothy he reinforces the fact that the local church has a responsibility to care for the widows in their midst (1 Tim. 5:3–16). Paul commands (Gr. present imperative) Timothy that the church is to, "Honor widows who are widows indeed." At its root, the Greek verb translated "honor" *(timaō)* means "to value" or "to set a price on." The context of our passage indicates that Paul is using it in the sense of material provision for the widows. He observes three ways to do this, through family, the church, and mutual support.

### The Responsibility of Godly Children

The first source of provision for the widows in the church is the adult children or grandchildren (probably male children) of that widow (v. 4). They have an explicit biblically-based responsibility to care for their mothers or grandmothers. Paul states that this gives them an opportunity "to make some return to their parents" (v. 4). Jesus also brought out that this responsibility to care for their parents was implied by the command, "Honor your father and mother" (Matt. 15:4). In Matthew 15, Jesus pointed out that the scribes and the Pharisees were violating the command. They did this in a clever way, as Barbieri explains:

> Jesus showed how these religious leaders had in effect nullified this commandment (Matt. 15:6). They could simply affirm that a particular item had been a gift devoted to God. Then the item could not be used by an individual but was kept separate. This was simply a clever way of keeping things from passing to one's parents. The person would of course continue to keep those things in his home where they had been supposedly set aside for God.

Such action was condemned by Jesus as hypocritical (v. 7), for while it appeared to be spiritual, it actually was done to keep one's possessions for himself. Thus this failure to help one's parents deliberately violated the fifth commandment of the Decalogue.[16]

Jesus indicates that honoring one's parents means a financial commitment to care for them also. As we saw earlier, this word *(timaō)* often carries with it the meaning of monetary help. MacArthur writes:

> So the Old Testament law of honoring one's parents meant that so long as a person lived he was to respect and support his parents. Let's face it, during the first half of our lives our parents give everything they have to supply their children's needs. The other side of the coin is that when they are no longer able to meet their own needs, it becomes their children's responsibility to take care of them. Do you see the overlapping of generations? The cycle never ends. It is God's way of producing families that stick together and pass along the inheritance of an unselfish love.[17]

Returning to 1 Timothy 5, we see that the responsibility of a child to financially care for his parents is also brought out clearly in Paul's discussion of the care for widows. In 5:4 he writes, "But if any widow has children or grandchildren, let them first learn to practice piety in regard to their own family, and to make some return to their parents; for this is acceptable in the sight of God." In verse 3, Paul has explained that widows are only to be put on the benevolence list if they are "widows indeed." In other words, if they are widows without children or grandchildren. If they have children or grandchildren, they are to "practice piety" and "make some return to their parents, *for this is acceptable in the sight of God.*"

In fact, Paul has strong words for the adult child or grandchild who does not provide for his parents or grandparents. He writes, "But if anyone does not provide for his own, and especially for those of his household, *he has denied the faith, and is worse than an unbeliever*" (1 Tim. 5:8). White writes, "The Christian who falls below the best heathen standard of family affection is the more blameworthy, since he has, what the heathen has not, the supreme example of love in Jesus Christ."[18] Lenski states, "This is the obligation of the church, to teach all children and all grandchildren what God wants them to do so that they may do it in every case and do it in the right spirit."[19]

Lenski notes of this section:

> Paul is not excluding from congregational help every widow
> with grown children and grandchildren lest the congregation be
> unduly burdened. Paul's words imply that *all* needy widows are
> to be provided for; the church has the obligation to see to that
> and to teach it to the members, in particular to children and to
> grandchildren who have needy parents. What the congregation
> is to do when children disregard this teaching need not be said;
> the church will take proper measures and will not abandon a
> widow who has heartless children.[20]

## *The Provision of the Church*

The natural question would be, "What about those widows who have no
children or grandchildren to care for them; those who are widows *indeed?*"
Paul makes it clear that the church must care for them. "The 'widow *indeed*' is
one who has been left utterly alone *(memonōmenē)* and has fixed her hope on
God *(ēlpiken,* 'fixed her hope in the direction of God'), and continues in en-
treaties and prayers night and day (v. 5; i.e. Luke 2:37). This godly woman
realizes that God is her only hope, especially since she 'has been left all alone'
or childless."[21] It is He who will ultimately supply her needs. She is in contrast
to the widow "who gives herself to wanton pleasure [and] is dead even while
she lives" (v. 6), which would have been a real temptation for widows in Paul's
day, as there were few opportunities for these women to earn a living. The
widow *indeed* who is to be honored by the church is that widow whose lifestyle
is above reproach. That this woman is worthy of the church's support is clear
from her godly character.

There is some disagreement among scholars whether Paul is addressing a
different group of widows in verses 9–15. Guthrie explains:

> The proviso of so high an age as sixty presents difficulty as to
> whether *widow* should be understood in the same sense as 3–8
> (i.e., of genuinely destitute Christian widows) or in the sense of
> widows belonging to an order. In the former case it is inconceiv-
> able that the church would set an arbitrary age in dispensing
> help to destitute widows, while in the latter case it is difficult to
> believe the entry age to an official ecclesiastical order would be
> as high as sixty, in the contemporary world a relatively more
> advanced age than in our own. It seems preferable, therefore, to
> suppose that special duties in the church were reserved for some
> of the old widows receiving aid, and some official recognition
> of this fact was given. Although the verb *katalegō,* translated

*taken into the number* [KJV], is used in Greek literature of the enrollment of soldiers, it can also mean "reckon," a sense which would support the explanation given above.[22]

If Guthrie is right, Paul now gives some specific guidelines for the widows to be "put on the list" *(katelegō)* of support by the church and to be involved in serving the church through special duties. These guidelines include:

1. She must be at least sixty years of age (v. 9). As MacArthur points out, "Such widows constituted an official group who represented the church in ministry—'staff widows,' if you will."[23] Some have taken this to mean that the widow must have been married only once, but the context shows the fallacy of that interpretation. Verse 14 clearly shows that widows were not forbidden to marry.

   In later centuries this body of widows developed into an official group in the church. Although there is much uncertainty regarding the details about these widows, Gustav Stählin discusses the development of this group in the community of believers:

   > Many aspects of this development are obscure and controversial. . . . In the Church Orders [Hippolytus, *Church Orders,* c. A.D. 160–235], which mostly have special sections on widows, there is often no clear-cut distinction between those living in *chēreia* widowhood, and those active in *chērikon,* the office of widows, so that in a given case it is hard to say whether the reference is to the one or the other. There are certain conditions for reception into the ranks of church widows; these partly adopt, partly change, and partly expand the rules of 1 Tim. 5. A specific time must elapse after the husband's death to give the widow a chance to test herself [Hippolytus, etc.]. She must have been only once married [Origen A.D. 185–254]. She must have led a blameless life as a widow, and must have proved herself in care for her family and upbringing of the children. As regards canonical age for acceptance the rule of 1 Tim. 5:9 is usually followed. . . . Installation was not by ordination but by benediction and prayer. When appointed a church widow, the woman takes a vow to remain a widow. If she breaks this she will be accountable to God.[24]

2. She must have been the wife of one husband (v. 9). The phrase here is *henos andros gynē,* literally "a one-man woman." This is the same qualification required of the overseer/elder (1 Tim. 3:2) and the deacons (v. 12). This does not mean that the widow is to only have been married once, it means she is to have been wholly committed to her husband. The *niv*

translates the phrase, "been faithful to her husband." Although not a literal translation, this brings out the meaning well.

3. She is known for her good works (v. 10). Examples of what Paul means are then given. They include: (1) the raising of children; (2) showing hospitality to strangers; (3) washing the saints' feet; and (4) assisting those in distress. In general her life has been characterized by being "devoted . . . to every good work."

Women younger than sixty are to be excluded from this "official" group. The answer to their plight, Paul states, is to remarry and fulfill their motherly duties (v. 14). This prevents the temptation of Satan to "set aside their previous pledge" (v. 12).

As we pointed out before, this group of widows became an official group of the church. Apparently, those in this group pledged themselves to a life of service to Christ. Paul states that women under sixty were not to be part of this group, since their natural desires to get married might become too intense to overcome. By marrying, they would break their commitment. Also, these young women might grow idle and become gossips. Paul's comment in verse 15 indicates that some of the younger women in the church at Ephesus, who were apparently placed on the list previous to his instruction, had already become involved in these things.

Thus, the church has a responsibility to care for the widows of the church and to help meet their basic needs. This responsibility should be met first by their adult children or grandchildren, but if they refuse then the church should not let these widows suffer as a result of their children's or grandchildren's neglect.

### *Provision by Other Widows*

Finally, Paul suggests a third way for the widows' needs to be met. There may be a rare case when there are no adult male children or grandchildren in the family to support the widow. In this case he states, "If any woman who is a believer has a *dependent* widow, let her assist them, and let not the church be burdened, so that it may assist those who are widows indeed" (v. 16). In other words, there may be a woman in the family who has the resources to provide the widow with a place to stay as well as to give food and clothing. This will take an extra financial burden off of the church and free up resources to use for others in need or in other areas of ministry.

In the New Testament era, we see that widows also banded together to meet each others' needs. Apparently in order to survive, widows banded together for emotional and maybe even financial security. When the widow Dorcas died in Joppa, Peter went down to where her body was laid out. Her many widow friends showed to him the coats and garments she had made when she was alive (Acts 9:39). Peter knelt by her and called out her Aramaic name, "Tabitha, arise" (v. 40). When she awakened from death Peter presented her alive to the saints and widows who were her Christian companions (v. 41).

## *The Local Church's Practical Response*

What should the local church do today for the women in the congregation who have lost husbands and are suddenly left alone without grown children to care for them? The church should quickly inquire as to what the widow needs and as to how she will make out financially. This is not to say that even a medium-size congregation could help totally in such a situation. But if there is no immediate family to help, the church should respond in doing what it can.

In most Western countries today, government-aid programs help pick up the tab. But because of this, churches have lost a sense of care and obligation for the individual, especially women who have lost a spouse. Some in the church feel the husband has well taken care of his wife. And many men have provided some life insurance for their wives. But not all. Yet also, many older women want to return, at least in a limited way, to the workforce and care for their own needs. However, with all this, the deacons working with the elders should make sure the widow is not neglected.

If financial help is not necessary, there should at least be spiritual and emotional help available. A widow often feels as if she is a fifth wheel and no longer fits in the church family. The church should make sure its widows are not forgotten spiritually. They should be included and invited to all appropriate church social functions.

Many assemblies provide an older women's guild for social contact and Bible study. But it must be remembered that if the women are in good health they can carry out their own ministries to the congregation. They can form visitation teams that minister to the sick. They can teach Sunday school classes and children's church. In other words, they can be found spiritually active, performing their God-given gifts in the midst of the church body. Being older does not mean they are put out to pasture or ignored. Their sense of usefulness may even be greater since they are now alone and have no one else to care for.

In biblical days, the widow was far more helpless unless she was fortunate to have a God-fearing and loving family who would bring her into the protection of their own household. Younger widows often sold themselves into prostitution or some other form of slavery simply for survival's sake. Since widows could be left unprotected, the apostle Paul says much about "remembering the widows."

The local church should take care to protect widows from those who might defraud her. Sometimes even today older unsuspecting widows can be cheated out of their very homes and estates by unscrupulous financial or religious hucksters. Jesus mentions this and refers to the scribes, who, like birds and locusts, settle on the ripe crops of the widows and "devoured" their property and homes "and for appearance's sake offer[ed] long prayers" (Mark 12:40).

> As the women who were attracted by our Lord's teaching ministered to Him of their substance ([Mark] xiv. 3, Lc. viii. 2, 3), so doubtless the Pharisaic rabbis had their female followers, whose generosity they grossly abused. Widows were specially

the object of their attack. . . . Men who devoured the property of widows could pray only in pretense. The word carries with it, however, the further sense of "pretext" . . . under color of a reputation for piety due to the length of their prayers . . . they insinuated themselves into the good opinion of their victims.[25]

The church needs to be reminded if they are to be Christlike they should show the same care for widows as Christ did. In Israel during the time of Christ, there were many widows (Luke 4:25) who were generally classified as poor (Mark 12:42–43), with some as young as forty (Luke 2:37). Jesus honored the poor widow who put into the temple treasury an offering out of her poverty because, as the Lord said, she "put in all that she had to live on" (21:4).

Today the local church, working through the deacons, should monitor what the widow truly needs. She should not be pampered but should be encouraged to be active and productive whenever possible. But she should never be ignored or forgotten.

A final note: As we have seen, though the Scriptures place the emphasis on widowed wives, the same principle should apply to widowers, and older men who may be physically limited and need the moral, spiritual, and financial aid of the church.

### The Orphan

Although there are no specific passages on the church's responsibility to orphans, this group was often included with widows as being specially favored by God. In the Law, God made special provision for them as stated in Deuteronomy 24:19–21. There we read:

> When you reap your harvest in your field and have forgotten a sheaf in the field, you shall not go back to get it; it shall be for the alien, for the orphan, and for the widow, in order that the Lord your God may bless you in all the work of your hands. When you beat your olive tree, you shall not go over the boughs again; it shall be for the alien, for the orphan, and for the widow. When you gather the grapes of your vineyard, you shall not go over it again; it shall be for the alien, for the orphan, and for the widow.

James states, "This is pure religion in the sight of our God and Father, to visit orphans and widows in their distress" (James 1:27). The Greek word translated "visit" (episkeptesthai) means "to provide for" or "to care for"[26] (cf. Matt. 25:36, 43; Acts 7:23; 15:36). Although there is no specific instruction concerning care of orphans, the whole of Scripture shows that God considers their welfare the responsibility of His people, regardless of dispensation. One would think this especially true of children left behind by believing parents who have died.

This verse in James is the only passage in the New Testament where the word *orphan (orphanos)* is used (James 1:27). Here it is translated "fatherless," possibly because the verse implies that by directly mentioning widows also. "Visit the fatherless and widows." Or, "visit the home where the mother is the only living parent."

Even today, single-parent mothers have great difficulty in dealing with their children. Could James have had that in mind when he urged that this kind of family be visited? Again, "visit" means more than simply dropping in. It implies care and concern, and even helping with whatever has to be done to alleviate the struggle of a home without a father.

Many churches have started Big Brother organizations in order to give spiritual and practical male mentoring to young men without fathers at home. More often than not it is divorce that brings on the one-parent family in today's culture. The young boy or girl in this environment needs role models to fill the gap left by the missing parent. Though this will never completely substitute for that parent, it is a task that the local church must take on.

Why does the New Testament mention the orphan or fatherless but once? Two answers may be given. (1) The early church saw quickly its obligation in this matter because charity to those in need was one of its instant hallmarks. (2) The Old Testament has much more to say about the fatherless. The believers in the early church were already doing what was commanded in that older text. They were providing obviously needed help to single-parent families.

Many Old Testament passages make it clear that God's people have a responsibility to the orphans. Believers in Christ can have no doubt as to how the Lord would have orphans treated. Today, local churches should take care to look after the same within their congregation but should also be working with reliable Christian orphanages. In like manner, they should be aware of child placement agencies that are hard at work rescuing babies from the abortion knife. Many Christian families see their ministry in adoption and foster care for the abandoned and helpless child overlooked and forgotten in this selfish society.

### The Sick

The most common word for sickness in the New Testament is the verb *astheneō* and its noun equivalents. The word is often translated *infirmities, impotent, weak,* and *feeble.* However, in the majority of the passages where the word is found, it has reference to a weak conscience (1 Cor. 8:12), weak in faith (Rom. 14:1), weak in temperament (Acts 20:35), weak in body (2 Cor. 10:10), weak spiritually (Rom. 5:6), the woman as a weaker vessel (1 Peter 3:7).

The Lord Jesus healed many as He went throughout the land of Israel, fulfilling a prophecy about the work of the promised Messiah in Isaiah 53:4: "He

Himself took our infirmities, and carried away our diseases" (Matt. 8:17). Many astounding healings were performed by the apostles in the early part of the book of Acts, which substantiated that these men were instruments of God in authenticating the gospel message (5:15–16).

By the time of Paul's Epistles, the apostles were not necessarily acting as healing agents. When Epaphroditus became ill, Paul's Philippian letter does not indicate a certainty that he would be healed. The apostle writes, "For indeed he was sick to the point of death, but God had mercy on him, and not on him only but also on me, lest I should have sorrow upon sorrow" (2:27–28). God did indeed restore his health but there does not appear to have been a guarantee.

When Timothy was suffering with a stomach illness, Paul prescribed "a little wine for the sake of your stomach and your frequent ailments" (1 Tim. 5:23). We can be sure that prayers were offered up but natural medicinals were also appropriate to take. The case of Trophimus is also mentioned in the Scriptures (Acts 20:15; 2 Tim. 4:20). Paul left him to convalesce in the seaport of Miletus as he journeyed on to Caesarea. Since prayers were probably also offered up for this man's illness, God answered with a "no" in terms of an instant cure. Trophimus was left behind by the traveling party in order to be healed over a period of time. The Word of God does not speak of the witnessing that he might have carried out at Miletus. The Lord has His reasons for not always healing dramatically as some Christians might think He should.

The apostle Paul himself was not cured of an infirmity that he must have carried for years. He writes that he pleaded with the Lord "three times that it might depart from me" (2 Cor. 12:7) but God answered, "'My grace is sufficient for you, for power is perfected (matured) in weaknesses (*astheneia*, "diseases").' Most gladly, therefore, I will rather boast about my weaknesses, that the power of Christ may dwell in me" (v. 9).

Believers in Christ always have a right to pray for personal healing. But it must be recognized that dramatic, instant healing is not always God's first desire when infirmity strikes. This in no way should blunt the petitioning of the Lord, but there must be an awareness that He may answer "yes," "no," or "later." His glory and hidden purposes must take precedence over the personal comfort of the believer. Suffering may be used to humble and teach tremendous spiritual lessons, both to the one who is ill but also to those who are witnessing the process.

James 5:13–18 is a powerful passage on sickness. James urges that the sick one may call on the church elders for healing prayer. They may anoint the ill brother with oil in the name of the Lord. The prayer offered in faith "will restore the one who is sick" (v. 15a). But James continues and implies there are times when the sickness comes by sins committed (v. 15b). Those sins can be forgiven, and prayer may be the agent of healing in light of this kind of sickness (v. 16). Though the apostle does not specify what the sin might be, Paul also mentions that some need to examine their life before taking the Lord's Supper lest the

Lord brings on weakness, then sickness, and ultimately "sleep" whereby the believer forfeits his life (1 Cor. 11:30).

On James 5:13–18 Ryrie notes:

> God may heal directly, through medicine, or in answer to prayer, as here. The oil is a symbol of the presence of God (cf. Ps. 23:5); it may also have been considered medicinal in James's day (cf. Luke 10:34), though hardly as being effective for all diseases. Prayers of faith are answered not simply because they are prayed in faith but only if they are prayed in the will of God (1 John 5:14). God does not always think it best to heal (cf. 2 Cor. 12:8). Here the healing is dependent on confession of sin.[27]

When it comes to the care of the sick, a church with a team of concerned elders is richly blessed. If that local body is but served by one minister, he may soon weary of calling on the many who may be ill, both in home visits and in the hospital. In order that the teaching ministry of the assembly be unhindered, it is beneficial to have those with the personal gift of relating to people and their problems carry out the main task of visitation. Though cards, letters, and phone calls may raise the spirits of those confined by infirmities, nothing can substitute for the personal touch.

Time with the sick may move slowly and drain the mental and physical resources of a single pastor. With a local congregation of any significant size, he cannot do it all. That is why Paul calls for multiple elders/pastors. However, it must be pointed out that this important visitation of the sick can be delegated and done by members of the congregation and by deacons as well. Yet it certainly is the responsibility of the elders to see to it that no one who is ill is neglected.

Common sense must rule in visiting the sick. The one who is calling on the ill person must not be too loud, boisterous, or pushy. The rule of thumb is to honor the quietness of the moment if the person who is sick is especially weak, tired, or in pain. Though most doctors maintain that pastoral visits are morale boosters, the medical attendants have the last say as to the time allotted for calling on a sick patient. As well, the wishes of the family should play a part in what constitutes help and attention given to the brother who is suffering. To stay too long on a hospital call is not necessary. Just the gesture of concern may be sufficient to lift the spirits. Reading of Scripture and prayer are certainly part of the calling process. At the right time, it is also appropriate to send to the sick person sermon tapes or devotional literature. In fact, this may be even better than loading a hospital room or sick room at home with flowers. The rule of thumb is to be thoughtful of the situation and also to be thinking ahead of what would be best to share, in light of the circumstances and the depth of the illness.

Again, lest the elder/pastor become bogged down in visitation, to have visiting teams or rotating visits by staff or other members of the church is certainly appropriate. It may also not be necessary to "overcall" on the sick. Allow days for quiet rest so that the ill person may get the right amount of rest. And clearly this may vary with the intensity or urgency of the sickness.

## *The Poor*

Scripture puts a heavy emphasis on caring for the poor. In giving instruction to Israel, God states the following in Deuteronomy 15:7–11:

> *If there is a poor man with you, one of your brothers, in any of your towns in your land which the Lord your God is giving you, you shall not harden your heart, nor close your hand from your poor brother; but you shall freely open your hand to him, and shall generously lend him sufficient for his need in whatever he lacks. Beware, lest there is a base thought in your heart, saying, "The seventh year, the year of remission, is near," and your eye is hostile toward your poor brother, and you give him nothing; then he may cry to the Lord against you, and it will be a sin in you. You shall generously give to him, and your heart shall not be grieved when you give to him, because for this thing the Lord your God will bless you in all your work and in all your undertakings. For the poor will never cease to be in the land; therefore I command you, saying, "You shall freely open your hand to your brother, to your needy and poor in your land."*

The Proverbs give the same exhortation.

> *One man gives freely, yet gains even more; another withholds unduly, but comes to poverty. (Prov. 11:24)*

> *He who despises his neighbor sins, but blessed is he who is kind to the needy. . . . He who oppresses the poor shows contempt for their Maker, but whoever is kind to the needy honors God. (Prov. 14:21, 31)*

> *He who is kind to the poor lends to the Lord, and he will reward him for what he has done. (Prov. 19:17)*

> *A generous man will himself be blessed, for he shared his food with the poor. (Prov. 22:9)*

> *If a man shuts his ears to the cry of the poor, he too will cry out and not be answered. (Prov. 21:13)*

As we saw at the beginning of this study, the early church felt a strong responsibility to share the resources they possessed with others in the body of Christ (i.e., Acts 2:44–47; 4:32–35). In 2 Corinthians 8:13–15 Paul gives a guiding principle for the exchange of material possessions among the brethren. He writes:

> *For this is not for the ease of others and for your affliction, but by way of equality—at this present time your abundance being a supply for their want, that their abundance also may become a supply for your want, that there may be equality; as it is written, "He who gathered much did not have too much, and he who gathered little had no lack."*

Whether as a church or on an individual basis, when our brethren are in need and we have surplus, we should share that surplus with them so that their basic needs are met. If we find ourselves in the same situation in the future, they can reciprocate. Lowery writes:

> A guiding principle for material exchange among churches is equality. Paul was not wanting some church to have relief (*anesis;* cf. 2:13; 7:5) while the Corinthians were hard pressed (*thlipsis;* cf. 1:4). That would be like robbing Peter to pay Paul! . . . Paul no doubt approved of the Jerusalem church's early efforts in meeting each other's needs by having everything in common (Acts 2:44). This expressed their mutual concern for all members of the body of Christ (1 Cor. 12:25). This principle was modeled after a divine pattern. When God gave food to the Israelites in the wilderness He did so equally according to their needs (Exod. 16:16–18). The church should not do less.[28]

With the state of our culture, more and more churches and charity organizations are in need of discerning the legitimately needy from panhandlers and sluggards. Dr. Vernon Grounds shows the directive of Scripture in our need to discern. He writes:

> Leaving aside all poverty-producing factors beyond human control, we must face the reality that some poverty is caused by personal traits like shiftlessness, waste, extravagance, lust and sheer stupidity. These are mentioned in the Book of Proverbs which, for example, warns against the consequences of being idle. A typical warning is given in Proverbs 24:30–34:

"I went past the field of the sluggard, past the vineyard of the man who lacks judgment; thorns had come up with weeds, and the stone wall was in ruins. I applied my heart to what I observed and learned a lesson from what I saw: A little sleep, a little slumber, a little folding of the hands to rest—and poverty will come on you like a bandit and scarcity like an armed man."

Another warning is given in Proverbs 19:15: "Laziness brings on deep sleep, and the shiftless man goes hungry." (See also Proverbs 6:9; 13:4; 18:19; 20:4; 26:15.)

Paul gives an emphatic command in 2 Thessalonians 3:8–12 regarding indolent believers. In short, we are cautioned, even commanded not to indulge in misguided sympathy for the poor who don't deserve our compassion. The God-obedient diligent are not to sacrifice for the care of the God-disobeying indolent.[29]

## *The Divorced*

No issue stirs passionate controversy in the local church more than the subject of divorce. Three issues are always in debate: (1) The central point of conflict has to do with the issue of divorced leadership, such as pastor or elder. (2) Another focus point has to do with having exclusive ministries to those who have undergone the breakup of the marriage. (3) And finally, the issue of re-marriage is always hotly contested by some sincere believers.

It is not the purpose of this section to deal with the burning theological issues about divorce. No single chapter could answer satisfactorily all questions about the subject. There are as many opinions on the subject as there are voices wishing to be heard on the matter.

It is enough here to say that anyone who has made mistakes in their marriage and has gone through divorce deserves restitution. Many factors have to be considered and weighed carefully, but if God forgives and restores, so ought the local assembly. No one takes divorce lightly or justifies it when it happens. No one can counsel divorce or ever say it is right. But the issue cannot be ignored nor will verses quickly quoted satisfy the complexity of the problem.

The evangelical Christian world has undergone the scourge of the split family. The statistics are almost equal with the secular culture; fifty percent of Christian families have been broken. This brings into the local body deep spiritual and emotional wounds that need to be attended.

With no desire to simply justify divorce, many sincere scholars have recently taken another look at the issue. For example, Baptist minister Walter Callison has taken a bold step to openly challenge the legalistic view that he believes has hung "like a dark cloud over the heads of divorced Christians."[30] He notes that the high divorce rate is not the real problem but that marriage failure should first be blamed. He argues that early new converts often had multiple wives, slave wives, and concubines.

Each of these relationships, though given the nicer title, polygamy, was adultery. Paul rejected the heads of such households as leaders in the church. The command to give a writing of divorcement in Deuteronomy 24 limited a man to only one wife and thus prohibited polygamy and the adultery inherent in it. Paul seemed to concur fully when he said, "A bishop then must be blameless, the husband of one wife" (1 Tim. 3:2). He rejected polygamy, not divorce.[31]

Callison goes on and argues that Jesus received all who came to Him. Yet today, many divorced people are afraid of the churches because of heavy, harsh teaching. Christ came to receive sinners which also includes the divorced. The only people the Lord ever rejected, Callison says, are the religious self-righteous.

One passage that has stirred such controversy is 1 Timothy 3:2, which reads, "An overseer, then, must be above reproach, the husband of one wife." The overseer or elder thus cannot be a divorced person, many argue. But in a most reputable and biblical publication, Ed Glasscock challenges this view. He writes:

First Timothy 3:2 does not say "an elder must be married only once" nor does it say "an elder cannot remarry." Since the phrase is admittedly somewhat ambiguous, to place this type of stern restriction on a godly man because of such an unclear phrase seems quite unjust. One should avoid the Pharisaical error of binding men with unnecessary and oppressive burdens (cf. Matt. 23:1–4; Acts 15:10) and should seek to be gracious at every opportunity.[32]

Glasscock continues:

Paul's concern in 1 Timothy 3:1–10 is that if a man desires the office of elder he must be qualified "at that time," not before his conversion. For those concerned with the testimony of the church, let them consider which glorifies God more—that He takes an unworthy, defiled human and makes him pure enough to become His own servant (cf. 1 Tim. 1:12–16). . . . Even divorced and remarried Christians can trust the great promises of Psalm 103:12–13 and Isaiah 38:17. If God has made a man clean how can the church consider him unworthy to serve God even on the highest levels?[33]

Glasscock concludes:

As one considers the many facets of the arguments related to the phrase "one-woman man," it must be admitted that there is no

simple absolute answer. One may assume Paul meant to pro-
hibit divorced and remarried men from serving as elders, but
one should honestly admit that Paul did not say "he cannot have
been previously married" or "he cannot have been divorced."
What he did say is that he must be a one-wife husband or a one-
woman type of man. Paul was clearly concerned with one's character [in the present] when a man is being considered for this
high office.[34]

Local churches open to placing divorced Christians into important positions
(whether pastor/elder, or Sunday teacher) should consider a list of guidelines
that should conform to the biblical standard but also take into consideration mercy
and restitution. For example:

1.  Has sufficient time passed for proper emotional and spiritual healing?
2.  Has the dust settled in regard to the issue so that this person is able to
    function properly without undue distraction?
3.  What is his attitude in regard to the matter? Has he been repentant
    about his part in the failed marriage? If needed, has he made proper
    restitution?
4.  As far as can be ascertained, has he grown spiritually and morally from the
    incident? Has it humbled him and is he using the experience to help others
    who are failing in their marriages?
5.  Is there a consensus among those who know him best that he is ready and
    able to serve and be used of the Lord again?
6.  As far as is humanly possible to know, if this is an issue, has he over-
    come any moral weakness that could trap him again in a compromising
    situation?

In most cases, restored servants of the Lord have been a credit to their Lord
and the ministry. They have a sensitivity about the tenacity and severity of sin.
They also serve with a sense of reality concerning sin and a quickness about
restoration and mercy for those who have fallen.

Congregations need to be open about this difficult issue. They need to look
again at all of the biblical testimony on the restoration of anyone who has fallen
into any trap of transgression.

### Other Ministries of Charity

Charles Ryrie comments on the ministry of the church to those in need:

> The circles of responsibility toward those in need spread out
> from the local church. Those whose needs we come in con-
> tact with in the church (whether believers or unbelievers) have

first claim (James 2:2–3; 15–16; 1 John 3:17). The early church was also concerned with the needs of believers in other places (Acts 11:27–30). Paul spent considerable effort and time collecting money for the poor believers in Jerusalem. It involved the cooperative effort of a number of churches. The money did not pass directly from donors to recipients but was supervised by a committee chosen by the churches and apparently distributed under the direction of the leadership (2 Cor. 8:18–22).[35]

As we saw at the beginning of this chapter, the early church felt a strong responsibility to share the resources they possessed with others in the body of Christ (i.e., Acts 2:44–47 and 4:32–35). In 2 Corinthians 8:13–15 Paul gives a guiding principle for the exchange of material possessions among the brethren. He writes:

> *For this is not for the ease of others and for your affliction, but by way of equality—at this present time your abundance being a supply for their want, that their abundance also may become a supply for your want, that there may be equality; as it is written, "He who gathered much did not have too much, and he who gathered little had no lack."*

Whether as a church or on an individual basis, when our brethren are in need and we have surplus, we should share that surplus with them so that their basic needs are met. If we find ourselves in the same situation in the future, they can reciprocate. Ironside closes our discussion:

> As children of God we are never to be selfish or niggardly in ministering to those who are in poverty or distress. But we are not to encourage laziness, nor should the church be held accountable to support those whose own children can assume their care (i.e. 2 Thess. 3:10).[36]

# Some Practical Suggestions

## *General Suggestions:*

1. Give regular biblical instruction on stewardship and the Christian's biblical responsibilities to widows, orphans, the sick, the poor, and the needy.
2. The leadership should provide opportunities to carry out ministry to these groups. This is important for all members of the body, but it is especially

important for those in the body who have the spiritual gifts of service or ministry, mercy, and helps.

### *Widows, Widowers, and the Elderly*

1. Teach children and grandchildren (especially the males) that they have a biblical responsibility to care for their parents and grandparents in their old age. This responsibility can be taken up by the female members of the family as well as by other widows who have the means.
2. The local church should care for widows who have no children, grand-children, or other caring member of the family to care for them.

Remember, in the early church it appears that some widows were taken on by the church to "earn their keep" through caring for some of the ministry responsibilities of the church. This is certainly an option for the local church today, as well.

In addition to providing for food (a "Meals-on-Wheels" local church program), clothing, and shelter for these widows, the church needs to try to provide companionship and activities for the widows and widowers as well as the elderly in general. This could be done through:

a. A seniors group that organizes regular trips and activities.
b. Regular planned interaction of the older and younger women of the church, as well as older men and younger men. This would provide fellowship for widowers and wisdom and insight for the younger generation.
c. Visits to elderly people by young couples and other times of fellowship, as around a meal.

### *Orphans*

Orphans and the fatherless in single-parent homes should be cared for by:

1. Providing a male role model through a Big Brother program (whether this be for single mothers within the congregation or by working with a local orphanage).
2. Providing in the congregational budget for the support of an orphanage. Ideally this orphanage is close enough that members can be personally involved, making regular organized trips during the year.
3. Being aware of the need of the orphan to be a part of a stable Christian home. Always make your congregation aware of the ministry of adoption.
4. Making information on foster care available.

### *The Sick*

1. Pray for the sick to be healed.
2. The elders are to visit the sick and pray for them. (It should be noted that in

James 5:13–18 the sick person is to contact the elder; the responsibility is not primarily on the elder.)
3. Cards, letters, and phone calls can lift the spirits of the sick and their family by communicating the concern of the congregation.

### The Poor
1. Be open-handed and generous with help for those who are truly in need.
2. Be sure to examine the situation, making sure the need is legitimate and the poverty is not simply the result of laziness or a sinful character. We are commanded to verify the need.

Sometimes the father is lazy and as a result children are suffering. In such a case food and clothing can be provided directly, but not cash, which may be misused.

### Benevolence in Balance
One final word must be said about charity and benevolence in the church. The history of Christianity is full of examples of churches and mission groups that began their ministry to needy people with their priorities straight and later lost their way. The fact that material help is only a benefit in this life ought to be at the forefront of our thinking. The material needs of the world are overwhelming, yet they eternally pale in comparison to the spiritual needs of those around us. When we lose that perspective, we have lost our way and the enemy has gained a victory. The charity and benevolence ministries of a church need always keep in mind that only the gospel of Jesus Christ can truly make an eternal difference in people's lives, and without salvation they have no hope.

## Pastoral Counseling
The field of counseling is drastically under fire by many evangelical leaders who feel that it is tainted with secular psychology. That charge is valid because many churches have been pulled into secular counseling, thinking they are providing an important ministry to the body of Christ. Too many local church counseling centers are staffed by Christian counselors with good intentions, yet they have been trained at state universities, where biblical principles are not taught. They may become integrationists, mixing biblical principles with the theories of Carl Jung, Abraham Maslow, Sigmund Freud, and others. John MacArthur writes:

> The word psychology literally means "the study of the soul."
> True soul-study cannot be done by unbelievers. After all, only
> Christians have the resources for comprehending the nature of
> the human soul and understanding how it can be transformed.
> The secular discipline of psychology is based on godless
> assumptions and evolutionary foundations and is capable of

dealing with people only superficially and only on the temporal level. Sigmund Freud, the father of modern psychology, was an unbelieving humanist who devised psychology as a substitute for religion.

Before Freud, the study of the soul was thought of as a spiritual discipline. In other words, it was inherently associated with religion. Freud's chief contribution was to define the human soul and the study of human behavior in wholly secular terms. He utterly divorced anthropology (the study of human beings) from the spiritual realm and thus made way for atheistic, humanistic, and rationalistic theories about human behavior.[38]

Because so many pastors today have been university trained, they received large doses of secular psychological principles in psychology, biology, philosophy, and educational classes. Going on to seminary, many were bombarded again with psychology in the Christian counseling courses. Without getting overly complicated and technical, it is enough to point out that, because of the lack of discernment, many pastors are unaware of how anti-biblical many of the theories used in psychology such as "self-esteem," "the little child within," "self-actualization," the "hierarchy of needs" really are.

There is a place for true and honest biblical counseling in the church setting. In fact, any exhortation and encouragement on a personal level is counseling. It should be noted that the word *counseling* is a legitimate biblical word, used as such in many Bible translations. The Greek verb *parakaleo*, which relates to counseling, actually means "to call alongside." The idea is that one is "called alongside" to give advice, to comfort, to encourage, to be an advocate, to exhort, and even correct.

Using the same word, the Holy Spirit is called the believer's Comforter (John 14:16, 26; 15:26; 16:7). Jesus is called the Advocate with God the Father (1 John 2:1). The Father Himself is called "the God of all comfort" (2 Cor. 1:3). Both Paul (1 Tim. 3:12) and Peter (1 Peter 5:1) "exhorted" the child of God.

Believers in trouble are comforted (2 Cor. 1:4), the downcast are comforted also (7:6), hearts are comforted (Col. 4:8). Christians are counseled as a group how they are to walk (Eph. 4:1), and individuals such as Euodia and Syntyche were counseled (beseeched) as to how they were to live together in harmony (Phil. 4:2).

Though all agree that biblical and ministerial counseling is needed, a raging controversy divides evangelical pastors over two questions: (1) Should there be a fee charged for ministry counseling? (2) And, should others counsel besides the elder/pastors?

Without at least a minimal donation or contribution to cover reasonable counseling expenses, those coming for spiritual help take the service for granted and often fail to follow through with assigned book or Bible reading, according to Dr. Lacy Couch of Tyndale Seminary in Ft. Worth, Texas. They more quickly throw off the process of seeking godly counsel and soon quit coming to sessions altogether. In other words, even a small donation becomes an investment and those seeking help become more responsible.

Others feel that no premium should be placed on godly counsel. It should be offered and given without charge. Few would argue with this idealistic position, except to say there may be a difference between those who require extensive time to dig through some very painful and extreme issues and those who need only an hour or two in the pastor's office. One could also argue that a Christian receiving such extensive and important spiritual help would want to contribute a donation for such dedicated service.

There is strong New Testament evidence that counseling is a shared responsibility of all believers to help hurting and grieving Christian friends. Most counseling through the centuries has been carried out by godly and prayerful friends and family who are trying to give wise advice from the Bible. To say that only pastors can do this is not supported by Scripture.

The apostle Paul writes of believers in Christ having the gift of counseling. "He who exhorts, [be active] in his exhortation" (Rom. 12:8). "Exhortation" here is the Greek word *parakaleo*. Thus, "He who counsels [comes alongside], [should be active] in his counseling." He further writes that the counselors in Thessalonica should "be counseling one another, and build up one another, just as you also are doing" (1 Thess. 5:11). The writer of Hebrews urges "not forsaking our own assembling together, ... but encouraging (counseling) one another" (10:25).

The most telling proof that counseling can be done by others besides the pastor is found in 2 Corinthians 1. The apostle writes of God who is our heavenly Comfort (v. 3), who comforts us in our afflictions "so that we may be able to comfort those who are in any affliction with the comfort with which we ourselves are comforted by God" (v. 4).

If formal counseling is carried out in the local church environment, and under the umbrella of the ministry, there is no question that this must be done under the supervision of the pastors. Some commonsense rules should be in place. No one is to counsel the opposite sex alone. A spouse should be present or another counselor. To further this protection, if the pastor alone is counseling, the counseling office should have windows. And none should be thrown into the position of a lay counselor unless they demonstrate personal and biblical maturity and have some kind of training or guidance to help others. As already argued, that training should not be secular or psychologically based.

Before venturing into ministerial counseling, elder/pastors should examine state laws for restrictions that may apply. Most states leave pastoral counseling alone. But pastors have been sued by disgruntled clients. Unfortunately pastors should consider counseling insurance for protection.

### *Premarital Counseling*

Premarital counseling certainly should be carried out by an elder/pastor. This should be thorough and can take as long as six months on a weekly basis. A few of the subjects that should be discussed are:

- "Waiting" until marriage
- Roles of husband and wife
- Making decisions
- Responsibility of the husband as head of the family
- When to have children
- Issues of sex
- Discipline of children
- The importance of a clean home
- Being aware of "the little things"
- How to fight fair
- Differences between men and women
- The wife: to work or not
- Dealing with in-laws
- Quality time for relaxation and fun
- Quality time for the spiritual life

In concluding, Adams notes:

> There are many fundamental presuppositions and principles of Scripture that bear upon counseling. . . . That is true since the subject matter of counseling is precisely the same as that of the Scriptures. It is, therefore, necessary for the counselor to be well grounded in the Word of God. Theological and biblical training, then, is the essential background for a counselor; not training in psychology or psychiatry.[38]

See "The Counseling Ministers," pp. 238–39.

## Strengthening the Family

The entire Sunday school program should be constructed to support the family, from newborns to those of retirement age. The pulpit ministry along with the Sunday school must be the teaching arm of the local assembly. Innovative programs and materials should keep up with the cultural onslaught against the Christian home. This does not mean that the training programs of the church simply extinguish fires. But it does mean that the Bible must be made relevant in regard to what Christian families are facing on a daily basis.

One of the problems with the Sunday school is that it may give parents a false sense of security that they do not have to lead their children in the spiritual learning process at home. The Sunday school then should be so constructed and programmed that it involves "homework" for the entire family.

Early church history points to the fact that there was religious education. Yet the father was responsible for the biblical lessons taught at home. Most scholars believe the early churches were following the patterns of Jewish religious training.

> The home was the center of religious education and an elementary education in reading and writing. . . . The primary school [outside the home] was known as the "*beth sepher*" (or *sopher*)— "house of reading" or "of the scribe." . . . The Jewish child was expected to be able to read the Hebrew Scriptures, to memorize a standard translation in his own language if not Hebrew (called a *Targum*), and to recite certain parts of the liturgy. There was a great emphasis on memorizing Scripture.[39]

Comparing the home life of a Jewish child with statements of the apostle Paul, we know that "the personality of his parents and the atmosphere of his home were among the most potent educative factors in his early life."[40]

> The mother kept the home. The chief responsibility for the education of the children fell upon the father as head of the household. On the other hand, the first duty of children was to honor and obey their parents absolutely. . . . Life in the Hebrew home was a series of object-lessons. Each symbol, ceremony, and festival in family observance exerted an educative influence. . . . The parents, seizing this moment of excited curiosity, imparted that knowledge to the child which was so dear to themselves; the origin of each festival, the meaning of each symbol and ceremony, as the case might be, in the history and religion of their race.[41]

The elder/pastors are responsible for the final approval of the Sunday school material that can be used on the home front to strengthen each member of the family. The material should have clear instructions about the way of salvation found only in Jesus Christ. There should be an ongoing cycle of doctrine taught, along with character studies and life issues.

A continual debate about Sunday school strategy surrounds whether men and women should be in separate classes? Married adults may stay together in classes, affording husbands and wives a conversational point of contact over the biblical material learned. But there are times when men simply need to hear from men and be able to ask hard questions about marriage and the coming of mid-life crisis difficulties. The same holds true for women. Both sexes may feel more free to speak up without their spouses.

Some see no problem for boys and girls together in the same classroom, at least until puberty. At that point it is appropriate to divide them because, despite the feminist philosophy, gender issues of sexual growth and moral issues become urgent and embarrassing with the opposite sex around. Young women need mature female teachers who have "been there" and know the temptations that are prevalent. Young men as well need strong male role models to steer and guide through rough moral and spiritual waters!

Young married couples may need to be divided from time to time by gender. Emotional and sexual problems are often taking their toll on newly married couples. Young married couples will listen intently to those who have gone before them and who have fought through very tough issues.

Paul in Titus 2:1–6 sets forth the importance for reaching every adult age group in the congregation with solid teaching. The apostle spells out for Titus the spiritual strategy as to how to address the specific gender and age needs of men and women. He urges, "As for you [Titus], speak the things which are fitting for sound doctrine" (v. 1).

The faithful pastor/teacher is mandated first to teach both doctrine and biblical truth; secondly, to teach them in relationship to each other and show how the practical fits with the theory. Finally, he must relate duty to doctrine, not in a general, abstract way but in detailed applications.

> *Older men are to be temperate, dignified, sensible, sound in faith, in love, in perseverance. (v. 2)*

Stott argues that the older men in the church

> . . . need special advice and encouragement. For, as Chrysostom puts it, "there are some failings which age has, that youth has not. Some indeed it has in common with youth, but in addition it has a slowness, a timidity, a forgetfulness, an insensibility, and an irritability." The older men are to receive two main exhortations, which may be summed up in the words "dignity" and "maturity." . . . That is, they are to exhibit a certain "*gravitas*," which is both appropriate to their seniority and expressive of their inner self-control.[42]

> *Older women likewise are to be reverent in their behavior, not malicious gossips, nor enslaved to much wine, teaching what is good, that they may encourage the young women. (vv. 3–4a)*

Likewise, older women in the church

are to "practise the presence of God" and to allow their sense of his presence to permeate their whole lives. . . . the older women are strenuously to avoid two moral failures with which they have sometimes been associated. They are not to be slanderers (back-biters or scandal-mongers) or to be addicted to much wine. Thirdly, and positively, instead of using their mouths for slander, they are to use them to teach which is good (3b). Whom are they to teach? Their own family no doubt (children and grandchildren), but also and specially they can train the younger women . . . (4a). There is a need in every congregation for the ministry of mature women.[43]

*The young women, to be sensible, pure, workers at home, kind, being subject to their own husbands, that the word of God may not be dishonored. (vv. 4b–5)*

As well, the younger women in the congregation

. . . are to be trained by the older women to love their husbands and children (4b). . . . The young wives are to be "trained" in this, which implies that it can be brought under their control. . . . younger women are to be kind, perhaps in the context meaning "hospitable" and to be subject to their husbands . . . This "sub-jection" contains no notion of inferiority and no demand for obedience, but rather a recognition that, within the equal value of the sexes, God has established a created order which includes a masculine "headship," not of authority, still less of autocracy, but of responsibility and loving care. And one of the reasons the younger women are to be encouraged to comply with this teach-ing is so that no-one will malign the word of God (5b).[44]

*Likewise urge the young men to be sensible. (v. 6)*

Finally, concerning the young men in the assembly,

Paul is thinking of the control of temper and tongue, of ambition and avarice, and especially of bodily appetites, including sexual urges, so that Christian young men remain committed to the unalterable Christian standard of chastity before marriage and fidelity after it.[45]

The apostle considers it important to speak to the needs of each age and gender group in the local church. No doubt this was partially done in private discussions, but more than likely there were also formal teaching sessions set aside for gathering these groups together for addressing the issues Paul feels a definite urgency about.

Though the particulars of a teaching method or setting are not spelled out in Titus 2, that can be determined in a practical way. What is important is that it is done and that these living issues are addressed. The local assembly indeed has its teaching mandate set before it in the church epistles.

# Questions for Discussion

1. How has modernity changed the thinking of evangelicals about the ministry of the church?
2. How can a church solve the problem of being both modern in its method but also true to the biblical guidelines for ministry?
3. Review the ways a congregation is made responsible for its own ministry outreach.
4. Why is the Word of God so central in setting the ministry direction of a church?
5. Why is it important that a church care for some of the basic needs of its own?
6. Why was the problem of widows so acute in biblical times?
7. How does the church put benevolence in balance?
8. How should the church handle the problem of divorce?
9. Discuss the revealing opinions of Glasscock in this chapter.
10. Can counseling be carried out by others as well as by the church pastors?
11. Is the gift of counseling given to the entire body of Christ?
12. What must a church avoid if counseling is part of its ministry?
13. Do churches do enough to strengthen families within their congregation?
14. Is it simply enough in providing for families to have a sports gym and a lot of extracurricular family activity?

# Endnotes

**Introduction**
1. William Ames, *The Marrow of Theology* (Grand Rapids: Baker, 1997), 180–81.

**Chapter 1**
1. Bernard Ramm, *Protestant Biblical Interpretation* (Grand Rapids: Baker, 1982), 11.
2. Roy Zuck, *Basic Bible Interpretation* (Wheaton: Victor, 1991), 19.
3. A. A. Hodge, *Outlines of Theology* (Grand Rapids: Eerdmans, 1957), 21.
4. Paul Lee Tan, *The Interpretation of Prophecy* (Rockville, Mass.: Assurance, 1988), 29.
5. Zuck, *Basic Bible Interpretation,* 19.
6. James Oliver Buswell, *A Systematic Theology of the Christian Religion* (Grand Rapids: Zondervan, 1977), 24–26.
7. Walter C. Kaiser, *Toward an Exegetical Theology* (Grand Rapids: Baker, 1981), 44–45.
8. Ramm, *Protestant Biblical Interpretation,* 12–16.
9. Zuck, *Basic Bible Interpretation,* 25.
10. Kaiser, *Toward an Exegetical Theology,* 45.
11. Ramm, *Protestant Biblical Interpretation,* 14.
12. Charles C. Ryrie, *Dispensationalism* (Chicago: Moody, 1995), 25.
13. Ibid., 28.
14. Clarence E. Mason, *Dispensationalism Made Simple* (Arnold, Mo.: Shield, 1976), 19.
15. Mal Couch, *God's Plan of the Ages* (Ft. Worth: Seminary Press, n.d.), 17.
16. Paul N. Benware, *Understanding End Times Prophecy* (Chicago: Moody, 1995), 84.
17. Paul Enns, *The Moody Handbook of Theology* (Chicago: Moody, 1989), 389.
18. W. Robertson Nicoll, *The Expositor's Greek Testament,* 5 vols. (Grand Rapids: Eerdmans, 1988), 3:259–60.

19. Ryrie, *Dispensationalism,* 142.
20. Enns, *The Moody Handbook of Theology,* 520–21.
21. Lewis S. Chafer, *Major Bible Themes,* rev. John F. Walvoord (Grand Rapids: Zondervan, 1974), 236.
22. Ibid., 240–41.

## Chapter 2

1. John Eadie, *Commentary on the Epistle to the Galatians* (Grand Rapids: Zondervan, 1984), 470–71.
2. Louis Berkhof, *Systematic Theology* (Grand Rapids: Eerdmans, 1994), 568.
3. Ibid., 569.
4. Ibid.
5. Ibid.
6. Ibid.
7. W. Robertson, Nicoll, ed., *The Expositor's Greek Testament,* 5 vols. (reprint, Grand Rapids: Eerdmans, 1990), 3:293.
8. Charles Hodge, *Commentary on the Epistle to the Ephesians* (Grand Rapids: Eerdmans, 1994), 131–39.
9. Simon J. Kistemaker, *Acts,* New Testament Commentary (Grand Rapids: Baker, 1995), 90–91.
10. J. A. Alexander, *Commentary on the Acts of the Apostles* (Grand Rapids: Zondervan, 1956), 61–63.
11. Horatio B. Hackett, *Commentary on Acts* (Grand Rapids: Kregel, 1992), 46–47.
12. Stanley D. Toussaint, "Acts," in *The Bible Knowledge Commentary, New Testament,* ed. John F. Walvoord and Roy B. Zuck (Wheaton: Victor, 1978), 358.
13. Charles C. Ryrie, *Dispensationalism Today* (Chicago: Moody, 1965), 123.
14. L. S. Chafer, "Inventing Heretics Through Misunderstanding," *Bibliotheca Sacra* 101 (July 1944): 259.
15. L. S. Chafer, *Grace* (Findlay, Ohio: Dunham, 1922), 113.
16. Ryrie, *Dispensationalism Today,* 109. For a more in-depth discussion of the relationship of Law and grace in the dispensation of Law see Ryrie's discussion in this excellent volume cited.
17. Ibid., 117.
18. Paul Enns, *The Moody Handbook of Theology* (Chicago: Moody, 1989), 522.
19. Lewis S. Chafer, *Systematic Theology,* 8 vols. in 4 (Grand Rapids: Kregel, 1993), 7:176, quoting C. I. Scofield, *Scofield Reference Bible,* 1343.
20. Ryrie, *Dispensationalism Today,* 123.
21. Charles C. Ryrie, *Dispensationalism* (Chicago: Moody, 1995), 120–21.
22. Ibid.
23. James Orr, *The Progress of Dogma* (Grand Rapids: Eerdmans, n.d.), 303–4.
24. Berkhof, *Systematic Theology,* 217.
25. Paul Benware, *Understanding End Times Prophecy* (Chicago: Moody, 1995), 79.

26. Berkhof, *Systematic Theology*, 265.
27. Hodge, *Commentary on the Epistle to the Ephesians,* 2:358.
28. Ibid.
29. Ibid., 359.
30. Ibid.
31. Ibid., 364.
32. Charles C. Ryrie, *Dispensationalism,* rev. ed. (Chicago: Moody, 1995), 190.
33. Ibid.
34. William Hendriksen, *The Gospel of Matthew* (Grand Rapids: Baker, 1982), 651.
35. A. T. Robertson, *Word Pictures in the New Testament,* 6 vols. (Nashville: Broadman, 1930), 1:133–34.
36. R. C. H. Lenski, *The Interpretation of Matthew* (Minneapolis: Augsburg, 1961), 628–29.
37. D. A. Carson, "Matthew," in *The Expositor's Bible Commentary,* 12 vols., ed. Frank E. Gaebelein (Grand Rapids: Zondervan, 1984), 8:369.
38. Hendriksen, *Gospel of Matthew,* 646.
39. Carson, "Matthew," 8:370–71.
40. Edward Denny, *Papalism* (London: Rivingtons, 1912), 30.
41. Ibid., 41.
42. Joseph Deharbe, *A Complete Catechism of the Catholic Religion* (New York: Schwartz, Kirwin & Fauss, 1912), 134.
43. Ibid.
44. Ibid., 135–36.
45. Ibid., 139.
46. Ibid., 141.
47. Ibid., 141–42.
48. Ibid., 142.
49. Ibid., 145.
50. Ibid., 146.
51. Ibid., 148–49.
52. Ibid., 149.
53. Ibid., 148.

## Chapter 3

1. Stanley Toussaint, "Matthew," in *The Bible Knowledge Commentary, New Testament*, ed. John F. Walvoord and Roy B. Zuck (Wheaton, Ill.: Victor, 1983), 354.
2. Charles C. Ryrie, *Ryrie Study Bible* (Chicago: Moody, 1986).
3. Toussaint, "Matthew," 358.
4. Walter Bauer, *A Greek-English Lexicon of the New Testament and Other Early Christian Literature,* 2nd ed., rev. F. Wilbur Gingrich and Frederick W. Danker, trans. (Chicago: University of Chicago Press, 1957, 1979), 766.
5. W. Robertson Nicoll, *The Expositor's Greek Testament,* 5 vols. (Grand Rapids: Eerdmans, 1988), 3:241–42.
6. Charles Hodge, *Commentary on the Epistle to the Ephesians* (Grand Rapids: Eerdmans, 1994), 222–23.

7. John MacArthur Jr., *Ephesians,* The MacArthur New Testament Commentary (Chicago: Moody, 1986), 1, 82.
8. Ibid., 142–43.
9. James Hastings, ed., *A Dictionary of the Bible* (Peabody, Mass.: Hendrickson, 1988), 1:103–4.
10. W. J. Conybeare and J. S. Howson, *The Life and Epistles of St. Paul* (Grand Rapids: Eerdmans, 1980), 103.
11. Bernard Ramm, *Protestant Biblical Interpretation* (Grand Rapids: Baker, 1986), 48.
12. Ibid., 49.
13. Ibid.
14. Ibid., 50.
15. Ibid.

## Chapter 4

1. R. C. H. Lenski, *The Interpretation of St. Paul's Epistles to the Galatians, Ephesians, and Philippians* (Minneapolis: Augsburg, 1961), 625.
2. Gerhard Kittel, ed., *Theological Dictionary of the New Testament,* trans. Geoffrey W. Bromiley, 10 vols. (Grand Rapids: Eerdmans, 1987 reprint), 8:37–45.
3. A. T. Robertson, *Word Pictures in the New Testament,* 6 vols. (Nashville: Broadman, 1930), 4:544.
4. T. K. Abbott, *Ephesians and Colossians,* The International Critical Commentary, ed. Charles Briggs, Samuel Driver, and Alfred Plummer (New York: Charles Scribner's Sons, 1911), 164.
5. Lenski, *Interpretation of St. Paul's Epistles,* 636–37.
6. Albert Barnes, *Acts,* Barnes on the New Testament, 14 vols. (Grand Rapids: Baker, 1956), 12:113.
7. H. E. Dana and Julius R. Mantey, *A Manual Grammar of the Greek New Testament* (New York: Macmillan, 1958), 241.
8. Lenski, *Interpretation of St. Paul's Epistles,* 627–28.
9. A. Skevington Wood, "Ephesians," in *The Expositor's Bible Commentary,* 12 vols., ed. Frank E. Gaebelein (Grand Rapids: Zondervan, 1978), 11:75.
10. Horst Balz and Gerhard Schneider, eds., *Exegetical Dictionary of the New Testament* (Grand Rapids: Eerdmans, 1991), 2:285.
11. Ibid., 286.
12. John MacArthur Jr., *Ephesians,* The MacArthur New Testament Commentary (Chicago: Moody, 1986), 288.
13. Ibid., 289.
14. Charles Hodge, *Commentary on the Epistle to the Ephesians* (Grand Rapids: Eerdmans, 1994), 313.
15. W. Robertson Nicoll, *The Expositor's Greek Testament,* 5 vols. (Grand Rapids: Eerdmans, 1988), 3:371.
16. Henry Alford, *Alford's Greek Testament: An Exegetical and Critical Commentary,* 6 vols. (Grand Rapids: Guardian, 1976 reprint), 3:139.

17. Everett F. Harrison and Charles F. Pfeiffer, eds., *The Wycliffe Bible Commentary* (Chicago: Moody, 1962), 1314.
18. Harold W. Hoehner, "Ephesians," in *The Bible Knowledge Commentary, New Testament,* ed. John F. Walvoord and Roy B. Zuck (Wheaton: Victor, 1983), 641.
19. Barnes, *Acts,* 12:113.
20. Ibid., 257.
21. Charles Ryrie, *The Basis of the Premillennial Faith* (New York: Loizeaux Brothers, 1953), 130–34.
22. Ibid.
23. Hoehner, "Ephesians," 641.

**Chapter 5**
1. Ronald E. Baxter, *Gifts of the Spirit* (Grand Rapids: Kregel, 1983), 11.
2. For instance Merrill F. Unger, *The Baptism and Gifts of the Holy Spirit* (Chicago: Moody, 1974); Ronald E. Baxter, *The Charismatic Gift of Tongues* (Grand Rapids: Kregel, 1981); Ronald E. Baxter, *Gifts of the Spirit* (Grand Rapids: Kregel, 1983); John F. MacArthur Jr., *Speaking in Tongues* (Panorama City, Calif.: Grace to You Communications, 1988); idem, *The Charismatics: A Doctrinal Perspective* (Grand Rapids: Zondervan, 1978); John F. Walvoord, *The Holy Spirit* (Grand Rapids: Zondervan, 1991); and Frederick Dale Bruner, *A Theology of the Holy Spirit* (Grand Rapids: Eerdmans, 1970).
3. Walvoord, *The Holy Spirit,* 164.
4. Thomas R. Edgar, *Satisfied by the Promise of the Spirit* (Grand Rapids: Kregel, 1996), 41.
5. Ibid.
6. Walter Bauer, *A Greek-English Lexicon of the New Testament and Other Early Christian Literature,* 2nd ed., rev. F. W. Gingrich and Frederick Danker, trans. William F. Arndt and F. W. Gingrich (Chicago: Chicago University Press, 1979), 780.
7. Walvoord, *The Holy Spirit,* 165.
8. Bauer, *Greek-English Lexicon of the New Testament,* 56.
9. Charles C. Ryrie, *Basic Theology* (Wheaton: Victor, 1986), 375.
10. Edgar, *Satisfied by the Promise of the Spirit,* 35.
11. Walvoord, *The Holy Spirit,* 164–65.
12. Ibid., 173.
13. D. Müller, "Apostle," in *The New International Dictionary of New Testament Theology,* 4 vols., ed. Colin Brown (Grand Rapids: Zondervan, 1975, 1986), 1:126.
14. Edgar, *Satisfied by the Promise of the Spirit,* 52.
15. Müller, "Apostle," 128–29.
16. For a discussion of whether these should be taken as "apostles" in the official sense see Edgar, *Satisfied by the Promise of the Spirit,* 52–65.
17. Edgar, *Satisfied by the Promise of the Spirit,* 59.
18. K. Hess, "Serve," in *The New International Dictionary of New Testament Theology,* 3:546.

19. Baxter, *Gifts of the Spirit,* 209.
20. C. Peter Wagner, *Your Spiritual Gifts Can Help Your Church* (Glendale, Calif.: Regal, 1979), 226.
21. Bauer, *Greek-English Lexicon of the New Testament,* 191.
22. Ibid.
23. Douglas Moo, "What Does It Mean Not to Teach or Have Authority over Men?" in *Recovering Biblical Manhood and Womanhood,* ed. John Piper and Wayne Grudem (Wheaton, Ill.: Crossway, 1991), 185.
24. Walvoord, *The Holy Spirit,* 168.
25. Ibid., 170.
26. Ibid.
27. G. Braumann, "Exhort," in *The New International Dictionary of New Testament Theology,* 4 vols., ed. Colin Brown (Grand Rapids: Zondervan, 1975, 1986), 1:570.
28. Walvoord, *The Holy Spirit,* 170–71.
29. Braumann, "Exhort," 570.
30. Leslie B. Flynn, *19 Gifts of the Spirit* (Wheaton, Ill.: Victor, 1974), 82–83.
31. Translation from R. C. H. Lenski, *The Interpretation of St. Paul's Epistle to the Romans* (Minneapolis: Augsburg, 1936), 55.
32. Bauer, *Greek-English Lexicon of the New Testament,* 85–86.
33. Flynn, *19 Gifts of the Spirit,* 118.
34. Bauer, *Greek-English Lexicon of the New Testament,* 707.
35. L. Coenen, "Bishop," in *The New International Dictionary of New Testament Theology,* 1:197.
36. Bauer, *Greek-English Lexicon of the New Testament,* 763.
37. Lenski, *Interpretation of St. Paul's Epistle to the Romans,* 765.
38. Flynn, *19 Gifts of the Spirit,* 127.
39. H. H. Esser, "Mercy," in *The New International Dictionary of New Testament Theology,* 2:594.
40. W. E. Vine, Merrill F. Unger, and William White Jr., eds., *Vine's Expository Dictionary of Biblical Words* (Nashville, Tenn.: Nelson, 1985), 403–4.
41. Baxter, *Gifts of the Spirit,* 223, quoting W. A. Criswell, *The Holy Spirit in Today's World* (Grand Rapids: Zondervan, 1967), 223.
42. Lenski, *Interpretation of St. Paul's Epistle to the Romans,* 765.
43. U. Becker, "Gospel, Evangelize, Evangelist," in *The New International Dictionary of New Testament Theology,* 2:107.
44. Walvoord, *The Holy Spirit,* 169–70.
45. Wagner, *Your Spiritual Gifts Can Help Your Church,* 224.
46. Baxter, *Gifts of the Spirit,* 221–22.
47. R. C. H. Lenski, *The Interpretation of I and II Corinthians* (Minneapolis: Augsburg, 1937), 540.
48. Baxter, *Gifts of the Spirit,* 205.
49. Ibid., 205–6.
50. Walvoord, *The Holy Spirit,* 172.
51. Baxter, *Gifts of the Spirit,* 67–74.

## Chapter 6

1. Horst Balz and Gerhard Schneider, eds., *Exegetical Dictionary of the New Testament,* 3 vols. (Grand Rapids: Eerdmans, 1993), 3:130.
2. J. B. Lightfoot, *Paul's Epistle to the Philippians* (Lynn, Mass.: Hendrickson, 1981), 156.
3. Martin Luther, *Commentary on Peter and Jude* (Grand Rapids: Kregel, 1990), 302.
4. Walter Bauer, *A Greek-English Lexicon of the New Testament and Other Early Christian Literature,* 2nd ed., rev. F. Wilbur Gingrich and Frederick W. Danker (Chicago: University of Chicago Press, 1957, 1979), 256.
5. Balz and Schneider, *Exegetical Dictionary,* 1:446.
6. David K. Lowery, "1 Corinthians," in *The Bible Knowledge Commentary, New Testament,* ed. John F. Walvoord and Roy B. Zuck (Wheaton: Victor, 1978), 515.
7. Arthur Stanley, *The Epistles of St. Paul to the Corinthians* (Minneapolis, Minn.: Klock & Klock, 1981), 94.
8. Thomas Edwards, *A Commentary on the First Epistle to the Corinthians* (Minneapolis, Minn.: Klock & Klock, 1979), 138.
9. Charles Hodge, *An Exposition of the First Epistle to the Corinthians* (Grand Rapids: Eerdmans, 1956), 94.
10. Ibid., 95–96.
11. Robert Thomas, *Revelation 1–7: An Exegetical Commentary* (Chicago: Moody, 1992), 233, 225–26.
12. J. Vernon McGee, *Reveling Through Revelation,* 2 vols. (Los Angeles: Church of the Open Door, n.d.), 1:47.
13. Thomas, *Revelation 1–7,* 484–85.
14. Ibid., 199.
15. John F. Walvoord, *The Revelation of Jesus Christ* (Chicago: Moody, 1966), 70.
16. Ibid., 70–71.
17. Thomas, *Revelation 1–7,* 292.
18. Ibid., 293.
19. Ibid., 462.
20. Walvoord, *Revelation of Jesus Christ,* 322.

## Chapter 7

1. John Horsch, *Modern Religious Liberalism* (Chicago: Bible Institute Colportage Assoc., 1921).
2. Ibid., 10.
3. Ibid.
4. Ibid., 10–11.
5. Ibid., 11.
6. Ibid., 220.
7. Ibid.
8. Ibid., 315.
9. Ibid., 315–16.
10. W. Robertson Nicoll, *The Expositor's Greek Testament* (Grand Rapids: Eerdmans, 1988), 120.

11.  Horst Balz and Gerhard Schneider, eds., *Exegetical Dictionary of the New Testament,* 3 vols. (Grand Rapids: Eerdmans, 1994), 3:211.

12.  Walter Bauer, *A Greek-English Lexicon of the New Testament and Other Early Christian Literature,* 2nd ed., rev. F. Wilbur Gingrich and Frederick W. Danker, trans. William F. Arndt and F. Wilbur Gingrich (Chicago: University of Chicago Press, 1957, 1979), 857.

13.  Nicoll, *The Expositor's Greek Testament,* 4:169.

14.  Bauer, *Greek-English Lexicon of the New Testament,* 126.

15.  Albert Barnes, *Notes on the New Testament,* 14 vols. (Grand Rapids: Baker, 1983), 12:158.

16.  R. C. H. Lenski, *The Interpretation of St. Paul's Epistles to the Colossians, to the Thessalonians, to Timothy, to Titus and to Philemon* (Minneapolis: Augsburg, 1961), 618–19.

17.  William Hendriksen, *Thessalonians, Timothy and Titus,* New Testament Commentary (Grand Rapids: Baker, 1983), 146.

18.  Lenski, *Interpretation of St. Paul's Epistles,* 623.

19.  Patrick Fairbairn, *Commentary on the Pastoral Epistles* (Grand Rapids: Zondervan, 1956), 172.

20.  Lenski, *Interpretation of St. Paul's Epistles,* 627.

21.  Barnes, *Notes on the New Testament,* 231.

22.  Lenski, *Interpretation of St. Paul's Epistles,* 820.

23.  Ibid., 819.

24.  Bauer, *Greek-English Lexicon of the New Testament,* 266.

25.  Barnes, *Notes on the New Testament,* 231.

26.  Lenski, *Interpretation of St. Paul's Epistles,* 821.

27.  Ibid., 822.

28.  Colin Brown, ed., *The New International Dictionary of New Testament Theology,* 3 vols. (Grand Rapids: Zondervan, 1977), 2:539.

29.  William Hendriksen, *Thessalonians, Timothy and Titus,* New Testament Commentaries (Grand Rapids: Baker, 1979), 285.

30.  Barnes, *Notes on the New Testament,* 232.

31.  Ibid., 233.

32.  Hendriksen, *Thessalonians, Timothy and Titus,* 285.

33.  Bauer, *Greek-English Lexicon of the New Testament,* 326.

34.  Hendriksen, *Thessalonians, Timothy and Titus,* 285.

35.  Lenski, *Interpretation of St. Paul's Epistles,* 618.

36.  Thomas Manton, *Commentary on Jude* (Grand Rapids: Kregel, 1988), 333.

### Chapter 8

1.  Mal Couch, "Major Rapture Terms and Passages," in *When the Trumpet Sounds,* ed. Thomas Ice and Timothy Demy (Eugene, Ore.: Harvest House, 1995), 26–56.

2.  Marvin R. Vincent, *Word Studies in the New Testament,* vol. 4 (McLean, Va.: MacDonald, 1888), 4:41.

3.  Fritz Reinecker, *Linguistic Key to the Greek New Testament,* rev. and trans. Cleon Rogers (Grand Rapids: Zondervan, 1976, 1980), 599.

4.  H. E. Dana and Julius R. Mantey, *A Manual Grammar of the Greek New Testament* (New York: Macmillan, 1957), 172.
5.  A. T. Robertson, *Word Pictures in the New Testament,* 6 vols. (Nashville: Broadman, 1931), 4:36.
6.  Walter Bauer, *A Greek-English Lexicon of the New Testament and Other Early Christian Literature,* 2nd ed., rev. F. W. Gingrich and Frederick Danker, trans. William F. Arndt and F. W. Gingrich (Chicago: Chicago University Press, 1979), 41.
7.  William Hendriksen, *1 Thessalonians,* New Testament Commentary (Grand Rapids: Baker, 1990), 128.
8.  Alfred Plummer and Arch Robertson, *1 Corinthians,* The International Critical Commentary (New York: Charles Scribner's Sons, 1911), 354.
9.  Charles John Ellicott, ed., *Ellicott's Commentary on the Whole Bible* (Grand Rapids: Zondervan, 1959), 8:348.
10. Henry Alford, *Alford's Greek Testament* (Grand Rapids: Guardian, 1976), 3:609.
11. Plummer and Robertson, *1 Corinthians,* 354.
12. Ibid.
13. Robertson, *Word Pictures,* 4:36.
14. Ibid., 4:61.
15. Albert Barnes, *Barnes' Notes on the New Testament* (repr. ed., Grand Rapids: Baker, 1996), 13:88.
16. Robertson, *Word Pictures,* 4:14.
17. Hendriksen, *1 Thessalonians,* 57.
18. *Barnes' Notes,* 12:18.
19. John Calvin, *Calvin's Commentaries* (Grand Rapids: Baker, 1989), 21:279.
20. Leon Morris, *The First and Second Epistles to the Thessalonians* (Grand Rapids: Eerdmans, 1979), 146.
21. Robertson, *Word Pictures,* 4:47.
22. David K. Lowery, "1 Corinthians," in *The Bible Knowledge Commentary, New Testament,* ed. John Walvoord and Roy Zuck (Wheaton: Victor, 1984), 543–44.
23. W. Robertson Nicoll, ed., *The Expositor's Greek Testament* (Grand Rapids: Eerdmans, 1988), 2:940.
24. Plummer and Robertson, *1 Corinthians,* 376.
25. Bauer, *Greek-English Lexicon of the New Testament,* 38.
26. Henry George Liddell and Robert Scott, comps., *A Greek-English Lexicon* (Oxford: At the Clarendon, 1968), 68.
27. *Barnes' Notes,* 11: 319–20.
28. Bauer, *Greek-English Lexicon of the New Testament,* 176.
29. Alford, *Alford's Greek Testament,* 186.
30. Robertson, *Word Pictures,* 4:547.
31. Alford, *Alford's Greek Testament,* 419.
32. Bauer, *Greek-English Lexicon of the New Testament,* 176.
33. Nicoll, *Expositor's Greek Testament,* 4:195.
34. Bauer, *Greek-English Lexicon of the New Testament,* 636.

35. Zane C. Hodges, "1 John," in *The Bible Knowledge Commentary, New Testament,* 893.
36. Liddell and Scott, *Greek-English Lexicon,* 68.
37. Ibid., 1117.
38. Ibid., 1757.
39. Homer A. Kent Jr., "Philippians," in *The Expositor's Bible Commentary,* 12 vols. (Grand Rapids: Zondervan, 1984), 11:148.
40. Dana and Mantey, *Manual Grammar,* 246.
41. *Barnes' Notes,* 13:312.
42. Robertson, *Word Pictures,* 5:249.
43. Dana and Mantey, *Manual Grammar,* 185.
44. Alford, *Alford's Greek Testament,* 288.
45. Ellicott, *Ellicott's Commentary on the Whole Bible,* 84.
46. Hendriksen, *1 Thessalonians,* 57.
47. Liddell and Scott, *Greek-English Lexicon,* 467.
48. Bauer, *Greek-English Lexicon of the New Testament,* 744.
49. Alford, *Alford's Greek Testament,* 253.
50. Robert L. Thomas, "1 Thessalonians," in *The Expositor's Bible Commentary,* 12 vols. (Grand Rapids: Zondervan, 1984), 11:248
51. Liddell and Scott, *Greek-English Lexicon,* 693.
52. Vincent, *Word Studies,* 4:20.
53. Morris, *First and Second Epistles to the Thessalonians,* 145.
54. Robertson, *Word Pictures,* 6:219.
55. Bauer, *Greek-English Lexicon of the New Testament,* 657.
56. Robertson, *Word Pictures,* 6:219.
57. Bauer, *Greek-English Lexicon of the New Testament,* 770.
58. Ibid., 64.
59. Robertson, *Word Pictures,* 6:219.
60. Hodges, "1 John," 893.
61. Adolf Deissmann, *Light from the Ancient East* (New York: Doran, 1927), 368.
62. Robertson, *Word Pictures,* 5:249.
63. Dana and Mantey, *Manual Grammar,* 185.
64. Liddell and Scott, *Greek-English Lexicon,* 467.
65. Gerhard Kittel, *The Theological Dictionary of the New Testament* (Grand Rapids: Eerdmans, 1987), 2:330.
66. *Barnes' Notes,* 13:89.
67. Ellicott, *Ellicott's Commentary on the Whole Bible,* 8:154.
68. Robertson, *Word Pictures,* 5:47.
69. Dana and Mantey, *Manual Grammar,* 115.
70. Vincent, *Word Studies,* 4:345.
71. D. Edmond Hiebert, "Titus," in *The Expositor's Bible Commentary,* 12 vols. (Grand Rapids: Zondervan, 1984), 11:440–41.
72. Dana and Mantey, *Manual Grammar,* 147.
73. Thomas, "1 Thessalonians," 11:285.
74. Kent, "Philippians," 11:148.
75. Thomas D. Ice, "Rapture, The History of," in *The Premillennial Dictionary of Theology,* ed. Mal Couch (Grand Rapids: Kregel, 1996), 344–47.

76. John F. Walvoord, *The Blessed Hope and the Tribulation* (Grand Rapids: Zondervan, 1976), 24–25.

77. Kurt Aland, *A History of Christianity,* vol. 1 (Philadelphia: Fortress, 1985), 87–93; Millard J. Erickson, *Contemporary Options in Eschatology* (Grand Rapids: Baker, 1977), 112; and J. Barton Payne, *The Imminent Appearing of Christ* (Grand Rapids: Eerdmans, 1962), 12–19.

78. Larry V. Crutchfield, "The Blessed Hope and the Tribulation in the Apostolic Fathers," in *When the Trumpet Sounds,* ed. Thomas Ice and Timothy Demy (Eugene, Ore.: Harvest House, 1995), 103.

79. Ibid., 88–101.

80. *The Shepherd of Hermas* 1.4.2.

81. For more information on this matter see Timothy J. Demy and Thomas D. Ice, "The Rapture and an Early Medieval Citation," *Bibliotheca Sacra* 152, no. 607 (July–September 1995), 306–17.

82. Dorothy deF. Abrahamse, introduction to *The Byzantine Apocalyptic Tradition,* by Paul J. Alexander (Berkeley: University of California Press, 1985), 1–2.

83. Paul Boyer, *When Time Shall Be No More: Prophecy Belief in Modern American Culture* (Cambridge, Mass.: Belknap, 1992), 75.

84. Paul N. Benware, *Understanding End Times Prophecy: A Comprehensive Approach* (Chicago: Moody, 1995), 197–98.

85. Frank Marotta, *Morgan Edwards: An Eighteenth Century Pretribulationist* (Morganville, N.J.: Present Truth, 1995), 10–12.

86. Ibid.

87. Roy A. Huebner, *Precious Truths Revived and Defended Through J. N. Darby,* vol. 1 (Morganville, N.J.: Present Truth, 1991), 63–77.

## Chapter 9

1. Albert Barnes, *Matthew and Mark,* Notes on the New Testament (Grand Rapids: Baker, 1983), 63.

2. Zane C. Hodges, "2 John," in *The Bible Knowledge Commentary, New Testament,* ed. John F. Walvoord and Roy B. Zuck (Wheaton: Victor, 1983), 907.

3. Douglas Moo, *The Wycliffe Exegetical Commentary, Romans 1–8* (Chicago: Moody, 1991), 504.

4. Colin Brown, ed., *The New International Dictionary of New Testament Theology,* 5 vols. (Grand Rapids: Zondervan, 1977), 2:369.

5. David R. Nicholas, "Various Judgments," in *The Dictionary of Premillennial Theology* (Grand Rapids: Kregel, 1997), 226.

6. David K. Lowery, "2 Corinthians," in *The Bible Knowledge Commentary, New Testament,* 566.

7. Charles Hodge, *Commentary on the First Epistle to the Corinthians* (repr. ed., Grand Rapids: Eerdmans, 1994), 68.

8. Walter Bauer, *A Greek-English Lexicon of the New Testament and Other Early Christian Literature,* 2nd ed., rev. F. Wilbur Gingrich and Frederick W. Danker (Chicago: University of Chicago Press, 1957, 1979), 443.

9.  A. T. Robertson, *Word Pictures in the New Testament,* 6 vols. (Nashville: Broadman, 1930), 4:229.
10. Ibid.
11. W. Robertson Nicoll, *The Expositor's Greek Testament,* 5 vols. (Grand Rapids: Eerdmans, 1988), 2:796–97.
12. John Eadie, *Commentary on the Epistle to the Colossians* (Grand Rapids: Zondervan, 1957), 267.
13. Nicoll, *Expositor's Greek Testament,* 2:792.
14. Ibid., 3:69–70.
15. Charles Hodge, *Commentary on the Second Epistle to the Corinthians* (Grand Rapids: Eerdmans, 1994), 132–33.
16. Paul Enns, *The Moody Handbook of Theology* (Chicago: Moody, 1989), 392.

## Chapter 10

1.  Philip Schaff, *History of the Christian Church,* 22 vols. (reprint, Grand Rapids: Eerdmans, 1988), 1:488, 491–92.
2.  Ibid., 7:529.
3.  Ibid., 8:153.
4.  Merrill C. Tenney, *The Zondervan Pictorial Encyclopedia of the Bible,* 5 vols. (Grand Rapids: Zondervan, 1975, 1976), 1:854.
5.  J. D. Douglas, ed., *New Bible Dictionary,* 2d ed. (Wheaton: Tyndale House, 1987), 208.

## Chapter 11

1.  S. Safrai and M. Stern, ed., *The Jewish People in the First Century* (Philadelphia: Fortress, 1974), 489–96.
2.  Francis Brown, ed., *The New Brown-Driver-Briggs Gesenius Hebrew and English Lexicon* (Peabody, Mass.: Hendrickson, 1979), 278.
3.  Merrill C. Tenney, *The Zondervan Pictorial Encyclopedia of the Bible,* 5 vols. (Grand Rapids: Zondervan, 1975, 1976), 2:269.
4.  A. T. Robertson, *Word Pictures in the New Testament,* 6 vols. (Nashville: Broadman, 1930), 4:537.
5.  John MacArthur Jr., *Ephesians,* The MacArthur New Testament Commentary (Chicago: Moody, 1986), 143.
6.  W. Robertson Nicoll, *The Expositor's Greek Testament,* 5 vols. (Grand Rapids: Eerdmans, 1988), 3:330.
7.  Henry Alford, *Alford's Greek Testament: An Exegetical and Critical Commentary,* 6 vols. (reprint, Grand Rapids: Guardian, 1976), 3:116.
8.  Robertson, *Word Pictures,* 4:537.
9.  H. A. Meyer, *Ephesians,* Commentary on the New Testament, rev. and ed. William P. Dickson (Edinburgh: T & T Clark, 1880), 219.
10. John Gill, *Ephesians,* Exposition of the Old and New Testaments, 9 vols. (Paris, Ark.: Baptist Standard Bearer, 1989), 9:89.
11. John Calvin, *Ephesians,* Calvin's Commentaries, 22 vols. (repr. ed., Grand Rapids: Baker, 1989), 21:279).
12. Robertson, *Word Pictures,* 4:390.

13. *The Pulpit Commentary,* 31 vols. (Grand Rapids: Baker, 1981), 20:164.
14. Harold W. Hoehner, "Ephesians," in *The Bible Knowledge Commentary, New Testament,* ed. John F. Walvoord and Roy B. Zuck (Wheaton: Victor, 1983), 635.
15. MacArthur, *Ephesians,* 145.
16. A. Skevington Wood, "Ephesians," in *The Expositor's Bible Commentary,* 12 vols., ed. Frank E. Gaebelein (Grand Rapids: Zondervan, 1978), 11:58.
17. MacArthur, *Ephesians,* 144.
18. Ibid.
19. Walter Bauer; *A Greek-English Lexicon of the New Testament and Other Early Christian Literature,* rev. F. Wilbur Gingrich and Frederich W. Danker, trans. William F. Arndt and William F. Gingrich (Chicago: The University of Chicago Press, 1979), 817.
20. Ralph Earle, "1, 2 Timothy," in *The Expositor's Bible Commentary,* 12 vols., ed. Frank E. Gaebelein (Grand Rapids: Zondervan, 1978), 11:380.
21. John Gill, *1 Timothy,* Exposition of the Old and New Testaments, 9:303.
22. A. Duane Litfin, "1 Timothy," in *The Bible Knowledge Commentary, New Testament,* 744.
23. Albert Barnes, *1 Timothy,* Barnes on the New Testament, 14 vols. (Grand Rapids: Baker, 1956), 12:182.
24. Patrick Fairbairn, *Commentary on the Pastoral Epistles* (Grand Rapids: Zondervan, 1956), 216.
25. William Hendriksen, *1 Timothy,* New Testament Commentary (Grand Rapids: Baker, 1982), 181.

## Chapter 12

1. Patrick Fairbairn, *Commentary on the Pastoral Epistles* (Grand Rapids: Zondervan, 1956), 136.
2. Ibid., 139.
3. Ibid., 418–19.
4. Albert Barnes, *1 Timothy,* Barnes on the New Testament, 14 vols. (Grand Rapids: Baker, 1956), 12:143.
5. William Hendriksen, *1 Timothy,* New Testament Commentary (Grand Rapids: Baker, 1982), 123.
6. Walter Bauer, *A Greek-English Lexicon of the New Testament and Other Early Christian Literature,* 2nd ed., rev. F. Wilbur Gingrich and Frederick W. Danker (Chicago: University of Chicago Press, 1957, 1979), 445.
7. Barnes, *1 Timothy,* 144.
8. Fairbairn, *Commentary on the Pastoral Epistles,* 141.
9. Bauer, *Greek-English Lexicon of the New Testament,* 292.
10. Hendriksen, *1 Timothy,* 125.
11. Fairbairn, *Commentary on the Pastoral Epistles,* 141.
12. Bauer, *Greek-English Lexicon of the New Testament,* 707.
13. Ibid., 400.
14. R. C. H. Lenski, *The Interpretation of St. Paul's Epistles to the Colossians, to the Thessalonians, to Timothy, to Titus and to Philemon* (Minneapolis: Augsburg, 1961), 585.

15. John Gill, *1 Timothy,* Exposition of the Old and New Testaments, 9 vols. (Paris, Ark.: Baptist Standard Bearer, 1989) 9:602.

16. Bauer, *Greek-English Lexicon of the New Testament,* 848.

17. Fairbairn, *Commentary on the Pastoral Epistles,* 142.

18. Barnes, *1 Timothy,* 145.

19. Ibid., 147.

20. Bauer, *Greek-English Lexicon of the New Testament,* 64.

21. John Gill, *Titus,* Exposition of the Old and New Testaments, 9:651.

22. Barnes, *Titus,* Barnes on the New Testament, 12:268.

23. Gill, *Titus,* 651.

24. Fairbairn, *Commentary on the Pastoral Epistles,* 261.

25. Barnes, *Titus,* 12:268.

26. Bauer, *Greek-English Lexicon of the New Testament,* 579.

27. Barnes, *Titus,* 12:268.

28. Bauer, *Greek-English Lexicon of the New Testament,* 585.

29. Barnes, *Titus,* 12:269.

30. Gill, *Titus,* 651.

31. John Stott, *Guard the Truth* (Downers Grove, Ill.: InterVarsity, 1996), 91.

32. Henry George Liddell and Robert Scott, comps., *A Greek-English Lexicon* (Oxford: Clarendon, 1990), 657.

33. Bauer, *Greek-English Lexicon of the New Testament,* 298.

34. Simon J. Kistemaker, *Acts,* New Testament Commentary (Grand Rapids: Baker, 1990), 224.

35. A. T. Robertson, *Word Pictures in the New Testament,* 6 vols. (Nashville: Broadman, 1930), 4:435.

36. Bauer, *Greek-English Lexicon of the New Testament,* 584.

37. W. Robertson Nicoll, *The Expositor's Greek Testament,* 5 vols. (Grand Rapids: Eerdmans, 1988), 114.

38. Ibid., 115.

39. Ibid.

40. Bauer, *Greek-English Lexicon of the New Testament,* 202.

41. Nicoll, *Expositor's Greek Testament,* 4:115.

42. A. Duane Litfin, "1 Timothy," in *The Bible Knowledge Commentary, New Testament,* ed. John F. Walvoord and Roy B. Zuck (Wheaton: Victor, 1983), 738.

43. Charles C. Ryrie, *Ryrie Study Bible* (Chicago: Moody, 1986), 1818.

44. Gill, *Titus,* 9:290.

45. Ibid.

46. Nicoll, *Expositor's Greek Testament,* 11:364.

47. Stott, *Guard the Truth,* 99.

48. Ibid., 102.

## Chapter 13

1. Patrick Fairbairn, *Commentary on the Pastoral Epistles* (repr. ed., Grand Rapids: Zondervan, 1965), 188.

2. Albert Barnes, *Acts,* Barnes' Notes on the New Testament (Grand Rapids: Baker, 1956), 170.

3. Ibid., 222.
4. Horatio Hackett, *Commentary on Acts* (Grand Rapids: Kregel, 1992), 169.
5. J. W. McGarvey, *New Commentary on Acts of Apostles* (Delight, Ark.: Gospel Light, n.d.), 50.
6. Charles C. Ryrie, *Ryrie Study Bible* (Chicago: Moody, 1986), 1723.
7. Howard Tillman Kuist, *The Pedagogy of St. Paul* (New York: Doran, 1925), 71–73.
8. R. C. H. Lenski, *The Interpretation of St. Paul's Epistles to the Colossians, to the Thessalonians, to Timothy, to Titus and to Philemon* (Minneapolis, Minn.: Augsburg, 1961), 854–55.
9. Fairbairn, *Pastoral Epistles*, 386.
10. Barnes, *2 Timothy,* Barnes on the New Testament, 12:244.
11. Barnes, *Titus,* Barnes on the New Testament, 12:274.
12. A. Duane Litfin, "Titus," in *The Bible Knowledge Commentary, New Testament,* ed. John F. Walvoord and Roy B. Zuck (Wheaton: Victor, 1983), 764.
13. Fairbairn, *Commentary on the Pastoral Epistles,* 270.

## Chapter 14

1. John F. Walvoord, *The Revelation of Jesus Christ* (Chicago: Moody, 1966), 58.
2. Dave Hunt, *A Woman Rides the Beast* (Eugene, Ore.: Harvest House, 1994), 441.
3. Martin Luther, *Commentary on the Epistle to the Galatians* (Westwood, N.J.: Revell, n.d.), 21.
4. John Eadie, *Galatians* (Grand Rapids: Zondervan, 1956), 459.
5. J. B. Lightfoot, *St. Paul's Epistle to the Philippians* (Lynn, Mass.: Hendrickson, 1981), 144.
6. Walter Bauer, *A Greek-English Lexicon of the New Testament and Other Early Christian Literature,* 2d ed., rev. F. Wilbur Gingrich and Frederick W. Danker (Chicago: University of Chicago Press, 1957, 1979), 98.
7. R. C. H. Lenski, *The Interpretation of St. Paul's Epistles to the Colossians, to the Thessalonians, to Timothy, to Titus and to Philemon* (Minneapolis: Augsburg, 1961), 901.
8. John Calvin, *Titus,* Calvin's Commentaries, 22 vols. (reprint, Grand Rapids: Baker, 1989), 21:303.
9. John Gill, *Titus,* Exposition of the Old and New Testaments, 9 vols. (Paris, Ark.: Baptist Standard Bearer, 1989), 9:351.

## Chapter 15

1. Wayne Grudem, "The Meaning of Kephalē," in *Recovering Biblical Manhood and Womanhood,* ed. John Piper and Wayne Grudem (Wheaton, Ill.: Crossway, 1991), 467–68.
2. Paul K. Jewett, *Man as Male and Female* (Grand Rapids: Zondervan,1975), 119.

3.  S. Lewis Johnson Jr., "Role Distinctions in the Church: Gal. 3:28," in *Recovering Biblical Manhood and Womanhood,* ed. John Piper and Wayne Grudem (Wheaton, Ill.: Crossway, 1991), 492, n. 49.
4.  James B. Hurley, *Man and Woman in Biblical Perspective* (Grand Rapids: Zondervan, 1981), 141.
5.  Piper and Grudem, *Recovering Biblical Manhood and Womanhood,* 493n.
6.  Ibid., 494.
7.  Jewett, *Man as Male and Female,* 146.
8.  Charles C. Ryrie, *The Role of Women in the Church* (Chicago: Moody, 1978), 90.
9.  Ibid., 89.
10. Ibid., 90.
11. Joseph Henry Thayer, *Greek-English Lexicon of the New Testament* (New York: American Book, 1889), 138, 322–23.
12. Piper and Grudem, *Recovering Biblical Manhood and Womanhood,* 79–80.
13. Kurt Aland, ed., *The Greek New Testament* (New York: American Bible Society, 1966), 574–75.
14. R. C. H. Lenski, *Interpretation of the Epistle to the Romans* (Columbus, Ohio: Wartburg, 1945), 906.
15. For example, see Dallas Theological Seminary's statement "Women in the Church," *Connections Extra,* July 1997, 4, 8.
16. Donald A. Carson, "Silence in the Churches," in *Recovering Biblical Manhood and Womanhood,* 152.
17. Thomas R. Schreiner, *Women in the Church,* ed. Andreas Kostenberger, Thomas R. Schreiner, and H. Scott Baldwin (Grand Rapids: Baker, 1995), 153–54.
18. Ann L. Bowman, "Women in Ministry: An Exegetical Study of 1 Tim. 2:11–15," *Bibliotheca Sacra* 149 (April–June 1992), 213.
19. H. Wayne House, *The Role of Women in Ministry Today* (Nashville: Nelson, 1990), 148.
20. This entire section was taken by permission from Russell L. Penney, *Equipping the Saints—Division II Basic Bible Knowledge* (Ft. Worth, Tex.: Tyndale Biblical Institute, 1997), 176–77.

## Chapter 16

1.  Charles C. Ryrie, *Basic Theology* (Wheaton, Ill.: Victor, 1986), 433.
2.  Fritz Rienecker, *Linguistic Key to the Greek New Testament,* ed. Cleon Rogers (Grand Rapids: Zondervan, 1980), 714.
3.  Gerhard Kittel, ed., *The Theological Dictionary of the New Testament,* trans. Geoffrey W. Bromiley (Grand Rapids: Eerdmans, 1964–1968), 5:596–625.
4.  Homer A. Kent Jr., *The Epistle to the Hebrews* (Grand Rapids: Baker, 1972), 261.
5.  Rienecker, 714.
6.  Ibid.
7.  Kent, *Epistle to the Hebrews,* 262.

8. Ibid., 261.
9. F. F. Bruce, *The Epistle to the Hebrews,* The New International Commentary on the New Testament (Grand Rapids: Eerdmans, 1964), 357–58.
10. Ibid., 358–59.
11. Ibid., 359.
12. D. A. Carson, "Matthew," in *The Expositor's Bible Commentary,* ed. Frank E. Gaebelein (Grand Rapids: Zondervan, 1984), 8:369.
13. Thomas D. Ice and Robert Dean Jr., *Overrun by Demons* (Eugene, Ore.: Harvest House, 1990), 101.
14. Ryrie, *Basic Theology,* 433–34.
15. Rienecker, *Basic Theology,* 518.
16. Ryrie, *Basic Theology,* 434.
17. A. T. Robertson, *Word Pictures in the New Testament* (Nashville, Tenn.: Broadman, 1931), 58.
18. Thomas L. Constable, "2 Thessalonians," in *The Bible Knowledge Commentary, New Testament,* ed. John F. Walvoord and Roy B. Zuck (Wheaton, Ill.: Victor, 1983), 724.
19. Ryrie, *Basic Theology,* 434.
20. Donald Guthrie, *The Pastoral Epistles,* Tyndale New Testament Commentaries, (repr. ed., Grand Rapids: Eerdmans, 1986), 208.
21. Ibid., 208–9.
22. Ibid., 106.

## Chapter 17
1. Adolph Saphir, *Epistle to the Hebrews* (Grand Rapids: Kregel, 1983), 879.
2. R. C. H. Lenski, *The Interpretation of St. Paul's Epistles to the Colossians, to the Thessalonians, to Timothy, to Titus and to Philemon* (Minneapolis, Minn.: Augsburg, 1961), 495.
3. Patrick Fairbairn, *Commentary on the Pastoral Epistles* (Grand Rapids: Zondervan, 1956), 104.
4. Ibid., 105.
5. John Stott, *Guard the Truth* (Downers Grove, Ill.: InterVarsity, 1996), 119.
6. George W. Knight III, *The Pastoral Epistles,* The International Greek Testament Commentary (Grand Rapids: Eerdmans, 1996), 208.
7. Albert Barnes, *1 Timothy,* Barnes on the New Testament, 14 vols. (Grand Rapids: Baker, 1956), 12:170.
8. Ibid.
9. W. Robertson Nicoll, *The Expositor's Greek Testament,* 5 vols. (Grand Rapids: Eerdmans, 1988), 127.
10. William Hendriksen, *1 Timothy,* New Testament Commentary (Grand Rapids: Baker, 1982), 236.
11. Knight, *Pastoral Epistles,* 382.
12. Nicoll, *Expositor's Greek Testament,* 160.
13. A. Duane Litfin, "2 Timothy," in *The Bible Knowledge Commentary, New Testament,* ed. John F. Walvoord and Roy B. Zuck (Wheaton: Victor, 1983), 752.

14. Hendriksen, *1 Timothy,* 273.
15. Lenski, *Interpretation of St. Paul's Epistles,* 852.
16. Charles Caldwell Ryrie, *Ryrie Study Bible,* exp. ed. (Chicago: Moody, 1995), 1937.
17. Walter Bauer, *A Greek-English Lexicon of the New Testament and Other Early Christian Literature,* 2nd ed., rev. F. Wilbur Gingrich and Frederick W. Danker (Chicago: University of Chicago Press, 1957, 1979), 180.
18. Ibid., 138–39.
19. Lenski, *Interpretation of St. Paul's Epistles,* 939.
20. Bauer, *Greek-English Lexicon of the New Testament,* 23.
21. Knight, *Pastoral Epistles,* 355.

## Chapter 18

1. George W. Peters, *A Biblical Theology of Missions* (Chicago: Moody, 1972), 15.
2. Paul Enns, *The Moody Handbook of Theology* (Chicago: Moody, 1989), 366.
3. Robert P. Lightner, *Handbook of Evangelical Theology: A Historical, Biblical, and Contemporary Survey and Review* (Grand Rapids: Kregel, 1995), 235–36.
4. See Cleon Rogers, "The Great Commission," *Bibliotheca Sacra* 130 (July 1973): 258–67; H. E. Dana and Julius R. Mantey, *A Manual Grammar of the Greek New Testament* (New York: MacMillan, 1927), 229; and Daniel B. Wallace, *Greek Grammar Beyond the Basics* (Grand Rapids: Zondervan, 1996), 645.
5. Walter Bauer, *A Greek-English Lexicon of the New Testament and Other Early Christian Literature,* 2nd ed., rev. F. W. Gingrich and Frederick Danker, trans. William F. Arndt and F. W. Gingrich (Chicago: Chicago University Press, 1979), 485.
6. Ibid.
7. Dana and Mantey, *Manual Grammar,* 228.
8. Louis A. Barbieri Jr., "Matthew," in *The Bible Knowledge Commentary, New Testament,* ed. John F. Walvoord and Roy B. Zuck (Wheaton, Ill.: Victor, 1983), 93–94.
9. Fritz Rienecker, *Linguistic Key to the Greek New Testament,* ed. Cleon Rogers (Grand Rapids: Zondervan, 1976, 1980), 87.
10. This author is not proposing that Christ or the early church equated baptism and faith in Christ. Baptism has no part in salvation! At the same time, the author does believe that it would have been unthinkable for someone to place faith in Christ and not desire to be baptized, which would be a sign of identification with Christ as Savior and Lord.
11. Bauer, *Greek-English Lexicon of the New Testament,* 370–71.
12. Ruth A. Tucker, *From Jerusalem to Irian Jaya* (Grand Rapids: Zondervan, 1983), 29, 31.
13. Roland Allen, *Missionary Methods: St. Paul's or Ours?* (reprint, Grand Rapids: Eerdmans, 1989), 12.

14. Ibid.
15. Ibid., 16.
16. Ibid., 13.
17. Rienecker, *Linguistic Key,* 87.
18. Allen, *Missionary Methods,* 81.
19. Ibid., 84.
20. Ibid., 13.
21. Ibid.
22. *Personal Support Raising Manual* (Prospect Heights, Ill.: International Teams, n.d.), 1.
23. Rienecker, *Linguistic Key,* 453.
24. Bauer, *Greek-English Lexicon of the New Testament,* 709.

## Chapter 19

1. Os Guinness, *Dancing with the Devil* (Grand Rapids: Baker, 1994), 12.
2. Ibid., 43.
3. Ibid.
4. Ibid., 45.
5. Ibid., 51.
6. Ibid., 67.
7. Ibid., 69–70.
8. Ibid., 71–72.
9. Colin Brown, ed., *The New International Dictionary of New Testament Theology,* 4 vols. (Grand Rapids: Zondervan, 1975), 1:188.
10. Ibid., 1:189.
11. Ibid., 1:191.
12. Ibid., 1:191–92.
13. R. C. H. Lenski, *The Interpretation of St. Paul's Epistles to the Thessalonians, to Timothy, to Titus, and to Philemon* (Minneapolis: Augsburg, 1964), 655.
14. L. Coenan, "Bishop, Presbyter, Elder," in *The New International Dictionary of New Testament Theology,* ed. Colin Brown (Grand Rapids: Zondervan, 1975, 1986), 191.
15. Walter Bauer, *A Greek-English Lexicon of the New Testament and Other Early Christian Literature,* rev. F. Wilbur Gingrich and Frederick W. Danker, trans. William F. Arndt and William F. Gingrich (Chicago: University of Chicago Press, 1979), 184.
16. Louis A. Barbieri Jr., "Matthew," in *The Bible Knowledge Commentary, New Testament,* ed. John F. Walvoord and Roy B. Zuck (Wheaton, Ill.: Victor, 1983), 55.
17. John MacArthur Jr., *The Family* (Chicago: Moody, 1982), 87.
18. Cited by Ralph Earle, "1 Timothy," in *The Expositor's Bible Commentary,* 12 vols., ed. Frank E. Gaebelein (Grand Rapids: Zondervan, 1978), 11:377.
19. Lenski, *Interpretation of St. Paul's Epistles,* 657.
20. Ibid., 657–58.
21. Earle, "1 Timothy," 11:377.

22. Donald Guthrie, *The Pastoral Epistles,* Tyndale New Testament Commentaries (reprint, Grand Rapids: Eerdmans, 1986), 102.

23. John F. MacArthur Jr., *The Family* (Chicago: Moody, 1982), 47.

24. Gustav Stählin, *"chēra,"* in *The Theological Dictionary of the New Testament,* 10 vols., ed. Gerhard Kittel, trans. Geoffrey W. Bromiley (Grand Rapids: Eerdmans, 1964), 9:463.

25. Henry Barclay Swete, *The Gospel According to St. Mark* (New York: Macmillan, 1905), 291–92.

26. Coenan, "Bishop, Presbyter, Elder," 191.

27. Charles C. Ryrie, *Ryrie Study Bible* (Chicago, Moody, 1986), 1863.

28. David K. Lowery, "2 Corinthians," in *The Bible Knowledge Commentary, New Testament,* 574.

29. Vernon C. Grounds, "Why Should We Help the Poor?" in *Moody Monthly,* November–December 1997, 14.

30. Walter L. Callison, *Divorce, Law, and Jesus,* unpub.

31. Ibid., 8.

32. Ed Glasscock, "The Husband of One Wife: Requirements in 1 Timothy 3:2," *Bibliotheca Sacra,* 145, no. 540 (July–September 1983): 247.

33. Ibid., 253.

34. Ibid., 256.

35. Charles C. Ryrie, *Basic Theology* (Wheaton: Victor, 1986), 435.

36. Harry A. Ironside, *Timothy, Titus and Philemon* (Neptune, N.J.: Loizeaux Brothers, 1947), 122.

37. John MacArthur Jr. and Wayne A. Mack, *Introduction to Biblical Counseling* (Dallas: Word, 1994), 8.

38. Jay E. Adams, *The Christian Counselor's Manual* (Grand Rapids: Zondervan, 1973), 33.

39. Everett Ferguson, *Backgrounds of Early Christianity* (Grand Rapids: Eerdmans, 1993), 102–3.

40. Howard Tillman Kuist, *The Pedagogy of St. Paul* (New York: George H. Doran, 1925), 31.

41. Ibid., 31–33.

42. John Stott, *Guard the Truth* (Downers Grove, Ill.: InterVarsity, 1996), 187.

43. Ibid., 188.

44. Ibid., 188–89.

45. Ibid., 189.

# Scripture Index

# Subject Index

doctrine, sound 195–96, 201, 209,
241–43, 263, 265–66. *See also
under* education; Scripture.

**E**

education 292–96
*ekklēsia* 25
elder 86–87, 161–200, 237
choosing of 62–63, 156–57, 170,
191, 198, 241, 247
civic 162, 164–65
discipline of 233
Jewish 62, 161–62
Old Testament 162–64
plurality 171–72
qualifications of 175–80, 189, 217–
19, 221, 241, 245–47, 268
task of 194, 242, 268
election of officers 198
episcopal government 157
error, doctrinal 196, 201–12, 240–45.
*See also under* doctrine, sound.
eternal life 105
evangelism, gift of 222, 246, 250–51.
*See also under* Spirit, gifts of.
evangelists 59, 240
exhortation, gift of. *See under* Spirit,
gifts of.

**F**

faith, content of 36
*See also under* Spirit, gifts of.
false teacher 65, 115–16, 205, 231–33
family
care for 279–87
strengthening of 292–96
feminism 216, 294
financial affairs 65, 257–63

**G**

gender roles 69–75, 213–23, 239
gifts. *See under* Spirit, gifts of.
giving. *See under* Spirit, gifts of.
Gnosticism 201, 203, 208
Great Commission 249, 251–52

**H**

headship 71–72, 213–17, 221–23, 295
helps. *See under* Spirit, gifts of.
hermeneutics
definition of 14
dispensational 24
literal 20
principles of 15
Holy Spirit. *See also under* Spirit,
gifts of.
baptism 50, 52, 242
in church 51
hospitality 177, 183
husband 179, 181, 188, 214, 216–17,
221, 246, 292
humanism 108, 290

**I**

interpretation, Scripture 14–18, 67, 197
interpreter of tongues 17
Israel, church and 29–33, 44–45, 99

**J**

Judaizers. *See under* legalism.
judgment
of church 97, 132–34, 147–52
of world 99–101

**K**

kingdom of heaven 44–45, 101–2

**L**

law, passing away of 34, 204–5. *See
also under* dispensationalism.
leadership. *See also under* Spirit, gifts
of.
building 237–48
charge to 240
extent of 217
training 239, 245
legalism 66, 182, 201, 203, 204–6, 285
Lord's Day. *See under* Sunday.

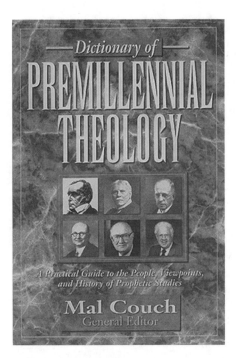

# Dictionary of Premillennial Theology

*A Practical Guide to the People, Viewpoints, and History of Prophetic Studies*

Mal Couch, general editor
448 pages, hardcover
ISBN 0-8254-2351-1

More than fifty scholars, authors, and Bible teachers have combined their expertise to present a historical and topical dictionary of premillennial theology. Included are articles on the major figures of prophetic studies such as Chafer, Darby, Ladd, Scofield, and Walvoord, as well as historical figures such as Augustine, Edwards, and Spurgeon. Additional articles cover major terms and concepts in premillennial theology as well as the eschatology of individual Bible books, Scripture passages, and extra-canonical writings.

Contributors include Robert Gromacki, John Hannah, Edward Hindson, H. Wayne House, Thomas Ice, Tim LaHaye, Robert Lightner, and Charles Ryrie.

Comprehensive in scope yet concise in its entries, *Dictionary of Premillennial Theology* will serve the needs of both the academic and lay reader as a practical reference book for prophetic studies.

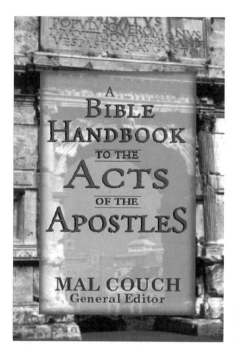

## A Bible Handbook to the Acts of the Apostles

Mal Couch, general editor
464 pages, hardcover
ISBN 0-8254-2360-0

Numerous evangelical scholars combine their talents to present an in-depth look at the major doctrinal themes of Acts from a dispensational perspective, as well as to provide definitions and identifications of the people, places, and terms used in the book. Includes numerous charts and maps. This book combines the best of a Bible handbook and a biblical theology.

Contributors include:

Paul Benware, Philadelphia College of the Bible
Thomas Figart, Lancaster Bible College
Arnold Fruchtenbaum, Ariel Ministries
Robert Lightner, Tyndale Theological Seminary
Stephen McAvoy, Institute for Biblical Studies
Randall Price, Liberty Baptist Theological Seminary

"For those with a special interest in Acts, this Bible handbook is must reading."
—*Christianity Today Biblical Reference*

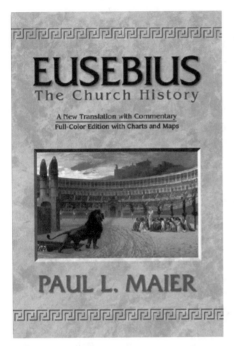

# Eusebius:
# The Church History

Paul Maier, translator
416 pages, hardcover
ISBN 0-8254-3328-2

Much of our knowledge of the first three centuries of Christianity—the terrible persecutions, the courageous martyrs, the theological controversies—comes from the writings of Eusebius, the first great historian of the Christian faith, who wrote in A.D. 325. Next to Josephus, Eusebius is the standard reference work on the early church.

Dr. Paul Maier's accurate yet thoroughly readable translation is further enhanced with a commentary following each chapter that explains the historical events and figures for the lay leader. Full-color photos with maps and charts throughout make this an insightful and rewarding reading experience.

The first new modern translation of this standard reference work in almost thirty years!

"There is no book more important to understanding the early church than Eusebius's *Church History*. And there is no edition more readable and engaging than this one."

—Mark Galli, editor
*Christian History*

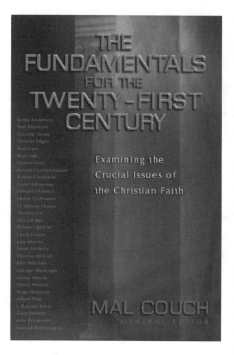

# The Fundamentals for the Twenty-First Century

*Examining the Crucial Issues of the Christian Faith*

Mal Couch, general editor
640 pages, hardcover
ISBN 0-8254-2368-6

At the turn of the last century, dozens of evangelical leaders contributed to *The Fundamentals,* now considered a classic work of Christian history. More than thirty leading evangelical authors and scholars now examine crucial issues facing the church at the end of the century and the dawn of the new millennium.

This new work addresses the cultural change and theological confusion facing today's believers and shows that God's Word is sufficient to meet the needs of every age.

Topics include: abortion, attributes of God, Bible prophecy, Christian family, the church, creation, eternity, ethics, evangelism, feminism, inerrancy of the Bible, inspiration of Scripture, millennial kingdom, nature of salvation, pluralism, raising children, Satan and the spirit world, and the uniqueness of Christianity. Contributors include:

Kerby Anderson • Paul Benware • Timothy Demy • Thomas Edgar • Paul Enns • Paul Fink • Harold Foos • Arnold Fruchtenbaum • Robert Gromacki • Gary Habermas • Ed Hindson • Henry Holloman • H. Wayne House • Thomas Ice • Tim LaHaye • Robert Lightner • Erwin Lutzer • Jobe Martin • Steve McAvoy • Tom McCall • John McLean • George Meisinger • Henry Morris • Dave Noebel • Paige Patterson • Al Platt • Randall Price • Gary Stewart • Harold Willmington • John Walvoord